CW01500534

To my nieces Maeve and Aisling,
great-great-granddaughters of "Molly Bloom,"
and Saoirse, her great-great-great-granddaughter

Joyce, Aristotle, and Aquinas

The Florida James Joyce Series

UNIVERSITY PRESS OF FLORIDA

Florida A&M University, Tallahassee
Florida Atlantic University, Boca Raton
Florida Gulf Coast University, Ft. Myers
Florida International University, Miami
Florida State University, Tallahassee
New College of Florida, Sarasota
University of Central Florida, Orlando
University of Florida, Gainesville
University of North Florida, Jacksonville
University of South Florida, Tampa
University of West Florida, Pensacola

JOYCE, ARISTOTLE, AND AQUINAS

❧

Fran O'Rourke

Foreword by Michael Patrick Gillespie

UNIVERSITY PRESS OF FLORIDA

Gainesville · Tallahassee · Tampa · Boca Raton
Pensacola · Orlando · Miami · Jacksonville · Ft. Myers · Sarasota

Publication of this book was aided by a grant from the National University of Ireland.

Copyright 2022 by Fran O'Rourke
All rights reserved
Published in the United States of America

27 26 25 24 23 22   6 5 4 3 2 1

Library of Congress Cataloging-in-Publication Data
Names: O'Rourke, Fran, author. | Gillespie, Michael Patrick, author of
   foreword.
Title: Joyce, Aristotle, and Aquinas / Fran O'Rourke ; foreword by Michael
   Patrick Gillespie.
Other titles: Florida James Joyce series.
Description: 1. | Gainesville : University Press of Florida, 2022. |
   Series: The Florida James Joyce series | Includes bibliographical
   references and index.
Identifiers: LCCN 2021040745 (print) | LCCN 2021040746 (ebook) | ISBN
   9780813069265 (hardback) | ISBN 9780813068633 (paperback) | ISBN
   9780813070056 (pdf) | ISBN 9780813072234 (ebook)
Subjects: LCSH: Joyce, James, 1882–1941. | Aristotle—Influence. | Thomas,
   Aquinas, Saint, 1225?–1274—Influence. | Philosophy, Ancient, in
   literature. | BISAC: LITERARY CRITICISM / European / English, Irish,
   Scottish, Welsh | LITERARY CRITICISM / Modern / 20th Century
Classification: LCC PR6019.O9 Z7737 2022 (print) | LCC PR6019.O9 (ebook)
   | DDC 823/.912—dc23/eng/20211013
LC record available at https://lccn.loc.gov/2021040745
LC ebook record available at https://lccn.loc.gov/2021040746

The University Press of Florida is the scholarly publishing agency for the State University System
of Florida, comprising Florida A&M University, Florida Atlantic University, Florida Gulf Coast
University, Florida International University, Florida State University, New College of Florida,
University of Central Florida, University of Florida, University of North Florida, University of
South Florida, and University of West Florida.

University Press of Florida
2046 NE Waldo Road
Suite 2100
Gainesville, FL 32609
http://upress.ufl.edu

Contents

Figures

Foreword

Reading Fran O'Rourke's *Joyce, Aristotle, and Aquinas* is akin to listening to Debussy's "The Girl with the Flaxen Hair," a beautifully constructed work, seemingly straightforward while full of complexities that convey the exuberance of the creation with grace and pleasure. Professor O'Rourke has written a marvelous scholarly study that offers, in lucid prose, profound insights into an important portion of the intellectual, imaginative, and creative contexts that inform the writings of James Joyce. O'Rourke disclaims direct interpretive intentions and instead makes the modest, though in my view quite important, assertion that his work is "concerned exclusively with philosophical themes which are of material significance for Joyce's writings, or which provide inspiration for their artistic construction; it is not concerned with the literary character or merit of the application in the writings of Joyce" (1). The pages that follow do just that, but in the process they provide the intelligent reader with a range of important explanations for the influence on Joyce of Aristotle and St. Thomas Aquinas. From this, one has the ability to construct one's own interpretation, as we all do anyway, based on philosophical perspectives quite familiar to Joyce but, given contemporary intellectual tastes and current university syllabi, foreign to most modern readers.

It would be easy to sum up this project by saying that it offers useful additional information to supplement current interpretations of Joyce's works. That would be true, but it would also run of risk of oversimplifying its impact. O'Rourke's study produces the same effect that Keats describes in "On First Looking into Chapman's Homer." The careful explanations of key philosophical positions held by Aristotle and Aquinas and the erudite delineation of how Joyce encountered these views open for readers narrative perspectives and dialogic nuances imbedded in the canon that would otherwise go unnoticed. This is not a polemic study attempting to proselytize a critic's ideology. This is a scholarly work that respects the intelligence of its readers and acknowledges the range of interpretive possibilities that can be supplemented by a greater sense of the elaborate and at times conflicted intellectual context from which Joyce's writing emerged.

Michael Patrick Gillespie
Florida International University

Acknowledgments

In preparing this work, I have received invaluable advice and encouragement from Professor Anne Fogarty of the School of English at University College Dublin; I express to her my most sincere thanks. I am also most grateful to Professor Declan Kiberd, who guided me in the early days of my research. Professor Luca Crispi generously provided expert advice during my investigation into Joyce's quotations from Aristotle.

I gratefully express my indebtedness to Jean-Michel Rabaté and Michael Patrick Gillespie, who generously shared their expertise with me on repeated occasions. I am grateful to my friends at the James Joyce Foundation in Zurich. Its founder and director, Fritz Senn, together with Ruth Frehner, Frances Ilmberger, and Ursula Zeller, made my visits to the Foundation fruitful and enjoyable on every occasion. I record my appreciation to Thomas Staley and the staff of the Harry Ransom Research Center at the University of Texas, Austin, for their exceptional help and courtesy during my visit.

I owe an inestimable debt of gratitude to Philip Kitcher, Sam Slote, and Catherine Clutterbuck for valuable comments that greatly improved the content. I am most grateful to Sebastian Knowles and Martin Brick, readers for University Press of Florida, for challenging and insightful recommendations that encouraged me to further explore important aspects of the topic. My friend Paddy Sammon made numerous suggestions that enhanced the text. For the digital image of "Aristotle's Experiment" I am grateful to Mihai Cucu. I express warmest thanks to the staff of University Press of Florida, especially Stephanye Hunter, Jenna Kolesari, Marthe J. Walters, and Rachel Doll, for their invaluable advice and cheerful patience. I owe special thanks to Penelope Cray for her excellent editorial work. For remaining shortcomings, I have only myself to thank.

I want in a special way to express heartfelt thanks to my friend Dr John Feeley for his collaboration in the wider field of Joycean activity; musical excursions in his cheerful company across the globe, from Shanghai to San Diego, have been a delight (www.joycesong.info).

A major part of the research was carried out during a sabbatical year funded by a President's Fellowship awarded by University College Dublin. I express my sincere gratitude for this support.

I should explain the dedication of the book to my adorable nieces Maeve and Aisling, and to Aisling's baby, Saoirse. In October 1858, Saoirse's great-great-great grandfather, nineteen-year-old Bernard Connor from Gorey, enlisted in the Royal Artillery in Dublin. In March 1861, he sailed on H.M.S. *Megaera* to Gibraltar, where he served for six years. On October 1, 1863, he married Amelia Capacete from nearby San Roque. Having served in Jamaica and Kent, he retired in 1879 at the rank of Brigade Sergeant Major and returned to live in Clonmel. In 1891, Bernard and his Spanish wife moved to 113 North Strand Road, Dublin, where they were near neighbors of Joyce's favorite aunt, Josephine Murray. Joyce was a frequent visitor to 103 North Strand Road; in September 1904, he wrote two letters to Nora Barnacle from that address. We may assume that Joyce not only heard of Amelia Connor but more than likely met her. Joyce characteristically based his literary inventions upon actual fact, and Amelia provided him with the minimal biography for the female protagonist of *Ulysses*. Their names even sound alike. In the Penelope monologue, Molly says that she "saw the Spanish cavalry at La Roque" and recalls the moods of Gibraltar. I am most grateful to Barry Sheehan for generously sharing the results of his research into the Connor family.

Publication Acknowledgments

I am grateful to the following for permission to reproduce material from previous publications.

National Library of Ireland: *Allwisest Stagyrite: Joyce's Quotations from Aristotle* (2005).

Cambridge University Press: "Joyce's Thomist Masters," in *Joyce in Context,* ed. John McCourt (2009).

Journal of Modern Literature: "Joyce's Early Aesthetic" (2011).

University College Dublin Press: "James Joyce and Aristotle," in *Voices on Joyce* (2015).

Palgrave Macmillan: "Knowledge and Identity in Joyce," in *Cognitive Joyce,* ed. Sylvain Belluc and Valérie Bénéjam (2018).

Abbreviations

Aristotle

CW1, CW2	*Complete Works of Aristotle,* vols. 1 & 2
An. Post	*Analytica Posteriora* (*Posterior Analytics*)
Phys.	*Physica* (*Physics*)
De An.	*De Anima* (*On the Soul*)
Hist. An.	*Historia Animalium* (*History of Animals*)
Part. An.	*De Partibus Animalium* (*Parts of Animals*)
Gen. An.	*De Generatione Animalium* (*Generation of Animals*)
Met.	*Metaphysica* (*Metaphysics*)
EN	*Ethica Nicomachea* (*Nicomachean Ethics*)
Pol.	*Politica* (*Politics*)
Rhet.	*Rhetorica* (*Rhetoric*)
Poet.	*Poetica* (*Poetics*)

Richard Ellmann

JJII	Richard Ellmann, *James Joyce* (revised edition)

James Joyce

CW	*The Critical Writings*
D	*Dubliners*
FW	*Finnegans Wake*
LI, LII, LIII	*Letters,* vols. 1, 2 & 3
OCPW	*Occasional, Critical, and Political Writings*
P	*A Portrait of the Artist as a Young Man*
PSW	*Poems and Shorter Writings*
SH	*Stephen Hero*

SL	*Selected Letters of James Joyce*
U	*Ulysses*

Thomas Aquinas

CG	*Summa Contra Gentiles*
De Spir. Creat.	*De spiritualibus creaturis*
De Ver.	*Quaestiones disputatae de veritate*
In Anal. Post.	*In libros Posteriorum Analyticorum*
In de Caelo	*In Libros de Caelo et Mundo*
In DN	*In Divinis Nominibus*
In Perihermeneias	*In libros Peri Hermeneias*
In Phys.	*In libros Physicorum*
In Sent.	*Scriptum super libros Sententiarum*
Q. Disp. De An.	*Quaestio disputata de anima*
ST	*Summa Theologiae*

Introduction

The present study aims to provide a comprehensive overview of the significance of Aristotle and Aquinas in the work of James Joyce. While it is universally recognized that both thinkers exerted profound influence on the author of *Ulysses*,[1] this area of inquiry has been neglected in recent decades. With the proliferation of research in other areas of Joycean studies and enhanced facilities for investigation, as well as access to new materials, it would be surprising if inquiry into both of these important sources were exhausted. It is more than sixty years since the publication of William T. Noon's excellent study on Joyce and St. Thomas; no equivalent work has been produced on Joyce and Aristotle.

The scope of my investigation is limited and specific. It is concerned exclusively with philosophical themes that are of material significance for Joyce's writings or that provide inspiration for their artistic construction; it is not concerned with the literary merit of their application by Joyce. To borrow from John Locke's aspiration, "It is ambition enough to be employed as an under-labourer in clearing the ground a little."[2] Much of what has been written on Joyce's relation to Aristotle and Aquinas is superficial and speculative, not looking beyond what is stated in his writings and lacking reference to the philosophers' own texts.[3] On the other hand, many studies in recent decades have progressed beyond the analysis of sources and influences to an interpretation of a "meta" character. The present investigation adheres to a more traditional style; convinced that a fundamental examination of Aristotle and Aquinas as sources of Joyce has been lacking, I have confined my study to explicit references and allusions and eschewed speculative exegesis. I aim to examine Joyce's use of these two important sources and to assess its accuracy and importance. This study is also intended to provide the nonphilosophical reader with a background to, and explanation of, the philosophical topics that occur.

James Joyce had a keen sense of the elemental and primordial questions. It is significant that many of the themes recurring throughout his work are precisely those that first emerged in early Greek philosophy: diversity and unity, identity, permanence and change, the nature and reliability of knowledge. While Joyce was a realist with regard to the basic philosophical questions, he exhibited throughout his life a keen interest in a variety of approaches. During his student years, he was a dedicated pupil of Aristotle and Aquinas. His early distrust of Platonism left him suspicious of idealism. Empiricism was unacceptable because of its skepticism, and his short-lived attraction to pragmatism turned to scorn because of the manner in which it debased the ideal of truth. For various aspects of their philosophies Joyce held Giordano Bruno, Giambattista Vico, and Nicholas of Cusa in high regard. He admired the rebellious Bruno as the father of modern philosophy; Vico probed the tangled web of thought and language into which Joyce would delve more deeply; Cusanus provided the logic of contradiction and the harmony of opposites that allowed Joyce to conceive of *Finnegans Wake.*

Joyce was acquainted with the philosophical trends of his day, many of which carried the trace of the Copernican revolution, which had inverted the compass of traditional philosophy. His own fundamental outlook was that of the *philosophia perennis,* and it is against the ancient background that we can best understand his approach, since the questions preoccupying him were essentially those first articulated in classical philosophy. In broad terms, the central theme of my inquiry is the meaning of identity as it surfaces in recurrent iterations throughout Joyce's writings. The question of identity is ultimately a philosophical question; the principle of identity is considered the first law of reality.

The ancient rhapsode introduced Odysseus to his audience as a "man of many turns": *polutropos,* literally "of many tropes." The hero wandered far and wide, saw many cities, learned the ways of many men, and suffered many sorrows. Odysseus's character unfurls gradually, almost organically, as his character grows in magnitude with each new adventure. By the time he arrives home to Ithaca, we have acquired a comprehensive picture of the individual, enlightened by many insights into his inner nature. Through a plethora of hints, dramatized through successive incidents, we are presented with a unified and integrated character. It was this completeness that attracted Joyce to Odysseus. His friend the sculptor Frank Budgen asked: "What do you mean by a complete man? For example, if a sculptor makes a figure of a man then that man is all-round, three-dimensional, but not necessarily complete in the sense of being ideal. All human bodies are imperfect, limited in some way, human beings too." Joyce replied: "Ulysses is both. I see him from all sides, and therefore he is all-round in the sense of your sculptor's figure. But he is a complete man as well—a good man."[4] Joyce regarded Odysseus as the most complete character in literature—more accomplished than either Faust or Hamlet. Joyce did not consider Christ a complete man: "He was a bachelor, and never lived with a woman. Surely living with a woman is one of the most difficult things a man can do, and he never did it."[5] Joyce declared that the most beautiful, all-embracing, theme was that of the *Odyssey,* and the subject of Odysseus the most human in world literature.[6] Odysseus's character comprises myriad aspects, revealed through a multiplicity of actions; Homer's success was to shape this diversity into a coherent unity and identity.

Lyrical poetry aside—unless a poet's work is considered as a whole—we expect a work of genuine literature to offer insights into the characters portrayed. A detective story must be exciting, full of suspense, intrigue, and anticipation, but we do not expect profound personality portraits: the plot's the thing. A novel or drama, however, should present complexity and depth of character, inherent tensions, and paradoxical traits, all somehow melded into a consistent whole, but without exhausting all the possibilities of the personalities portrayed.

Any attempt to appreciate the work of James Joyce prompts the question of authenticity and identity at various levels and from multiple perspectives. From the early portraits of *Dubliners,* through the self-searching of the burgeoning artist in *A Portrait of the Artist as a Young Man* and the constellation of characters in *Ulysses,* to the diverse and disparate personalities that remorph, Proteus-like, in the pages of *Finnegans Wake,* Joyce dramatized the inexhaustible miscellany of daily lives. To what extent are his personae invested with credible authentic self-identity? Are they complete and rounded, unified and integrated? To engage with the writings of James Joyce is to wrestle with multiple identities, to sift the flowing sands of alterity and alteration in search of permanence and individuality.

As a vector of value and meaning, the question of identity is vital to assessing the objective merit of Joyce's oeuvre, but it is central also to our understanding of the author himself. Critics disagree as to the authorial identity that sustains his work: Irish national or British passport-bearer, colonial subject or anti-colonial rebel, Catholic or apostate, classicist or modernist? There is little agreement as to Joyce's definitive, abiding identity, such was the rich complexity of the person and artist. Critics have argued against the "reification" of any supposed national or cultural authenticity.[7] Emer Nolan suggests, for example, that for Joyce "Irishness" is a heterogeneous notion but "a kind of originary heterogeneity [whose] definitive characteristic is its quality of eluding definition."[8] Vincent J. Cheng proposes that "Joyce's works become increasingly informed by his sensitivity towards the nature of the hybridity, ambivalences, and interpretations involved in cultural and discursive formations."[9] Thus many layers and strands of allegiance and experimental identities, at times conflictual, must be acknowledged. Nolan pertinently observes that while "authenticity" remains an important theme in the work of such critics as Richard Kearney and Declan Kiberd, the theorists to whom they are indebted "attack the very idea of a self to which one might be true or false."[10] The philosophical question of authentic selfhood and authorial identity is what is ultimately at stake. Whether it is personal selfhood or national identity that has been deconstructed or abandoned by poststructuralist or alternative theories, the originary concept must first be confronted.

As they walk from the Tower to the Forty Foot bathing place, Stephen and Haines discuss exalted questions such as creation from nothing, miracles, and a personal God. Stephen declares himself to be "a horrible example of free thought." Haines approves: "I should think you are able to free yourself. You are your own master, it seems to me." Stephen protests his restrictions: "I am a servant of two masters [. . .] an English and an Italian [. . .] The imperial British state [. . .] and the holy Roman catholic and apostolic church" (U 1.636–44). Haines's commendation of Stephen as his "own master" is an exact translation of what for Aquinas it is to be a person: *dominus sui,* one who is master of oneself.[11] A person possesses him- or herself in the order of knowledge through the power of self-consciousness, and in the order of action through self-determination or free will. James Joyce and his fictional counter-self were alike obliged to negotiate the constraints upon their thought and action in shaping their individuality. Cultural, political, social, and religious identity finally rest upon that of selfhood and personal authenticity. Those identities that continually vie beneath the surface for validation are derivative.

Literature was for Joyce a vehicle for articulating and asserting his personal, and in particular his artistic, identity. His was a conflicted growth, as he sought to escape the snares of nationality, language, and religion, the traps of home, fatherland, and church (P V.1047–50, 2576–77). Like the mythical Daedalus, he sought to fashion artful wings to flee those nets that held him down. Torn between allegiances, impulses, and antipathies, he sought in art to liberate his authentic self. To establish who he really was, he needed to affirm himself vis-à-vis nationality, social class, race, place, language, religion, and ideology. Each element is significant within his comprehensive makeup. Identity is a mille-feuille term connoting a multiplicity of radiating meanings. Many of these have been the focus of Joyce scholarship. Each approach offers a particular optic for understanding the author but can provide only a limited perspective. The present study only marginally considers these tangential or supervenient aspects, concerning itself instead with the core philosophical question of identity as prompted by a reading of Joyce. A philosophical elucidation will help to illuminate derivatory instances of relative identity, but these are beyond the scope of my inquiry. Questions of cultural, colonial, postcolonial, or ethnic identity are secondary to the primal nature of identity in existence, knowledge, and personhood.

The question of identity points to the twin dualities of unity and diversity, permanence and change. The twin phenomena that present the first challenge to philosophy are the diversity and change of immediate sense experience. We are confronted in perception by a bewildering plurality of seemingly unrelated objects that are, furthermore, subject to continuous and apparently haphazard change. Reflecting on the apparent chaos of physical data, the mind instinctively seeks unity underlying diversity and a permanence persisting through change.[12] If there is a unity beyond the plurality, it is not one of utter simplicity but one that is structured within a differentiated whole. The question is how to conceive and articulate unity in difference, and difference in unity.

How can a thing be unified if composed of diverse elements? How is it possible for something to change, yet retain an enduring integrity? These questions are essential to our interpretation of the real. Only when the things we experience are somehow embraced within a unifying totality are we satisfied that they have been understood. Each philosophical discipline somehow aims at a comprehensive, unified integration of diverse elements. Ethics aims at a harmonious ordering of the diverse, often conflicting, values and demands of human action; psychology seeks to integrate the various aspects of human behavior within the unity of personality; epistemology evaluates the polarity of subject and object throughout the successive stages of a single, complete, act of cognition as it proceeds from sensation to intellectual insight. At the widest possible horizon of experience and reality, metaphysics or ontology aims to order all things within the unity of being, the most fundamental and common aspect shared by all things.

Just as Odysseus was a man "of many turns" (*polutropos*), Aristotle declared that "being is said in many ways" (*pollachôs*). The universe manifests none-theless an underlying unity. As the need to unify the data of experience is deeply embedded in the human mind, order is likewise an axiom of lit-erature, when the world is retold and re-created in imagination; there is a deep analogy between the two. As Aristotle noted, in a phrase copied by Joyce into his Paris notebook, nature is a unified whole, not a haphazard aggregate of unrelated episodes, like a badly composed tragedy.

To the different approaches in the search for unity just outlined, corre-sponding themes may be identified in the work of James Joyce. The ques-tion of personal or ethical harmony is the key to the authenticity of char-acter of those individuals whose inner drama is depicted in *Dubliners, A Portrait,* and *Ulysses;* more fundamentally, the unity sought by psychology is the key to the enduring identity of those characters. The stability and union of subject and object in cognition is fundamental to the search for certainty, a problem that preoccupies Stephen in *Ulysses* and is repeatedly questioned in *Finnegans Wake.* The search for an overall unifying pattern to embrace all things is reflected in Joyce's attempts to give symbolic expres-sion to the totality, first in *Ulysses,* where the commonplace is given cosmic dimensions, and then in *Finnegans Wake,* with its ambitious scheme that through polyvalent allusion and endless pluralities betokens the multiple possibilities of human history and existence.

Questions of identity, unity, and permanence first emerged in Greek philosophy. The same questions animate the writings of James Joyce. We may identify the following specific themes, which will be the subject of central chapters of the present study.

(1) The question of permanence and identity as it relates to knowledge is dramatized in the "Proteus" episode: Is there a stable, enduring subject, a self-identical permanent knowing self, that transcends the flux of the changing world? Is there an enduring object that ensures the fixity necessary for reliable knowledge? A secondary question, prompted in modern philosophy by the experiment of Descartes's cogito, was the ability of the senses themselves to give direct ac-cess to the world. This question is enacted in the opening scenes of *Ulysses.*

(2) The question of self-identity arises with regard to the continuity of the individual person: Is there a permanent acting agent who per-sists during change, remaining constant throughout the stages of

life? Stephen and Bloom—and even Molly to a lesser degree—repeatedly interrogate their identity as they reflect upon the changes in their lives.

(3) The question of an overall unifying totality arises in various forms for Joyce and acquires particular application in his attempt to encapsulate the entirety of human life and reality in a synthetic manner in *Ulysses* and *Finnegans Wake*. Analogy is the key to Joyce's attempt to span the divisions of unity and diversity, permanence and change, in an overall understanding of the identity that pervades the totality of existence itself.

These three philosophical topics are considered in chapters titled "Knowledge and Permanence," "Identity, Soul, and Substance," and "Totality, Diversity, and Order: The Unity of Analogy." With respect to each theme, the influence of Aristotle and Aquinas is analyzed and documented. These central chapters are preceded by preliminary chapters with the self-explanatory titles "Aristotelian Joyce" and "Joyce's Thomist Formation." A detailed examination of Joyce's "Thomist" aesthetics is presented in chapter 6. Chapter 7 reproduces with commentary the quotations transcribed by Joyce from Aristotle during his stay in Paris in 1902.

* * *

The unspoken question framing the background to our inquiry asks in what measure Joyce may be regarded as a philosopher as well as an artist.[13] What is the relation between his implicit philosophical attitude and his artistic credo? Sartre observes, "The novelist's aesthetic always sends us back to his metaphysic."[14] This is particularly true of Joyce. Richard M. Kain described *Ulysses* as "a metaphysical novel";[15] according to Yeats, it "incites to philosophy."[16] Cheryl Temple Herr has remarked, "I view Joyce as a philosopher: his writing was motivated by issues that he encountered as metaphysical issues. Joyce's abiding interest was in the relations between the material and incorporeal (whether construed as thought or as spirit)." Most significantly for our investigation, she continues: "His works engage directly with Aristotle's concept of 'substance,' itself a much-debated category among philosophers. Joyce's philosophy of substance is, in fact, a crucial missing chapter in the history of twentieth-century thought. Like the pre-Socratics, Joyce developed his distinctively complex modes of expression to convey his evolving understanding of the nature of being."[17] Herr's approval of Joyce's interest in Aristotle's theory of substance could not be more relevant, since here, I suggest, we may detect the tacit core of Joyce's philosophical outlook. Joyce gave frequent and fervent expression to a charter-like Aristotelianism, which remained (at least for much of his career) the inherent, hidden, foundation of his thought. He also adopted certain tenets of Thomist aesthetics. Our purpose is to assess the extent of his commitment and to ask if it was anything more than a case of banner-waving or the miming of barren shibboleths.

While exposing his interest in philosophical themes, I will argue that although Joyce had a philosophical predisposition, that proclivity remained latent. Denis Donoghue's assessment is perhaps overly severe: "James Joyce was an amateur student of the philosophers, but his work shows little of that love of wisdom which constitutes the philosophic habit."[18] Joyce had undoubtedly a love of wisdom and was—indisputably—philosophically inclined. This was to the advantage of his creative work, but here's the rub: because he did not fully appreciate the richness and relevance of Aristotle's metaphysics, he remained perplexed by the fundamental questions of knowledge and identity. In his early works, Joyce sketched basic Aristotelian doctrines with seeming fidelity but with no deep understanding; in *Finnegans Wake,* more often than not, he controverted them. He contemplated the perennial mysteries with literary imagination rather than philosophical reason: that was the secret of his success.

1

Aristotelian Joyce

Joyce and Aristotle

Part 1 of this chapter offers an account of Joyce's acquaintance with Aristotle.[1] Part 2 sketches the background to some basic concepts of Aristotle's philosophy that are indispensable for an understanding of the writings of James Joyce.

It is arguable that Aristotle—next to Homer—was Joyce's greatest master. Without the *Odyssey,* Joyce could never have conceived *Ulysses;* had he not written the book celebrating his first rendezvous with a beautiful girl from Galway, whatever he wrote would have been profoundly marked by the philosopher of Stagira. There is, I suggest, a profound affinity of mind between Joyce and Aristotle; perhaps part of this kinship may be explained by its Homeric parentage. Aristotle too was profoundly influenced by Homer; he cites him more than one hundred times, second in frequency only to Plato. Many of these citations are in those works of Aristotle that Joyce would read. One of the most moving documents that we possess from the entire corpus of ancient philosophy is the fragment of a letter written by Aristotle toward the end of his life: "The more solitary and isolated I am, the more I have come to love myths."[2] One recalls Rembrandt's famous painting of Aristotle contemplating the bust of Homer.

It is noteworthy that in *Gulliver's Travels,* Jonathan Swift places Homer and Aristotle in the same company: "Having a desire to see those ancients, who were most renowned for wit and learning, I set apart one day on purpose. I proposed that Homer and Aristotle might appear at the head of all their commentators. [. . .] I had a whisper from a ghost, who shall be nameless, that these commentators always kept in the most distant quarter from their principals, in the lower world, through a consciousness of shame and guilt, because they had so horribly misrepresented the meaning of those authors to posterity."[3] Joyce would bear no such guilt in the company of Homer and Aristotle.

Joyce set out to emulate Homer, and his success is beyond dispute. He was also a true and sympathetic follower of Aristotle. He regarded Aristotle as the greatest thinker of all time, declaring: "In the last two hundred years we have had no great thinker. My judgment is daring, since Kant is included. All the great thinkers of the past centuries from Kant to Benedetto Croce have only recultivated the garden. In my opinion the greatest thinker of all times is Aristotle. He defines everything with wonderful clarity and simplicity. Volumes were written later to define the same things."[4]

How did Joyce come to know Aristotle? Why such great esteem? I will presently assess the most obvious avenue of influence—his Catholic upbringing and Jesuit education—but would first like to mention one that is perhaps overlooked. For generations in Ireland, the name of Aristotle has been synonymous with wisdom and erudition. The following account by the German travel writer J. G. Kohl of his visit to Ireland (1842) in *Travels in Ireland,* a copy of which Joyce had in Trieste, illustrates how well Aristotle had become established in the Irish vernacular tradition over the centuries:

> I have already mentioned the somewhat antiquated learning, even of the lower classes of the people of Kerry; and I now met with a remarkable instance of it. In the bow of the boat sat a Kerryman, reading an old manuscript, which was written in the Irish language, and in the Celtic character. [. . .] Some, the man told me, he had added himself; some he had inherited from his father and grandfather; and some had, in all probability, been in his family long before then. I asked him what were its contents? "They are," answered he, "the most beautiful old Irish poems, histories of wonderful events, and stories and treatises of antiquity; for instance, the translation of a treatise by Aristotle on some subject of natural history!" [. . .] Twice, methought, I heard them speak of Aristotle as a wise and mighty king of Greece, as if they had the same conception of him as of King Solomon.[5]

Aristotle's renown was clearly alive in the Irish mind. My own great-grandmother from West Cork, born within a generation of the scene described, spoke reverently of "Harry Stackle." The Irish, however, did not regard Aristotle as omniscient. Joyce copied in *Scribbledehobble,* his workbook for *FW,* the widespread traditional Irish triad: "3 things Aristotle didn't know labour of bees, flow of tide, mind of women."[6]

More than by any other influence, Joyce's philosophical outlook was profoundly shaped by his Catholic education. The presuppositions of any theology have far-reaching implications for the philosophy advanced in its support. Christian theology in the medieval period developed a sophisticated philosophical system, elaborated by natural reason, which served as a handmaid (*ancilla theologiae*) to elucidate the truths of Revelation. The newly translated works of Aristotle provided Scholastic philosophers, particularly St. Thomas Aquinas, with the categories and concepts to formulate Christian doctrine. Although banned upon his introduction into the West in the thirteenth century, when his writings had been translated, Aristotle received the approval of Aquinas, and it was largely under his influence that the Stagirite gained universal renown as "master of those who know."

Aristotle provided the philosophical substratum for Christian theology, with a metaphysics to establish the existence of God and a psychology to prove the immortality of the human soul. He bequeathed in particular the categories necessary to articulate sacramental doctrine. In the traditional vocabulary of the catechism, the sacraments are described through Aristotelian concepts: each has its matter and form, while the Eucharist is described in the vocabulary of substance and accident. Throughout his entire Catholic education, Joyce was exposed unwittingly but obligatorily to Aristotle's categories, concepts, and principles. Like many Irish youngsters before and since, he imbibed the practicality of Aristotle's metaphysics. Such Aristotelian formation endured. Thomas Merton rightly remarked of Joyce, "If he had abandoned St Thomas, he had not stepped much further down than Aristotle."[7]

Joyce's Catholicism was therefore decisive, introducing him to the Aristotelian mode of interpreting the world. His mind had been decisively shaped to the Aristotelian mold, and while he rejected the Catholic religion, he retained its core philosophical tenets. It is inconceivable that, were he a Protestant, he would have received this intellectual imprint or written as he did. Philosophy occupies a lower place for Protestant theology, with its almost exclusive emphasis on faith based on Scripture. Leaving aside St. Thomas, Aristotle did not enjoy the same status in the Protestant tradition, which placed less value on reason as the helpful handmaid of theology. Far from being the "master of those who know," Aristotle was for Luther the "chief of all charlatans."[8] Luther did not disguise his contempt for "that cursed heathen": "What will they not believe who have credited that ridiculous and injurious blasphemer Aristotle? His propositions are so absurd that an ass or a stone would cry out at them . . . My soul longs for nothing so ardently as to expose and publicly shame that Greek buffoon, who like a spectre has befooled the Church . . . If Aristotle had not lived in the flesh, I should not hesitate to call him a devil."[9]

It has been suggested that Joyce may have absorbed some of Aristotle's aesthetic ideas (the *Poetics*) while at Belvedere College; he was certainly introduced to Aristotle in a formal manner at University College under the guidance of his Jesuit professors. Not only did he choose logic as one of his subjects, but he was also exposed throughout the entire curriculum to the Scholastic mode of deliberation, which owed much to Aristotle. Buck Mulligan remarks to Stephen: "[Y]ou have the cursed jesuit strain in you, only it's injected the wrong way" (*U* 1.209). Joyce rejected much of his Jesuit education but was in many ways grateful for it. It is interesting to recall that from the foundation of their order, the Jesuits were committed followers of Aquinas and Aristotle. Their founder, St. Ignatius of Loyola, stipulated as follows in the *Constitutions of the Society of Jesus* (1553): "In theology there should be lectures on the Old and New Testaments and on the scholastic doctrine of St Thomas. [. . .] In logic, natural and moral philosophy, and metaphysics, the doctrine of Aristotle should be followed, as also in the other liberal arts."[10]

Joyce began to discover the philosophy of Aristotle in a formal academic manner from his early days at university, if not before.[11] He graduated in English, French, and Italian, taking courses also in mathematics, physics, and logic. His studies, however, took place within an atmosphere permeated by Aristotelian Scholasticism. It is worth recalling that for the founder of the university, John Henry Newman, Aristotle was the "oracle of nature and of truth"; he declared that "to think correctly, is to think like Aristotle."[12] Herbert S. Gorman, author of a biography written very much under Joyce's own direction, refers to Joyce's readings of Aristotle in Paris as "rereadings," which, he says, "were but a continuance of the road he had naturally found and followed under Jesuitical direction."[13] Constantine Curran recalls the first lecture in English Literature in 1899: "The professor was Father Darlington, the Dean of Studies, and his opening words were from Aristotle's *Poetics*."[14] The following year, Darlington moved from English to a chair in philosophy.

William Dawson, auditor of the College Literary and Historical Society, 1902–1903, and also a past pupil of Belvedere, recalled: "The influences strongest upon us in those young days were Father Delany, Father Tom Finlay and Professor Magennis. And the greatest of these was Finlay. We strove to talk like him; perhaps, even, to think like him."[15] Interestingly, in my own copy of the *Logic* handbook used in the College at the time, the first owner recorded the following quotation from Fr. Finlay: "I look upon scholasticism as the most perfect training for the mind that can be perceived."

We gain some insight into Joyce's evaluation of the Aristotelian roots of medieval Scholasticism from a comment in a lecture delivered in Padua in 1912, titled "The Universal Literary Influence of the Renaissance": "In the age of the Renaissance the human spirit struggled against scholastic absolutism, against that immense (and in many ways admirable) system of philosophy that has its fundamental origins in Aristotelian thought, cold, clear, and imperturbable, while its summit stretched upwards towards the vague and mysterious light of Christian ideology" (*OCPW* 187).[16]

Of the broader picture, Felix E. Hackett, another classmate of Joyce's, writes as follows (playing on the original sense of the Greek word "peripatetic," from the verb "to walk," and its transferred meaning, referring to Aristotle, who lectured as he strolled):

> Dublin at that time could well have been described as a city of peripatetic discourse. The university atmosphere around 86 St. Stephen's Green was indeed peripatetic also in the philosophic sense, as is evident from the description given by Joyce in *A Portrait of the Artist as a Young Man*. The aesthetic discussion with Father Darlington may be an idealized or a synthetic version of many such talks but it conveys the essence of the spirit of reference to Aristotle, which was the salient characteristic of Father Darlington's interventions in the discussions of the Literary & Historical and other societies such as the Library Conference and the Academy of St Thomas Aquinas. [. . .] Father Darlington, it is not too much to say, tempered the mind of that generation of students by the philosophy of Aristotle and Aquinas.[17]

For Joyce's commitment to Aristotle, we have ample evidence. Stanislaus Joyce, James's younger brother, informs us in his diary: "He upholds Aristotle against his friends, and boasts himself an Aristotelian."[18] In *A Portrait*, Stephen declares, "For my purpose I can work on at present by the light of one or two ideas of Aristotle and Aquinas" (*P* V.466–67). In the "Ithaca" episode, Aristotle is referred to by Stephen as a "seeker of pure truth" (*U* 17.716).

Shortly after his arrival in Paris, Joyce abandoned plans to study medicine, on learning that fees were to be paid in advance. He turned his attention, as it were, from physic to metaphysic, applying himself seriously to the study of Aristotle. On February 8, 1903, he wrote to Stanislaus: "I am feeling very intellectual these times and up to my eyes in Aristotle's Psychology" (*LII* 28). The following month, on March 20, 1903, he wrote to his mother: "I read every day in the Bibliothèque Nationale and every night in the Bibliothèque Sainte-Geneviève. [. . .] I am at present up to my neck in Aristotle's *Metaphysics* and read only him and Ben Jonson" (*LII* 38). The following year, on November 19, 1904, he wrote to Stanislaus from Pola: "I think that after a short course in Aristotle I will shut up the books and examine for myself in a cafe"(*LII* 71).

Joyce's Paris experiences are faithfully mirrored, as we shall see, in Stephen's reflections in *Ulysses*. The quotations from Aristotle copied into his notebook are a valuable insight into what Joyce found significant in the writings of Aristotle and into the way Joyce's understanding of the world was formed.[19] The choice of passages, confirmed by his effort to transcribe them, attest to a tacit sympathy of mind. All aspects of Joyce's life and experience find expression in his work, either as material transmuted through artistic creation or as principles of that very creation. This is particularly the case with Joyce's assimilation of Aristotle: the principles of the philosopher are not only put to work in the construction but also provide multiple elements of content.

Joyce's first published pronouncement on Aristotle was a review, sent from Paris and published in the *Daily Express* on September 3, 1903, of John Burnet's book *Aristotle on Education,* a compilation drawn from Aristotle's *Ethics* and *Politics.* What is revealing in an otherwise unenthusiastic review is the conclusion: "This book can hardly be considered a valuable addition to philosophical literature, but it has a contemporary value in view of recent developments in France, and at the present time, when the scientific specialists and the whole cohort of Materialists are cheapening the good name of philosophy, it is very useful to give heed to one who has been wisely named *maestro di color che sanno*" (*CW* 109–10). In a forceful declaration, Joyce affirms the power of Aristotle's timeless wisdom against the emergent materialism of his day.[20]

Aristotle also appears as an authority in "The Holy Office," the famous satirical poem written by Joyce shortly before he left Dublin in 1904 lampooning Yeats and other leading figures of the Irish literary revival; he criticizes in particular their spurious spirituality and false ethereal Celtic mysticism. He asks: "Ruling one's life by commonsense / How can one fail to be intense?" In a literal interpretation of the doctrine of catharsis, Joyce sees it as his task to cleanse literary Ireland, appealing to Aristotle even in the most inauspicious surroundings:

Myself unto myself will give
This name, Katharsis-Purgative.
I, who dishevelled ways forsook
To hold the poets' grammar-book,
Bringing to tavern and to brothel
The mind of witty Aristotle,
Lest bards in the attempt should err
Must here be my interpreter:
Wherefore receive now from my lip
Peripatetic scholarship.

(*CW* 149–50)

Anyone who has read Aristotle may well wonder about the phrase "witty Aristotle." He is not exactly the most lighthearted, although there are two or three passages where there might be the hint of intellectual playfulness. Hugh Kenner points out however that Joyce is translating Dante's description of Aristotle as *maestro di color che sanno* ("master of those who know") into a Saxon idiom; from the verb "witan," "witty" means "knowing."[21] As noted earlier, Swift also refers in *Gulliver's Travels* to Aristotle as "renowned for wit and learning."[22]

Joyce's natural sympathy with Aristotle also comes across in his review of a book by one of those figures targeted in "The Holy Office," Lady Gregory's *Poets and Dreamers*. One might wonder why he should start a review with the name of Aristotle. The review was published on March 26, 1903, six days after he wrote that he was up to his neck in Aristotle's *Metaphysics;* drawing out the essence of the early pages of that treatise, he sketches the trajectory from childhood wonder to the wisdom of old age. He writes: "Aristotle finds at the beginning of all speculation the feeling of wonder, a feeling proper to childhood, and if speculation be proper to the middle period of life it is natural that one should look to the crowning period of life for the fruit of speculation, wisdom itself" (*CW* 103).

It would seem that Joyce absorbed from Aristotle a firm belief in the absolute character of truth. According to Richard M. Kain, the two basic themes of *Ulysses* were social criticism and philosophical relativity.[23] The following declaration from *Stephen Hero* is indicative of Joyce's diagnosis: "It is a mark of the modern spirit to be shy in the presence of all absolute statements. However sure you may be now of the reasonableness of your convictions you cannot be sure that you will always think them reasonable"

(*SH* 205). In a review of Ibsen's *Catalina,* published in March 1903, Joyce wrote: "As the breaking-up of tradition, which is the work of the modern era, discountenances the absolute, and as no writer can escape the spirit of his time, the writer of dramas must remember now more than ever a principle of all patient and perfect art which bids him express his fable in terms of his characters" (*CW* 100).[24] Here, in his recipe for the role of art in counteracting the relativism of the day, Joyce invokes Aristotle's use of character as exemplar.[25] Typical of this general frame of mind to which Joyce refers is the empiricist attitude, according to which we live in a world not of realities but of relativities. Aristotle's stance was diametrically opposed. Concerning his brother's passing curiosity in pragmatism, Stanislaus Joyce noted: "The asserted relativity of truth and the practical test of knowledge by its usefulness to an end ran counter not only to his Aristotelian principles of logic, but still more to his character."[26]

To borrow a phrase from Descartes, founder of the modern philosophic spirit, Aristotle had sought the *fundamentum inconcussum veritatis,* the unshaken ground of truth. This is recognized by Stephen Dedalus: "Aristotle's entire system of philosophy rests upon his book of psychology and that, I think, rests on his statement that the same attribute cannot at the same time and in the same connection belong to and not belong to the same subject" (*P* V.1215–19). In fact, Stephen is mistaken—perhaps this is intentional on Joyce's part; it is in the *Metaphysics,* not his treatise on the soul, that Aristotle declares, "The same thing cannot at the same time both belong and not belong to the same object and in the same respect."[27] Aristotle wanted an absolute, necessary, nonhypothetical principle that would guarantee all discourse. Thus he formulated the famous law of noncontradiction. Stephen is clearly struck by the luminous power of this fundamental law governing all thought and pervading all reality: insofar as something is, it cannot not-be; insofar as we affirm, we cannot simultaneously deny. It is rigorous and compelling; it is absolutist. According to Aristotle, whoever denies it reduces himself to the status of the plant. Stanislaus, Joyce's brother, interestingly, invokes the evidence of the principle of noncontradiction when scorning the idea of belief in mystery: "One would laugh at the ridiculous idea of Aristotle covering his face with his hands and praying to God in agony of spirit to remove the temptation to disbelieve in the principle that at the same time and in the same connection the same attribute cannot belong and not belong to the same object."[28]

The first question on Joyce's second-year logic examination at University College asked: "What position in Logic is assigned to the principles of

Contradiction and Identity? Can these principles be said to constitute the Criteria of Truth?" The principle of noncontradiction is changed almost beyond recognition in *Finnegans Wake*: "dime *is* cash and the cash system (you must not be allowed to forget that this is all contained, I mean the systems in the dogmarks of origen on spurios) means that I cannot now have or nothave a piece of cheeps in your pocket at the same time and with the same manners as you can now nothalf or half the cheek apiece I've in mind unless Burrus and Caseous have not or not have seemaultaneously sysentangled themselves, selldear to soldthere, once in the dairy days of buy and buy" (*FW* 161.06–14).

In *Stephen Hero,* the protagonist expresses a criticism of the modern intellectual and moral climate: "The modern spirit is vivisective. Vivisection itself is the most modern process one can conceive" (*SH* 186). Prompted by mention of the investigative method of the life sciences, Cranly rejoins presently: "I suppose you know that Aristotle founded the science of biology" (Joyce knew this from John Burnet's book *Aristotle on Education*).[29] Stephen replies, "I would not say a word against Aristotle for the world but I think his spirit would hardly do itself justice in treating of the 'inexact' sciences" (*SH* 186). Joyce may have been familiar with Aristotle's comment that it is the mark of the wise person to seek only the degree of exactness that the subject allows;[30] this is quoted by Aquinas in the *Summa Contra Gentiles.*[31]

Richard Ellmann put it well when he stated that for Joyce, "What the universe was had been laid down by Aristotle."[32] One might well respond that in this he was no exception to the majority of the human race. Henri Bergson—of Irish-Jewish extraction, who died in the same year as Joyce— wrote that if we remove from Aristotle's philosophy everything derived from poetry and religion, as well as from a rudimentary physics and biology, we are left with a solid framework that is the "natural metaphysic of the human intellect."[33] What is this natural metaphysics of the human intellect? It is the spontaneous urge to accept the visible world around us as real and intelligible; most of us do not hold with Plato that the things we see are but images of higher essences, which abide in separation beyond our experience. We are accustomed, moreover, by our Western education to interpret the world through the categories first elaborated by Aristotle.

Stephen proclaims "a genuine predisposition in favour of all but the 'premisses' of scholasticism" (*SH* 77). Speaking of Joyce, Harry Levin sharply remarks: "He lost his faith, but he kept his categories."[34] These were the categories of Aristotle, that is, the philosophical concepts of Scholasticism viewed independently of the theological premises upon which they were ultimately founded. The very term "category" (meaning accusation or attribution) was borrowed by Aristotle from the law courts to express the diverse ways we interpret things. These categories, first named by Aristotle, are the labels of our daily discourse: substances, accidents, quality, quantity, relation, and so on. They are, in a phrase coined by Sidney Hook and beloved of Arthur Koestler, the "grammar of existence."[35] Aristotle's vocabulary has shaped our daily concepts and the ways we view the world.

What makes Joyce unique in his Aristotelianism is that he consciously made it his own, applying it to his art, as material content or principle of organization. A number of doctrines impact upon the consciousness of Stephen, who frequently comes across with the naive and admirable enthusiasm of one who names the world for the first time, having discovered the illuminating language of the philosopher. He is not yet the doctrinaire Aristotelian: there is an element of parody, perhaps even a touch of caricature. He brings to bear all the mentality and jargon of Aristotle in his encounter with the world in the "Nestor" and "Proteus" episodes. Aristotle too provides the stylistic wherewithal for "Aeolus," which relies heavily on Aristotle's *Rhetoric*. "Scylla and Charybdis" throws up perilous dilemmas that lurk within the deep. Stephen is set adrift as his Aristotelianism is confronted by the radical alternative of Platonism; as he clings to the rock of Aristotelian realism, he is challenged by the modern rejection of self that threatens to unsettle the traditional solidity of substance.

Aristotelian metaphysics and psychology provide Stephen in *Ulysses* with the vocabulary and categories he needs to understand himself and to interpret the world. Aristotle inspires Stephen's musings upon a series of enigmas presented to his consciousness throughout the course of the day. We are privy to his thoughts on the meaning of history (in the classroom), the nature of perception and knowledge (on Sandymount Strand), and the identity of the self (in the National Library).

Aristotelian Concepts

To appreciate the Aristotelian context for the philosophical reflections in Joyce's writings, it will be helpful to outline a few elementary concepts from both Aristotle's metaphysics and Aristotle's psychology. As I have pointed out, one of the earliest questions to emerge in Greek philosophy was how to make sense of change. Heraclitus gave classic expression to the unsettling theory that nothing whatsoever is permanent and that all is flux (a motif frequently pondered throughout Joyce's work). Reality resembles a stream that never remains the same. (Plato applied the flux theory to the natural world and stated that it was impossible to attain stable knowledge of changing realities.) Precisely the opposite was asserted by Parmenides, who rejected all change as involving the contradiction that, in order to change, being must become other; and since the only alternative to being is nonbeing, if something were to change, logically it must cease to exist.

The central philosophical question facing Aristotle was thus to explain, on the one hand (against Parmenides), how reality could change without thereby incurring contradiction and, on the other hand (against Plato, who took too seriously Heraclitus's view of physical nature in perpetual flux), how it is possible to attain stable knowledge concerning changing realities. One of Aristotle's greatest insights was that "being is said in many ways."[36] He recognized the distinction between what things are and what they can be and formulated the distinction between actual and potential being. According to Aristotle, the primary meaning of being is actuality: potency only makes sense in light of its possible actualization. He defines change or movement as "the act of the potential as potential"; this can only be effected through the agency of a cause that is itself actual. Joyce copied this definition into his notebook in Paris in 1903: "Movement is the actuality of the possible as possible." The importance of Aristotle's distinction was emphasized—perhaps overstated—by Hugh Kenner when he suggests: "The sharpest exegetical instrument we can bring to the work of Joyce is Aristotle's great conception of potency and act. His awareness of it helps distinguish Joyce from every other writer who has used the conventions of naturalist fiction."[37]

Aristotle further distinguished two related meanings of actuality. There is firstly the word *energeia* (our word "energy"), meaning to be active or literally "at work." He also coined the term *entelecheia* to denote the fully actualized perfection of something once it has completed its action and attained its goal.[38] In this sense "entelechy" also denotes the actuality of an individual insofar as it is fundamentally determined as a definite kind of substance. Another word used to describe this is essence or "form" (Greek *eidos*). Both terms, as we shall see, are central to Stephen's theorizing. Unfortunately the word "form" suggests to the ordinary ear the notion of the external or superficial: "outline" or "shape." Form or *eidos* is for Aristotle, by contrast, the most intrinsic actualizing principle that determines the very essence of things. It is the basic perfection or actualization of an individual in itself—its first determination. The most significant instance of form for

Aristotle is the soul, which he defines as "the first actuality (*entelechy*) of a natural body endowed with organs."[39] The body will act and further actualize itself by means of its organs, but in order to do so, these must first be determined and coordinated as the organs of this particular body. Before it can do anything whatsoever, the body must itself be actualized and constituted as a unity: this precisely is the work of the soul.

The soul fashions the body with all its components into an individual and is therefore its basic, most rudimentary, determination. Soul is for Aristotle the most significant instance of form; it is the soul that first molds the body into a unitary, self-subsistent, living being. The body's activities are a second actualization, but without the first actualization by soul, there is no thinking or perception, movement or rest, reproduction or nutrition, growth or decay. "It is the soul by which we primarily live, perceive, and think; so that soul is the *logos* or form, and not the matter."[40]

Aristotle provides the radical explanation for the unity of the body when he defines the soul as the "first actuality of a natural body which potentially possesses life."[41] The soul gives to the body actual existence, unity, and life. It is fundamental for Aristotle that the soul governs all vital activities of the human individual: vegetal, sensitive, and intellective. Aristotle's notion of form is well conveyed by Edmund Spenser: "For of the soul the body form doth take / For soul is form and doth the body make."[42] With the rise of the scientific method and its influence in modern philosophy, the Aristotelian principle of form was abandoned, as evidenced by the preface to Newton's *Principia:* "the moderns, rejecting substantial forms and occult qualities, have endeavoured to subject the phenomena of nature to the laws of mathematics."[43] Substance was rejected by the British empiricists, prompting doubts regarding self-identity, such as those that trouble Stephen in "Scylla and Charybdis."

"The soul is the first entelechy of a naturally organic body": this is the first quotation noted by Joyce in his notebook in February 1903, as he read Aristotle in the library of Sainte-Geneviève in Paris. The definition was to become crucial for his formulation of personal identity in *Ulysses*. Aristotle made use of other related concepts in his psychology to explain the nature of the soul and its cognitive activity. Joyce adopted many of these into his vocabulary. Among the phrases that he copied from Aristotle's *De Anima,* the following are particularly relevant to our topic:

A sense receives the form without the matter.
The sensation of particular things is always true.

The intellect conceives the forms of the images presented to it.
The intellectual soul is the form of forms.
The soul is in a manner all that is.[44]

According to Aristotle, while a sense faculty assimilates the sensible form of a material body, it is confined to one object. Intellect is not so restricted, since it can receive immaterially the forms of all things. That is what is meant by the phrase cited by Joyce: "The intellectual soul is the form of forms."[45] It has unrestricted cognitive openness toward the entirety of reality, with the capacity to grasp intellectively the essence or form of every substance that it encounters. This is stated in another phrase from *De Anima* that Joyce entered in his cahier: "Summing up what we have said about the soul, let us assert once more that the soul is in a manner all that is."[46]

It is impossible to exaggerate the importance for Joyce of the Aristotelian concepts of form, actuality, and potency and their application to the soul. In the metaphysical context, the soul is defined as the "entelechy," the first form or actualization of the body, which constitutes the human individual as a real single entity; epistemologically, it is the "form of forms," allowing the individual to know all reality.[47] We will return to these concepts as they relate to the identity of what is known and of the person who knows.

The human soul is for Aristotle a unique kind of form, *eidos,* or entelechy: whereas the form of every other kind of living thing is limited to itself, the human form has the capacity to receive immaterially into itself, in both sensation and intellection, the forms of everything that it knows.[48] Aristotle thus calls it the "form of forms"—as the hand is the "tool of tools," because it literally "*manu*-factures" every other tool or instrument. Although for Aristotle all intellectual knowledge depends for its content upon sensation, its activity is to some degree independent of the senses; in this mode of separation, it is, according to Aristotle,[49] "immortal and eternal"—incorrectly transcribed by Joyce in his Paris notebook as "immortal and *divine.*"[50]

Theoharis Constantine Theoharis sums up the significance for Joyce of Aristotle's treatise on the soul:

Aristotle's *De Anima* is an account of the nature and activity of life in the here and now. Vitality's functions, not the personality's, are the subjects of Aristotle's *Psychology.* Joyce the novelist found there not a philosophy of character that could be drawn on for the creation of fictional people, but a general account of life itself, a description of the fundamental laws governing organic existence, and of the process by which human beings experience and understand those laws.

De Anima must have appealed to Joyce the infidel largely because its analysis of the soul is general and impersonal, scientific rather than religious. I think he absorbed the treatise's general principles, used them as primary structural devices in his novel, and, according to habit, insinuated in *Ulysses* that he had done so.[51]

∗　∗　∗

To conclude this chapter, I will treat summarily of an important passage in "Nestor," in which Stephen engages in prolonged reflections that are entirely Aristotelian in content and character, with one paragraph consisting wholly of Aristotelian allusion and association. In the classroom, Stephen reflects upon the nature of time and of history, then on knowledge, mind, and the soul. Pondering the significance of historical events, he asks what their ultimate ontological status is. To begin with, they are real facts that cannot be ignored: "Had Pyrrhus not fallen by a beldam's hand in Argos or Julius Caesar not been knifed to death? They are not to be thought away. Time has branded them and fettered they are lodged in the room of the infinite possibilities they have ousted. But can those have been possible seeing that they never were? Or was that only possible which came to pass?" (*U* 2.48–52). Stephen's reflections recall Aristotle's explanation in the *Poetics* of the difference between poetry and history. The poet describes not what has happened but what might happen—"what is possible as being probable or necessary"; the historian in contrast relates what has in fact happened.[52] The terminology here masks a confusion among related terms, with crucial implications for Stephen's definition of history a few moments later. Aristotle himself declares, "What has happened cannot be made not to have happened."[53]

Stephen's school colleague and headmaster, Mr. Deasy, views history *sub specie aeternitatis*. His perspective is eschatological, in the fanciful view of some commentators, even Hegelian: "All human history moves towards one great goal, the manifestation of God" (*U* 2.380–81). Stephen experiences history differently. Subjectively, it is the nightmare from which he is trying to awake; objectively, it is the actualization of possible contingencies, and in this regard, his interpretation is Aristotelian. Past events are possibilities that have been actualized and thus removed from the world of possible contingency—excised from time and forever inscribed on the scroll of history. Historical facts are caught in the "niche of time" (*FW* 290.01). In "Scylla and Charybdis" (again with Caesar as an example), Stephen reflects upon the imponderable reality of unfulfilled contingencies of the past and the status of unrealized possibilities: "Here he ponders things that were not: what Caesar would have lived to do had he believed the soothsayer: what might have been: possibilities of the possible as possible: things not known: what name Achilles bore when he lived among women" (*U* 9.348–51).[54]

Stephen expresses his understanding of history in a phrase recalled from his reading of Aristotle's *Metaphysics:* "It must be a movement then, an actuality of the possible as possible. Aristotle's phrase formed itself within the gabbled verses and floated out into the studious silence of the library of Sainte Genevieve where he had read, sheltered from the sin of Paris, night by night" (*U* 2.67–70). This is an autobiographical fact: in February 1902, Joyce spent evenings reading the works of Aristotle in the Bibliothèque Sainte-Geneviève. One of the phrases that he copied into his notebook was: "Movement is the actuality of the possible as possible."[55] Joyce's rendition of Aristotle is itself a little garbled, caused by a substitution in the French translation of "possible" for "potential." The translation he used, that of J. Barthélemy-Saint-Hilaire,[56] was, in the words of a later French translator, "*très défectueuse.*"[57] Correctly, the text reads: "Movement is the actuality of the potential as potential." Aristotle defines motion or change as the actuality, or actualization, not of the *possible as the possible,* but of the *potential as potential.* The correct French equivalent is "*potentialité,*" not "*possibilité.*"

Is this not mere semantics? Perhaps, but there is literally a world of difference between the "potential" and the "possible." Anything that is potential must also be possible; however, not everything that is in any sense possible is thereby potentially real. Philosophers have distinguished between logical and metaphysical possibility, also called objective and subjective possibility. Objective possibility is what is logically possible, insofar as it contains no contradiction. Subjective possibility is what has within itself the potential to be realized. The notion of a railway line to Saturn involves no inherent contradiction and is in that sense logically possible; strange as it may sound, it is "objectively possible." Subjectively, however, there are no individual existing entities that have intrinsically within themselves the wherewithal required to make it an actual reality. It has no potency in reality.

What difference could this apparently simple difference between "potency" and "possibility" have made to the composition of *Ulysses?* What are the consequences of the fact that Joyce was misled with regard to one of the most fundamental doctrines of Aristotle's metaphysics? Perhaps none, other than a change of word that reoccurs throughout the book. The phrase "actuality of the potential as potential," it must be said, does not have the same flowing cadence; perhaps the error is *bien trouvé*.

The remainder of the paragraph from "Nestor" is rich in Aristotelian connotation. Having theorized about history in the light of Aristotle's metaphysics, Stephen proceeds to reflect upon knowledge, thought, and the soul, inspired both by Aristotle's *Metaphysics* and *De Anima*: "Thought is the thought of thought. Tranquil brightness. The soul is in a manner all that is: the soul is the form of forms. Tranquillity sudden, vast, candescent: form of forms" (*U* 2.74–76). Joyce once more draws from his treasury of quotations, taking license, however, in fusing—if not indeed confusing—aspects of Aristotle's psychology with his metaphysics and theology. As we have seen, the soul is for Aristotle the "form of forms," because it uniquely has the power to assimilate in an immaterial mode the essences or forms of everything it knows. God is defined by Aristotle as self-thinking thought, or the "thought of thought." Thinking is the highest act of which humans are capable, hence the best activity we can ascribe to the Prime Mover. The only proper object of God's thinking can be God himself, that is, the being whose nature is itself the plenitude of thought—hence the definition of God as *noêsis noêseôs,* self-thinking thought.

Joyce here applies the phrase "thought of thought" to the activity of intellect. There is no need to suggest, as does Sheldon Brivic, that "form of forms" is "clearly a definition of godhead, the first cause of everything else" and that Joyce equates mind with God.[58] "Form of forms" is Aristotle's definition of soul; "thought of thought" is his description of the Prime Mover. Stephen merely assimilates both phrases—a natural association, but there can be no identification of the human mind with God. The self-reflection of intellectual knowledge (the "form of forms" reflecting upon its contents), while clearly different from the self-thinking thought of God, may equally be described as "thought of thought." In our intellectual activity, humans most resemble the nature of divinity; Aristotle remarks that we sometimes do what God does always. There is no reason, however, to read this identification into Stephen's musings.

*   *   *

Later chapters will consider in detail the influence of Aristotle throughout the writings of James Joyce. This is evident in *A Portrait* and *Ulysses,* less so in *Finnegans Wake.* Seamus Deane has remarked, "In the *Wake,* the Greeks don't get a look-in."[59] Aristotle's strict logic of noncontradiction, based on the absolute opposition of "either-or," gives way to the *coincidentia opposi-torum* of Nicholas of Cusa, "a collideorscope" (*FW* 143.28) in which di-chotomies "by the coincidance of their contraries reamalgamerge." (*FW* 49.36) Aristotle is given his correct name only once, in connection with the law of universal order: "A Place for Everything and Everything in its Place" (*FW* 306.17–18). We have already seen how his formulation of the principle of noncontradiction is the subject of parody. Also parodied is the statement from the *Poetics* that "a probable impossibility is to be preferred to a thing improbable and yet possible."[60] There is reference to Aristotle's ambulant manner of teaching in the phrase "veripatetic imago of the impossible" (*FW* 417.32). With oblique allusion to John Pentland Mahaffy's clever quip that "in Ireland the inevitable never happens, the unexpected always," the author of the *Wake* writes:

> in this madh vaal of tares [. . .] where the possible was the improb-able and the improbable the inevitable. [. . .] we are in for a sequen-tiality of improbable possibles though possibly nobody after having grubbed up a lock of cwold cworn above his subject probably in Har-rystotalies or the vivle will go out of his way to applaud him on the onboiassed back of his remark for utterly impossible as are all these events they are probably as like those which may have taken place as any others which never took person at all are ever likely to be. Ahahn! (*FW* 110.09–21)

Joyce pokes fun here at Aristotle, as well as the Bible. The Ondt is described later as a "conformed aceticist and aristotaller" (*FW* 417.16).

Although Joyce's final masterpiece contains but few explicit references, Aristotelian motifs remain operative in the constant enigmas that compel the text. These will emerge as we observe Joyce's engagement with the re-lated questions of knowledge and identity in the pages of *Finnegans Wake*.

We may well ask how Joyce the "Aristotelian" can reconcile his technique of free association with the ineluctable modalities not only of the audible, visible, and other sensibles, but more crucially the ineluctability of the laws of thought. Can the analytic/synthetic/dialectic mentality of Aristotle host the idiosyncratic idiom of the *monologue intérieur*? One recalls Coleridge's remark about "the streamy nature of association, which thinking = reason curbs and rudders."[61] Does not the flow of consciousness, as Anthony Bur-gess suggests, follow "subterranean laws of association rather than logic"?[62] Joyce's technique dramatizes the problem of identity that intrigued Stephen.

But Aristotle also recognized the power of association—indispensable for metaphor. It is a gift of nature, free and spontaneous, the true sign of genius. For Aristotle, there is no conflict, only the difference between two levels of human activity: the primary order of natural reality and the derivative order of creative imitation. In Joyce, we find rich examples of both.

2

Thomist Joyce

Famously declaring loyalty to the school of old Aquinas, Joyce praised the saint as "perhaps the keenest and most lucid mind known to human history" (*CW* 161). In his Trieste notebook, he refers to Aquinas as "the lucid sensual Latin."[1] The influence of St. Thomas may be viewed broadly under three aspects. As theologian and official teacher of the Catholic Church, he was, symbolically, the figure of authority whom Joyce confronted on the battlefield of belief and doubt. As philosopher, he was an important channel of Aristotelian thought. As saint praising the beauty of God, Aquinas provided Joyce with the categories for his secular aesthetics. I will discuss these matters of philosophical or artistic content and survey the historical-educational circumstances of Joyce's initiation into the thought of St. Thomas; I will also adduce available evidence for his familiarity with specific writings of Aquinas.

Joyce's debt to both Aristotle and Aquinas went far beyond what Stephen declared was "only a garner of slender sentences from Aristotle's poetics and psychology and a *Synopsis Philosophiae Scholasticae ad mentem divi Thomae*" (*P* V.99–100). The significance of Aquinas in Joyce's intellectual formation is considerable. According to S. Foster Damon, Joyce's alter ego, Stephen, "has mastered Aquinas and Aristotle so well that he saw the whole world through their eyes."[2] Joyce's biographer remarked: "[I]n the back of Stephen's mind that instinctive, deeply-planted Aquinianism constantly manifests itself. He is an astonishing modern product of scholastic philosophy."[3] Referring to Joyce, Herbert S. Gorman comments: "Here was a young man who had been flung head-foremost into the writings of Aristotle and St Thomas Aquinas in a Jesuit school and therefore naturally a dialectician. The hair-splitting strangeness of scholastic philosophy (long dormant in modern letters) had been bred in him. His scheme of things was based upon these men and together with it went his self-disillusionment in the Roman-Catholic Church."[4]

Symptomatic of Joyce's complex character is the fact that, at the time he was consciously rejecting the authority of the Catholic Church, and seeking a replacement, he invoked her greatest magisterial authority, St. Thomas Aquinas, in the service of his artistic creed. Anthony Burgess remarks: "It is typical of Joyce that, creating a religion of art to replace his Catholicism, he has to formulate his aesthetic in the terms of the schoolmen, and that his very premises come out of Aquinas."[5] In the overarching project to shape his role as conscience-maker of his race through the medium of art, while rejecting the core beliefs of Aquinas's Catholic system, he retained much of its intellectual equipment to authorize the principles of artistic creation. Aquinas's brief reflections on aesthetics occur in relation to beauty as a name and quality of divine nature; Joyce unties them from their original context and applies them to the context of human creativity.

Opinions vary widely regarding the importance of Aquinas and his Greek master Aristotle in the work of Joyce. One commentator refers critically to "those scholars who see Joyce as an Aristotelian for all seasons."[6] Harry Levin refers to the "central" influence of Shakespeare and Aquinas, as opposed to the "tangential" influence of Mallarmé.[7] His friend Padraic Colum writes: "Aristotle and St Thomas Aquinas had shown him everything, and who was there who could show him any more?"[8] Frank O'Connor regarded A Portrait as "a study in differentiation based on Aristotle's De Anima and St Thomas's Commentary." The first page, which looks like a long passage of baby talk, is, he suggests, "an elaborate construct that relates the development of the senses to the development of the arts, a device later used in Ulysses, when we find the transmigration of souls discussed over an underlying metaphor of the transmutation of matter."[9] Robert Scholes and Richard M. Kain, on the other hand, suggest that "Joyce's practice with Aristotle and Aquinas was not to work out their theories but to borrow single phrases which caught his fancy and work out his own interpretations of the possibilities inherent in those phrases."[10]

The testimony of Joyce's brother Stanislaus is informative: "The interest that my brother always retained in the philosophy of the Catholic Church sprang from the fact that he considered Catholic philosophy to be the most coherent attempt to establish such an intellectual and material stability. [. . .] My brother was undoubtedly interested more in the Catholic Church than in any other organized system in Europe. He found its theologians ruthlessly logical, granting their premises, and suggestive of thought even when he did not agree with them."[11]

In "The Holy Office," the youthful and rebellious Joyce publicly declares his debt to Aquinas, confessing that his intellectual strength is derived from St. Thomas:

> So distantly I turn to view
> The shamblings of that motley crew,
> Those souls that hate the strength that mine has
> Steeled in the school of old Aquinas. (*CW* 152)

This self-recognition is most significant, leaving no doubt as to where his allegiance lay. His adherence to Aquinas, however strong, was limited to certain fundamental philosophical notions and principles, the "premisses" (*SH* 77) upon which Scholasticism was grounded. Rejecting his theology, Joyce adhered to Aquinas the philosopher, which meant essentially Aquinas the Aristotelian. In this respect, his picture of Aquinas was that portrayed by scholars at the start of the twentieth century, who assumed that Aquinas's purpose as philosopher was to adapt Aristotle's system to Christian teaching.

The relation of Aquinas to Aristotle prompts the question of their respective attitudes toward Platonism, often viewed as the other great, alternative, and rival philosophical approach within the tradition of philosophy. Joyce was avowedly Aristotelian; in this, he was typical of the Thomists of his day, since Aquinas was also by repute an avowed Aristotelian. According to general contemporary interpretation, Aquinas's greatest achievement was to enlist the philosopher of Stagira into the service of Christian theology while rejecting every trace of Platonism. This view was clearly stated by Canon Sheehan in a book published in 1903.[12] Referring to Platonism, Sheehan writes:

> Yet, it always haunted the East with its poetic splendours, until the tremendous reaction of mediaeval times towards the Aristotelian method of reasoning drove Platonism back into the shades of history and tradition. And from these mediaeval times downwards, the Aristotelian philosophy with its contempt for poetry, its hard, dry analysis, and the rigid formalism of the syllogism, has been accepted informally as the philosophic method of the Church. The *Summa* of St. Thomas, the impregnable bulwark of Catholic philosophic teaching, is founded on it. The spirit of the Stagyrite passed into the "dumb Sicilian ox," and through his mouth spoke to the world.[13]

Leaving aside the many inaccuracies in this view—for one thing, Aristotle held poetry in high regard—this passage indicates perfectly the understanding of the time. There is something of this, certainly exaggerated, in Stephen's remarks to Cranly in *Stephen Hero:* "But what is the Church? It is not Jesus, the magnificent solitary with his inimitable abstinences. The Church is made by you and my like—her services, legends, practices, paintings, music, traditions. These her artists gave her. They made her what she is. They accepted Aquinas' commentary on Aristotle as the Word of God and made her what she is" (*SH* 143).

The picture of the philosopher Aquinas as a quasi-doctrinaire Aristotelian endured until the mid-twentieth century, by which time the profound influence of Plato was finally and generally recognized. Etienne Gilson, one of the greatest Thomist scholars of the twentieth century and who was at the center of a revolution in Thomist studies in Paris in the 1920s, had claimed that Aquinas made a conscious option for Aristotle and against Plato. The picture current in Joyce's day of Aquinas as a strict Aristotelian has been largely revised in the last century to recognize the important elements assimilated from Platonism.[14] It is agreed, nonetheless, that Aquinas relied on Aristotle in matters of method and epistemology; Aristotle was simply *philosophus* (*the* philosopher)—the figure most singularly deserving of the name. Aristotle was the master of method, a sure guide and teacher.

Typical for the Thomist of his day, Joyce would in fact have seen minimal difference between the philosophies of St. Thomas and Aristotle. According to accepted opinion, Aquinas had merely baptized the philosophical system of the Stagirite; Thomist philosophy completed Aristotelian thought. Trained by Thomist masters, Joyce entered the conceptual worlds of both without concern for overlapping or extending borderlines but absorbed the two together. Aristotle and Aquinas furnished Joyce with an applied aesthetic and provided his characters with multifarious themes of discourse as they reflect on daily life. In grossly simplistic terms, we may say that Aristotle's metaphysics and psychology supply Stephen with the concepts and categories needed to understand himself and to interpret the world, while Aquinas inspired the aesthetic reflections that were his central concern in *A Portrait.*

The Thomist Revival

It will be of interest to consider the historical and intellectual circumstances of Joyce's introduction to Aquinas. While this may seem a boundless landscape, the conditions are so definitive and particular that the following account might be accurately summed up: "Gioacchino Pecci and James Joyce." Pecci was elected Pope on February 20, 1878, as Leo XIII; on August 4, 1879, he issued the encyclical *Aeterni Patris,* which was arguably the single most decisive factor in shaping the intellectual milieu in which two decades later James Joyce would—albeit informally—receive his philosophical and aesthetic education. The Catholic commitment to philosophy was given a vigorous boost through the renaissance in Scholastic philosophy inspired by the encyclical. Pope Leo encouraged Catholic schools and universities to "restore the renowned teaching of Thomas Aquinas to its ancient beauty." He exhorted:

> Let carefully selected teachers endeavor to implant the doctrine of Thomas Aquinas in the minds of students, and set forth clearly his solidity and excellence over others. Let the universities already founded or to be founded by you illustrate and defend this doctrine, and use it for the refutation of prevailing errors. But, lest the false for the true or the corrupt for the pure be drunk in, be ye watchful that the doctrine of Thomas be drawn from his own fountains, or at least from those rivulets which, derived from the very fount, have thus far flowed, according to the established agreement of learned men, pure and clear.[15]

The encyclical inspired a remarkable revival of Scholastic philosophy; new centres of Thomist philosophy were established, journals and instructional handbooks were published for the dissemination of Thomistic thought. Within two decades, the Thomist renaissance would in large measure mold the mind of the young Joyce, providing the kernel of his aesthetic and the philosophical concepts that would be credited to his literary hero.

While he was most likely unaware of the role of Gioacchino Pecci,[16] by Joyce's own testimony Aquinas was one of his greatest influences. In assessing the importance of the Pope's encyclical for the Catholic educational milieu of the time, it will be helpful to present the background to its promulgation in the late nineteenth century. Although Aquinas, who died in 1274 and was canonized in 1323, was the most preeminent Doctor of the Catholic Church, his importance had greatly diminished over the centuries. The reasons why the Pope thought it necessary to issue an encyclical are well illustrated by the reply received in November 1846 by John Henry Newman when he asked an Italian Jesuit if their young students studied Aristotle: "Oh no," he said, "Aristotle is in no favour here—no, not in Rome—nor St Thomas. I have read Aristotle and St Thomas and owe a great deal to them, but they are out of favour here and throughout Italy. St Thomas is a great saint, people don't care to speak against him; they profess to reverence him, but put him aside." In reply to Newman's question, concerning what philosophy they adopted, "He said none. 'Odds and ends, whatever seems to them best, like St Clement's *Stromata*. They have no philosophy. Facts are the great things, and nothing else. Exegesis, but not doctrine.'"[17] Against this background of ignorance, apathy, and antipathy, the encyclical *Aeterni Patris* brought about a remarkable renaissance of Scholastic philosophy, particularly in Europe. Succeeding decades saw a great revival of research into the writings and system of Aquinas. One direct result of this was the initiation of an attractively produced series of manuals by professors of philosophy at the historic Jesuit college at Stonyhurst in Lancashire; these were, as I will illustrate, the primary instruments of Joyce's education in logic, aesthetics, and philosophy.

To understand the impact of the Thomist revival upon the philosophical milieu that directly influenced Joyce, it is necessary to clarify the status of philosophy at University College, especially since conflicting and contradictory accounts have been given. On the one hand, Kristian Smidt, while partly correct with respect to the importance of Aristotle and Aquinas, exaggerates Joyce's exposure to their thought:

> At the university, which he entered in 1898, Joyce began to study Aristotle and Aquinas thoroughly. These two were of the greatest importance to him, and for a time they probably satisfied his intellectual curiosity. Aristotle seems to have inspired much of the thinking that lay behind *Ulysses* and *Finnegans Wake*. And Aquinas's aesthetic theories formed Joyce's point of departure in his own aesthetic speculations. The fact that Aristotle and Aquinas were pillars of Roman Catholic theology places Joyce's intellectual starting point, like his metaphysical origin, within the confines of the Church.[18]

At the other extreme, some commentators have entirely denied Joyce's debt to Aquinas. It is not true, as claimed by Jacques Aubert, that Scholastic philosophy was barred from the state-supported university.[19] While William T. Noon is correct in saying that Joyce never formally studied philosophy, he ignores the importance of his exposure to Aristotelian Thomism at University College.[20]

Noon's *Joyce and Aquinas,* published in 1957, is to date the most comprehensive study on Joyce and Aquinas. As a Jesuit, Noon had obvious advantages; intimately familiar with the spirit and background of Joyce's education, he also had direct access to relevant records of the Irish Jesuits. Noon was, most surprisingly, misinformed by his fellow Jesuit Fergal McGrath, who stated: "No regular course in scholastic philosophy was offered at all in the old University College during Joyce's attendance."[21] Noon moreover missed some crucial items of evidence and engaged instead in vain speculation regarding putative sources of influence.[22] Thus it is worth recalling some relevant facts and circumstances that either directly or indirectly influenced Joyce's philosophical education during his formative years. Of particular relevance are the philosophical teaching manuals at University College, which, I contend, were the main source for Joyce's knowledge of Aristotle and Aquinas and arguably the primary source for his aesthetic ideas.

Joyce's Jesuit Masters

Because of the close spirit of the academic *communitas* between the small body of students and professors at University College, it is of definite interest to supply some information about the personalities who enliven the pages of *Stephen Hero* and *A Portrait of the Artist as a Young Man*. This will provide an insight into the ambience of Aristotelian Thomism that influenced Joyce. The background to his philosophical "formation" is also inextricably linked to the Jesuits' governance of the College and its relationship with the Royal University.

One of the central figures in *A Portrait* is the College president; the person behind the character played an even greater role in reality. William Delany (1835–1924)[23] attended St. Patrick's College, the Irish national seminary in Maynooth, before deciding to join the Jesuits as the best way of serving the cause of Irish Catholic education. He studied at Saint-Acheul in France and Stonyhurst in Lancashire; after ordination, he studied theology in Rome. Appointed rector of St. Stanislaus College, Tullabeg, in 1870, he brought rapid fame to the school, and it was largely as a result of Fr. Delany's reputation as an educationalist that the bishops transferred the Catholic University to the Jesuits. Delany was greatly influential in the establishment of the Royal University by the Disraeli Conservative Government in 1879. This was not a teaching institution but an examining body, with which were affiliated a number of colleges, staffed by fellows paid by the Royal University—a formula that allowed indirect funding of Catholic colleges. Its charter was approved on April 27, 1880, and its senate appointed: eighteen Catholics and eighteen non-Catholics. In October

1883, the bishops transferred the Catholic University to the Jesuits, with Fr. Delany in charge. An early controversy to assail Delany arose from a complaint by the bishops, meeting at Clonliffe College on October 1, 1884, that the questions in the metaphysics examinations of the Royal University necessitated "the reading of anti-Catholic works, most dangerous to Catholic faith."[24] The problem arose from the lack of suitable literature dealing with modern philosophy from the Scholastic point of view.

Partly to blame for this problem, and responsible in turn for its solution, was another remarkable Jesuit, Thomas A. Finlay (1848–1940). Finlay studied in France, Italy, and Germany and in 1883 was appointed professor of mental philosophy at University College. He was concurrently rector of Belvedere, the Jesuits' secondary school, and it was perhaps the onerous obligations of his joint appointment that caused him soon to be embroiled in the dispute with the bishops that, in the words of his biographer, "threatened the future of the college."[25] The examination paper in metaphysics had been set by Fr. Finlay together with Professor Park of Queen's College, Belfast, and was intended for a wide range of students: those who had studied philosophy in the light of modern approaches, and those (particularly in Catholic seminaries) who had been taught from the traditional, Scholastic, point of view. Finlay himself accepted as "a deplorable blunder"[26] the failure to take the latter sufficiently into account, especially as no suitable textbooks were available in English. The senate of the Royal University quickly set up a committee to devise a program of studies that would be fair to all candidates.

In early 1885, "largely through the efforts of Finlay, a satisfactory and effective compromise was worked out. Some changes were made in the courses, and a choice of alternative questions was offered."[27] The chairman of the senate, Lord Emly, would have preferred to face down the bishops but was persuaded by Fr. Delany to satisfy them temporarily, "even at the risk of narrowing temporarily our course of mental philosophy."[28] He was confident that suitable handbooks would become available within a few years, by which time "the Royal University, 'now on its trial and suspected,' would have grown and established itself, and Catholics would have won such a position at University College that it would be plain that the system involved no unfairness and no religious danger."[29] Delany's biographer notes significantly that "in accordance with the lines laid down by the pope, he was committed to making the college's philosophical teaching 'distinctly and thoroughly Scholastic and Thomistic.'"[30] Constantine Curran, a classmate of Joyce, recalled that while philosophy courses attracted "a large portion of the best brains in the College . . . it was not so easy for any student to escape some tincture of divine philosophy."[31] Thomas Finlay's biographer also remarks: "The Aristotelian and Thomist undercurrent ran through the institution, and influenced those like James Joyce and Curran who did not follow any course in philosophy."[32]

Delany's confidence regarding philosophical handbooks was well-founded; within a few years, a comprehensive series of manuals, written by professors of Stonyhurst, the English Jesuit seminary, provided the core of the philosophy curriculum at University College. The volume in psychology was written by Delany's nephew, Michael Maher, past pupil of St. Stanislaus College, Tullabeg, and now a member of the English Jesuit province.[33] Thomas Finlay, for his part, responded to the crisis—for which he felt responsible—by translating *A Handbook of the History of Philosophy* by the German priest, Albert Stöckl.[34] Finlay was either founder or cofounder of six journals and editor of three. The choice of the name *Lyceum,* so called after the school of Aristotle, for a monthly literary and educational magazine is indicative of his philosophical leanings.

A key figure who played an important part in Joyce's education was Fr. Joseph Darlington (1850–1939). Darlington received a master's degree from Brasenose College, Oxford, in 1876[35] and ministered for a short time in the Anglican Church. After a year of reflection spent in the Rhineland, he was received into the Catholic Church and in 1880 joined the Irish Jesuits. In 1890, he became dean of studies at University College and university examiner in English. Darlington taught both English and philosophy in turn. Constantine Curran commented: "His teaching of each subject profited from his experience of the other. Perhaps he was not so very distinguished as a philosopher, but his approach to Hamlet through Aristotle and Aquinas had a particular savour for one student bored with the solemnities of Dowden and Bradley. This Aristotelian under-current emerged whenever the Dean spoke, as he often did, at the College Societies, and indeed it fits in with what Father Delany used to say, that the Faculty of Philosophy should be at the heart of any university."[36]

Another person who contributed decisively to Joyce's philosophical development was William Magennis (1867–1946). An early student of Thomas Finlay's, he graduated in 1888,[37] and during Joyce's time at University College held a fellowship in mental and moral philosophy.[38] There is reference in *A Portrait* to "the tall form of the young professor of mental science discussing on the landing a case of conscience with his class like a giraffe cropping high leafage among a herd of antelopes" (*P* V.650–53). The official history of University College, Dublin, under the Jesuits describes a similar scene: "During the day sometimes the metaphysicians were observed still hammering out their arguments, in the College corridors, and giving the Philistines an opportunity to jeer."[39] Such accounts suggest the philosophical enthusiasm and vitality that pervaded the student body.

As a student, Magennis had assimilated an ardent brand of Thomism from the French Jesuit Père Jacques Mallac (1829–1891), who taught at University College from 1884 to 1890. A freethinker until middle age, Mallac joined the Jesuits upon his conversion. A "fierce follower of Aristotle," he found the curriculum insufficiently "Scholastic" or "Peripatetic" and, in his zeal to rectify the situation, managed to split the student body into opposing camps of "broader and narrower Aristotelians." As a result of this divisive influence, he was recalled to France.[40] William Magennis appears to have assumed the mantle of Thomist zealot; closely involved in student activities, he championed the philosophy of St. Thomas on every occasion. Referring to a new society within the College, the Academy of St. Thomas Aquinas, in November 1901, the history of the College states: "The leading spirit of this new development was Professor Magennis, who was at this time surrounded by a militant group of his own philosophical students, just as he himself had been a prominent member of the early group."[41] His contribution to the inaugural debate was a proclamation of Aquinas's timeless supremacy:

> The principles of St Thomas Aquinas are the true principles of reason in every department. There can be no changing what is unchangeable. St Thomas' philosophy needs no reconstruction or readaptation, but we should attend to the form of its delivery; we should speak and write not in an unknown tongue but in language understandable. Whilst so many systems are attracting attention for their style, and so many books are written to support other systems, Catholic principles are unstudied by these writers and the general public because untranslated into modern jargon.[42]

Significant from our point of view is the fact that Joyce was one of the few students present at that inaugural meeting. The American scholar Kevin Sullivan had carefully examined the minutes of the Academy of St. Thomas Aquinas before they unfortunately went missing; he corrected William T. Noon's statement that Joyce appeared to have taken no part in the foundation of this society.[43] Sullivan emphasizes the "specifically Thomistic atmosphere in which Joyce chose to move while at the university."[44]

According to Joyce's classmate, William G. Fallon, Magennis exercised considerable influence on the young writer: "Joyce availed of opportunities to meet Professor William Magennis and during the succeeding years they frequently conversed in the precincts of the College or following a meeting of the Literary and Historical Society." It was Magennis who advised Joyce to read Cardinal Newman's autobiography *Apologia Pro Vita Sua*.[45] The minutes of the Library Conference of the Sodality show that Magennis presided on February 2, 1902, when Joyce attended—on the evening of his twentieth birthday—a paper delivered by his friend J. F. Byrne on *The Imitation of Christ*.[46] Magennis was also in the chair for both of Joyce's papers to the Literary & Historical Society, "Drama and Life," and that on James Clarence Mangan. He later told Constantine Curran that he admired both performances.[47] It is unlikely the independent-minded Joyce would have frequently engaged with Magennis were he not to some degree sympathetic to his ardent Thomism; this explains perhaps the background for the profession that he was "steeled in the school of old Aquinas."

Professor Magennis makes an appearance in "Aeolus," where he is described as "a man of the very highest morale." Subsequent events would indeed bear this out. As chairman of the Censorship Board and a member of the Irish Senate, Magennis was for decades the archconservative guardian of national morals. Commenting on the task of the Censorship Board, he remarked: "Beelzebub's demons of hell could not write worse than some works we have been obliged to read and report on to the Minister. They are vile beyond description."[48] We can only imagine what Magennis, "of the very highest morale," made of the most famous novel of the century, penned by the former pupil of Belvedere—his own alma mater—to whom he had, as examiner, awarded the Intermediate Senior Grade prize for English composition.

Thomist Atmosphere

Based on the wide variety of testimonies, it is evident that the influence of Aquinas was all-pervasive at Joyce's university, not only among the philosophers but also in classes of literature and even economics. The strength and power of the Thomistic atmosphere at University College can be conveyed by the following most strange confession by J. F. Byrne, who would feature as "Cranly," Stephen's co-discussant of aesthetic theory: "I have always held Saint Thomas in affectionate regard. When I was very young—say in University College, Stephen's Green—I often day-dreamed of how delightful it would be to walk out with him over the Dublin and Wicklow mountains and maybe talk as we went, or maybe not utter a word."[49]

Responding to the remark that he was quintessentially Catholic, Joyce riposted that he should really be described as a Jesuit. He had in effect received his entire education at the hands of Jesuits; for these masters, whose teaching he disavowed, he always held the greatest esteem; "I don't think you will easily find anyone to equal them," he told the composer Philipp Jarnach (*JJII* 27). Vivian Mercier has offered the following insightful evaluation of Joyce's intellectual debt to his Jesuit education:

> Joyce is the quintessence of University College; his intellectual virtues and vices are both the products of Jesuit training; the pedantry is Jesuit, and so is the continual seeking after first principles. If Trinity were to give the world a great writer today, he would never trouble to arrive at an esthetic theory before producing his works of art; still less would he base that theory upon Aristotle and Aquinas. Gorman tells us that Synge, a Trinity man, was very impatient with Joyce's pedantry when they knew each other in Paris. I wonder whether Joyce acquired his extraordinary memory partly because of the Jesuit school-discipline of repeating last day's lesson before commencing today's?[50]

William Kirkpatrick Magee ("John Eglinton" of *Ulysses*) referred to Joyce as "one of a group of lively and eager-minded young men in University College" who through their interest "in everything new in literature and philosophy far surpassed the students of Trinity College."[51]

Noteworthy is Joyce's high regard for his Jesuit teachers. According to Jacques Mercanton, he spoke of them "with a certain admiration: a distinguished order, efficacious, remarkable educators, far more likeable than the Dominicans, whom he considered narrow, obtuse, tangled up in their own theology, truly the barking dogs of the Lord."[52] This remark is echoed in Stephen's reference in "Scylla and Charybdis" to "the bulldog of Aquin" (*U* 9.863).

Thomistic Philosophical Handbooks

We now turn our attention to those philosophical handbooks that William Delany believed would assure the Catholic character of philosophy at University College and that I suggest were the primary instruments of Joyce's education in logic, aesthetics, and philosophy. Joyce himself mentions these volumes in *Stephen Hero*, referring to Cranly's friend O'Neill, whom he observed in the National Library: "He was very busy all the summer reading philosophical handbooks" (*SH* 148). Published throughout the 1890s under the general rubric of "Manuals of Catholic Philosophy"—printed in gold letters across the top, with the Jesuit motto IHS, crowned by a cross from which emanated rays of gold—the handbooks gained wide circulation and went through numerous reprints in subsequent years.[53]

The Stonyhurst series became the prescribed texts for philosophy courses in University College. It is beyond doubt that these handbooks were the primary source not only for Joyce's aesthetic ideas but also for most of his knowledge of both Aristotle and Aquinas. Constantine Curran confirms, "These Stonyhurst manuals would have escaped the attention of no intelligent student in the College; Joyce could have got what he wanted from them in half an hour."[54] Their importance, however, has been largely ignored. Curran's remarks are worth citing at length; having spoken of Fr. Darlington's importance, he states:

> As to Aquinas, I must also mention Boedder's *Natural Theology,* the textbook used in the class of religious doctrine open to all students. He had a page or two on Thomistic aesthetics starting out with *pulchra enim dicuntur ea quae visa placent.* [John] Rickaby's *General Metaphysics* was read in the philosophy classes. Joyce could not but have seen it in the hands of his friends who were reading philosophy, including, for example, J. F. Byrne (Cranly), who sat at the same table with him in the National Library and at least in the first week of the term would have opened its pages. Rickaby, between pages 148 and 151, holds the marrow of Joyce's aesthetics. It is Rickaby who quotes from St. Thomas well-nigh all that Joyce uses touching the good and the beautiful which by its mere contemplation sets the appetite at rest. He discusses its unity, or *integritas,* its harmony of parts or *consonantia,* and its clear lustre, or *claritas;* commonplaces, it may be said. But for me an intriguing detail is that Rickaby illustrates part of his argument by an unlikely reference to a barn,[55] just as Joyce, in his talk with Lynch, suddenly invokes the basket on the head of a passing butcher's boy.[56]

Proverbially, one can understand a person by knowing who his friends are or what books he reads. If we are to believe Constantine Curran, this is verified on both counts in the case of the young Joyce, who was in the habit of reading the books of his friends and fellow students.[57] Eugene Sheehy describes the atmosphere of intellectual exchange in Joyce's circle: "The real Alma Mater at this time was the National Library in Kildare Street. We read for our examinations in the Library upstairs, but there were rather prolonged adjournments to the steps outside, where we heard the views on art and life and literature of Joyce, Kettle, Skeffington, Arthur Clery, John Marcus O'Sullivan, William Dawson, Constantine Curran and many other well-read and cultured men."[58] Many of these were students of philosophy; John Marcus O'Sullivan distinguished himself as a philosophy scholar and later became a professor of history and the Minister for Education. I have in my possession a copy of the *Logic* handbook by Richard F. Clarke, S.J., signed by its owner, Joyce's classmate, Thomas Kettle, dated 1899.[59]

Curran mentions only two of the series: John Rickaby's *General Metaphysics* and Boedder's *Natural Theology.*[60] More than likely Joyce was familiar with other volumes. Later, in his library in Trieste, he had Michael Maher's manual *Psychology: Empirical and Rational,* first published in 1890 and republished six times by 1906.[61] He could find here an exposé of Aristotle's principles of matter and form as well as his definition of soul as the "first entelechy" of the body.[62]

Taking logic as a subject in his second year, Joyce was required to study the *Logic* manual by Richard F. Clarke, S.J. We read in *A Portrait*: "He saw the heads of his classmates meekly bent as they wrote in their notebooks the points they were bidden to note, nominal definitions, essential definitions and examples or dates of birth or death, chief works, a favourable and an unfavourable criticism side by side" (*P* V.134–38). Although he received a mark of 26 percent in the logic examination of 1901,[63] Joyce must have had some acquaintance with the prescribed textbook. In part 1, chapter 10, he would have found a detailed elaboration of nominal and essential definitions, which go back to Aristotle's *Posterior Analytics.*[64] He could also read in this book a comprehensive treatment of the syllogism, codified by Aristotle in its various modes.[65] Years later, in Paris, he declared to Mary Colum: "The equation in mathematics and the syllogism in logic are the great intellectual inventions."[66] Joyce was required to treat of syllogistic forms in his logic examination. The *Logic* handbook contained a lengthy exposition on the enthymeme, a rhetorical technique adopted in the "Aeolus" episode.

Due to his rejection of Catholic moral teaching, it is less likely that Joyce consulted the Stonyhurst volume on *Moral Philosophy* (*Ethics and Natural Law*) written by Joseph Rickaby, S.J., brother and religious confrere of John Rickaby, author of the two volumes mentioned above. In 1913 or 1914, Joyce went to the expense of ordering Joseph Rickaby's magnificent folio-sized translation, with copious notes, of Aquinas's *Summa Contra Gentiles* (*Of God and His Creatures*), published in 1905.[67] Responding in November 1927 to a query from Ezra Pound (who presumed that Joyce was an authority on Aquinas) regarding the phrase "*natural dimostramento*" from Guido Cavalcanti's canzone "*Donna me prega,*" Joyce replied that he could not find the phrase "in Father Rickeby's [*sic*] enormous edition of Aquinas or in the French one I have." He continues: "The scholastic machinery of the process of thought is very intricate, *verbum mentale* and all the rest of it. [. . .] These philosophical terms are such tricky bombs that I am shy of handling them, being afraid they may go off in my hands" (*LIII* 166). Had he consulted Joseph Rickaby's two-volume publication of texts from Aquinas's ethics, Joyce could have found an alternative translation of one of Aquinas's central texts on aesthetics to that provided by John Rickaby in his *General Metaphysics* manual.[68]

In John Rickaby's *General Metaphysics,*[69] Joyce would have read, possibly for the first time, the words *integritas, consonantia,* and *claritas*—the requisite elements that feature so prominently in his reflections on beauty. In Bernard Boedder's *Natural Theology,*[70] he could read Aquinas's definition of beauty: "*Pulchra dicuntur quae visa placent.*" In both manuals, he would also have encountered the definition of beauty as *splendor veri,*[71] attributed to Plato, and which he would later encounter in Flaubert. In John Rickaby's *General Metaphysics,*[72] he could read a critique of Locke's theory that personal identity is grounded in memory, a reflection that occurs in "Scylla and Charybdis." An interesting insight into the nature of these volumes may be gleaned from a remark in the *General Metaphysics* volume: "The opponents whom we shall seek to encounter will be mainly our English Empiricists, because they represent the most natural aberrations of British intellect; whereas other aberrations are of an imported character, being borrowed especially from Hegel."[73] In John Rickaby's other volume, *First Principles of Knowledge,*[74] Joyce could read, among other important quotations, Aristotle's phrase "The soul is in a manner all things," which features prominently in the "Nestor" episode of *Ulysses.*

William Noon names only one of the Stonyhurst volumes but seems not to have known it firsthand. Discussing the status, real or fictitious, of the *Synopsis Philosophiae Scholasticae ad mentem divi Thomae,* he adds: "Two other textbooks which appeared while Joyce was working out the aesthetics of the *Portrait* are the Jesuit Joseph Rickaby's *Scholasticism* (London, Constable, 1908) and his *General Metaphysics* which had appeared in 1898 in a third edition." Noon was clearly not very familiar with either of these two works. Joseph Rickaby's little book on Scholasticism would have been of little use for Joyce's aesthetics; the *General Metaphysics* volume was written not by Joseph Rickaby but by his brother John and gives lengthy quotations from Aquinas's *Summa* dealing with beauty, which Noon fails to mention. Instead, he suggests that the most likely source for Joyce's Thomist aesthetics was Maurice De Wulf's comprehensive study, *Les théories esthétiques propres à saint Thomas.*[75] It is my surmise that Joyce never read De Wulf, simply because he had already found the Thomist elements needed for his aesthetic theories in ample measure in the philosophy manuals used at University College, as confirmed by Constantine Curran.[76] It is gratuitous moreover to assume that Joyce read De Wulf, and not an equally important and more elaborate, older, work by P. Vallet, *L'idée du beau dans la philosophie de saint Thomas d'Aquin,* which deals in a variety of ways with many of the themes that concern Joyce.

It is surprising that not more attention has been paid to these handbooks by those scholars who have expended so much energy in excavating the raw materials for the literary and aesthetic theories of the young Joyce. Scholars have speculated unnecessarily about the sources for Joyce's "pennyworth of thomism." It seems strange that Fr. Noon, S.J., should have gone to such lengths to find out whether Joyce might have been able to read the very important articles by Maurice De Wulf on Aquinas's aesthetics that appeared during these years and failed to notice that, as Curran points out, a few pages in one of these handbooks contains "the marrow of Joyce's aesthetics."[77] Everything Joyce needed was available in the Manuals of Catholic Philosophy. There is perhaps feigned modesty in Stephen's claim to the Dean of Studies: "For my purpose I can work on at present by the light of one or two ideas of Aristotle and Aquinas" (*P* V.466–67). Ellmann tellingly observes: "Inspired cribbing was always part of James's talent; his gift was for transforming material, not for originating it . . . As he remarked in later life to Frank Budgen, 'Have you ever noticed, when you get an idea, how much *I* can make of it?'"[78] Joyce did not require exhaustive knowledge of the Thomist corpus to convince himself that his theories were essentially Thomist, although adapted to his own secular aesthetic. Aquinas occupied for him a position of great authority.

We get an idea of Joyce's high regard for Aquinas from his reference in the lecture "Ireland, Island of Saints and Sages" (1907) to Petrus Hibernicus (Peter of Ireland), "the theologian who had the supreme task of educating the mind of the author of the scholastic apology, *Summa Contra Gentiles,* St Thomas Aquinas, perhaps the keenest and most lucid mind known to human history" (*CW* 161). It is significant that Joyce refers to the *Summa Contra Gentiles* rather than Aquinas's more famous *Summa Theologiae.* He even borrowed the title. Gogarty described life in the Martello Tower at Sandycove: "Thus we lived in privacy and profanity. I could take it easy on the roof, for I shunned work; Joyce could remain downstairs forever reading and rereading his '*Contra Gentiles*,' an early essay against everybody."[79] The *Contra Gentiles* receives dubious mention, moreover, in *Ulysses:* "I called upon the bard Kinch at his summer residence in upper Mecklenburgh street and found him deep in the study of the *Summa contra Gentiles* in the company of two gonorrheal ladies, Fresh Nelly and Rosalie, the coalquay whore" (*U* 9.1088–91).

It seems that Joyce was quite familiar with the *Contra Gentiles;* his Trieste library included an edition published in Paris in 1906.[80] Unlike Aquinas's enormous *Summa Theologiae*, the *Contra Gentiles* was contained in a compact volume and could serve as an ideal vade mecum. We have evidence from Stanislaus Joyce that James was reading the *Summa Contra Gentiles* in 1903. Prompted either by Yeats's encouragement or the desire to earn money, James asked Stanislaus to suggest titles for some essays. Stanislaus later recorded:

> I made out a list of half a dozen or so, of which I remember "Revellers," "Athletic Beauty," "A Portrait of the Artist" (I was then reading *The Portrait of a Lady* with boundless admiration), "*Contra Gentiles*" (Jim was reading the *Summa;* I knew only the title, but it struck me as a good one for a modern essay) . . . Nothing came of it for the moment; he wrote no essay then, but he spoke to Gogarty of his intention to write an essay and call it "*Contra Gentiles.*" A short time afterwards Gogarty produced an essay with that title, and showed it to my brother. Jim read the essay, and then turned down and creased and neatly tore off the top of the page that bore the title. Gogarty pooh-poohed the gesture, and made some rambling statement about "all of us using the same alphabet."[81]

Interestingly Stanislaus also uses this title to explain his brother's motivation in writing "Drama and Life"; as with "The Day of the Rabblement," and the essay on Mangan, "his reason for doing so was also the same. In it he was defining his position to himself and against others—*contra Gentiles.*"[82]

There is even mention of the treatise in *Giacomo Joyce:* "Her father and his son sit in the carriage. They have owls' eyes and owls' wisdom. Owlish wisdom stares from their eyes brooding upon the lore of their *Summa contra Gentiles*" (*PSW* 234). In "Scylla and Charybdis" (*U* 9.770–71), a phrase is quoted from *Contra Gentiles*—referred to in standard commentaries as "source unknown." The passage in question is from book 3, chapter 125, where Aquinas argues that marriage should not take place between blood relatives: "*Amplius. In societate humana hoc est maxime necessarium ut sit amicitia inter multos.*" Joseph Rickaby's translation of the passage ("In human society the widening of friendships is of the first importance")[83] is rather loose, which confirms the suggestion in *Ulysses* that Joyce was relying on the original text: "Saint Thomas, Stephen, smiling, said, whose gorbellied works I enjoy reading in the original, writing of incest from a standpoint different from that of the new Viennese school Mr Magee spoke of, likens it in his wise and curious way to an avarice of the emotions" (*U* 9.778–81).

We have the evidence for Joyce's enthusiasm for Aquinas from some of his English language pupils on the continent. Ellmann records that he tried to choke one pupil's enthusiasm for Schopenhauer and Nietzsche "by urging that Thomas Aquinas was the greatest philosopher because his reasoning was 'like a sharp sword.' He read him, he said, in Latin, a page a day" (*JJII* 342). Another pupil reported: "A favourite subject was Thomistic morality, about which Joyce theorized with precision and ingenuity" (*JJII* 340). Joyce acknowledged to Robert McAlmon (1896–1956), an American writer whose company he enjoyed in Paris, that "his favourite authors were Cardinal Newman and St Thomas Aquinas."[84] Ellmann reported that when Joyce was discussing Aquinas, someone objected, "That has nothing to do with us," to which Joyce replied: "It has everything to do with us." Ellmann also recorded that Thomas Kettle pleased Joyce with the remark, "The difficulty about Aquinas is that what he says is so much like what the man in the street says" (*JJII* 63).

A survey of Joyce's sources would be incomplete without reference to the only Thomistic work mentioned by name in *A Portrait*. We are told that in his search for the essence of beauty, Stephen's inspiration was "only a garner of slender sentences from Aristotle's poetics and psychology and a *Synopsis Philosophiae Scholasticae ad mentem divi Thomae*" (*P* V.98–100). Jacques Aubert, to whom we are greatly indebted for having discovered the actual work, correctly explains that "this *Synopsis* is not fictional; it has actual bibliographic existence."[85] Although it has physical existence, its use in *A Portrait* is in all likelihood no more than fictional: the title suited Joyce's purpose, as it suggested pithily the kind of volume likely to contain the pennyworth of Thomism needed to creatively stimulate a personal aesthetic. Joyce entered in his Paris notebook the title and call number in the Bibliothèque Sainte-Geneviève: FOL R SUP 5—the number still in use today. There is no evidence that he drew any influence from the work; the only hint that he may have consulted it is the word "slender." The work summarizes in telegrammatic style ("slender sentences"?) the main doctrines of Thomist philosophy in its various branches, followed by a catalogue listing the errors of subsequent thinkers. The *Synopsis* is not strictly a book, rather a folio-sized aide-memoire intended for use by seminarists in the diocese of Cambrai; it contains 71 pages and measures approx. 35 cm (horizontal) by 25 cm. The copy in the Bibliothèque Sainte-Geneviève is of the second edition (1892), published by Roger and Chernoviz, publisher of many books on Scholastic philosophy. No author is given, but the catalogue of the Bibliothèque Nationale attributes it to Abbé D. Choisnard. Apart from the copy in the Bibliothèque Sainte-Geneviève, a microfilm (of poor quality) may be consulted in the Bibliothèque Nationale. Happily, I can report that I discovered a pristine copy of the publication in the library of the Centre Culturel Irlandais in Paris and secured sponsorship for it to be digitized. It may be viewed on the website of the Centre Culturel.[86]

Joyce's protestation that he was "steeled in the school of old Aquinas" was more than just a shibboleth. The frequent references in his writings to St. Thomas, in particular Stephen's appeal to Aquinas in support of his aesthetic program, provide sufficient proof of Joyce's debt to the medieval master. The extrinsic evidence, with which I have been concerned, is a less important confirmation. Jacques Aubert proposes a different scenario, suggesting that hasty and oversimplified references to Thomas Aquinas constitute "a particularly bright red herring."[87] He has argued that the real inspiration for Joyce's aesthetic theories is Hegel, filtered through scholars such as Butcher and Bosanquet. This is a daring interpretation, particularly since Joyce nowhere appeals to Hegel, referring to him only obliquely with humor on one occasion ("hegelstomes," *FW* 416.33). The case for Aquinas is overwhelming. Repeated allusions by the author, a wealth of evidences, the ambience of his educational environment, and the reports of classmates, friends, and pupils: these are more than a false scent to put us off our track. There can be little doubt about Joyce's considerable debt to his Thomist masters or in the first place to Aquinas himself.

Joyce's Knowledge of Aquinas

Joyce was clearly interested in Aquinas's intellectual ideas but not in his monastic ideals; his attitude to the apostolic virtues of which the Angelic Doctor was a paragon might be summarized by Stephen's attitude: "Obedience in the womb, chastity in the tomb but involuntary poverty all his days" (U 14.336–37). Sharing little by way of personality, St. Thomas and Joyce had in common a deep fear of lightning. Aquinas's younger sister was killed by a fork of lightning that shot through the window of the room where they were both sleeping with their nurse.[88] Understandably, this event affected the usually imperturbable saint for the remainder of his days. As a child, Joyce was taught by his governess, Elizabeth Conway (the fictional "Dante"), to fear thunder as the wrath of God. (She took the Joyce children to see Francis Danby's painting "The Opening of the Sixth Seal" in the National Gallery of Ireland, which heralded the end of the world with a flash of lightning.) To his European friends who did not understand his irrational fear of thunder (closing the shutters and hiding in his bed), he replied that they had not been raised in Catholic Ireland. But as Peter Costello points out: "The thunder that rolls through *Finnegans Wake* had its remote origin here in the fevered visions of both Mrs Conway and Francis Danby."[89]

Joyce was familiar with another episode from the life of Aquinas. Robert McAlmon characterized Joyce as not only a "Dublin-Irish provincial" but also a "Jesuit-Catholic provincial in revolt." He relates:

> He refused to understand that questions of theology did not disturb or interest me, and never had. When I assured him that instead of the usual "religious crises" in one's adolescent life I had studied logic and metaphysics and remained agnostic, he did not listen. He would talk about the fine points of religion and ethics as he had been taught by the Jesuits. His favourite authors were Cardinal Newman and St Thomas Aquinas, and I had read neither. He told me some tale of how St Thomas once cracked a woman—possibly a prostitute—over the head with a chair, and explained that the Jesuits were clever at logic. They could justify anything if it suited their purposes.[90]

Referred to is an attempt by the family of the young Dominican monk to seduce him from the clerical life by the temptations of a harlot. It was with a burning log from the fire that the young Thomas chased her from his cell; he burned a sign of the cross on the door and pleaded with God to preserve his chastity. It is said that in response to his prayer, he was at that moment tied so tightly with a belt that he fainted. Joyce, as is well known, did not share the saint's zeal for the virtue of chastity and, although he regarded Thomas very highly for his intellect, had no great sympathy for the saint.

Joyce was by no means a doctrinaire or submissive Thomist. Yeats describes his remarkable first meeting with Joyce, when the younger writer displayed an exuberant condescension toward his elder:

> [H]e began to explain all his objections to everything I had ever done. Why had I concerned myself with politics, with folklore, with the historical setting of events and so on? Above all why had I condescended to make generalizations? These things were all the sign of the cooling of the iron, of the fading out of inspiration. I had been puzzled, but now I was confident again. He is from the Royal University, I thought, and he thinks that everything has been settled by Thomas Aquinas, so we need not trouble about it. I have met so many like him. He would probably review my book in the newspapers if I sent it there. But the next moment he spoke of a friend of mine [Aubrey Beardsley] who after a wild life had turned Catholic on his deathbed. He said that he hoped his conversion was not sincere. He did not like to think that he had been untrue to himself at the end. No, I had not understood him yet.[91]

It appears that for some reason Joyce greatly disliked the modern advocates of Aquinas. He was aware through Mary Colum of the burgeoning Thomist movement in Paris; Jacques Maritain was one of its leading exponents, another was Etienne Gilson.[92] These were the leading and most creative readers of Aquinas at the time and would later acquire international renown. The name "Étienne chanson" (*U* 14.401), besides referring to himself, "Stephen Song," possibly includes a reference also to this preeminent Thomist scholar. Joyce's attitude to the pioneers of the Thomist revival was hostile. Mary Colum records: "In some ways Joyce could be very difficult and even intolerable. He was angry with me because I made friends with some French people who were Thomists in a different way from himself, who was 'steeled in the school of old Aquinas.'"[93]

Joyce seems to have been familiar with some of the finer points of Thomist thought, including the angelology of Aquinas. In his letter (September 21, 1920) to Carlo Linati on the structure and design of *Ulysses,* he illustrates the unity and variety of each adventure and episode by comparing it to Aquinas's notion of angelic community: "Each adventure is so to say one person although it is composed of persons—as Aquinas relates of the heavenly hosts."[94]

Joyce received a strongly Thomist-oriented education from his Jesuit professors at University College. Hugh Kenner does not exaggerate when he suggests: "The *Ratio Studiorum* of St Ignatius governed Joyce's education." However, assuming that Constantine Curran's recollections, cited earlier, are trustworthy, Kenner's evaluation of this education is less accurate: "Aristotle's *Ethics* and *Politics,* the *Summa* of St Thomas Aquinas, the intertwined disciplines of grammar, logic, and rhetoric, trivium and quadrivium, came to him through the musty rote of anachronistic classrooms, solid as they had been when they informed the mind of Europe, realities of the mind evading their jailers the school-masters."[95] Nor does Kenner's reference to "phrases and definitions pickled in Jesuit textbooks"[96] accord with the experience of Joyce's classmates, as earlier outlined. Aristotelian Thomism enlivened the entire curriculum, finding particular expression in the literature and language syllabi. While he did not study philosophy formally as an undergraduate, Joyce was exposed to philosophical doctrines, which he absorbed, it would appear, with conviction and enthusiasm. His knowledge of both Aristotle and Aquinas was that of a genuine amateur, interested in exploring their thought for his own purposes. In succeeding chapters, we will examine how well he achieved this.

It is worth noting in advance that while Aquinas is central to both *A Portrait* and *Ulysses,* his presence in *Finnegans Wake* is minimal. As Donald Phillip Verene notes, it is difficult to make his "arrahquinonthiance" (*FW* 296.20).[97] Invited, "Please by acquiester to meek my acquointance!" (*FW* 145.10), we are encouraged: "Yet an I saw a sign of him, if you could scrape out his acquinntence?" (*FW* 514.16–17). But as Verene explains: "In *Finnegans Wake* Aquinas appears, not as the great wielder of the sharp mental sword of philosophical reasoning but as the embodied philosopher of great corpulence."[98] The phrase "latten stomach even of a tumass equinous" (*FW* 93.09) suggests that the writer of limpid Latin has the bulk and appetite of a horse. He is "tunnibelly," (*FW* 113.36) with "tumescinquinance in the thight of his tumstull" (*FW* 240.08–09). The reference in *Ulysses* to "Aquinas tunbelly" (*U* 3.385), suggesting both a potbelly and giant fermenting vat, is echoed in *Finnegans Wake*: "the whole stock company of the old house of the Leaking Barrel, was thomistically drunk" (*FW* 510.17–18).[99]

3

Knowledge and Permanence

The philosophical problem of knowledge is thematized in the opening pages of both *A Portrait of the Artist as a Young Man* and *Ulysses,* as well as in the final pages of *Finnegans Wake.*[1] Such protracted interest confirms Joyce's lifelong preoccupation with the philosophical question of cognition. Educated in the tradition of classic realism, Joyce was tested by the challenges of modern philosophy. The dilemma of direct versus indirect (immediate vs. mediate) realism—the divergent positions of ancient and modern philosophy—is dramatized in the opening scene of *Ulysses,* where Buck Mulligan declares: "I can't remember anything. I remember only ideas and sensations" (*U* 1.192–93). Mulligan espouses Locke's corpuscular theory of ideas, as well as Descartes's axiom that in sensation we perceive not things but ideas. Stephen's position is one of robust realism: we know things themselves directly and immediately. He will put this to the empirical test on Sandymount Strand.

A number of fundamental assumptions distinguish modern from classical philosophy. Whereas ancient philosophy sought to disclose the hidden meaning of the cosmos, confident in the faith that objective meaning could be discovered, albeit imperfectly, the concern for modern philosophy was whether we can know anything whatsoever with certainty. The modern question centers not upon the world but upon human cognition; this preoccupation eventually led to the skepticism that Joyce criticized in his contemporaries. A. N. Whitehead remarks: "The ancient world takes its stand upon the drama of the Universe, the modern world upon the inward drama of the Soul."[2] For Descartes, the unshaken ground of truth (*fundamentum inconcussum veritatis*) is the self-experience of subjective thought, as conveyed in his famous "*Cogito ergo sum*": "I think, therefore I am."[3] For Aristotle and Aquinas, the foundation of truth is prior: *Aliquid est,* "Something is." Rather than Descartes's cogito, their motto would read: "*Sunt res, ergo cognosco, deinde cogito*": "Things are, therefore I know, then

I think." Descartes not only placed knowledge of the independent world in doubt but, as we shall see in the next chapter, sowed the seeds for the demise of the self as autonomous substance. For Descartes, consciousness is a closed world, limited to internal ideas or representations: we can know only what is *in* the mind. This assumption was adopted unquestioningly by both the British empiricists and Kant. What I know directly are not things themselves but impressions or ideas of things within the mind. The direct realism of traditional philosophy gave way to an indirect realism, a position shared equally by Continental idealism and British empiricism. In the words of John Locke, "the mind, in all its thoughts and reasonings, hath no other immediate object but its own ideas, which it alone does or can contemplate."[4] If all we know are the contents of our mind, what grounds have we to affirm the reality of an independent world? The logical conclusion, drawn by the Irishman George Berkeley, is that reality itself consists of nothing but perceptions; being consistent, he rejected the reality beyond the idea. Joyce's Stephen would engage with Berkeley's theory that the being of things consists in their being perceived, *esse est percipi.* The question will be prominent in the final pages of *Finnegans Wake.*

Dilemmas of knowledge and identity are center stage in the opening paragraphs of *Ulysses,* with the contrast between Stephen and Buck Mulligan evident from the outset: Mulligan is the crass empiricist for whom life is a beastly affair; Stephen Dedalus the sensitive, realist, introspective, reflective Aristotelian.[5] Mulligan intones: "For this, O dearly beloved, is the genuine christine: body and soul and blood and ouns. Slow music, please. Shut your eyes, gents. One moment. A little trouble about those white corpuscles. Silence, all" (*U* 1.21–23). In this parody of the Mass, Mulligan ridicules the transubstantiation of bread into the body of Christ (*corpus Christi*). The mockery alludes to the theory of corpuscles that was central to the empiricist theory of John Locke. According to Locke, natural bodies are composed of particles that give to bodies the primary qualities of solidity, extension, figure, motion or rest, and number, which are retained even after repeated division of bodies. These primary qualities also cause our simple ideas.[6]

The theory of corpuscles had been proposed by Robert Boyle, Irish scientist and friend of John Locke.[7] In his address, "Of the Origins of Forms and Qualities," to the Royal Society in 1665, he declared: "There are in the world great store of particles of matter, each of which is too small to be, whilst single, sensible, and being entire or undivided, must needs both have its determinate shape and be very solid."[8] Boyle was praised by the German theologian Henry Oldenburg for having "driven out yt Divell of Substantiall Forms [. . .] that has stopt ye progres of true Philosophy, and made the best of Schollars not more knowing as to ye nature of particular bodies than the meanest ploughman."[9] The modern rejection of substantial form was another major challenge to the dominant role of Aristotelian *eidos* or form that had occupied a central place in the world view of the medieval period and beyond. It was the latter theory that provided Stephen with solutions to the theoretical questions about himself and the world.

Locke's theory of enclosed consciousness and indirect realism is invoked when Mulligan plays down his insult to Stephen: "What? Where? I can't remember anything. I remember only ideas and sensations. Why? What happened in the name of God?" (*U* 1.192–93). Stephen's direct memory of the actuality of the experience by contrast is still raw: "I am not thinking of the offence to my mother.—Of what then? Buck Mulligan asked.—Of the offence to me, Stephen answered" (*U* 1.218–20). The response is cruel: "O, an impossible person!" (*U* 1.222). Mulligan embodies the "vivisective" (*SH* 186) mentality that typifies the modern age: "To me it's all a mockery and beastly. Her cerebral lobes are not functioning" (*U* 1.210–21). The death of his mother affects Stephen profoundly and personally. For Mulligan, it is a physiological event that happens to everyone, a "beastly" event devoid of personal meaning. The question of identity, of personal life and personal death, is to the fore: "And what is death, he asked, your mother's or yours or my own? You saw only your mother die. I see them pop off every day in the Mater and Richmond and cut up into tripes in the dissectingroom. It's a beastly thing and nothing else. It simply doesn't matter" (*U* 1.204–07). The contrast between Stephen and Mulligan could not be greater.

In the "Proteus" episode, striding Sandymount Strand, Stephen explicitly ponders the nature of knowledge, as well as the fundamental questions of stability and identity. Aristotle is the philosophical rock upon which he can rely, conscious that the real challenge is not so much Locke's mediate realism but the subtle idealism of George Berkeley. Stephen attempts to reconcile the Greek realist and Irish idealist but fails since their positions are radically antithetical. His reflections are complicated, even contorted. Frank Delaney has described "Proteus" as the *pons asinorum* of *Ulysses*.[10] Declan Kiberd states: "Many readers drop *Ulysses* at this point, finding themselves unable to keep up with Stephen's remorseless and obscure pedantry." Kiberd's judgment is harsh: "This entire episode is a mocking study of the lethal after-effects of a recent university degree [. . .] a schooling ill-suited to real human needs. [. . .] Suffering too much information, carrying too great a learning, Stephen is weighed down rather than illuminated by his knowledge. He is the adolescent as narcissist, but at least his learned quotations are all internalized, impressing nobody but himself."[11] All of this, Kiberd however suggests, is not without purpose: "[T]he truth is that Joyce is laughing at the pitiful pretentiousness of the youth he once was. *Nobody* could understand all that Stephen says or thinks. *Nobody* could take all of his ideas with utter seriousness."[12] Joyce is seen as mocking his earlier self, represented by his literary alter ego in a prolongation of the irony that characterized his treatment of Dedalus in *A Portrait*—a suggestion championed by Hugh Kenner.[13] It may be true that Joyce increasingly lost interest in Stephen and concentrated on the character of Leopold Bloom, still an unknown quantity. I suggest, nonetheless, that the portrayal of Stephen in "Proteus" is credible for the philosophically minded, attentive reader.

The opening lines of "Proteus" cast up in precipitous fashion virtually every philosophical problem associated with sense perception. Although the presentation may seem chaotic, the passage is a careful and exciting dramatization of elements drawn from conflicting theories of sensation. The chapter is a farrago of part-theories adapted from Aristotle, George Berkeley, and Jacob Boehme,[14] as well as the Austrian psychologist Otto Weininger (1880–1903).[15] Aristotle is center stage, but Berkeley summons critically from the wings, challenging Stephen with radical doubts regarding the reliability of human cognition; other philosophical elements add piquancy to the conflict. The text is as follows:

> Ineluctable modality of the visible: at least that if no more, thought through my eyes. Signatures of all things I am here to read, seaspawn and seawrack, the nearing tide, that rusty boot. Snotgreen, bluesilver, rust: coloured signs. Limits of the diaphane. But he adds: in bodies. Then he was aware of them bodies before of them coloured. How? By knocking his sconce against them, sure. Go easy. Bald he was and a millionaire,[16] *maestro di color che sanno*. Limit of the diaphane in. Why in? Diaphane, adiaphane. If you can put your five fingers through it, it is a gate, if not a door. Shut your eyes and see.
>
>   Stephen closed his eyes to hear his boots crush crackling wrack and shells. You are walking through it howsomever, I am, a stride at a time. A very short space of time through very short times of space. Five, six: the *Nacheinander*. Exactly: and that is the ineluctable modality of the audible. Open your eyes. No. Jesus! If I fell over a cliff

that beetles o'er his base, fell through the *Nebeneinander* ineluctably! (*U* 3.01–15)[17]

The first paragraph deals with sight, the second with hearing; the "ineluctable modality" of each is interrogated in turn. Stephen is struck by the motley variety and range of objects to be observed: "seaspawn and seawrack, the nearing tide, that rusty boot." He reflects that thought begins in the senses—"thought through my eyes"—but recognizes that his task is to grasp and interpret the essence of what he sees: "Signatures of all things I am here to read." The ubiquitous and ever-present phenomenon of movement is of particular interest. The reader quickly recognizes that Joyce was well acquainted with many details of Aristotle's theories.

Stephen is recurrently concerned with the nature and process of knowledge and our understanding of its objects. The focus of "Proteus" are the senses, particularly those regarded as most important: sight, hearing, and touch. The latter, Aristotle points out, is the most basic and elementary: "Sensation must be attributed to all animals as such, for by its presence or absence we distinguish between what is and what is not an animal";[18] and "Without a sense of touch it is impossible to have any other sensation."[19] Aristotle claims that while humans lag behind other animals in regard to the power of all other senses, they excel in discrimination of touch.[20] Stephen emphasizes its importance, with a possible erotic connotation: "Touch me [. . .] O, touch me soon, now [. . .] Touch, touch me."[21] But it is sight and hearing that are his primary focus. Aristotle states that sight is the most treasured sense because it is the most informative.[22] Hearing is most important for the enhancement of understanding because of its primary function in the process whereby we learn from others.[23]

The preeminent phrase in Stephen's interpretation of sensation are the words "ineluctable modality," one of the most famous expressions in Joyce's entire work.[24] "Ineluctable modality of the visible" (*U* 3.01) and "ineluctable modality of the audible" (*U* 3.13) are unmistaken allusions to Aristotle's doctrine of sense knowledge, outlined in *De Anima,* which Joyce had studied in the Bibliothèque Sainte-Geneviève. Implicit also is the distinction that through our eyes we see things simultaneously in space, spread out and contiguous to one another, whereas with our ears we perceive sounds successively in time as they endure from one moment to the next. These aspects of contiguity and succession are aptly expressed by the German adverbs *nebeneinander* and *nacheinander.*

While it is possible that scholars may discover an identifiable source for the phrase "ineluctable modality," I believe that it is Joyce's own coinage. Robert McAlmon spotted in Joyce what he himself recognized as the professional malady of young writers, from which Joyce never recovered, namely, a penchant toward particular words. McAlmon mentioned in particular the words "ineluctable" and "metempsychosis"—"grey, clear, abstract, fine-sounding words that are a bit 'ineluctable' themselves."[25] The common French word *modalité* is, I suggest, a "fine-sounding" word that even today strikes the anglophone visitor as conferring added elegance to everyday French conversation. It is unnecessary to seek Joyce's penchant for the word in the Kantian vocabulary of the categories.[26]

Joyce captures the kernel of Aristotle's theory of sensation in the twin phrases "ineluctable modality of the visible" (*U* 3.01)[27] and "ineluctable modality of the audible" (*U* 3.13). Each sense, in accordance with its accidental mode of time and space, inescapably and of its very nature, delivers knowledge of its physical datum that is by necessity true. Each of the senses is infallible with respect to its specific object within its own particular, very restricted, domain. In the simple apprehension of their respective objects, the senses cannot err.[28] The dedicated objects of each individual sense Aristotle calls the "proper sensibles." Joyce had transcribed in his notebook Aristotle's phrase, "The sensation of particular things is always true." The full text reads: "For the perception of the proper objects is always true, and this is found in all animals; it is possible to think erroneously, however, but this occurs only in beings which have reason."[29]

Color is the proper sensible of the eye, sound the proper sensible of the ear. Size, shape, quantity, speed, and distance, on the other hand, are what Aristotle calls "common perceptibles." The latter may be grasped by more than one sense faculty and the perceiver risks error if he judges hastily on the evidence of one sense alone. Prior to interpretation and judgment, the raw sensation as such is always objectively true and free from error. The necessity attaching to our knowledge of the proper sensibles derives from the very nature of the sense faculty itself: the eye is the organ uniquely and exclusively equipped to grasp color; the ear is the organ that necessarily and inevitably grasps sound. To suggest that a particular sense faculty, operating according to its nature, is deceived in its grasp of its proper object is contradictory: it would be to deny the existence of such a faculty.

Whereas only my eyes perceive an object's color as it passes, its movement can be grasped not only by sight but also by the ear, touch, perhaps even smell. Familiar examples of illusions attending common sensibles are the stick that appears broken when immersed in water, or the railway lines that seem to converge in the distance. These are simple optical illusions. I am mistaken if I judge that the train tracks really do converge, or that the stick is broken, even though this is how they inevitably appear. My eyes necessarily convey the correct impression; my interpretation errs if I affirm the object to be really as it appears. I must distinguish—usually unconsciously—between single-sense certitude (which inevitably and by necessity reveals the proper sensibles) and the multisense impressions of the common sensibles. In the latter, there is no automatic certainty; I must interpret and integrate messages from distinct and diverse perceptual antennae. I am aware of the train's movement both by means of my ear as it tracks the passing sound and by means of my eye as it perceives the colored shape in its changing relation to the surrounding countryside. I am open to error, however, if I judge too hastily the speed or distance of the train. Careful attention is required before I pronounce judgment.

Aristotle grounds the certainty of knowledge in sensation. The senses supply material to the intellect, which resembles a blank tablet (*tabula rasa*, *FW* 50.12) on which nothing has yet been written. The intellect is void of content and must be first activated by the senses. Sense knowledge, however, especially the common sensibles, must be interpreted by the intellect. The phrase "thought through my eyes" at the start of "Proteus" confirms the Aristotelian doctrine of cooperation between sense and intellect (*U* 3.01– 02). Interestingly, the Buffalo manuscript reveals two earlier variations, as if Joyce hesitated regarding the respective roles of sense and intellect: "My eyes do not see it; they think it rather than see."[30] The mutual dependence of sensation and thought is repeated when Stephen reflects upon the difficulty of seeing correctly with defective eyes: "Distance. The eye sees all flat. Brain thinks. Near: far. Ineluctable modality of the visible" (*U* 15.3629–31). The eye necessarily perceives according to its condition; erroneous impressions are corrected by a judgment of intellect. Even if I am color-blind, my eye faithfully conveys to me the light reflected from the object as I must receive it, given the deficient capacity of my visual organ; my incapacity is itself proof of the necessary character of sensation and its infallibility, insofar as it obeys the condition of my fallible sense. Error occurs only when I judge my subjective experience to be identical with that of someone with regular vision. A person with normal vision may be similarly compared to those animals that are endowed with a greater range and more acute powers of sight. We find this reflection in "Scylla and Charybdis," in the debate between Platonism and Aristotelianism: "God: noise in the street: very peripatetic. Space: what you damn well have to see" (U 9.85–86).

Essential to the modality of sight and hearing are their spatial and temporal contexts. Joyce places the core psychological and epistemological aspect of the visible and audible within the ontological categories of time and space, which further define each faculty, respectively. In A Portrait, Stephen had already asserted: "An esthetic image is presented to us either in space or in time. What is audible is presented in time, what is visible is presented in space" (P V.1362–63).

In a reversal of Aristotle, who gave primacy of certainty to the evidence of the single senses, John Locke attached primacy to data such as extension and number, since they are supported by multiple senses. Because they are less dependent upon the subjective condition of the observer, he regarded them as primary qualities. Experiences such as color and taste, he argued, are less reliable and therefore considered "secondary qualities."

The difficulty involved in the perception of the common sensibles is dramatized in "Lestrygonians," as Bloom admires the field glasses in the window of Yeates and Son on Nassau Street: "Must get those old glasses of mine set right" (U 8.554). Distance appears to distort size; the clock on the top of the bank appears no larger than a watch: "There's a little watch up there on the roof of the bank to test those glasses by" (U 8.560–61). Distance, size, shape, perspective: these are all situation-dependent. Bloom improvises the experiment suggested by the Irish astronomer Sir Robert Ball in The Story of the Heavens (first published 1885) to illustrate "the conception known to astronomers by the name of parallax; for it is by parallax that the distance of the sun, or, indeed, the distance of any celestial body, must be determined." It is, notes Ball, "a geometrical problem of no little complexity."[31]

"What's parallax?," Bloom wonders (U 8.578). Parallax may be explained as the apparent displacement of an object in the foreground relative to a distant background because of a change in the observer's point of view, or when viewed separately by the right eye and left eye. The optical displacement increases as one approaches and decreases as one moves away.[32] This is because distance, perspective, size, and shape are not the proper sensibles of any one of the senses alone; they are what Aristotle calls "common sensibles," since we can grasp these data not only by sight but also by touch.

Limit of the Diaphane: Color and Space

Analyzing the activity of sight, Stephen attributes great importance to color ("snotgreen, bluesilver, rust: coloured signs"); this is playfully reinforced by quoting Dante's praise of Aristotle as "master of those who know (*color che sanno*)." Consideration of the role of color in perception prompts a reflection on the nature of bodies, space, and place. One is reminded of Cézanne's comment that "Colour is the place where our brain meets the universe."[33] Analyzing subsequently the act of hearing, Stephen emphasizes movement: "I am, a stride at a time. A very short space of time through very short times of space. Five, six: the *Nacheinander*." *Solvitur ambulando*. Taking sight and sound together, it would be more accurate to say that *color* is the ineluctable modality of the visible and *movement* the ineluctable modality of the audible.

Stephen is fascinated by the process through which we perceive the appearance or "epiphany" of the world. Implicit in his language is both a metaphysic and metaphoric of light. "Diaphane," the Greek word for "translucent" or "transparent," holds special attraction. According to Aristotle, light may be described incidentally as the color of whatever is transparent. Light is caused by the presence of something fiery in a translucent body; its absence is darkness. We associate translucence with water and air, but it is potentially present to a greater or lesser extent in all bodies. Color is the boundary that limits translucence. It coincides with the periphery of a body, which has its own determinate limits. Color is indispensable for our visual perception of physical objects; without difference of color, the eye could not distinguish between diverse objects. Stephen's dependence on Aristotle as he interprets the perception of color and of bodies is evident in the following lines, which merit repetition:

> Snotgreen, bluesilver, rust: coloured signs. Limits of the diaphane. But he adds: in bodies. Then he was aware of them bodies before of them coloured. How? By knocking his sconce against them, sure. [. . .] Limit of the diaphane in. Why in? Diaphane, adiaphane. If you can put your five fingers through it, it is a gate, if not a door. Shut your eyes and see.
>
> (*U* 3.03–09)

One of the quotations in Joyce's student notebook reads: "Colour is the limit of the diaphane in any determined body."[34] This is from Aristotle's treatise on sensation, *On Sense and Sensible Objects.* The full sentence reads: "But since the colour is at the extremity of the body, it must be at the extremity of the translucent/transparent in the body. Whence it follows that we may define colour as the limit of the translucent/transparent in a determinately bounded body."[35] An earlier passage from the treatise provides the full Aristotelian context for Stephen's reflections:

> Light is incidentally the colour of the translucent (διαφανὲς). [. . .] What we call translucent is not peculiar to air or water or any other so-called body, but a common nature and power, which does not exist separately but resides in these and other bodies, to a greater or lesser extent. Now just as every body must have some limit, so too must this. Of its nature, light exists in a transparency which has no limit; but obviously there must be some limit to the translucent which inheres in bodies, and it is clear from the facts that this limit is colour; for colour either is in the limit or is the limit itself.[36]

Aristotle is stating that the transparency of light has of itself no limitation: its limit coincides with the surface of bodies: and this limitation is precisely what color is. Stephen registers "snotgreen, bluesilver, rust" as the colored signs that constitute the limits of the diaphanous, the perceptible boundaries of physical bodies that he observes.

Since Aristotle's definition of color as the limit of translucence in a body includes the concept of body, Stephen suggests there must be a prior grasp of body, given in touch: "Limits of the diaphane. But he adds: in bodies. Then he was aware of them bodies before of them coloured. How? By knocking his sconce against them, sure" (*U* 3.04–06). Stephen's explanation of Aristotle's certainty regarding the existence of bodies is a clear reference to Dr. Johnson's refutation of Berkeley's denial of material existence. Boswell relates the occasion in his *Life of Johnson:* "After we came out of the church, we stood talking for some time together of Bishop Berkeley's ingenious sophistry to prove the non-existence of matter, and that every thing in the universe is merely ideal. I observed, that though we are satisfied his doctrine is not true, it is impossible to refute it. I never shall forget the alacrity with which Johnson answered, striking his foot with mighty force against a large stone, till he rebounded from it—'I refute it *thus.*'"[37] In Stephen's mind, Aristotle "knocked his sconce" against bodies. Exploiting the double meaning of the word "sconce" as skull and as candle or oil-lamp holder, Joyce conveys what Stephen recognized as the cerebral challenge posed for some philosophers by the existence of matter, requiring both physical evidence as well as optical and intellectual illumination. The challenge is of course entirely in Stephen's mind, since for Aristotle a demonstration of the existence of physical bodies was as futile as it was unnecessary: it is impossible to prove what is already evident.

In assuming that in order to define color as the limit of translucence in bodies, Aristotle first needed a prior concept of body acquired through touch, Stephen is mistaken. He confuses discovery with definition: in human knowledge, there is an inverse relation between the order of experience and that of explanation, between what is prior in itself (*prius quoad se*) and what is evident to us (*prius quoad nos*). Stephen mistakes perceptual experience for the conceptual interpretation of the relation between color and the bodies to which they belong. For Aristotle, sight simultaneously grasps colors and the bodily surfaces in which they inhere. Subsequent reflection upon the simultaneous perception of color and shape may arrive at a definition of color that employs the concept of body and that recognizes body as logically prior, without reference to touch; the perception of color is, however, prior. Body is prior in the order of definition, color first in the order of discovery.

It is true that we most frequently associate perception of bodies with the sense of touch (as borne out by Dr. Johnson's "refutation" of Berkeley). There is a bruteness of fact attached to the immobility of a physical object. I can however arrive equally realistically at a knowledge of a body through the perception of color, in which case my affirmation of a body depends upon a prior experience of color. Sight, however, cannot grasp the existence of a body prior to, or in isolation from, color. It is also true that I cannot define color without including reference to a body. Color is perceived at the boundary, limit, or surface (*superficies*) of a body. The notion of physical boundary or limit is central to the definition of color, space, and body. Perhaps Stephen envisages that I initially perceive a body through the separate sense of touch—with eyes shut—and subsequently observe its color: in which case, my knowledge of the body does indeed precede my perception of color. That, however, would involve separate acts of perception; the philosophical question concerns the order of priority in a single act of perception. Even if there were no sense of touch, we could derive the concept of body from our initial perception of color.

Stephen wonders about the precise location of color: "Limit of the diaphane in. Why in? Diaphane, adiaphane. If you can put your five fingers through it, it is a gate, if not a door. Shut your eyes and see" (*U* 3.07–09). Where does color actually reside? What is the difference between transparent and opaque? The contrast between "diaphane" and "adiaphane" expresses the phenomenological difference between the perceptual experience of a gate and the perceptual experience of a door. Touch is a substitute for sight: "If you can put your five fingers through it, it is a gate, if not a door." With the aid of touch, it is possible to "shut your eyes and see." There is allusion once again to Johnson, with a reference to his *Dictionary of the English Language*: "*Door* is used of house, and *gates* of cities and public buildings except in the license of poetry."[38]

Time and Space

Interesting tangential issues are raised by Frank Budgen's remarks on "Proteus." He writes: "With open eyes [Stephen] walks through space. In it things lie *nebeneinander*. He calls it the 'ineluctable modality of the visible.' With eyes shut he walks through space in time. 'Time is the ineluctable modality of the audible.' One happening follows the other *nacheinander*." Budgen quotes Joyce: "My definitions of space and time are good. What?"[39] What is interesting is not only that Budgen expands Joyce's phrase to explicitly identify *space* as the "ineluctable modality of the visible" and *time* as the "ineluctable modality of the audible" but also that Joyce believes he has provided good definitions of space and time. If that was Joyce's intention, then he underestimated the problems involved. Stephen does not provide a definition for space and time but only recognizes space and time as the required correlates for the visible and audible. We perceive sounds along a temporal dimension, allied to movement; we perceive visible objects juxtaposed in space when we grasp objects as colored.

Aristotle remarks: "Place appears to be something important and hard to grasp."[40] He defines it in the *Physics* as "the innermost immobile surface of a surrounding body."[41] This has been translated into Latin as "*corporis ambientis terminus immobilis primus.*" In his *General Metaphysics,* John Rickaby provides the following intimidating formula when he defines it as "the superficies of the containing body considered as immoveable and immediately contiguous to the body located."[42] A more comprehensible English version reads, "The place of a thing is the innermost motionless boundary of what contains it."[43] Rickaby illustrates the meaning with the following examples: "The place of a body immersed in water is the immediate watery surface which touches it all round, and which is considered, for convenience, as unchangeable. A fossil immoveably imbedded in a rock, if it were suddenly annihilated would leave a perfect definition of its place."[44]

A modern artistic illustration would be the cire perdue process of sculpture. Place is thus conceived as the outer physical limit of the body itself envisaged as a container of the object. Bodies stand toward each other in a relationship of mutual limitation. Aristotle's category of place depends therefore upon a multiplicity of bodies: if we were to imagine, or conceive of, a uniquely existing body—tantamount to the universe itself—it would have no real "place" in the Aristotelian sense.[45]

Having discussed Aristotle's definition of place, we may consider his interpretation of time, which he famously defines as "the number of movement with respect to before and after" (ἀριθμὸς κινήσεως κατὰ τὸ πρότερον καὶ ὕστερον).[46] Time is the "calculable measure or dimension" by which we distinguish and identify earlier and later stages in the course of any unfolding change or movement. It is not identical with motion but is that by which motion is counted, the measurable dimension proper to motion. Aristotle's concept of time as the measurable aspect of before and after is suitably conveyed in the German word "nacheinander." Aristotle emphasizes that without the sensation of change or movement, there would be no awareness of time. He notes importantly that time is neither identical with movement nor capable of being separated from it; the two are indivisible. He states: "Not only do we measure movement by time, but also time by movement, because they define each other."[47] Significant for an Aristotelian interpretation of "Proteus" is the question raised by Aristotle: "The relation of time to consciousness deserves examination [. . .] whether or not time would exist if there were no consciousness."[48] He replies that "if nothing can count except consciousness, and consciousness only as intellect, it is impossible that time should exist if consciousness did not."[49] Particularly relevant for readers of Joyce is Aristotle's emphasis on the perception of change in the awareness of conscious states and activities: "When we are aware of movement we are thereby aware of time, since, even if it were dark and we were conscious of no bodily sensations, but something were 'going on' in our minds, we should, from that very experience, recognize the passage of time. And conversely, whenever we recognize that there has been a lapse of time, we by that act recognize that something 'has been going on.'"[50] While most of the activity shared with the reader is the flow of Stephen's conscious introspection, in closing his eyes Stephen's action is only partly verification of this, as he continues to move and "hear his boots crush crackling wrack and shells" (U 3.10–11).

The inseparable relation between spatial movement and time is expressed in the following question and answer in "Ithaca": "What would render such return irrational? An unsatisfactory equation between an exodus and return in time through reversible space and an exodus and return in space through irreversible time" (*U* 17.2024–27).

Stephen relates the passage of time to movement of place, deriving temporal from local succession: "You are walking through it howsomever, I am, a stride at a time. A very short space of time through very short times of space" (*U* 3.11–12). The expression "space of time" is common; the phrase "times of space" is enigmatic. Joyce cleverly suggests the chiasmic relation involved in the perception of both. While it is true that it takes a short period of time to traverse a short distance, we do not primarily measure spatial distance in terms of the temporal interval: there are more objective means of calculation. Space is one of Aristotle's "common sensibles" but is particularly amenable to measurement via sight and touch; without specialized apparatus, measurement of spatial distance by reference to a time interval is a matter of imprecise estimation. Time is not measured by any of the five external senses but by an internal sense of awareness involving both memory and intellect.

It must also be remembered that whereas locomotion is physically the most obvious kind of movement, it is not the only one. Whereas we most frequently associate movement with spatial or local motion, there is not only change of place but also change of quantity (e.g., without changing location, an individual can increase in size) and change of quality (e.g., an individual can acquire new characteristics, such as wisdom or virtue). In the self-awareness of one's mental activity, one is concomitantly and simultaneously aware of oneself as the persisting and identical subject of that activity. One is not primarily aware of oneself as changing but rather as the abiding foundation of enduring activity. One has, nonetheless, undergone a process of change, inasmuch as one has reflected or deliberated on a series of mental contents. Joyce's writings are, in their entirety, proof that awareness of mental activity conveys the passage of time.

According to Aristotle and Aquinas, time and space do not have separate or independent existence: they are not distinct entities. (Kant, on the other hand, regarded space and time as subjective a priori forms of the senses without objective validity, albeit with a foundation in physical bodies.) We must not be misled by the imagination, which suggests that sound is perceived "in time" and that color is perceived "in space." Time and space are not independent realities within which events and bodies occur and are situated. Space is the mutual relationship that holds between material or extended bodies (*partes extra partes*) deriving from the physical limits of their bodies. Extension is the position of parts outside parts (*partium extra partes positio*). We must not be misled by the image of space as a void or empty receptacle into which material bodies are placed, like toys in a box or furniture in a room. Similarly, time is not, as it were, a separate context or arena in which events occur; it is the measurable aspect of the progression of individuals as they pass from potentiality to actuality in the course of change.

Stephen's self-observation in the activity of sense perception rightly highlights the temporal character of auditory sensation and the spatial context within which visual perception occurs. He observes himself as operating and enduring through a succession of events, in a world of objects that are related through mutual physical limitation. Time is continuous succession; space is the coexistent, simultaneous contiguity of extended bodies. To express the sequence of time and the contiguity of space, Joyce adopted from Weininger—with echoes of Lessing—the words *nacheinander* and *nebeneinander*.

Nebeneinander and *Nacheinander*

Joyce enlists the terms from the Austrian psychologist Otto Weininger to indicate the relations of sight and hearing to space and time, respectively. Hearing takes place in time and perceives that which is successive, *nacheinander;* seeing takes place in space, perceiving objects that are mutually adjacent, *nebeneinander.* Joyce's so-called Subject Notebook,[51] preserved in the National Library of Ireland, contains a densely filled half page with disparate phrases from Weininger's book *Über die Letzten Dinge* (*On Last Things*).[52] The text relevant to the "Proteus" passage is as follows: "Der Raum enthält im Nebeneinander, was nur im zeitlichen Nacheinander erlebt werden kann." Joyce's selective quotation from Weininger is noteworthy, here indicated in bold:

> **Der Raum** ist also eine Projektion des Ich (aus dem Reich der Freiheit ins Reich der Notwendigkeit). Er **enthält im Nebeneinander, was nur im zeitlichen Nacheinander erlebt werden kann**. Der Raum ist symbolisch für das vollendete, die Zeit für das sich wollende Ich.[53]
> **Space** is thus a projection of the I (out of the realm of freedom into the realm of necessity). It **contains in the contiguous what can only be experienced in temporal succession**. Space is symbolic for what is completed, time for the desiring I.[54]

Joyce partly eschews the idealist suggestions of the text, to emphasize the commonsense meaning of Aristotle.

A number of allusions and associations conjoin in the adverbial modalities "*nacheinander*" and "*nebeneinander*," which occur in the second paragraph of "Proteus." Their conceptual content is truly Aristotelian. Hearing involves a listening to movement; it relies upon temporal change: the ear is stimulated by the action of a vibrating body which occurs in time. *Nacheinander* accurately conveys the temporal and successive nature of the changing body in this activity. The psychology of perception rests upon a metaphysics of action, that is, transition from potency to act. The phenomenology of the consequent subjective experience is suitably summed up in its mode of reception as *nacheinander:* one thing after another. Sight, on the other hand, can be instantaneous: it does not require change or movement. We observe bodies located beside one another; we are aware of them by their difference in color. While the philosophical idea behind this distinction is in keeping with Aristotle's metaphysics, epistemology, and psychology, Joyce was prompted to find the appropriate terms elsewhere. The earliest source for his choice may have been the treatise *Laocoön: An Essay on the Limits of Painting and Poetry* (1767), written by the German theorist and dramaturg Gotthold Ephraim Lessing.[55]

Joyce was apparently well acquainted with Lessing's *Laocoön*,[56] but—assuming some element of author-hero identity—was far from enthusiastic. In *Stephen Hero* we read: "The treatises which were recommended to him he found valueless and trifling; the Laocoon of Lessing irritated him. He wondered how the world could accept such fanciful generalisations as valuable contributions. What finer certitude could be attained by the artist if he believed that ancient art was plastic and that modern art was pictorial" (*SH* 33). In *A Portrait,* it is Stephen's classmate Donovan who speaks with some eagerness of Lessing: "Goethe and Lessing, said Donovan, have written a lot on that subject, the classical school and the romantic school and all that. The Laocoon interested me very much when I read it. Of course it is idealistic, German, ultra-profound" (*P* V.1323–26). Stephen does not share his enthusiasm: "Lessing, said Stephen, should not have taken a group of statues to write of. The art, being inferior, does not present the forms I spoke of distinguished clearly one from another" (*P* V.1440–42).

Although Joyce does not seem to have found Lessing's *Laocoön* greatly inspiring, and while an extensive quotation in his Subject Notebook suggests Otto Weininger as his immediate source for the adverbial pair "*nacheinander*" and "*nebeneinander*"—Lessing uses *aufeinander* rather than *nacheinander*—we find in *Laocoön* a detailed analysis of the differences between auditory and visual artistic execution and perception, which are remarkably close to Stephen's thoughts on Sandymount Strand. Joyce may well have been more influenced in these reflections than he was consciously aware or prepared to admit. Lessing contends that poetry deals with actions (*Handlungen*), which unfold successively one after the other (*aufeinander*) in time, while the plastic arts represent objects that exist side by side (*nebeneinander*) in space:

> There is this important difference between them, that the action of one is visible and progressive, its different parts happening one after another (*nach und nach*), in the sequence of time; while the action of the other is visible and stationary, its different parts developing themselves near one another (*nebeneinander*), in space. [. . .] If it is true that painting and poetry, in their imitations, make use of entirely different media of expression, or signs—the first, namely, of form and colour in space, the second of articulated sounds in time;—if these signs indisputably require a suitable relation to the thing betokened, then it is clear, that signs arranged near to one another (*nebeneinander*), can only express objects, of which the wholes or parts exist near one another (*nebeneinander*); while consecutive (*aufeinander*) signs can only express objects, of which the wholes or parts are themselves consecutive (*aufeinander*). Objects, whose wholes or parts exist near one another (*nebeneinander*) are called bodies (*Körper*). Consequently, bodies, with their visible properties, are the peculiar objects of painting. Objects, whose wholes or parts are consecutive (*aufeinander*), are called actions. Consequently, actions (*Handlungen*) are the peculiar subject of poetry.[57]

The adverbial modalities of '*nacheinander*' and '*nebeneinander*' characterize respectively the differences between auditory and visual perception. The coinciding axes of time and space constitute the coordinates of our experience: in the absence of *nacheinander/aufeinander* and *nebeneinander,* everything would be utter confusion—a total *Durcheinander*. The world around us can be seen at a glance, when in an eyeblink we observe the visible minutiae of diverse bodies located side by side. Hearing requires an interval of time—no matter how short—in which the world changes. There is awareness of movement, both retention and anticipation. This recognition,

with an allusion to Lessing, recurs later in the work, when Stephen ponders: "Why striking eleven? Proparoxyton. Moment before the next Lessing
says" (*U* 15.3609). This motif has already been aired in two quite different contexts: "Expecting every moment will be his next, says Lenehan" (*U*
12.1649), and in the style of fifteenth-century prose of Sir Thomas Malory's
compilation of the Arthurian legend: "Expecting each moment to be her
next" (*U* 14.178).

Modality and Perception

Some commentators have made heavy weather explaining the opening
lines of "Proteus." Joseph E. Duncan, for example, assumed that Joyce
conceived the phrase "ineluctable modality" in the light of modern modal
logic, which distinguishes the various qualities or moods of propositions,
according as they assert possibility, necessity, or certainty. He applies this
interpretation to Aristotle's metaphysics and epistemology, which in turn
he reads into Joyce's phrase:

> Stephen is developing the implications of Aristotle and his scholas-
> tic commentators in associating changing, unpredictable sights and
> sounds with Aristotelian theories of modal logic which deal with the
> uncertainty, potentiality, and variability of the sublunary world. In
> the logic of Aristotle and his scholastic interpreters, modality always
> raises the problem of the relative certainty or uncertainty of judg-
> ments or events. Modal propositions are either apodictic [i.e. self-
> evident] or problematic. The apodictic statement is a kind of univer-
> sal proposition treating necessity or impossibility; the problematic
> statement is a kind of particular proposition treating possibility in the
> realm of the actual. Both are distinguished from assertoric proposi-
> tions dealing with matters of fact. In the field of logic, then, modality
> is a qualification as to certainty or uncertainty in a statement.

Duncan continues:

> It is with the problematic proposition and its implications that Joyce
> is most concerned in his use of modality in *Ulysses*. In this kind of
> proposition, Aristotle explains, the possible can refer to what hap-
> pens generally but falls short of necessity, like a man's turning gray,
> or to indefinite and chance occurrences, like being caught in an
> earthquake.

He concludes:

> For Stephen, then, the ineluctable modality of the visible and the audible refers chiefly to the changing appearances and irregular sequences of the sublunary world, the product of potentiality and uncertainty, as these are perceived through seeing and hearing and are remembered.[58]

I agree with John Killham's assessment that Duncan's interpretation is "a misunderstanding of the whole of Stephen's intellectual position."[59] However, I do not see any grounds for Killham's suggestion that Stephen's reflections are not intended as a serious reflection upon the problems of change and perception in light of Aristotle, despite its element of parody or mockery. Killham proposes:

> Stephen is in the mood for relaxed and irreverent intellectual sport, a coruscation of the mind on questions as old as the hills. Starting from an infinitely more refined knowledge of the problems of perception than was to be found in Aristotle, he amuses himself with a little persiflage (which he gravely pretends to rebuke himself for—"Go easy. Bald he was and a millionaire") on one of the philosopher's less successful theories. [. . .] Stephen is far from commending Aristotle's ideas on how we see things; he rather wittily seizes upon their obvious weakness.[60]

Stephen is certainly poking fun at Aristotle, by conflating his theory with Johnson's refutation of Berkeley: "Then he was aware of them bodies before of them coloured. How? By knocking his sconce against them, sure" (U 3.04–06). But, as Theoharis puts it,

> Stephen reproves himself with a mocking parody of the voice of restraint and kindly reverence. "Go easy" he tells himself. "Bald he was and a millionaire." These of course are not reasons for Stephen to let up the ridicule—they merely characterize Aristotle as old and rich in addition to doddering. The two details are from traditional ancient and medieval biographies of Aristotle. Stephen includes them as part of flippant ridicule for the reverence of the philosopher he has enjoined upon himself.[61]

Killham, for his part, does not explain what he sees as the obvious weakness of Aristotle's theory of sensation. Even today, many would hold that in its essentials his theory is eminently defensible as the best commonsense explanation of sense knowledge. Such a defense presupposes the superiority of his immediate realism over modern theories that assume with Descartes that what we directly know are not realities but ideas.

Killham's interpretation of the opening lines of the episode is puzzling. Referring to Stephen he writes:

> His remark, "Then he was aware of them bodies before of them coloured" is a shrewd and palpable hit at Aristotle's seeming assumption that we can know objects by means other than those provided by our senses. This was Berkeley's whole objection to traditional theories of perception in a nutshell—ultimately we are forced to admit that matter is unknowable, since all we receive through the senses is impressions. Stephen's jocular explanation of Aristotle's certainty that things have a knowable existence independently of perceiving them is the charmingly absurd one that he must have bumped his head on them, and glances at Aristotle's theory that touch is the basic sense, possessed by all animals whatever.[62]

The matter is in fact quite the reverse. Killham is both partially correct in his presentation of Berkeley and partially mistaken in his portrayal of Aristotle. Berkeley's doubts present no difficulty for Aristotle, who differs greatly in his metaphysical presuppositions and epistemological commitments. Whereas for Berkeley the reality of objects depends on their being perceived, according to Aristotle, "The things which produce the exercise of sensation are objects from outside, the visible and audible, and similarly with all the other objects of sense."[63]

Aristotle's direct realism is clearly stated in his remark, "Perception is a form of being acted upon."[64] In other words, while imagination and intellect have a certain autonomy or control over content, operating upon what has been previously perceived, imagined, and understood, the senses are in a condition of dependent potency and require the action of a physical body acting directly upon them in order to function. Aristotle's immediate realism is guaranteed by the unity and identity of direct action between the object perceived and the perceiver.[65] According to Aristotle's metaphysics of causation, the action occurs within the patient. "The activity of the sensible object and of the sensation is one and the same."[66]

It is true that, according to Berkeley, we can only know impressions; he is thus committed to the view that we cannot know the existence of material bodies; for Aristotle, these are never in doubt. Aristotle, however, is adamant that we can know bodies only by the senses; he does not believe, as Killham suggests, that "we can know objects by means other than those provided by the senses." Things do not have "a knowable existence independently of perceiving them": Aristotle could never accept such an absurdity, despite its alleged charm; that would be a contradiction in itself. It is true that in a certain important sense for Aristotle "prime matter," as distinct from material objects, is unknowable. Prime matter, however, is not a "thing" but a principle at the foundation of existing physical things, which it is necessary to affirm in order to make sense of substantial change. Aristotle is somewhat hesitant regarding its knowability. In *Metaphysics 7*, where he seeks to identify what is most real, he even considers matter as a possible candidate. He concludes, however, that matter is not directly known as such but only and always insofar as it is determined by some particular substantial form. Matter, considered in itself as a radical principle of being, is sheer potency and thus imperceptible. Material bodies, however, as distinct from prime matter, are never in doubt for Aristotle, as they are for Berkeley.

Perception and Change

Stephen's interrogation of perception and its reliability takes place against the backdrop of one of the most intractable problems to challenge the very possibility of reliable knowledge, namely, change. Emphasizing the volatility of experience, Joyce intentionally made his task of validating knowledge more difficult. Budgen's report is valuable: "'You catch the drift of the thing?' said Joyce. 'It's the struggle with Proteus. Change is the theme. Everything changes—sea, sky, man, animals. The words change, too.'"[67] In reply to Budgen's question about the meaning of the word "almosting," Joyce replied: "That's all in the Protean character of the thing. Everything changes: land, water, dog, time of day. Parts of speech change too. Adverb becomes verb."[68]

For Aristotle change was essential to life; quoting Euripides, he remarks that "change in all things is sweet."[69] He defines change as the transition from potency to act. Although he does not explicitly make the distinction, we may differentiate in Aristotelian terms between two kinds of change. The more frequent is *accidental* change, when a substance changes in respect of one of its accidents (e.g., I grow older or wiser, the tadpole becomes a frog, the caterpillar becomes a butterfly); this is less profound and occurs gradually over time. More radical is *substantial* change, where one substance ceases and another comes to be; this occurs instantaneously. The explanation of substantial change in Aristotelian terms is known as the "Hylomorphic Theory," from ὕλη/*hylê* (matter) and μορφή/*morphê* (shape/form). Examples of substantial change are death, nutrition,[70] generation; a modern example is photosynthesis, the process whereby plants transform light and oxygen into glucose.

In substantial change, one substance changes into or becomes another, different, substance. However, some element of the first substance must continue to exist in the second—what was A is now B; change is a succession within an identity. Thus in all substances that are subject to change, Aristotle distinguished two elements or principles: a common element that remains unchanged—what was substance A and is now substance B—and a second element that is proper to each and that makes each the kind of substance it is. Since every substance is a single substance, these two elements cannot themselves be substances, that is, have a separate existence of their own. They are co-principles, which together constitute a substance. It is this substance alone that exists and acts.

Every material substance, living and nonliving, is subject to substantial change and is therefore composed of these two substantial principles, which Aristotle called "Prime Matter" (πρωτή ὕλη/*prôtê hulê*)[71] and "Substantial Form" (μορφή/*morphê* = form, shape). Matter is a principle of determinability, form a principle of determination. Form is the principle of actuality with respect to its corresponding matter. Form enters into the very nature of substance as its immanent, determining principle. Matter is potency; form is actuality. A banal illustration of this is the shape of a statue that organizes the marble or wood. The most important instance of this is the unity of body and soul that together constitute a single individual. Soul (*psuchê*) is the principle of life, the first actuality of a living body. *Psuchê* distinguishes living from nonliving: a cadaver is not a body but only the remains, an aggregate of disparate chemicals. "A corpse has the same shape and fashion as a living body; and yet it is not a man."[72]

Probably unaware of the distinction, Joyce was confronted with both kinds of change, substantial and accidental, that are to be observed in the natural world. In "Proteus," he gives a graphic description of the former:

> Bag of corpsegas sopping in foul brine. A quiver of minnows, fat of a spongy titbit, flash through the slits of his buttoned trouserfly. God becomes man becomes fish becomes barnacle goose becomes feather-erbed mountain. Dead breaths I living breathe, tread dead dust, devour a urinous offal from all dead. Hauled stark over the gunwale he

breathes upward the stench of his green grave, his leprous nosehole snoring to the sun. A seachange this, brown eyes saltblue.

(U 3.476–82)

With his choice of the Shakespearean word "seachange," Joyce consciously recalls the eerie lines of *The Tempest*, in which Ariel tells Ferdinand of his father's fate:

Full fathom five thy father lies
Of his bones are coral made;
Those are pearls that were his eyes;
Nothing of him that doth fade
But doth suffer a sea-change
Into something rich and strange.[73]

Another stark example of substantial change is instanced in *Hamlet:* "A man may fish with the worm that hath eat of a king, and eat of the fish that hath fed of that worm."[74]

As the personification of change Joyce chose the minor sea-god Proteus (Πρωτεύς), Poseidon's son and herdsman of his seals.[75] Called by Homer the "Old Man of the Sea," he knew all the secrets of nature, the properties of matter, and the processes of change. He had knowledge of all things past and could tell the future, but only to whoever would hold him fast; he thus changed his shape continually to avoid capture. Menelaus encounters Proteus on the island of Pharos on the Egyptian coast and wishes to learn the fate of his fellow countrymen and how he should best return home. Although Proteus changed into a lion, a serpent, a leopard, a pig, water, and a tree, Menelaus held him fast and forced him to answer questions. Proteus is the symbolic embodiment of change, alteration, and metamorphosis; as an adjective, "protean" is more significant of change than "polytropic" ("of many turns"), since Proteus is not only versatile in action but also repeatedly changes his essential form and nature.[76] Daniel Schwarz remarks: "Just as Menelaus had to wrestle with the continually changing Proteus, Stephen must wrestle with the protean nature of his experience."[77] Figuratively, Stephen was likewise made less forlorn by the sight of "Proteus rising from the sea."

The name "Proteus" is cognate with Greek "primary" or "first" and had also for Joyce the connotation of πρωτή ὕλη (*prôtê hulê*), prime matter, the malleable elemental principle intrinsic to all natural substances referred to in Aristotle's hylomorphic theory. Of itself prime matter possesses no

nature or determination but may become any material substance whatsoever. Without such a principle of sheer potency, the material universe could
not undergo its evident process of constant renewal. The cyclic movement
of extinction and renewal, grounded in matter, is aptly illustrated: "God
becomes man becomes fish becomes barnacle goose becomes featherbed
mountain" (*U* 3.477–79). Matter receives the determination of multiple
successive forms in a ceaseless flow of substantial change. This is one of
Aristotle's most important principles of explanation. Aristotle's recognition
of the metaphysical importance of matter, with the allied discovery of potency, merited high praise from the Thomistic theologian and Dominican
Thomas de Vio Cajetan (1469–1534), who referred to him as "*divus Ar-
istotelis, quia invenit materiam*" ("divine Aristotle, because he discovered
matter").[78]

In confirmation of the link between Proteus and primal matter, Stuart
Gilbert refers to Marcus Aurelius:

> The nature of the universe delights not in anything so much as to alter
> all things, and present them under another form. This is her conceit
> to play one game and begin another. Matter is placed before her like
> a piece of wax, and she shapes it to all forms and figures. Now she
> makes a bird, then out of the bird a beast—now a flower, then a frog,
> and she is pleased with her own magical performances as men are
> with their own fancies.[79]

Joyce may also have received this association from Francis Bacon, whose
writings he studied as an undergraduate.[80] This is the account given in his
De Veterum Sapientia (*Of the Wisdom of the Ancients*), in the chapter titled
"*Proteus sive Materia*" ("Proteus or Matter"):

> The sense of the fable relates, it would seem, to the secrets of nature
> and the conditions of matter. For under the person of Proteus, Mat-
> ter—the most ancient of all things, next to God—is meant to be rep-
> resented. Now matter has its habitation under the vault of heaven, as
> under a cave. And it may be called the servant of Neptune, inasmuch
> as all the operation and dispensation of matter is effected principally
> in a fluid state. The herd or flock of Proteus, seems to be nothing else
> than the ordinary species of animals, plants, minerals, etc. in which
> matter may be said to diffuse and use itself up; insomuch that hav-
> ing once made up and finished those species it seems to sleep and
> rest, as if its task were done; without applying itself or attempting or

preparing to make any more. And this is what is meant by Proteus counting his herd and then going to sleep.[81]

Like Proteus, movement is the most elusive of phenomena, difficult to pin down. This is because to define movement or change, we must refer to the notion of potency, the antithesis of a clear and distinct idea. Potency opens up an extra dimension that comports a surplus of existential depth, a surcharge of inner wealth.

Ralph Waldo Emerson refers to the beauty of Greek fables, which, "being proper creations of the imagination and not of the fancy, are universal verities. What a range of meanings and what perpetual pertinence has the story of Prometheus!" He refers to the truths of human nature symbolized by Prometheus, Orpheus, and Tantalus. His remarks on Proteus have a convincing ring for readers of *Ulysses:* "The philosophical perception of identity through endless mutations of form makes [man] know Proteus. What else am I who laughed or wept yesterday, who slept last night like a corpse, and this morning stood and ran? And what see I on any side but the transmigrations of Proteus?"[82]

Both Stephen and Bloom are, each in his own way, struck by the phenomenon of change. In "Lotus Eaters," Bloom reflects: "Won't last. Always passing, the stream of life, which in the stream of life we trace is dearer thaaan them all" (*U* 5.563–64). In "Lestrygonians," he muses: "How can you own water really? It's always flowing in a stream, never the same, which in the stream of life we trace. Because life is a stream" (*U* 8.93–95). The phrase is repeated shortly afterward: "The stream of life" (*U* 8.176). Later in the same episode, we find him reflecting upon the fluidity of the world, in a passage strongly reminiscent of Heraclitus. In a powerful reflection on the constancy of change, Bloom ponders the tableau vivant of the living city as he perambulates:

Trams passed one another, ingoing, outgoing, clanging. Useless words. Things go on same, day after day: squads of police marching out, back: trams in, out. Those two loonies mooching about. Dignam carted off. Mina Purefoy swollen belly on a bed groaning to have a child tugged out of her. One born every second somewhere. Other dying every second. Since I fed the birds five minutes. Three hundred kicked the bucket. Other three hundred born, washing the blood off, all are washed in the blood of the lamb, bawling maaaaaa.

Cityful passing away, other cityful coming, passing away too: other coming on, passing on. Houses, lines of houses, streets, miles of pavements, piledup bricks, stones. Changing hands. This owner, that. Landlord never dies they say. Other steps into his shoes when he gets his notice to quit. They buy the place up with gold and still they have all the gold. Swindle in it somewhere. Piled up in cities, worn away age after age. Pyramids in sand. Built on bread and onions. Slaves Chinese wall. Babylon. Big stones left. Round towers. Rest rubble, sprawling suburbs, jerrybuilt. Kerwan's mushroom houses built of breeze. Shelter, for the night. No-one is anything. (*U* 8.476–93)

This highly theoretical passage is perhaps not quite in keeping with the mentality of Bloom, of whom one would not expect such a philosophical exposé. It would be more in keeping with the anonymous narrator.

The account is a stunningly accurate repetition of the "secret doctrine" attributed by Plato in the dialogue *Theaetetus* to the Sophists, who apply Heraclitus's theory of ubiquitous and all-pervasive change both to the process of knowledge and to the objects of knowledge: nothing is ever itself, with the result that things are "not even nohow." "All things are always in every kind of motion. [. . .] One must not use even the word 'thus,' nor yet 'not thus.'"[83] According to this theory, it is impossible either to think or speak about anything, since nothing ever remains constant, neither the knower nor the known. The Greek word for knowledge, *epistêmê*, is related to the verb "to stand," implying fixity. Socrates's phrase in *Theaetetus* has exactly the same meaning as Bloom's "No-one is anything."[84] Because Plato believed there could be no stable knowledge of changing things, he posited a separate world of unchanging Ideas. With his theory of form (*eidos*) as the abiding, defining, principle of natural beings, Aristotle explained how there can be stable knowledge of changing things: form guarantees the underlying identity of the individual even as it changes accidentally. With his theory of soul, which is metaphysically the entelechy of the body, and cognitively the "form of forms," he provided an explanation of the continuity and identity of the knowing subject.[85]

Stephen's reflections on change, which dominate "Proteus," are those of the intellectual who theorizes about what he observes. He goes beneath the perceptible to seek an underlying and enduring undercurrent. In his analysis of change, he was, perhaps unawares, searching for a common element analogous to Aristotle's "prime matter." Prime matter, *prôtê hulê*, a principle of pure potency, allows Aristotle to make sense of radical, substantial, change: since change is a succession within an identity, there must be an underlying element that persists throughout the process and that is receptive to all possible transformation.[86]

Aristotle or Berkeley?

The thinkers with whom Stephen mentally engages, as he ponders the phenomena of sensation and the processes of perception, are in the first place Aristotle and Berkeley. In attempting to fuse them, however, he manages only to confuse them without ever reconciling their quite different perspectives. It is indeed noteworthy that different commentators have highlighted one of the philosophers, to the exclusion of the other. In his important study of *Ulysses*, Joyce's friend Stuart Gilbert makes no reference whatsoever to Aristotle in his discussion of "Proteus." Referring to the opening lines, he states: "Surely the 'signature' of Bishop Berkeley is on this passage!"[87] By contrast, Joseph E. Duncan suggests that "the guiding influence on Stephen's thought is not Berkeley, but Aristotle."[88] The fact is that Joyce aims to blend—rather unsuccessfully—the reflections of both on the nature and operation of sense perception. Allusions to both alternate with one another, ignoring the quite distinct context and purpose of the axioms that are cited. As John Killham aptly remarks, Stephen's mind "flows from association to association as freely and fondly as the waves of the sea mix and merge near at hand."[89]

We have already noted that the following lines in the opening paragraph present a special challenge for the exegete: "Limits of the diaphane. But he adds: in bodies. Then he was aware of them bodies before of them coloured. How? By knocking his sconce against them, sure" (*U* 3.04–06). We have seen that for Aristotle, color is the diaphanous medium through which corporeal reality is perceived. Color is the visible surface of the material reality itself, a patina that directly and immediately reveals the independent reality of the object. It is neither a barrier in, nor a veil to, the perception of something outside the mind, a material physical body with independent existence. Matters later become more complicated with the introduction of the Berkeleyan problematic. Here is the passage in full:

> I throw this ended shadow from me, manshape ineluctable, call it back. Endless, would it be mine, form of my form? Who watches me here? Who ever anywhere will read these written words? Signs on a white field. Somewhere to someone in your flutiest voice. The good

bishop of Cloyne took the veil of the temple out of his shovel hat: veil of space with coloured emblems hatched on its field. Hold hard. Coloured on a flat: yes, that's right. Flat I see, then think distance, near, far, flat I see, east, back. Ah, see now! Falls back suddenly, frozen in stereoscope. Click does the trick. You find my words dark. Darkness is in our souls do you not think? Flutier. Our souls, shamewounded by our sins, cling to us yet more, a woman to her lover clinging, the more the more. (*U* 3.412–23)

It is to be expected that the writings of the idealist philosopher George Berkeley would hold strong fascination for Joyce. He might have been attracted by the self-declared independence of the Kilkenny philosopher, who took pride in asserting the intellectual independence of the Irish who, he declared, often think differently about matters.[90] Joyce could have been intrigued by the ingenious way Berkeley rejected the empiricism and mechanism of British philosophy, in a manner congenial with his own Aristotelian rejection of skeptical relativism. Together with Locke, Berkeley accepted Descartes's assumption that what we directly know are not things themselves but rather impressions or ideas of things. He was, however, more consistent than Locke: if we directly know only what are contents of mind, we have no grounds for asserting extramental realities. According to Berkeley's famous definition, "to be is to be perceived": *esse est percipi*. This is only part of his reasoning, which must be extended to include reference to the divine mind, the omnipotent ground that maintains everything in existence. To be is thus "either to perceive or be perceived."

In Stephen's worry "Who watches me here?" (*U* 3.414), we may recognize a reference to the Berkeleyan riddle: do things cease to be when they are no longer perceived? What guarantees the persistence and continued existence of mental objects? Joyce may have been familiar with Ronald Knox's widely cited limerick stating and solving the crux of Berkeley's theory:

There was a young man who said "God
Must think it exceedingly odd
If he finds that this tree
Continues to be
When there's no one about in the Quad."
"Dear Sir, your astonishment's odd;
I am always about in the Quad
And that's why this tree

Will continue to be
Since observed by Yours faithfully, God."

Stephen's references to Berkeley are rich and significant. The sentence "The good bishop of Cloyne took the veil of the temple out of his shovel hat" harbors a wealth of both associations and challenges. "Shovel hat" may be no more than a reference to the shape of the episcopal tiara. The phrase "veil of the temple" is possibly an anatomical reference to the skull (sconce) mentioned in the first paragraph and its opaque impact with material objects; more importantly, it carries all the references to the biblical veil, woven of blue, purple, and scarlet, that shrouded the holy of holies (Exodus 26:31–33). One of the most dramatic signs of the redemption was the physical scission of this barrier at the time of Christ's death: "And the veil of the temple was rent in twain from the top to the bottom" (Mark 15:38). Reference to the "veil of space" sums up the entire problematic of the representationalist theory of perception: we must draw back the veil that occludes our vision of things in themselves.

The perception of space is problematic for Aristotle and Berkeley alike. For Aristotle, as already explained, space is an aspect of material objects that is not the exclusive domain of a single sense faculty but may be perceived alike through sight, hearing, and touch. Our impression of space is hence not infallible but susceptible to error, unless we take into account the circumstantial conditions, of both our subjective situation and that of the viewed object. Interestingly, what Aristotle terms the "common sensibles"—features attainable by more than one sense—are precisely what Locke terms "primary qualities," those that inhere independently in objects themselves, as distinct from "secondary qualities," which are subjective affections of the perceiver. These "subjective" affections are for Aristotle the proper sensibles, whose truth and objectivity are guaranteed both by the essential nature of the sense organs and the data they are uniquely equipped to receive.

Of Aristotle's common sensibles, space presents the most intractable problems. While he does not refer to Aristotle's approach, Berkeley is beset with similar difficulties. As we consider these, it will be helpful to have again before us the lines from "Proteus":

Who watches me here? Who ever anywhere will read these written words? Signs on a white field. Somewhere to someone in your flutiest voice. The good bishop of Cloyne took the veil of the temple out of his shovel hat: veil of space with coloured emblems hatched on its field. Hold hard. Coloured on a flat: yes, that's right. Flat I see, then think distance, near, far, flat I see, east, back. Ah, see now! Falls back suddenly, frozen in stereoscope. Click does the trick. (*U* 3.414–20)

As J. Mitchell Morse remarks, these lines are explicitly Berkeleyan.[91] *An Essay Towards a New Theory of Vision* is a searching contribution to the psychology of vision. Berkeley proposes to "shew the manner wherein we perceive by sight the distance, magnitude, and situation of objects."[92] Of particular relevance to "Proteus" is his statement that "distance, of itself and immediately, cannot be seen" (§ 2). The reason is as follows: "For distance being a line directed end-wise to the eye, it projects only one point in the fund of the eye, which point remains invariably the same, whether the distance be longer or shorter" (§ 2). According to Berkeley, our estimation of distance is a matter of experience rather than sense.[93] The renowned Berkeley scholar, A. A. Luce, has commented: "Berkeley gives great prominence to the principle that distance, size, and situation are judged, not seen, and that principle is sometimes regarded as Berkeley's theory; but that principle is at least as old as Aristotle."[94] There is also an echo of Aristotle in Berkeley's statement: "The proper, immediate object of vision is light, in all its modes and variations."[95] He emphasizes the importance of vision in his conclusion to the *Theory of Vision* by stating that "the proper objects of vision constitute an universal language of the Author of Nature."[96]

Unsettled by Berkeley's theory that the reality of things depends on being perceived (*esse est percipi*), Stephen lapses momentarily into uncertainty. Having closed his eyes so as to experience sensually the temporality of hearing, he fears the visible world may have disappeared. But on opening his eyes, he reaffirms the world's independent and eternal existence. "Open your eyes now. I will. One moment. Has all vanished since? If I open and am for ever in the black adiaphane. *Basta!* I will see if I can see. See now. There all the time without you: and ever shall be, world without end" (*U* 3.25–28). Reality does not depend on the childish game, "Peekaboo. I see you" (*U* 3.298). Stephen is more concerned that someone may see him depositing the dry snot picked from his nostril on a rock ledge: "For the rest let look who will. Behind. Perhaps there is someone" (*U* 3.501–02).

Knowledge in "Scylla and Charybdis"

Sense knowledge was contemplated at great length in "Proteus" against the background of radical and continuous change. The status and value of intellectual ideas are raised in "Scylla and Charybdis,"[97] which sets out the opposing positions of Plato and Aristotle.[98] "The brain," Joyce told Frank Budgen, "is the organ presiding over *Scylla and Charybdis*. The Aristotelian and Platonic philosophies are the monsters that lie in wait in the narrows for the thinker."[99] The German romantic philosopher Friedrich Schlegel (1772–1829) remarked that every man is born either a Platonist or an Aristotelian, an aphorism Joyce may have known via Coleridge (1772–1834). He was himself a committed Aristotelian; Yeats was the devoted Platonist, represented in the episode by Eglinton and Russell. The contrast is dramatized in a conversation regarding the purpose of art. Russell declares: "Art has to reveal to us ideas, formless spiritual essences. The supreme question about a work of art is out of how deep a life does it spring. The painting of Gustave Moreau is the painting of ideas. The deepest poetry of Shelley, the words of Hamlet bring us into contact with the eternal wisdom, Plato's world of ideas. All the rest is the speculation of schoolboys for schoolboys" (*U* 9.48–53).[100]

Russell describes Plato's ideas as "formless," although they are frequently referred to as "Forms," an alternative translation for *eidos* (plural *eidê*). Presumably what he has in mind is that Plato's transcendent essences are not limited to any particular finite mode or concrete form. Otherwise he correctly summarizes the Platonic theory of artistic creation. Stephen does not engage in a debate on the purpose of art, although a little later he reminds Eglinton that it was Plato rather than Aristotle who banished artists from the ideal republic.

From *Stephen Hero* we are familiar with Stephen's sympathetic grasp of Aristotle's definition of art as the imitation of nature, although he does not refer to the manner in which it portrays universal nature or essence.[101] For Aristotle, this was crucial to the distinction between poetry and history: "The difference is this: that the one relates actual events, the other the kinds of things that might occur. Consequently, poetry is more philosophical and more elevated than history, since poetry relates more of the universal, while history relates particulars."[102] To say that poetry is more universal is not to say that it is a contemplation of universal essences, as Russell demanded. For Aristotle, what really exist are concrete living individuals of a similar nature (*phusis*), which are grasped in a single universal idea;[103] poetry does not contemplate the universal but presents the actions of particular beings, in which the universal nature is exemplified.

When Russell dismisses anything other than the eternal wisdom of formless spiritual essences as mere "speculation of schoolboys for schoolboys" (U 9.53), Stephen "superpolitely" replies that the "schoolmen were schoolboys first. [. . .] Aristotle was once Plato's schoolboy" (U 9.56–57). To Eglinton's condescending remark that he hopefully remained "a model schoolboy with his diploma under his arm," (U 9.59) Stephen replies with sharp irony: "That model schoolboy would find Hamlet's musings about the afterlife of his princely soul, the improbable, insignificant and undramatic monologue, as shallow as Plato's" (U 9.76–78). No longer the schoolboy, Aristotle dismisses his master's doctrine of immortality as shallow and insignificant. Aristotle's hylomorphism implies that with the corruption of the human person at death, the soul as form of the body cannot survive on its own but must also perish. Stephen knows that Aristotle rejects the immortality of the soul, with the possible exception of the active intellect.

John Eglinton becomes impassioned: "Upon my word it makes my blood boil to hear anyone compare Aristotle with Plato" (U 9.80–81). Stephen is not interested in speculation about the survival of the soul: "Hold to the now, the here, through which all future plunges to the past" (U 9.89). The reality is here and now, the instant when history occurs. In the spirit of the young Stephen Hero, aiming "to pierce to the significant heart of everything," (SH 33) he resolves: "Unsheathe your dagger definitions. Horseness is the whatness of allhorse" (U 9.84–85). The example of a horse is frequent in explaining the difference between the concrete empirical individual and the universal idea, although Joyce was probably not familiar with Simplicius's anecdote about Antisthenes, who challenged Plato's theory of Ideas: "I see a horse, but I don't see horseness." Plato replied: "No, for you have the eye with which a horse is seen, but you have not yet acquired the eye to see horseness."[104]

With his reflection, "Unsheathe your dagger definitions. Horseness is the whatness of allhorse," Stephen alludes to two ways in which something may be known. There is, first, the definition, which expresses the logical reference of the word, and, second, the intellectual content of the idea to which the word refers. (P V.136: "nominal and essential definitions") Stephen's statement "Horseness is the whatness of allhorse" is a peculiar but unmistakably Aristotelian response to an age-old problem of universals in epistemology, which asks: to what do general ideas refer? The question goes to the root of knowledge, since it touches upon the relation between sense and intellect and between the particular and the general. The concept "horse" is supposed to refer to an endless number of individuals, but there exists in reality nothing corresponding exactly to the content of the idea "horse." What then is its value? What is the connection between my intellectual idea and the things that really exist in the natural world of change and imperfection?

At stake is the validity of cognition itself. As noted already, the Greek word for knowledge, "*epistêmê*," connotes fixity. Without permanence, there is no true knowledge. We ourselves, however, are constantly undergoing change, and everything around us is in continual flux; change characterizes both the knower and the known. Inverting the metaphor, we could say that the Scylla and Charybdis of knowledge are the rock of immutability and the maelstrom of unceasing flux. Plato and Aristotle give radically divergent answers to the question of universals and to what ultimately guarantees scientific knowledge. Plato applied the Heraclitean theory of flux to the natural world of nature and concluded that the world of the senses was an unsuitable object for stable knowledge. He solved the problem by postulating the existence of a separate world of perfect essences, "Forms" or "Ideas," which are not subject to the changes and imperfections of the natural world. These superior realities are known by the intellect independently of sense knowledge. The latter grasps only the changing things of the natural world, which are in a state of continual flux and ultimate decay.

Aristotle solved the problem of stable knowledge with his notion of form, as well as with his understanding of the soul and how the intellect works. He believed with Plato that the object of true knowledge is "form," but understood in a completely different sense. Form is the principle *within* every individual that determines what it is: its essence. Plato's Forms are transcendent, general, and separate; Aristotle's are immanent, individual, and intrinsic. According to Plato, the Form exists "apart from the many"; for Aristotle, it is within and common to the many individuals that share a similar essence.

Essence, according to Aristotle, is the proper object of intellect, as color is the proper object of the eye. The mind, he maintains, intuitively grasps the defining characteristic of the object that is perceived. This the intellect does by mentally abstracting the essential aspect of the object, divested of its accidental features of time and place and so on. Aristotle expressed the difference between sense and intellectual knowledge: "Sensation grasps individuals, intellect understands universals."[105] Abstraction is the key to the passage from sense to intellect.[106] In abstractive intuition, the intellect grasps the essence or form of the individual. Referring to Aristotle's invented phrase for "essence," Hugh Kenner accurately remarks that Joyce "reached for the Philosopher's solid, the rock: τὸ τί ἦν εἶναι [what it was to be]," that is, the essence of the individual that he identified as substance.[107]

Just as the individual senses are infallible in their domain, the intellect too has its privileged infallibility. It has the intuitive power to grasp "what" an object of experience is. If, for example, I were presented for the first time with a horse and a dog, I would spontaneously form a basic notion of the uniqueness of each and could never confuse the two. This is to grasp—however inadequately—the nature, essence, or "whatness" of the individual, viewed simply in itself as indivisible. Aristotle states in *De Anima*: "The thinking of indivisible objects of thought occurs among things concerning which there is no possibility of falsehood."[108] The mind is always true when thinking of the definition of something in its essence.[109] Put most simply: "Mind is always right."[110] The intellect is infallible in its specific capacity when it forms a notion of what something is. This is summarized in Aristotle's statement, noted by Joyce in his Paris notebook: "Error is not found apart from combination."[111] Just as the senses do not err in grasping their proper object at the accidental physical level, the intellect does not err in its intuition of the object's intelligible essence. Error occurs only at the level of judgment, when intellect combines diverse data and mentally affirms a wrong combination.

Knowledge in *Finnegans Wake*

Richard Beckman asserts optimistically: "One passage that would seem to settle questions about epistemology in the *Wake* once and for all is the debate between Saint Patrick and the Archdruid."[112] If only it were so simple! Especially in light of the threat that we may be "dead certain however of neuthing whatever" (*FW* 455.21–22)[113]. The work suggests rather an "Epistlemadethemology for deep dorfy doubtlings" (*FW* 374.17–18). William York Tindall states that this passage is "as obscure as anything in the *Wake*."[114] While the "Paddrock and bookley chat" (*FW* 611.2) brings to a climax many of the philosophical antagonisms heralded within the work, it leaves unresolved the great problems of epistemology.[115] It confirms, however, Joyce's persistent fixation with questions of certainty, identity, and existence. As Beckman notes, "The great themes in philosophy—being and knowledge—are intrinsic to a book that is itself philosophic."[116] While neither Aristotle nor Aquinas features in the discussion, the question regarding the portals of perception (*FW* 612.24 "gnosegates," *gnosis* = knowledge) was for each a matter of primary significance and may be assessed from their point of view. Patrick/Paddrock stands on the rock of Aristotelian common sense and on the founding stone of the Roman Church; rock also suggests the stone kicked by Johnson to refute Berkeley's immaterialism. The bookish and "bookley" archdruid, by contrast, is enclosed in an idealist world of subjective ideas, according to the Berkeleyan principle that "to be" is "to be known."[117]

There is optimistic promise also in the preamble to the discussion, which suggests it will be conducted rationally in the clear light of day, aided by a superior or infused illumination: "By the light of the bright reason which daysends to us from the high" (*FW* 610.28–29). The episode occurs at sunrise, as daylight dissolves the shades of night. We are awakening from dream to the wide-awake world: "From sleep we are passing. [. . .] Into the wikeawades warld from sleep we are passing" (*FW* 608.33–34). The dispute between "saint and sage," (*FW* 613.16)[118] however, is a confrontation between two crude and seemingly irreconcilable positions. Apart from a rudimentary realism, Patrick displays none of Aristotle's refined insight, while Buckley lacks the Bishop's subtlety.[119]

The archdruid is avatar of George Berkeley,[120] the Irish philosopher whose extreme idealism (*esse est percipi*: "to be is to be perceived"), as we have seen, held fascination for Joyce,[121] who was familiar with "the phyllisophies of Bussup Bulkeley" (*FW* 435.10–11). Earlier in the *Wake*, we read that "Berkeley showed the reason genrously" (*FW* 423.32–33); he now appears as Bilkilly-Belkelly-Balkally, the archdruid of High King Leary, last non-Christian king of Ireland. His name also recalls Buckley, the Irish soldier who shot the Russian general in the Crimean War. Speaking Chinese pidgin, Patrick is presented as the Eurasian Generalissimo (*FW* 610.12–13). In a larger perspective, the debate is between pagan Celtic Ireland and the newly announced message of Christianity (referenced by the "four three two agreement," [*FW* 612.26] *anno Domini* of Patrick's arrival as bishop). In an ironic turn, the dispute is between the Bishop of Cloyne and his first predecessor on the island of Ireland, Patrick the Bishop of Armagh.

Anticipating the debate between Bulkily/burkeley (*FW* 610.1, 12) and Paddrock, Muta suggests that the archdruid will seek unity, Patrick diversity, before they engage in dispute and finally reconcile: "So that when we shall have acquired unification we shall pass on to diversity and when we shall have passed on to diversity we shall have acquired the instinct of combat and when we shall have acquired the instinct of combat we shall pass back to the spirit of appeasement?" (*FW* 610.23–27). Here is represented once again the classic polarity of the One and the Many. Susan Shaw Sailer suggests that the archdruid "sees the continuity of reality from one object to another and realizes that it is only their surfaces that differ"; Patrick sees "the daytime distinctions between things," while "the archdruid's [reality] is that in which one sees the unity of all that is."[122] This difference is illustrated by the druid's claim to behold the diversity of all colors in a single perception.[123]

Balkelly is dressed in the seven colors of the rainbow (*FW* 611.06–07: "heptachromatic sevenhued septicoloured roranyellgreenlindigan [= red, orange, yellow, green, blue, indigo] mantle),"[124] Patrick in a simple white-colored alb.[125] The contrast symbolizes the druid's claim that only the privileged seer can behold reality in its full resplendence, whereas fallen man has a monochromatic perception of the world: he perceives its "furniture"—animals, vegetables, and minerals—under a single color, that is, the one that they reflect because they cannot absorb it. According to Balkelly, God's richly multicolored world ("hueful panepiphanal [Greek: *panepiphanês,* completely manifest] world spectacurum of Lord Joss") is concealed under many illusions that distort the full spectrum and spectacle (*FW* 611.12–14, "all too many much illusiones through photoprismic velamina"). The archdruid declares that only a visionary gifted with the highest grade of wisdom knows reality as it truly is in itself (*FW* 611.20–21: "numpa one paraduxed seer in seventh degree of wisdom of Entis-Onton he savvy inside true inwardness of reality, the Ding hvad in idself id est"). The high-minded druid alone can with special insight (*FW* 611.32: "throughsighty": German, *durchsichtig*) behold in their unity the totality of all things in the world in their full glory, including the six colors of light, which are hidden to normal vision: "all objects (of panepiwor) allside showed themselves in trues coloribus resplendent with sextuple gloria of light actually retained, untisintus, inside them (obs of epiwo)" (*FW* 611.22–24). (The word "untisintus" combines the Greek genitive of "being" and the Latin "intus," within.) By inner vision he perceives within himself the remaining six colors inherent in the "furniture" of the "hueful panepiphanal world" (*FW* 611.18: "furnit of heupanepi world"). which are hidden from common sight under the apparent color. Fallen man, on the other hand, perceives "but one photoreflection of the several iridals gradations of solar light" (*FW* 611.16–17).

With his repeated references to "furniture," "furnit," and "fur," we may presume that besides *A New Theory of Vision,* in which Berkeley criticizes Locke's distinction between primary and secondary qualities, Joyce alludes to a well-known passage in section 6 of *A Treatise Concerning the Principles of Human Knowledge:*

> Some truths there are so near and obvious to the mind that a man need only open his eyes to see them. Such I take this important one to be, viz., that all the choir of heaven and furniture of the earth, in a word all those bodies which compose the mighty frame of the world, have not any subsistence without a mind, that their *being* is to be perceived or known; that consequently so long as they are not actually perceived by me, or do not exist in my mind or that of any other created spirit, they must either have no existence at all, or else subsist in the mind of some Eternal Spirit—it being perfectly unintelligible, and involving all the absurdity of abstraction, to attribute to any single part of them an existence independent of a spirit.[126]

The phrase "photoreflection of the several iridals gradationes of solar light" (*FW* 611.16–17) recalls the theory of Isaac Newton, according to which colors are not as such located within bodies but caused by the manner in which they variously reflect the light: "Some natural bodies reflect some sorts of rays, others other sorts more copiously than the rest. [. . .] Every body reflects the rays of its own colour more copiously than the rest, and from their excess and predominance in the reflected light has its colour."[127] This phenomenon may be obversely explained as the ability of bodies to "stop and stifle in themselves the rays which they do not reflect or transmit."[128] The color of an object is, therefore, "that one which that part of it (furnit of heupanepi world) had shown itself (part of fur of huepanwor) unable to absorbere" (*FW* 611.17–19). Endowed with inner vision, the privileged seer perceives all colors not in their diverse manifestations but concentrated in rich simplicity, "with pure hueglut intensely saturated one, tinged uniformly allaroundside upinandoutdown" (*FW* 612.13–14).[129] No doubt he perceives also "nighthood's unseen violet . . . nonviewable to human watchers" (*FW* 403.22–24).

As well as Berkeley, Joyce introduces into later versions and the final text a distinction that was central in the complex epistemology of Immanuel Kant (1724–1804). Beneath the sense phenomena experienced in space and time, the German rationalist posited the *Ding an sich* ("thing in itself"), which lies beyond the range of our perception. This assertion accords with the druid's suggestion that we know only appearances (*FW* 611.12–14: "illusiones through photprismic velamina") and are unable to grasp the "inside true inwardness of reality, the Ding hvad in idself id est" (*FW* 611.21). The distinction served Joyce well. Kant's vast system was an attempt to synthe-size the idealism of René Descartes with the empiricism of David Hume (*FW* 606.16: "something to right hume about"). With his distinction be-tween noumenon and phenomenon, Kant reified the distinction between appearance and reality, agreeing with both Descartes and Hume that we can know only what is in the mind. The search thus continued for the true inwardness of reality, with a call to "roll away the reel world, the reel world, the reel world!" (*FW* 64.25–26).

Among exponents of philosophical paradox, Immanuel Kant was cer-tainly a leader, a "puraduxed" seer (*FW* 611.19–20). His early work on Emanuel Swedenborg (1766) was titled *Dreams of a Spirit-Seer* (*Träume eines Geistersehers*). It is the height of paradox to affirm as real an object that is independent of observation and unknowable in itself, an "Unknun!" (*FW* 353.15). Richard Beckman comments: "*Finnegans Wake* can be taken as a parody version of Kant's idea of how limited human knowledge is, nothing but a kind of seeming."[130] Joyce was familiar with Kant's phenom-enalism, but as Beckman points out, "Kant's Ding-an-sich, thing in itself, is all but useless to Joyce because it implies a sharp distinction between the phenomenal, or knowable, world and the noumenal, or realm of the unknowable. But the two are not distinguishable in *Finnegans Wake,* where the knowable and the unknowable are alike uncertain."[131] Whereas *Ulysses* unfolds in the light of day, *Finnegans Wake* is the "book of the dark" (*FW* 251.24). The *lumen naturale* of intellect, exemplified in the luminous guide-lines of identity, noncontradiction, and excluded middle, is sacrificed for the *coincidentia oppositorum,* where dichotomies merge in coinciding con-traries (*FW* 49.36).

The potent references to the "wisdom of Entis-Onton" (a combination of Latin and Greek genitives, singular and plural, of "being"),[132] the "true inwardness of reality" (an echo perhaps of Hopkins), and "the Ding hvad in idself id est": these all combine to emphasize Joyce's concern with the real in itself. They recall Aristotle's statement: "The question which, both now and of old, has always been raised, and always been the subject of doubt, viz. what being is, is just the question, what is substance?"[133] There is an as-sertion of the primacy of existence in the words "This exists that isits after having been said we know" (*FW* 186.08–09). The enigmatic questions of certainty and identity continue to perplex the author of *Finnegans Wake* but are never conclusively resolved.

Patrick has not fully understood the archdruid's speech (*FW* 611.25: "no catch all that preachybook") but does not hesitate to dismiss it as nonsense ("tripeness," *FW* 611.17). The druid's speech is introduced with the word "Tunc" (Then), recalling one of the most beautiful illustrations in the Book of Kells ("*book of kills*," *FW* 482.33); Patrick's blunt retort begins: "Punc," suggesting that the druid's speech is bunkum. In Anthony Burgess's words, "'Bilkilly-Belkelly' spouts sesquipedalian idealism which makes as much sense as blackfellow's gibberish."[134] To add injury to insult, the dismissal is bookended with a crushing "Thud" (*FW* 612.36). Patrick addresses the druid sarcastically as "Bigseer," although unaware he has misunderstood his position. He is wrong in stating that the archdruid claims to know true celestial reality through a posteriori experience (when it is exactly the opposite) and that he sees things only in a chiaroscuro of black and white (*FW* 612.18–19: "you pore shiroskuro blackinwhitepaddynger,[135] by thiswis aposterioprismically[136] apatstrophied [turned away and bereft of nourishment]"). He is more on the mark when he claims that the druid's reasoning is paralyzed by faulty logic and sham synthesis (*FW* 612.19–20, 25: "paralogically periparolysed [. . .] synthetic shammyrag").[137] This prompts incredulity among the bystanders, who hesitate between the apparent truthfulness of the Druid and the seeming upper hand of the Saint (*FW* 612.22–24: "murkblankered in their neutrolysis between the possible viritude of the sager and the probable eruberuption [*Eroberung*, Ger. conquest] of the saint").[138]

Patrick's position is to proclaim the doctrine of the divine Trinity, which he illustrates with a hand-plucked sheaf of three-leafed shamrock, symbolizing the triune synthesis of divine persons. The phrase "Me wipenmeselps gnosegates a handcaughtscheaf of synthetic shammyrag" (*FW* 612.24–25) could also be a rebuttal of Kant's theory of scientific knowledge as synthetic a priori: the realist wipes the idealist's nose with a chamois handkerchief while unlocking to him the portals of perception ("gnosegates"). Patrick finally invokes the panoply and panorama of power, light, fire, and color to proclaim the Christian Trinity, genuflecting to hail it with ascending reverence as Balenoarch, Great Balenoarch, and Greatest Great Balenoarch. These names are inversions of the Italian compound for rainbow, "arcobaleno"; the inversion is appropriate, since "baleno" means "flash of lightning," while Greek "arch" (ἀρχή) is principle or origin, in this case the ground and summit of all hierarchy.[139] While he does not have much respect for the Irish druid's celestial rainbow, the palest of all (*FW* 612.20–21: "celestial from principalest of Iro's Irismans ruinboon [*Regenbogen*, Ger. rainbow] pot before"), Patrick himself sees in the light and fire of the rainbow a symbol of the Trinity: "The Son is the radiance of God's glory and the exact image of his nature."[140] Along with the shamrock—which is no sham—the rainbow is a genuine symbol of the Blessed Trinity, Father, Son, and Holy Ghost (*FW* 612.29–30: "the sound sense sympol in a weedwayed-wold of the firethere the sun in his halo cast. Onmen."). To the symbols of fire and sun is joined the image of Christ's holocaust for the salvation of mankind. Spurning the druid's belief in the "hueful panepiphanal world," he kneels to worship the rainbow as visible symbol of God's covenant with mankind. "Balenoarch" contains audible mention of Noah's Ark, who received God's pledge: "I have set my bow in the clouds, and it will be the sign of the covenant between me and the earth."[141] Let us not forget that Patrick lit the paschal fire on the Hill of Tara in direct provocation of the druids.[142]

Patrick proceeds to reject the archdruid's premises, with an axiomatic assertion of *res* (thing) as the *primum datum* of experience, the *Ding an sich*: "That was thing, bygotter, the thing, bogcotton, the very thing, begad" (*FW* 612.31–32). Patrick's point of view echoes Aristotle's theory of the "proper sensibles," according to which the color you see is the genuine color of the object as it truly appears. The object seen is the real thing. To knowingly posit the existence of an unknown something is absurd.[143] The druid, on the other hand, dismissing the evidence of the senses, seeks a metaphysical reality beneath the surface, an invisible reality beneath the veil of appearances ("hueful panepiphanal world"). The words "bygotter, bogcotton, begad," add a deep religious connotation, referring to the doctrine that Christ was "begotten, not made," the doctrine that was canonized in the Nicene and Apostles' Creeds.

Patrick has put it up to pompous, "uptoputty Bilkilly-Belkelly-Balkally" (*FW* 612.32), who falls in defeat with a "Thud" (*FW* 612.36); but he is not finished. Patrick condemns the druid's world of false appearances in the world of true color (*FW* 613.10–12: "Shamwork, be in our scheinung! [*Schein*, Ger. Illusion; *Erscheinung*, appearance/revelation] [. . .] in a farbiger [Ger. 'colorful'] pancosmos"). It could also refer to the revelation of the true meaning of the shamrock. Patrick sums up his common sense: "Yet is no body present here which was not there before. Only is order othered. Nought is nulled. *Fuitfiat!*" (*FW* 613.13–14). Knowledge does not invent realities but adds a new order toward the world. There is, however, a primacy in the order: things come first. The ultimate affirmation is: "As it was, let it be!" The exhilaration of Patrick's proclamation echoes the command of divine creation: *Fiat lux!*

There are clearly diverse and conflicting philosophical principles and presuppositions operative in the discussion between the druid and the saint. Traces of Berkeley, Newton, and Kant are undoubtedly present. Our interest is in possible influences of Aristotle and Aquinas, and these are less obvious. Alistair Cormack refers to the "pious Aristotelianism" of the saint and suggests that "St Patrick embodies a devout scholastic realism, in which identities are clear and logic can mark out causality."[144] Michael Patrick Gillespie's suggests: "To illustrate the efficacy of his system, the druid presents his theory of colors, a mixture of the views of Aristotle, Berkeley, and Kant with an adumbration of Freudian psychology."[145] It is true that in the arguments of both druid and saint one may recognize features that recall aspects of Aristotle and Aquinas. These are, I suggest, however, too general to attribute particular reliance. Aspects of Balkelly's theory of colors may recall Aristotelian terminology, while, for his part, St. Patrick shares with Aristotle and Aquinas a basic and universal commonsense realism. Anything more is to read too much into the text.

The role of Kant in the dialogue, on the other hand, is far more significant. Joyce was understandably fascinated by Kant's intriguing and ingenious theory of knowledge. He was already familiar with the distinctions and vocabulary of the cognitive process, from his reading of both Aristotle and Aquinas. He had some familiarity with the entire process of cognition from Scholastic philosophy manuals.[146] Joyce certainly had some familiarity with Kant's vocabulary but was, I suggest, "categorically unimperatived by the maxims" (*FW* 176.25) of the Kantian system. While greatly intrigued by it, he could not have found it congenial, as it would offend his deeply ingrained realism. Harry Levin has pertinently remarked: "There are times, even in his maturest writing, when he still seems to be a realist in the most medieval sense."[147]

In *Finnegans Wake*, Joyce was engaged in a playful but impossible experiment. As we shall see in a later chapter, he wanted to create a universe that would be free of all the rules, surpassing the cut-and-dried logic of "either/or" in a synthesis of "both/and." Kant contributed toward the skepticism that encouraged such an enterprise, precisely because his system was also a fruitless attempt to achieve the impossible. He failed in his ambition to overcome the division between idealism and empiricism, managing only to juxtapose the two antithetical positions, each of which emphasized to exclusivity one of the complementary poles of cognition: dependence on the sensible, on the one hand, and the a priori element that transcends space and time, on the other. Agreeing with both Descartes and Hume that we can know only what is in the mind, Kant nonetheless posited the *Ding an sich,* the "thing in itself" beyond experience. Richard Beckman remarks:

"What *Finnegans Wake* most has in common with Kant's *Critique of Pure Reason* is the proposition that direct knowledge is not attainable. [. . .] Direct knowledge would be stable and certain. But *Finnegans Wake* presents the world in a darker light, where only indirect and flickering images exist, where the real is known only by means of the 'celluloid art' (*FW* 534.25), images stored on a 'reel' (*FW* 64.25)."[148] On the contrast between the cognitive contexts of *Ulysses* and *Finnegans Wake,* respectively, Beckman writes:

> The streams of associations in *Ulysses* represent the mutable but coherent contents of the mind. The representation of the mind in *Finnegans Wake* is far more accidental, arbitrary, and the grounds of association verge, or seem to verge, on the unknowable. The spirit of skepticism rules, or misrules. In *Ulysses,* everything—with occasional exceptions, and sometimes only by inference—seems knowable. The reader has never known so much about the world; and the sense of selfhood, no matter how much disturbed by random associations and unwelcome thoughts, is secure. But in *Finnegans Wake,* selves merge and shift like currents of water or the flights of bats. The accidental quality of selfhood, consciousness, and thought is prominent, and the knowability of history and objects is treated from the point of view of an almost anarchic skepticism—just what Kant was afraid of.[149]

All of this confirms that, apart from some tangential mentions, and St. Patrick's rudimentary realism, neither Aristotle nor Aquinas occupies any significant place in Joyce's book of the night.

4

Identity, Soul, and Substance

The opening lines of Joyce's youthful essay "A Portrait of the Artist" (1904) allude to themes of personal identity, continuity, and self-definition—questions that would continue to occupy him throughout his life. The paragraph merits quotation in full, with significant phrases emphasized in bold:

> The **features of infancy** are not commonly reproduced in the **adolescent portrait** for, so capricious are we, that we cannot or will not **conceive the past** in any other than its iron **memorial aspect**. Yet **the past assuredly implies a fluid succession of presents**, the **development of an entity of which our actual present is a phase only**. Our world, again, recognises its acquaintance chiefly by the **characters of beard and inches** and is, for the most part, estranged from those of its members who seek **through some art**, by some **process of the mind as yet untabulated**, to **liberate from the personalised lumps of matter** that which is their **individuating rhythm**, the **first or formal relation of their parts**. But for such as these a **portrait is not an identificative paper** but the **curve of an emotion**. (*PSW* 211)

The question under consideration is how to depict the self as it matures and develops. Features of infancy are often neglected in portraying the adolescent, because we focus on the present and rigidly consign the past to memory. But the past and "actual present" are both phases in a "fluid succession of presents." A portrait should also go beyond superficial features to grasp the self-determining shape ("rhythm") imposed by the artist on the raw material of his emotions. Joyce makes use of the Aristotelian concepts of matter and form when stating that the artist's aim is "to liberate from the personalised lumps of matter that which is their individuating rhythm, the first or formal relation of their parts."[1]

This early essay, written at a single stroke but undoubtedly the culmination of much reflection, foreshadows Joyce's lifelong concern with the question of the identity of the self and its permanence through change, as well as the definition of artistic personality. The opening paragraph signals his awareness of the difficulties he would encounter during an entire life of artistic and creative work. Although it does not feature in this paragraph, the word "soul" is the pivotal concept in Joyce's reflections about individuality, identity, and permanence. He was from first to last fascinated, intrigued, and challenged by the idea and reality of the soul. In a letter to Lady Gregory in November 1902 Joyce wrote: "All things are inconstant except the faith in the soul, which changes all things and fills their inconstancy with light" (*LI* 53). The narcissistic dedication of his first work indicates almost obsessive self-absorption:

To

My own Soul I

dedicate the first

true work of my

life.[2]

It is highly significant that "soul" is one of the words most frequently used by Joyce, occurring twenty times in *Dubliners,* thirty-five in *Stephen Hero,* 204 times in *A Portrait,* 106 in *Ulysses,* fourteen in *Exiles,* and thirty-four in *Finnegans Wake,* a total of more than four hundred.[3] Joyce was "a student of the human soul if anything" (*U* 16.1047).

An outline of Aristotle's theory of the soul has already been given. A summary will suffice here, to include added nuances of Aquinas's, since it was with their combined theory that Joyce was familiar. In light of his theory of act and potency, Aristotle identified the soul as the actualizing principle of the body, in union with which it constitutes the individual living substance. Synonymous with "soul" (*psuchê*) are the words "nature" (*phusis*), "form" (*eidos*), and in certain contexts "substance" (*ousia, to ti ên einai*). Aristotle's invented term "entelechy" denotes the soul in its primary perfection and fundamental activity as determining principle of the living substance.[4] Aristotle considered the metaphysics of human nature in his treatise on psychology (*Peri tês Psuchês,* Latin, *De Anima*). He distinguished between vegetative, animal, and human souls, each respective level exhibiting a higher degree of perfection. Plants are endowed with powers of growth and nutrition; animals have movement and sensation; in addition, humans are capable of intellectual cognition.

In his treatise on the soul, Aristotle left a number of questions ambiguous. His indication that the soul in its intellectual activity could be regarded as "separate," and possibly immortal, was inconclusive, giving rise to the suggestion by Averroes (1126–1198) that all humankind shares a single intellect. Much debate and controversy would have been spared if Aristotle had explained more carefully what he meant by "separate." Aquinas, however, had no doubts about its meaning and expressed surprise at the controversy it provoked:

> Indeed it is astonishing how easily some have let themselves be deceived by his calling the intellect "separate"; for the text itself makes it perfectly clear what he means,—namely that, unlike the senses, the intellect has no bodily organ. For the nobility of the human soul transcends the scope and limits of bodily matter. Hence it enjoys a certain activity in which bodily matter has no share; the potentiality to which activity is without a bodily organ; and in this sense only is it a "separate" intellect.[5]

Since the soul is nonmaterial, it is free from the disintegration that affects the body and is therefore immortal. It is not composed of parts but is simple in nature, as Stephen would try to explain to Bloom.[6]

Questions concerning the soul arise in "Oxen of the Sun," the theme of which is gestation and birth. Stephen refers to "those Godpossibled souls that we nightly impossibilise" (U 14.225–26).[7] Presumably he has in mind the possible souls that are neutralized through masturbation or contraceptive sex. He describes this as the "sin against the Holy Ghost, Very God, Lord and Giver of Life" (U 14.26–27). Blasphemy was traditionally regarded as the sin against the Holy Spirit, but Stephen may have understood the elimination of possible souls as an offence against the author of life.

Stephen also pronounces on the disputed question as to when the embryo becomes human: "He said also how at the end of the second month a human soul was infused" (U 14.247–48). There is no authoritative source for such a precise statement, although it has a background in the embryology of Hippocrates, as developed by Aristotle and interpreted by Aquinas. The discussion concerns the different stages of embryonic development and the related question of the point in time when the corresponding soul is present. Is the rational soul fully present in the early stages of pregnancy even before the fetus is recognizably human?

In his treatise *The Nature of the Child*, Hippocrates placed the differentiation of limbs in the male embryo at thirty days, in the female at forty-two.[8]

The quickening process, that is, when the fetus starts to move, he suggests, occurs at three months in the male, at four in the female.[9] Aristotle considered the soul's biology in his *History of Animals* and *Generation of Animals*. Based on empirical observation and experiment he traced the development of the embryo through all its stages from conception to birth. He argued that the human embryo is a sentient animal before becoming a rational human.[10] The reason for the delayed emergence of the sensitive and rational soul can be understood in light of Aristotle's definition of soul as the actuality of the body endowed with organs and having the potency for life. The embryo can only receive the more perfect soul when it has developed the appropriate organ. Aristotle placed the completion of the bodily form at forty days for the male embryo, ninety for the female embryo.[11] The question of greatest difficulty, he stated, concerns the origin of the rational soul; because it is independent of any physical organ, it cannot derive from the animal soul: "It remains, then, that reason alone enters in, as an additional factor, from outside, and that it alone is divine, because physical activity has nothing whatsoever to do with the activity of reason."[12] By "from outside," he understands that it derives from the paternal seed.[13] The solution proposed by Aquinas is that the rational soul is immediately created by God, albeit through the instrumentality of the body.

Aquinas follows Aristotle in stating that there is a succession of distinct souls. One of the objections to his own position affirming the unicity of the soul refers to Aristotle's view that the embryo is an animal before it is a man.[14] In his reply, Aquinas states: "The embryo has first of all a soul which is merely sensitive, and when this is removed, it is supplanted by a more perfect soul, which is both sensitive and intellectual."[15] In his commentary on Peter Lombard's *Sentences* (an early work), Aquinas cites Aristotle's view that the conception of the male is perfected at forty days, that of the female at ninety.[16] As distinct from Aristotle, however, Aquinas maintained that the soul is created by God and not generated. This takes place when the embryo is fully formed (40/90 days), that is, sufficiently developed to receive the intellectual soul, in other words, when it is a complete human body. David Albert Jones sums up the standard medieval doctrine: "The infusion of the rational soul, as it was termed, was understood as a divine intervention that took place upon completion of a natural process—the formation of the body."[17]

Aquinas is concerned to emphasize that there is only one single soul in each individual, that is, the intellectual soul, which contains virtually the perfections and powers of the earlier forms: it is one and the same soul that is the principle of nutrition, sensation, and intellection:

> We must therefore conclude that in man the sensitive soul, the intellectual soul, and the nutritive soul are numerically one soul.[18]
>
> And so we must conclude that there is no other substantial form in man besides the intellectual soul, and that the soul, as it virtually contains the sensitive and nutritive souls, so does it virtually contain all inferior forms, and itself alone does whatever the imperfect forms do in other things. The same is to be said of the sensitive soul in brute animals, and of the nutritive soul in plants, and universally of all more perfect forms with regard to the imperfect.[19]

As to how the distinct souls become present one after another, that is, the progression from vegetative to sentient to rational, Aquinas maintains that the one replaces the other through a process of generation and corruption. Thus when the sentient soul supervenes upon the embryo, the vegetative soul is destroyed; similarly, the infusion of the rational soul results in corruption of the sentient soul. The rational or intellectual soul is endowed with all the powers and perfection of the lesser souls. Aquinas expresses this as follows:

> It must be said that the soul is in the embryo, the nutritive soul from the beginning, then the sensitive, lastly the intellectual soul. [. . .] We must therefore say that since the generation of one thing is the corruption of another, it follows of necessity that both in men and in other animals, when a more perfect form supervenes the previous form is corrupted, yet so that the succeeding form contains the perfection of the previous form, and something in addition. It is in this way that through many generations and corruptions we arrive at the ultimate substantial form, both in man and other animals. This indeed is apparent to the senses in animals generated from putrefaction. We conclude therefore that the intellectual soul is created by God at the end of human generation, and this soul is at the same time sensitive and nutritive, the pre-existing forms being corrupted.[20]

Aquinas's theory of the soul is summed up in the definition "*anima forma corporis*": the soul is form of the body. Verbally this is identical with Aristotle's view; the radical difference is that for Aquinas the soul subsists in itself (*subsistens in se*), which is proved by the fact that it has activities that are independent of the body, such as self-reflection and the formation of universal ideas. Of its nature it is simple, that is, devoid of parts, and is therefore immune from corruption and is immortal.

As well as Stephen's references to the soul in "Oxen of the Sun," there is a reference in *Finnegans Wake*—"middayevil down to his vegetable soul" (*FW* 423.27–28)—and perhaps also in Stephen's remark "We don't want any of your medieval abstrusiosities" (*U* 3.319–20).

We noted earlier how St. Ignatius decreed that members of the Jesuit order should be trained in the philosophy of Aristotle. A decade later, Francisco Borgia, third Superior General (1565–1572), specified a number of precise doctrines concerning the soul:

> The intellective soul is truly the substantial form of the body, according to Aristotle and the true philosophy. The intellective soul is not numerically one in all men, but there is a distinct and proper soul in each man, according to Aristotle and the true philosophy. The intellective soul is immortal, according to Aristotle and the true philosophy. There are not several souls in man, intellective, sensitive, and vegetative souls, and neither are there two kinds of souls in animals, sensitive and vegetative souls, according to Aristotle and the true philosophy.[21]

By "true philosophy" was meant a Thomist interpretation of those aspects of the nature, and the status of the soul, regarding which Aristotle had been ambiguous. These precisions were already contained in Aquinas but not universally accepted. They became in succeeding centuries the standard Catholic teaching on the soul, which was the doctrine Joyce received.

Besides Aristotelian-Thomist thinking on the soul, Joyce was doubtless also familiar with the Catholic doctrine of the "Communion of Saints," namely, the fellowship existing between all members of the Mystical Body of Christ, comprising those still living on earth (the Church militant), those in Purgatory (the Church suffering), and those who have attained eternal salvation (the Church triumphant). Catholics are encouraged to seek through prayer the intercession of the saints in Heaven and to pray and offer sacrifice for the "Holy Souls in Purgatory." In "The Sisters," the pious aunt twice prays for the happy repose of the soul of Father O'Rourke: "God have mercy on his soul," "The Lord have mercy on his soul!"[22] In "Ivy Day in the Committee Room," Mr. Henchy expresses the opposite sentiment toward Mr. Lyons: "Blast your soul!"[23]

As someone who grew up in the fifties in Ireland and who received the traditional Catholic upbringing of the day, I can from personal experience attest to the importance placed upon the soul. From an early age, we were taught that what mattered in the end was to save one's immortal soul. We were created by God, who through love made us out of nothing; our entire purpose in life was to know him, so we could spend eternity in his glorious and bliss-filled presence in Heaven. Our soul was our most precious part, and our greatest concern was to keep it clean and pure, always in the state of grace. The Holy Souls were as much a reality as the children in the classroom next door. You could not see them, but they were present in your awareness because they needed you, to pray for them so they would soon pass from Purgatory, brightly cleansed, into Heaven for all eternity. They were your neighbors or relatives who had died, your friends who had been kind to you and now it was your turn. This was the religious education received by Irish children for generations, until it was diluted in the sixties, in the wake of Vatican II. It was the education that was received by James Joyce and that, I suggest, best explains his abiding interest in the concept and reality of the soul.

In *A Portrait*, we read of Stephen's concern for the Holy Souls: "His daily life was laid out in devotional areas. By means of ejaculations and prayers he stored up ungrudgingly for the souls in purgatory centuries of days and quarantines of years" (*P* IV.17–19).[24] In "Wandering Rocks," Fr. John Conmee, S.J., dwells on matters of life and death and the ultimate salvation of souls. He regrets what in Catholic prayer would be called the "sudden and unprovided death" of victims in a dreadful catastrophe in New York, which he reads about on a newsboard. He reflects that an act of perfect contrition or sorrow for their sins would gain them eternal salvation. Later, he reflects on "the souls of black and brown and yellow men" and "millions of black and brown and yellow souls that had not received the baptism of water when their last hour came like a thief in the night." He reflects on the "millions of human souls created by God in His Own likeness to whom the faith had not (D.V.) been brought. But they were God's souls, created by God. It seemed to Father Conmee a pity that they should all be lost, a waste, if one might say" (*U* 10.143–52).

The closing mood of "The Dead" is marked by an awareness of the universal fellowship of souls. The penultimate paragraph, which conveys the inner thoughts and feelings of Gabriel, is a profound meditation on final questions of life and death, personal identity, and the finitude of existence itself. Reading the text, one should keep in mind that Aristotelian "form" is a synonym for "soul'":

> The tears gathered more thickly in his eyes and in the partial dark-ness he imagined he saw the form of a young man standing under a dripping tree. Other forms were near. His soul had approached that region where dwell the vast hosts of the dead. He was conscious of, but could not apprehend, their wayward and flickering existence. His own identity was fading out into a grey impalpable world: the solid world itself, which these dead had one time reared and lived in, was dissolving and dwindling (D 194, 1590–600).[25]

Gabriel is overwhelmed, not only by the memory of Michael Furey but also by the presence of all the living and the dead. The ultimacy of existence and the soul's final destiny are foremost in his mind.

The challenge for philosophy is to justify the commonsense belief that there is an abiding unity in each of us while also accounting for the interac-tion of that self-unity with the ever-changing flux of experience. The dyadic character of human nature is aptly conveyed by the "composite asymmetri-cal image" that Bloom sees reflected in the mirror—"The image of a solitary (ipsorelative) mutable (aliorelative) man" (U 17.1348–50). The self must be incommunicable in itself, yet open and receptive to others in reciprocal communion. It must be at once constant and dynamic: is this not a contra-diction? Must we choose between solitude and solidarity? It is clear that the individual must be inalienable and self-possessed. This is illustrated in "A Painful Case," where Mr. Duffy realizes that the self is a solitary and isolated entity: "as he attached the fervent nature of his companion more and more closely to him, he heard the strange impersonal voice which he recognised as his own, insisting on the soul's incurable loneliness. We cannot give our-selves, it said: we are our own" (D 93.143–45). Duffy is incapable of sharing and remains in self-imposed isolation. In Finnegans Wake, such isolation becomes exile, conveyed in a very powerful passage: "the whirling dervish, Tumult, son of Thunder, self exiled in upon his ego, a nightlong a shaking betwixtween white or reddr hawrors, noondayterrorised to skin and bone by an ineluctable phantom (may the Shaper have mercery on him!) writing the mystery of himsel in furniture" (FW 184.05–10). This isolation is also suggested by Anna Livia, who in her concluding introspective reflections recognizes this fundamental fact of life: "Ourselves, oursouls alone" (FW 623.28–29).

Aristotle's understanding of a living thing's essence as "nature" (*phusis*) accounts for the polar aspects of the individual: its persistent identity whereby it remains constant, and its openness to change. *Phusis* derives from the Greek verb "to grow"; Aristotle defines "nature" as the "principle of motion and rest" within the living individual.[26] Nature is the source of both the entity's introverted activity and its extroverted activity. As the renowned Aristotle scholar Joseph Owens has observed, Aristotle exploits two basic significations of nature in the Greek tradition, "the stable constitution of a thing and the thing's growth and development. Against this historical background of both change and permanence, Aristotle seems to take the best of both worlds. He finds the basic philosophical meaning of 'nature' to be the *unchangeable* components of *changeable* things."[27]

It is in *A Portrait* that the soul is given greatest prominence. Not only does the word appear with the greatest frequency, but according to Richard Ellmann, "*A Portrait of the Artist as a Young Man* is in fact the gestation of a soul, and in the metaphor Joyce found his new principle of order" (*JJII* 296–97).[28] That the soul's gestation provides the principle of order is confirmed if we examine the manner in which the hero's growth and development are portrayed. The soul, Stephen declares, "has a slow and dark birth, more mysterious than the birth of the body" (*P* V.1046–47). As the book advances, the narrative style and language exhibit a progression corresponding to Stephen's personal growth and maturation. Chapter 1 of *A Portrait* describes Stephen's infancy in childish language as he slowly awakens to the world through the senses. This is followed in chapter 2 by a growth in self-awareness as Stephen becomes conscious of changes in his surrounding world as, for example, when his family is forced to move: "For some time he had felt the slight changes in his house; and these changes in what he had deemed unchangeable were so many slight shocks to his boyish conception of the world" (*P* II.158–60; see *FW* 486.10: "The old order changeth"). He is challenged by the conflict between his inner and outer worlds: "He did not want to play. He wanted to meet in the real world the unsubstantial image which his soul so constantly beheld" (*P* II.174–75).

In chapter 3, the brooding adolescent withdraws into himself, described in the following passage referring to Stephen's soul, and also to Aristotelian "form," the inmost principle of individual nature and identity:

He pressed his face against the pane of the window and gazed out into the darkening street. Forms passed this way and that through the dull light. And that was life. [. . .] His soul was fattening and congealing into a gross grease, plunging ever deeper in its dull fear into a sombre threatening dusk while the body that was his stood, listless and dishonoured, gazing out of darkened eyes, helpless, perturbed, and human for a bovine god to stare upon. (*P* III.341–50)

In chapter 4 is described a real awareness of the soul and its ultimate value:

But he could no longer disbelieve in the reality of love, since God Himself had loved his individual **soul** with divine love from all eternity. Gradually, as his **soul** was enriched with spiritual knowledge, he saw the whole world forming one vast symmetrical expression of God's power and love. Life became a divine gift for every moment and sensation of which, were it even the sight of a single leaf hanging on the twig of a tree, his **soul** should praise and thank the Giver. The world for all its solid substance and complexity no longer existed for his **soul** save as a theorem of divine power and love and universality. So entire and unquestionable was this sense of the divine meaning in all nature granted to his **soul** that he could scarcely understand why it was in any way necessary that he should continue to live. Yet that was part of the divine purpose and he dared not question its use, he above all others who had sinned so deeply and so foully against the divine purpose. Meek and abased by this consciousness of the one eternal omnipresent perfect reality his **soul** took up again her burden of pieties, masses and prayers and sacraments and mortifications: and only then for the first time since he had brooded on the great mystery of love did he feel within him a warm movement like that of some newly born life or virtue of the **soul** itself. The attitude of rapture in sacred art, the raised and parted hands, the parted lips and eyes as of one about to swoon, became for him an image of the **soul** in prayer, humiliated and faint before her Creator. (*P* IV.92–117)

This passage contains the entire panorama of Catholic doctrine on the gift of Creation and the struggle to achieve salvation.

The final chapter of *A Portrait* presents the ultimate challenge, as the full gravity of self-responsibility is realized: "The soul is born, he said vaguely, first in those moments I told you of. It has a slow and dark birth, more mysterious than the birth of the body. When the soul of a man is born in this country there are nets flung at it to hold it back from flight. You talk to me of nationality, language, religion. I shall try to fly by those nets"

(*P* V.1045–50). *A Portrait* depicts Stephen's uninterrupted struggle for self-identity. Though the description is not intended to refer to him, we may recognize in Stephen "a batlike soul waking to the consciousness of itself in darkness and secrecy and loneliness" (*P* V.331–32, 1667–69).[29]

When speaking of himself in *A Portrait,* Stephen frequently does so by referring to his soul. One of Aquinas's best-known statements is *Anima mea non est ego* ("My soul is not I").[30] Nonetheless, for Aristotle, the soul is what essentially constitutes the real self.[31] "It is the soul by which we primarily live, perceive, and think."[32] The intellect *is* man: "It is our reasoned acts that are felt to be in the fullest sense our own acts and voluntary acts."[33] The good man acts "for the sake of the intellectual element in him, which is thought to be the man himself."[34]

*   *   *

It is interesting that Joyce's own use of the stream of consciousness as a literary device ("the steady monologuy of the interiors," *FW* 119.32–33) is itself an incarnate example of one of the central problems of modern philosophy, namely, the existence and nature of the self as subject and substance. Is there an abiding substantial self underlying the flux of consciousness and its contents? The dominant modern belief is that there is not. Traditional philosophy had rooted the self as a substance in the soul, but this changed radically with Descartes. Besides placing doubt upon our knowledge of the external world, another decisive consequence followed from the methodic primacy of the cogito. In his obsession with clear and distinct ideas, Descartes identified the soul with conscious activity, defining the self as *res cogitans,* a thinking thing. In doing so, he dislocated the self from the sure and solid ground that it had previously enjoyed as an independent and autonomous subject, defined in the language of metaphysical principles. In Aristotelian terms, Descartes equated substance with one of its accidental or secondary modes, separating activity from its underlying, abiding, and enduring agent.

Moreover, by identifying the body as *res extensa,* Descartes introduced an insoluble dualism into human nature. He had no place for the traditional notion of individual personal substance as a metaphysical principle. The substantial unity of the person was abandoned, the self dissipated and dispersed. The English empiricist John Locke dealt a further blow to the role and identity of the self when he defined substance as the obscure, unknown support of qualities that cause our simple ideas. Substance is, according to Locke, "but a supposed, I know not what, to support those ideas, we call accidents."[35] The traditional notion of substance was intended to provide a positive idea of something for which "we have no Idea of what it is, but only a confused obscure one of what it does."[36] It presupposes what it aims to assert and must be dismissed as circular.

David Hume inherited Descartes's fixation with clarity and distinction. He also adopted Locke's criterion that an idea must be "clear and intelligible,"[37] and since there is no clear and intelligible idea of the self as an enduring, single, simple entity, there can be no such reality. In a famous passage from his *Treatise of Human Nature* (to which we will have reason to return), Hume drew the logical consequence of Descartes's equation of the ego with thought. The personal, individual, substantial self disappears: "For my part, when I enter most intimately into what I call myself, I always stumble on some particular perception or other, of heat or cold, light or shade, love or hatred, pain or pleasure. I never can catch myself at any time without a perception, and never can observe any thing but the perception."[38] According to Hume, what is observed are perceptions, not a self that has those perceptions. His explanation of the self as nothing more than a bundle of perceptions in perpetual flux, without inner core or ground, became known as the "bundle theory" of the self, a theory that has since remained popular. According to William James, whose pragmatist theories held passing interest for Joyce,[39] "The passing Thought is the only Thinker which Psychology requires."[40] This is essentially the narrative technique employed by Joyce. Daniel Dennett even adopted the term "Joycean machine" to describe what he regards as the illusion of a self beneath the flow of consciousness.[41]

In the classical tradition, the notion of self was inseparable from that of soul. In a lecture at Oxford in 1908, William James however declared: "Souls are out of fashion."[42] James was commenting on the increased popularity of materialist interpretations of humanity and the decline of religion in the West. Qualifying Virginia Woolf's provocative claim that "on or about December 1910 human character changed,"[43] Richard Rorty has suggested that "the big change in the outlook of intellectuals—as opposed to a change in human nature—that happened around 1910 was that they began to be confident that human beings had only bodies, and no souls."[44] This was the climate in which Joyce was forming his intellectual outlook, often in reaction to the dominant influences around him.

The enigma of the soul is its elusive nature; St. Augustine remarked on its abyss-like character[45] (*FW* 40.23: "selfabyss"). The early Greek thinker

Heraclitus declared: "You could not in your going find the ends of the soul, though you travelled the whole way, so deep is its *Logos*."[46] It was of course Heraclitus who gave classic expression to the unsettling theory that nothing whatsoever is permanent, but that all is flux. This is a common motif pondered throughout Joyce's work. Reality resembles a stream that never remains the same.

∗ ∗ ∗

The question of identity remained central throughout Joyce's writing, from *Stephen Hero* to *Finnegans Wake,* where Shaun tires in his effort "to isolate i from my multiple Mes" (*FW* 410.12).[47] Questions of identity are of concern to the protagonists of Joyce's works. Both Stephen and Bloom are exercised by the enigma of self-identity as well as the challenge of a changing world. Each speculates whether he persists as the same individual in a stable world. For Stephen this already occurs in *A Portrait,* when he confirms his own sense of selfhood and self-creation when asked about his attitude to his abandoned religion and if he was now happier:

> —It's a curious thing, do you know, Cranly said dispassionately, how your mind is supersaturated with the religion in which you say you disbelieve. Did you believe in it when you were at school? I bet you did.
> —I did, Stephen answered.
> —And were you happier then? Cranly asked softly, happier than you are now, for instance?
> —Often happy, Stephen said, and often unhappy. I was someone else then.
> —How someone else? What do you mean by that statement?
> —I mean, said Stephen, that I was not myself as I am now, as I had to become. (*P* V.2334–45)

Stephen is faced here with an instance of accidental change but does not have the vocabulary and concepts to deal with it. He remains the same individual but changes in respect of one of his accidental modes. He abides in enduring selfhood. Aristotle's distinction between substance and accidents explains how a single individual, while remaining identically the selfsame, can successively receive different and contrary qualities. The self becomes "other," but not "an other"/"another." The notion of becoming "someone else" makes no sense for Aristotle: it would be absurd to desire to live as another. Referring to intellect as what is deepest within each individual, he states: "It may even be held this is the true self of each, inasmuch as it is the dominant and better part; and therefore it would be a strange thing if a man should choose to live not his own life but a life of some other than himself."[48] Stephen's assertion "I was not myself as I am now, as I had to become," is in keeping with what is for Aristotle a fundamental principle of nature: "What a thing is potentially, its work reveals in actuality."[49] This is also Bloom's observation, who "saw in a quick young male familiar form the predestination of a future" (*U* 17.780).

Philip Kitcher rightly comments: "The challenge, for ALP and HCE, indeed for all of us, is to find a human identity to which we can adhere during the course of life."[50] The ideal of the well-integrated individual is timeless and universal. Plato's successful citizen was one who "attained to self-mastery and beautiful order within himself," harmonizing the conflicting elements within his soul. "When he has bound these elements into a disciplined and harmonious whole, and so become fully one instead of many (ἕνα γενόμενον ἐκ πολλῶν), he will be ready for action of any kind."[51] The challenge of selfhood and identity was well penned by Robert McAlmon, confidant of Joyce in Paris:

> Oh, let me gather myself together.
> Where are the pieces
> quivering and staring and muttering
> that are all to be a part of me?[52]

Stephen Dedalus's first reflection on self-identity in *Ulysses* occurs in the opening scene in which Mulligan enacts a mock liturgy. Stephen recalls how years earlier he participated in a religious ceremony: "So I carried the boat of incense then at Clongowes. I am another now and yet the same. A servant too. A server of a servant" (*U* 1.310–12). Later, he refers back to past events to interpret current experiences. He sympathizes with the struggling pupil, Cyril Sargent, by comparing him to himself: "Like him was I, these sloping shoulders, this gracelessness. My childhood bends beside me" (*U* 2.168–69). The subsequent conversation with Mr. Deasy likewise triggers memories of the self and attendant problems: "The same room and hour, the same wisdom: and I the same. Three times now. Three nooses round me here. Well? I can break them in this instant if I will" (*U* 2.233–35). This is an interesting indication of Joyce's persisting struggle for personal identity in self-liberation from the nets of nationality, language, and religion, famously challenged at the end of *A Portrait*.

Stephen's reminiscences in "Proteus" emphasize the flux of life. He is walking through life and time, "a stride at a time" (*U* 3.11). Some past events are of little importance, others radical and fundamental, which prompt deliberation on the course of life itself from birth to death and the ultimate end of all flesh: "Bridebed, childbed, bed of death, ghostcandled. *Omnis caro ad te veniet*" (*U* 3.396–97). Stephen considers even a more awesome possibility: "I moved among them on the frozen Liffey, that I, a changeling, among the spluttering resin fires. I spoke to no-one: none to me" (*U* 3.307–09).

The "Proteus" episode highlights the relativity of knowledge. As he observes the ever-shifting world of appearances and the dissolution of life (*U* 3.105–07: "Houses of decay, mine, his and all. [. . .] Beauty is not there"), Stephen likewise interrogates the ground of his constant and consistent self-identity. Beyond the ineluctable certainty of knowledge rooted in the necessity of the audible and visible, he seeks the ineluctable necessity of selfhood, which, he fears, may be as insubstantial as his shadow on the rocks. Will it be always he? What is the guarantee? The question may inconveniently arise in the case of mistaken identity: "We thought you were someone else" (*U* 3.75), or conveniently if an alibi is required: "Other fellow did it: other me. Hat, tie, overcoat, nose. *Lui, c'est moi*" (*U* 3.182–83).

The question of individual identity and continuity arises most visibly due to physical transformation, that is, renewal by replacement, but is this accidental or substantial change? In "Scylla and Charybdis," Stephen ponders his self-identity as he recalls the pound he once borrowed from Russell:

> Five months. Molecules all change. I am other I now. Other I got pound. Buzz. Buzz. But I, entelechy, form of forms, am I by memory because under everchanging forms. I that sinned and prayed and fasted. A child Conmee saved from pandies. I, I and I. I. A.E.I.O.U. (*U* 9.205–13)[53]

With the passage of time, does he, as lender, still exist? Put crassly, have not all his molecules changed? More subtly: is he still the same individual, despite his discrete memories. Is he the same enduring "I"—indicated punctually: "I, I"—or are there disjointed successive selves: "I. I"?. The dilemma is resolved by recourse to Aristotle: Stephen endures in his identity by virtue of his personal entelechy—persisting under the ever-changing forms that pass and are remembered, because the soul is the primordial "form of forms." Contemplating his debt to Russell, whose pseudonym was

'AE,' Stephen concludes his musings with what is surely the most brilliant literary joke in any language, a sentence consisting entirely of the vowels: "A.E.I.O.U."

The question of identity arises for Stephen at two levels: that of the individual self as an abiding entity, and that of the development of the individual artistic persona. The following passage, also from "Scylla and Charybdis," presents this twofold challenge:

> As we, or mother Dana, weave and unweave our bodies, Stephen said, from day to day, their molecules shuttled to and fro, so does the artist weave and unweave his image.[54] And as the mole on my right breast is where it was when I was born, though all my body has been woven of new stuff time after time, so through the ghost of the unquiet father the image of the unliving son looks forth. In the intense instant of imagination, when the mind, Shelley says, is a fading coal, **that which I was is that which I am and that which in possibility I may come to be. So in the future, the sister of the past, I may see myself as I sit here now but by reflection from that which then I shall be.** (*U* 9.376–85)

Stephen briefly entertains Locke's theory of self-identity as grounded in memory but holds fast to his belief in soul, the primary determination (entelechy) that governs the exchange of molecules and gives actuality to memory. In one of his metaphysical insights in Nighttown, Stephen brilliantly describes first entelechy, the soul, as "the structural rhythm" (*U* 15.107). With this principle, Aristotle could respond to the *panta rhei* ("all is flux") of Heraclitus; one could step twice into the same stream, indeed step out of it, while the stream itself flows on: "human nature was a constant quantity," we read in *Stephen Hero* (175).[55]

That Stephen's solution to personal identity is the Aristotelian soul or entelechy ("form of forms") is already announced in "Proteus": "Take all, keep all. My soul walks with me, form of forms. [. . .] The flood is following me. I can watch it flow past from here" (*U* 3.279–82). The "I" necessarily stands above the flow, stable and constant, otherwise it could not observe the flow itself. Stephen confirms his conviction that the self is rooted in the soul as "form of forms": "I throw this ended shadow from me, manshape ineluctable, call it back. Endless, would it be mine, form of my form?" (*U* 3.412–14). The word "manshape" echoes Hopkins's poem "That Nature Is a Heraclitean Fire":

Man, how fast his firedint, his mark on mind, is gone!
Both are in an unfathomable, all is in an enormous dark
Drowned. O pity and indignation! Manshape, that shone.

Aristotle occasionally used the word "shape" (*morphê*) as synonymous with
"form" (*eidos*); combined with one of Joyce's favorite words, "ineluctable," it
conveys what for Aristotle is essential, necessary, and inalienable within the
human individual. The phrase "form of forms" conveys the soul's powerful cognitive role as receptive of all reality. Shortly afterward, in the same
episode, we have an obstinate affirmation of self-confidence in Stephen's
ultimate existential self-affirmation: "As I am. As I am. All or not at all" (*U*
3.452).

Even in his inebriated state, Stephen manages to come up with a remarkable formula for the development of self:

What went forth to the ends of the world to traverse not itself, God,
the sun, Shakespeare, a commercial traveller, having itself traversed
in reality itself becomes that self. Wait a moment. Wait a second.
Damn that fellow's noise in the street. Self which it itself was ineluctably preconditioned to become. *Ecco!* (*U* 15.2117–21)

It is highly revealing of Joyce's preoccupation with permanence and self-
identity that Stephen and Bloom are both challenged by the phenomenon
of change, which features so centrally in "Proteus," "Lestrygonians," and
"Scylla and Charybdis." The approaches of Bloom and Stephen are significantly different. While Bloom is equally baffled by the question of self-
identity through time, he does not have Stephen's theoretical apparatus
to resolve the question. Michael Groden observes, "Leopold Bloom is
no intellectual like Stephen Dedalus, but he lives actively in his mind."[56]
Committed positivist, he is skeptical of Stephen's metaphysical tendencies:
"Bloom dissented tacitly from Stephen's views on the eternal affirmation of
the spirit of man in literature" (*U* 17.29–30).

Bloom reflects on his past life: "Happy. Happier then" (*U* 8.170), but has
difficulty recalling his past: "My memory is getting. Pen . . . ? Of course it's
years ago" (*U* 8.178–79). Bloom compares the changes of life to the fluidity
of water: "How can you own water really? It's always flowing in a stream,
never the same, which in the stream of life we trace. Because life is a stream"
(*U* 8.93–95). A little while later, as he struggles with memory, he again reflects: "Stream of life" (*U* 8.176).[57] As well as puzzlement with a Heraclitean

vision of the world in constant flux, Bloom is also troubled by the question of his own personal permanence and identity:

> I was happier then. Or was that I? Or am I now I? Twentyeight I was. She twentythree. When we left Lombard street west something changed. Could never like it again after Rudy. Can't bring back time. Like holding water in your hand. Would you go back to then? Just beginning then. Would you? (*U* 8.608–12)

Reminiscing about his amorous adventures with Molly on Ben of Howth, he muses: "Me. And me now" (*U* 8.917). He also wonders about the identity of his personality: "Am I like that? See ourselves as others see us!" (*U* 8.662). His self-doubt is illustrated in the final scene of "Nausicaa" by his failure to trace his identity in the sand, in the hope of arranging another encounter with Gerty MacDowell: "I. [. . .] AM. A. No room. Let it go. Mr Bloom effaced the letters with his slow boot. Hopeless thing sand. Nothing grows in it. All fades" (*U* 13.1258, 1264–67). Bloom somehow seems uncertain of his identity and muses at the graveside in Glasnevin, "If we were all suddenly somebody else" (*U* 6.836). This is, of course, a futile and contradictory exercise. The illusory assumption is that while remaining oneself, one might also become another, which is a complete impossibility. Aristotle remarks (in a phrase reminiscent of that cited earlier to similar effect): "No one would choose to possess every good in the world on condition of becoming somebody else [. . .] but only while remaining himself, whatever he may be."[58] The impossible presumption is that one could become someone else, while remaining oneself—a manifest contradiction.

In Holles Street maternity hospital, Bloom ponders the meandering course of the soul through the passage of time, in a lengthy reflection upon his own life's history:

> What is the age of the soul of man? As she hath the virtue of the chameleon[59] to change her hue at every new approach, to be gay with the merry and mournful with the downcast, so too is her age changeable as her mood. No longer is Leopold, as he sits there, ruminating, chewing the cud of reminiscence, that staid agent of publicity and holder of a modest substance in the funds. A score of years are blown away. He is young Leopold. There, as in a retrospective arrangement, a mirror within a mirror (hey, presto!), he beholdeth himself. That young figure of then is seen, precociously manly, walking on a nipping morning from the old house in Clanbrassil street to the high

school, his booksatchel on him bandolierwise, and in it a goodly
hunk of wheaten loaf, a mother's thought. Or it is the same figure, a
year or so gone over, in his first hard hat (ah, that was a day!), already
on the road, a fullfledged traveller for the family firm. [. . .] But hey,
presto, the mirror is breathed on and the young knighterrant recedes,
shrivels, dwindles to a tiny speck within the mist. Now he is himself
paternal and these about him might be his sons. Who can say? (*U*
14.1038–63)

It is interesting to compare Bloom's self-image with the perception others
have of him. Molly, who presumably knows him better than anyone, on the
one hand recognizes his uniqueness—"I suppose there isnt in all creation
another man with the habits he has" (*U* 18.1197–98)—but also raises a trou-
bling question regarding Bloom's core personality: "hes always imitating
everybody" (*U* 18.1204–05). Hoppy Holohan exclaims in "Circe": "Good
old Bloom! There's nobody like him after all" (*U* 15.1727).

Stephen and Bloom are alike concerned with the question of permanence and personal identity. But while Stephen is compelled to theorize
about everything, Bloom is more practical. We might apply the words from
Finnegans Wake: "Let us leave theories there and return to here's here" (*FW*
76.10). Not that he is averse to a modicum of theory: "Intellectual stimulation, as such, was, he felt, from time to time a firstrate tonic for the mind"
(*U* 16.1221–22). In Glasnevin Cemetery, Bloom reflects upon the decay of
the body. Whereas Stephen finds permanence in Aristotle's principles of
form and prime matter, Bloom (whose mentality is more scientific than
philosophical)[60] finds ultimate stability in the cells that go on living:

I daresay the soil would be quite fat with corpsemanure, bones, flesh,
nails. Charnelhouses. Dreadful. Turning green and pink decompos-
ing. Rot quick in damp earth. The lean old ones tougher. Then a kind
of a tallowy kind of a cheesy. Then begin to get black, black treacle
oozing out of them. Then dried up. Deathmoths. Of course the cells
or whatever they are go on living. Changing about. Live for ever practically. Nothing to feed on feed on themselves. (*U* 6.775–82)

As he passes between graves in the cemetery, Bloom reflects on death and
the departed: "How many! All these here once walked round Dublin. Faithful departed." He imagines them addressing him: "As you are now so once
were we" (*U* 6.960–61).

Bloom, just like Stephen, observes such "phenomena" as the passage of time and his changes in life, but, unlike Stephen, he does not subject these to philosophical analysis. His contented attitude is conveyed in "Cyclops": "That can be explained by science, says Bloom. It's only a natural phenomenon, don't you see, because on account of the . . . And then he starts with his jawbreakers about phenomenon and science and this phenomenon and the other phenomenon" (*U* 12.464–67).[61] His scientific method contrasts with the "perverted transcendentalism" (*U* 14.1223–24) of Stephen: "Science, it cannot be too often repeated, deals with tangible phenomena. The man of science like the man in the street has to face hardheaded facts that cannot be blinked and explain them as best he can" (*U* 14.1226–29).[62]

Bloom views all happenings in the world from a scientific point of view; the world is composed entirely of natural phenomena that can be explained through natural causes and events. Stephen is the Aristotelian philosopher.[63] He finds the guarantee of self-identity in Aristotle's theory of the soul as the entelechy, or first actualization, which is the substantial form of the human individual. He grounds the reliability of knowledge in Aristotle's theory of sensation and develops it through Aristotle's theory of the soul as "form of forms." The intellectual soul apprehends the essential form of the object, its whatness or quiddity, which it expresses in definition: "Unsheathe your dagger definitions. Horseness is the whatness of allhorse" (*U* 9.84–89).

Not only are both Stephen and Leopold perplexed by the question of their individuality and continued identity, but they are also equally concerned with how others perceive them, how they appear to others. Stephen wonders as he beholds his distorted reflection in the cracked mirror: "As he and others see me. Who chose this face for me?" (*U* 1.136–37). Bloom: "Am I like that? See ourselves as others see us" (*U* 8.662).[64] And again: "See ourselves as others see us. So long as women don't mock what matter?" (*U* 13.1058–59). He even speculates how his cat perceives him: "Wonder what I look like to her. Height of a tower? No, she can jump me" (*U* 4.28–29).[65]

In a delightful and cleverly worded exchange in "Eumaeus," we are given a clear insight into the contrasting outlooks of Bloom and Stephen concerning human nature and the foundation of human thought. Bloom is forthright in his challenge:

You, as a good catholic, he observed, talking of body and soul, believe in the soul. Or do you mean the intelligence, the brainpower as such, as distinct from any outside object, the table, let us say, that cup? I believe in that myself because it has been explained by competent men as the convolutions of the grey matter. (*U* 16.748–52)

Stephen is obliged to recall what he has learned about the ultimate metaphysical ground of the soul and its enduring identity:

> Thus cornered, Stephen had to make a superhuman effort of memory to try and concentrate and remember before he could say: "They tell me on the best authority it is a simple substance and therefore incorruptible. It would be immortal, I understand, but for the possibility of its annihilation by its First Cause, Who, from all I can hear, is quite capable of adding that to the number of His other practical jokes, *corruptio per se* and *corruptio per accidens* both being excluded by court etiquette." (*U* 16.754–60)[66]

Bloom's reaction is one of the most clever-amusing characterizations in the entire book: "Mr Bloom thoroughly acquiesced in the general gist of this though the mystical finesse involved was a bit out of his sublunary depth" (*U* 16.761–62). He entirely misunderstands Stephen's use of the word "simple": "Simple? I shouldn't think that is the proper word. Of course, I grant you, to concede a point, you do knock across a simple soul once in a blue moon" (*U* 16.764–65). Bloom innocently assumes that "simple" means weak-minded, innocent, or naive, whereas Stephen intends it in its original sense of undivided. He correctly outlines the Thomist argument that since the human soul is not composed of parts, it is of its nature incorruptible. The only conceivable possibility is that God would annihilate it or reduce it to nonbeing. But since God has out of love created souls in his own image and likeness, it would negate his divine goodness if he were to do so. Such a practical joke on God's part would intrinsically be a contradiction, since he would be destroying his own work; the purpose of Creation would be annulled.

Selfhood in *Finnegans Wake*

Margot Norris remarks that, like *Ulysses,* "*Finnegans Wake* is a quest for the nature of the self." It is, however, "a quest conducted in error and doubt because the truth will not be comforting or reassuring."[67] Self-identity is "the first riddle of the universe: asking, when is a man not a man?" (*FW* 170.04–05). The intractable question, "How can I change while remaining the same?" is "the farst wriggle of the ubivence, whereom is man, that old offender, nother man, wheile he is asame" (*FW* 356.12–14). Bloom had heard Molly sing Rossini's *Stabat Mater*: "*Quis est homo?*" (*U* 5.402). Here is asked: "Fas est dass [*Was ist das?* = German, 'What is that'] and foe err you?" (*FW* 273.6). Alternatively: "To me or not to me. Satis thy quest on" (*FW* 269.19–20). The entire work deals with "the untireties of livesliving being the one substance of a streamsbecoming" (*FW* 597.07–08). Given the constantly changing prosopography ("intermutuomergent," *FW* 55.11–12) inhabiting its dreamworld, the conflict between identity and plurality of personality is repeatedly dramatized but, unsurprisingly, never resolved.[68] The question of continuity, unity, and integrity is presented strikingly in *Finnegans Wake*. Characterized by "inharmonious detail" (*FW* 188.26) and "dislocated reason" (*FW* 189.30), it is populated by "all kinds of promiscious individuals" (*FW* 66.04–05). The "charictures in the drame" (*FW* 303.31–32) multiply and proliferate, appear and disappear, only to reemerge transformed and disguised. Margot Norris observes: "The singularity of individual experience—its uniqueness—is undermined by the replication of events and the instability of characters. The causal relationship of events in novelistic narration is replaced in *Finnegans Wake* by contiguous associations on the order of psychoanalytic free associations."[69] In the bifurcation of selfhood, identities are distorted and dissolved; the unity and coherence of character is lost (*U* 15.2523: "Reduplication of personality"). As Patrick McCarthy points out, "Joyce intended this style to underscore the book's universality and to imitate the logic of dreams."[70] We are faced with the impossible challenge of reconciling "nobodyatall with Wholyphamous" (*FW* 73.09).

The following description of the blend of chaos and cosmos fits the work itself: "every person, place and thing in the chaosmos of Alle anyway connected with the gobblydumped turkery was moving and changing every part of the time" (*FW* 118.21–23). Throughout the work, identities fluctuate in a "constant of fluxion" (*FW* 297.29). The challenge, to borrow from Adeline Glasheen, is to decipher who is who when everybody is somebody else.[71] Such protean multiplicity and mutability of personality are exemplified in HCE: "They know him, the covenanter, by rote at least, for a chameleon at last, in his true falseheaven colours from ultraviolent to subred tissues" (*FW* 590.07–09). Anna Livia's name "Plurabelle" denotes a multiplicity of personality. Her essence perpetually changes: "*I'se so silly to be flowing but I no canna stay!*" (*FW* 159.18). Yet she is "Loonely in me loneness," lamenting in her isolation: "A hundred cares, a tithe of troubles and is there one who understands me? [. . .] They'll never see. Nor know. Nor miss me" (*FW* 627.14–15, 34–36). Her monologue, like Molly's, is a fluid and turbulent stream of consciousness.

Tim Finnegan, the "hero" of the ballad, had his forerunner in the mythical phoenix, who rose from death in even more dramatic fashion. The mystery of continuity and identity is conveyed in the poem "*Carmen de ave Phoenice*" attributed to Lactantius (ca. 250–ca. 325): "She is indeed herself, but not the same; and she is the same, but not herself" (*Est eadem sed non eadem, quae est ipsa nec ipsa est*). How is it possible for diverse aspects of a character to coexist and cohere in a single character? How does an individual change while remaining the same? This is the philosophical paradox that may be solved by reference to Aristotle's theory of substance and accidents, according to which the fundamentally identical and selfsame substance can successively receive and shed accidental or secondary modes of being. Familiarity with his short treatise *The Categories* would have offered the solution. Were Joyce familiar with its contents, he would not have experienced the challenge that he so ingeniously reiterated with great originality in his final work. The germ of a solution might indeed be gleaned from one of his early writings. Adopting Joyce's comparison of a nation with the ego, from his lecture "Ireland, Island of Saints and Sages," we can say that the human individual is likewise "a vast fabric, in which the most diverse elements are mingled."[72] The vast fabric may be interpreted metaphorically as the Aristotelian ground substance in which multiple, changing, aspects of personality change and replace one another in a dynamic process of self-fulfillment.

Joyce presents his account of Shem ("self exiled in upon his own ego [. . .] writing the mystery of himsel," *FW* 184.6–10) in Aristotelian-Thomist concepts, raising in novel form all the questions of persons, individuation, persistence through time, alteration, self-consciousness, and loss of individuality. Shem writes the mystery of himself

over every square inch of the only foolscap available, his own body, till by its corrosive sublimation one continuous present tense integument slowly unfolded all marryvoising moodmoulded cyclewheeling history (thereby, he said, reflecting from his own individual person life unlivable, transaccidentated through the slow fires of consciousness into a dividual chaos, perilous, potent, common to allflesh, human only, mortal) but with each word that would not pass away the squidself which he had squirtscreened from the crystalline world

> waned chagreenold and doriangrayer in its dudhud. This exists that
> isits after having been said we know. (*FW* 185.35–186.09)

The word "transaccidentated" is coined from the Eucharistic doctrine according to which bread and wine are changed into the body and blood of
Christ. In transubstantiation, the substance of the elements is changed, but
the appearances remain. Aquinas explains the real presence of Christ under
the appearance of bread and wine by saying that the accidents receive their
own act of existence.

On Joyce's portrayal of selfhood in *Finnegans Wake*, C. H. Peake remarks:

> Like the inhabitants of a dream, all the figures of the comedy are
> the manifold and protean night-forms adopted [. . .] by the mind
> of the one dreamer, and between them there are no sharp divisions.
> The very notions of a distinct self and of a mankind composed of
> innumerable selves, each unique, consistent, and as identifiable as
> a fingerprint are questioned, and it is impossible "to identifine the
> individuone."[73]

Sigmund Freud cites English psychologist James Sully, who writes that "our
dreams are a means of conserving [previous] successive personalities."[74]
This presumes that at least the dreamer is the same. But by the author's
admission, in *Finnegans Wake* "[t]here are no individual characters. [. . .]
If one had to name a character, it would be just an old man."[75] On the other
hand, he presents a "multiplicity of personalities," whose "traits featuring
the *chiaroscuro* coalesce, their contrarieties eliminated, in one stable somebody" (*FW* 107.24–30). It is no use to appeal to either Aristotle or Aquinas,
since concrete facts give way to the realm of the imagination: "It's like a
dream. The style is also changing, and unrealistic, like the dream world"
(*JJII* 696). And yet the work is in a very real sense a testament to the profound mystery of selfhood and its multiple manifestations: ever most real,
despite myriad allusions it remains elusive and beyond defining. Its most
important lesson is, perhaps, that it is impossible "to identifine the indi-
viduone" (*FW* 51.06). This coincides indeed with the deepest sentiment of
both Aristotle and Aquinas, who joyfully affirm the mystery of concrete
reality: *individuum est ineffabile.*

On the matter of identity, Richard Ellmann has summed it up well:

> Like Margaret Fuller, Joyce could say, "I accept the universe." What
> the universe was had been laid down by Aristotle. Joyce found in
> Aristotle someone to whom he could go to school, for in *De Anima*

Aristotle addressed himself to that very question of idealism versus materialism which to Joyce seemed basic. Aristotle rejected both positions. Against idealism, he declared that the soul was inextricably bound up with matter. He rejected the transmigration of souls, with which Joyce disports a little in *Ulysses*, on the ground that the soul is only the soul of its particular body and can't survive a transplant. He also specifically ruled out, as Stephen Dedalus does, the conception of one man's having a succession of souls. Stephen clings to western, Aristotelian notions of identity.[76]

"Substance" and its Variants

A term closely associated with "soul" (ψυχή/*psuchê*) for Aristotle is "substance" (οὐσία/*ousia*). Compound variations of the word appear in significant contexts in Joyce's writings. "Substance" is the inadequate translation of the Greek word οὐσία, which unfortunately became part of the philosophical vocabulary of medieval philosophy and the perennial tradition. Οὐσία literally means "beingness" and was used by Plato and Aristotle in their search for the deepest determining principle in all beings, namely, that in virtue of which something primarily is said to be. In book 7 of the *Metaphysics,* Aristotle considered the requirements for the primacy of such a principle. One requirement for οὐσία was the function of "standing under," or underlying the changes that occur in individuals; this role was conveyed by the Greek term ὑποκείμενον (*hupokeimenon* = "that which underlies"). In the transmission of thought from Greek to Latin, οὐσία was thus translated as "*substantia*." A more accurate translation would have been "*essentia*," which instead came to signify "what" something is. To convey what historically has been understood as the "essence" of a being, Aristotle invented a clumsy circumlocution, τὸ τί ἦν εἶναι / *to ti ên einai* ("that which it was to be"), namely, the basic determination of what something in its origin was destined to be. He equated this in turn with "form" (εἶδος/ *eidos*). Aristotle concluded his discussion by stating that form or essence is οὐσία/*ousia*, that is, the deepest principle of being. As we have seen, depending on the context, εἶδος/*eidos* is interchangeable with "soul," "nature," and "entelechy." Each term has its nuanced meaning, denoting a particular aspect or function of the individual being. For example, nature (φύσις/ *phusis*) denotes the form of a growing body and is defined by Aristotle in the *Physics* as the "principle of that which has within itself its own source of motion and change."[77] Φύσις/*Phusis* can also be taken as synonymous with ἐντελέχεια/*entelecheia,* the fulfilment of εἶδος/*eidos.* Aristotle moreover on occasion uses "shape" (μορφή/*morphê*) as interchangeable with "form" (εἶδος). All of these are cognate with the concept that we have come to understand as "substance"; they appear in various contexts in Joyce's work.

The term "consubstantial," which originated in theological debate concerning relations between the persons of the Blessed Trinity, features in Stephen's vocabulary when explaining the father/son relationship between Stephen Dedalus and Leopold Bloom and also in his theory regarding the relation of paternity between Shakespeare and Hamlet (the hypothesis that Shakespeare was "ghost-father to Hamlet as son").[78]

In continuation of the mock celebration of the Mass in "Telemachus," Stephen recalls the chanting of the Apostles' Creed ("Symbol of the apostles," *U* 1.653) with its resounding confession of belief in the one, holy, catholic, and apostolic church: "*et unam sanctam catholicam et apostolicam ecclesiam*" (*U* 1.651). He calls to mind the "horde of heresies fleeing with mitres awry" (*U* 1.656) that assailed the church in the early centuries, in particular those of Arius and Sabellius. Arius (256–336) maintained that Jesus Christ, the Son, was not coequal with the Father but created, and that in turn he created the Holy Spirit. In the previous century, Sabellius (fl. ca. 220), at the other extreme, had exaggerated divine unity to the point of denying the real distinction between the divine persons. "Father," "Son," and "Holy Spirit" were, he believed, different modes of the one divine person. Exploiting the etymology of the word "person" (*prosôpon*), he suggested that they were different "masks" of the divine being.

To combat Arianism, the Council of Nicaea in 325 added clarifications to the Credo (indicated in bold):

> We believe in one God the Father all-powerful, maker of all things both seen and unseen. And in one Lord Jesus Christ, the Son of God, the only-begotten from the Father, **that is from the substance (ἐκ τῆς οὐσίας) of the Father, God from God, light from light, true God from true God, begotten not made (γεννηθέντα οὐ ποιηθέντα) consubstantial (ὁμοούσιον)** with the Father, through whom all things came to be.

The Council also condemned the teaching of Arius with the following words:

> And those who say "there once was when he was not," and "before he was begotten he was not," and that he came to be from things that

were not, or from another hypostasis (*hypostaseôs*) or substance (*ousias*), affirming that the Son of God is subject to change or alteration, these the catholic and apostolic church anathematizes.[79]

The Council of Nicaea thus decreed that all three Persons were equal and fully divine. According to the Catechism of the Catholic Church, to say that the Son is "consubstantial" with the Father means that he is "one only God with him" (*unum Deum cum Illo*).[80] The phrase "begotten not made" means that the Son is not a creature but shares the selfsame ontological existence as the Father. He is fully divine and equal to the Father. The Council of Chalcedon (451) used the term "consubstantial" to declare that the Son was also fully human, with an essence similar to ours; it decreed that the second person of the Trinity, being fully human, was "consubstantial with us as to his humanity."[81]

Stephen twice reflects on Arius's theological battles concerning the Trinity: "warring his life long upon the consubstantiality of the Son with the Father" (*U* 1.657–58) and "upon the contransmagnificandjewbangtantiality" (*U* 3.50–51). Arius's heresy denying the consubstantiality of Christ with the Father has been explained; Joyce emphasizes the complexity of the question by employing the jawbreaker "contransmagnificandjewbangtantiality."[82] Richard Ellmann offers the following explanation: "Stephen is obsessed by questions of the relative degrees of ghostliness and substance in the persons of the Trinity; he lumps them together under the rubric of 'contransmagnificandjewbangtantiality' (the consubstantiation, transubstantiation, magnification of a Jewish, explosively begotten God-man)."[83]

Reflecting on the relationship of father and son in "Scylla and Charybdis," Stephen recalls: "Sabellius, the African, subtlest heresiarch of all the beasts of the field, held that the Father was Himself His Own Son. The bulldog of Aquin, with whom no word shall be impossible, refutes him" (*U* 9.862–64). In his *Summa Theologiae*, Aquinas gave a comprehensive assessment of the views of both Arius and Sabellius, whom he viewed as presenting two opposite errors. He neatly summed up his critique by saying that while Arius confused the Trinity of persons with a Trinity of substance, Sabellius confused unity of essence with unity of person.[84] Stephen's reference to St. Thomas as the "bulldog of Aquin" is a pun on the Dominican order as "*Domini canis*," "dog of the Lord."[85]

In the debate on the relationships between Shakespearean characters, we read that King Hamlet's ghost is "a voice heard only in the heart of him who is the substance of his shadow, the son consubstantial with the father" (*U*

9.480–81). Bloom is the "transubstantial" heir of Rudolf Virag, because his father is dead; Stephen is "consubstantial" heir of Simon Dedalus, because his father is alive.[86] Simon Dedalus is referred to both as a consubstantial father (*U* 3.62) and as an "unsubstantial father" (*U* 9.552–53), presumably because he has no material wealth. As both God and Man, Christ is substance in a unique manner, either by transubstantiation in the Eucharist or in consubstantial union in the Trinity but, as Stephen puts it in "Oxen of the Sun," never anything less than substance: "*Entweder* transubstantiality *oder* consubstantiality but in no case subsubstantiality" (*U* 14.307–08).

Joyce's Concept of Self

Before discussing Joyce's concept of personal identity in further detail, I wish to refer to two important studies on the nature of human subjectivity: those of John S. Rickard and of Judith Ryan. In his excellent monograph *Joyce's Book of Memory: The Mnemotechnic of Ulysses,* Rickard states: "Joyce was profoundly interested in and affected by models of mind that are no longer taken seriously."[87] As examples of outmoded models, he mentions such theories as invoke ancestral knowledge, innate ideas, or racial memory. Contemporary approaches by contrast, he states, "privilege either personal experience or the power of linguistic and ideological systems over questions of 'nature' or inheritance."[88] To favor culture and experience over nature is consistent with John Locke's view of the human subject as a "white paper, void of all characters," that must first be inscribed by individual experience. This view contrasts with what Rickard terms "more essential models of subjectivity."[89] I will argue to the contrary, however, that the theory most invoked by Joyce was precisely one of those "essential" models.

In her comprehensive study titled *The Vanishing Subject: Early Psychology and Literary Modernism,* Judith Ryan examines various psychologies of self that influenced literature in the late nineteenth and early twentieth centuries. Espoused positions range from that of the American pragmatist William James, who, she suggests, favored a "real and verifiable personal identity which we feel,"[90] to that of Austrian positivist Ernst Mach, for whom "the self is unsalvageable."[91] James Joyce is one of the authors whom she lists as "salvaging the self."[92] Of the different philosophical conceptions of the self explored by Joyce in *Ulysses,* she highlights three: "the self that exists as 'ideas and sensations,' the self that finds its continuity in memory, [and] the self that moves towards a predetermined goal ('entelechy')." All three, she suggests, are playfully suggested in the course of the novel, but none is given final preference: "Joyce makes it clear that he has been following the debates about the self but that he is not fully prepared to settle for any one 'solution.' The ground of Joyce's novel is constantly shifting, and even its most ambitious mythic structures, the fundamental patterns that hold it together, are subject at one moment or another to ironic distancing and internal self-parody."[93] Commenting on these concepts of self, I will argue that Joyce favored the third model, the one that was centered on entelechy, although not quite as understood by Judith Ryan.

The theories of self-identity based respectively on "ideas and sensations" and the continuity of memory may be considered together, since they share essential elements inspired by the British empiricist philosophers John Locke and David Hume. The concept of self as "ideas and sensations" derived from Hume's so-called bundle theory and is represented in *Ulysses* by Buck Mulligan, who declares: "I can't remember anything. I remember only ideas and sensations" (*U* 1.192–93). The theory of self as rooted in memory is shared by Locke and Hume.

Locke defines "person" as "a thinking intelligent being, that has reason and reflection, and can consider itself as itself, the same thinking thing, in different times and places; which it does only by that consciousness which is inseparable from thinking, and as it seems to me, essential to it; it being impossible for any one to perceive without perceiving that he does perceive."[94] Locke equates personal identity with consciousness: "For since consciousness always accompanies thinking, and it is that which makes everyone to be what he calls *self*, and thereby distinguishes himself from all other thinking things, in this alone consists *personal identity*, i.e. the sameness of a rational being."[95] In brief, consciousness constitutes personal identity.

Two particular aspects of Locke's doctrine must be recalled. There is first his assumption, adopted from Descartes, that we do not know things directly but only representations of things. Second, he makes no distinction between sensation and the intuitive (analytic or synthetic) activity of intellect. While his axiom that, prior to stimulation by the senses, the mind resembles a blank sheet of paper (tabula rasa), seems to be a repetition of Aristotle's view, it is radically different. He rejects Aristotle's theory that the intellect has a power that surpasses the senses. Certainty for Locke attaches only to the most vivid of sensations: there is no intellectual knowledge of universal ideas.

Locke retains substance as the underlying principle of unification, needed to explain why we attribute diverse qualities to the same subject.

Substance is not known through its activities but inferred as a support of qualities and activities: "If anyone will examine himself concerning his notion of pure substance in general, he will find he has no other idea of it at all, but only a supposition of *he knows not what* support of such qualities which are capable of producing simple ideas in us; which qualities are commonly called accidents."[96] Substance is thus for Locke an inert, unknowable, underlying "something" whose sole role is to support accidents; we have no direct knowledge of its nature. Likewise, in the case of the human person, we can only infer the existence of the self. Hume takes this a step further. Some philosophers, he tells us, imagine that we are at "every moment intimately conscious of what we call our self; that we feel its existence and its continuance in existence; and are certain, beyond the evidence of a demonstration, both of its perfect identity and simplicity." He rejects such privileged knowledge:

> For my part, when I enter most intimately into what I call *myself*, I always stumble on some particular perception or other, of heat or cold, light or shade, love or hatred, pain or pleasure. I never can catch *myself* at any time without a perception, and never can observe any thing but the perception. [. . .] I may venture to affirm to the rest of mankind, that they are nothing but a bundle or collection of different perceptions, which succeed each other with an inconceivable rapidity, and are in a perpetual flux and movement. [. . .] The mind is a kind of theatre, where several perceptions successively make their appearance, pass, re-pass, glide away, and mingle in an infinite variety of postures and situations.[97]

The comparison of the theater, he warns, must not mislead us: there is neither stage nor theater, only the succession of scenes. What we experience is a stream of impressions or perceptions and we mistakenly take this succession as identity. Memory produces the relation of resemblance between passing impressions, "acquaints us with the continuance and extent of this succession of perceptions,"[98] and is therefore the chief source of personal identity. Hume's position is that a clear and intelligible idea of the self could derive only from a constant and invariable impression and that we have no such impression. He denies the possibility of ultimately solving the problem of self-identity and dismisses it as a grammatical fiction. In the end he "must plead the privilege of a sceptic."[99]

In rejecting the notion of a clearly identifiable self, Hume has Descartes in mind, and in this he is undeniably correct: we have no direct introspective grasp of the self as such. This is also the position of Aquinas, according to whom God alone, whose act of existing is identical with his act of knowing, has direct knowledge of himself.[100] Given our nature as psycho-physical beings, our knowledge of self is formed through reflection upon the activity whereby we know the sense objects that initially awaken and actualize our capacity to know. Sense objects inscribe the tabula rasa of the soul, but the soul's intellective power raises these to the universal level. Aquinas, in his moderate realism, explicitly states: "The substantial forms of things, which, according as they are in themselves, are unknown to us, shine forth to us (*innotescunt*) through their accidental properties."[101] He states: "The operation of a thing manifests both its substance [essence] and its existence."[102] Again: "The operation of a thing shows forth its power, which in turn points to (*indicat*) its essence."[103] Thus for Aquinas it is through action that "the object achieves its epiphany" (*SH* 213).

For St. Thomas, we have no intuitive knowledge of essences, not even of our own. We know them discursively through their actions. For Aquinas, substance is not, as for Locke, inert and unknown: it is precisely through activity that it makes itself known.[104] Accidents are not separate from substance but inhere in, perfect, and reveal it. Action is the self-manifestation of substance. This also means that, contrary to Hume, we cannot have a separable notion of substance: we cannot isolate the substance of the self from the accidental modalities that reveal it. Action, W. Norris Clarke argues, "does reveal something of the inner nature; otherwise it would not be action at all. But it also leaves unrevealed further depths or aspects of the reservoir of active potency within it; and though finite in itself, the latter is still inexhaustible to our knowledge because of its hidden ontological connections with every other being in the universe."[105]

Thus, viewed from the point of view of Aquinas's theory of knowledge, there is validity in the answer to the question regarding Bloom's knowledge: "How did he elucidate the mystery of an invisible attractive person?": "With indirect and direct verbal allusions or affirmations: with subdued affection and admiration: with description: with impediment: with suggestion" (*U* 17.1177–81). There is also genuine insight in the following assertion in *Finnegans Wake* regarding the value of action: "A true friend is known much more easily, and better into the bargain, by his personal touch, habits of full or undress, movements, response to appeals for charity than by his footware, say" (*FW* 115.08–11). According to Aristotle's theory of knowledge, developed by Aquinas, while a substance is unknowable (*ignotum*) in its hidden depth, its properties become manifest through its operations.

Action is the primary portal and avenue of discovery. For Aristotle and Aquinas, an individual is revealed from multiple perspectives, all of which are manifestations of the acting substance.

According to Locke, consciousness defines the self; both for Locke and Hume, memory is the guarantee of self-identity. Memory is without doubt the indispensable source for our *awareness* of self-continuity. Without memory, we could not recall or reminisce or recognize past deeds as our own; we would have no history. The question, however, goes deeper: who or what is the unifying subject of disparate and diverse memories? If there is neither stage nor theater, only a succession of scenes, we may ask with Stephen "Who watches me here?" (*U* 3.414). Awareness does not constitute continuity: there must be a prior existing, persistent entity that is conscious of itself as enduring through time.[106] This is the view of the self that, beginning with Aristotle, was adopted and developed by Aquinas and the Scholastics. In his reflection on identity in "Scylla and Charybdis," Stephen acknowledges the importance of memory but immediately recognizes that the soul is the prior and ultimate principle of persistent personal identity. Locke echoes in his ear, but Stephen stands with Aristotle on solid ground: "But I, entelechy, form of forms, am I by memory because under everchanging forms." The individual soul is, in Aristotle's terminology, "entelechy, form of forms" (*U* 9.215–19).

Richard Ellmann summarizes well:

> Hume was the master of those who do not know. Hume is not prepared to assert, as Stephen is, that the soul is the form of forms, and instead declares that questions about the soul's essence, such as its degree of materiality, are unintelligible. Although he agrees with Aristotle, and Stephen, that memory is a source of personal identity, he insists that "all the nice and subtle questions concerning personal identity can never possibly be decided, and are to be regarded rather as grammatical than as philosophical difficulties."[107] Against Stephen's theory of persons and things having each its signature, Hume refuses to concede uninterrupted identity.[108]

Hume is looking for a concrete object that he can identify as the self and that can be observed independently of the flow of experience. And since, predictably, he cannot find it, he denies the reality of a permanent self. The tradition of Aristotle suggests that the self is not grasped directly and immediately in itself but is observed in and through its activities. Aquinas states: "The understanding is first aware of its object; secondly, it is aware of the act by which it is aware of the object; and through the act it is aware of itself."[109] The self is not an object observed independently of our changing experience; we are simultaneously aware of an element of permanence as well as of variations within it. We cannot think of the self apart from experience, but neither can we consider experiences as atomic, detached, events. We concretely experience an identical self in a succession of actual states. There is an element of permanence in ourselves and in the changing persons and things with which we are in contact. This lived experience is illuminated by Aristotle's theory of substance and accident. Substance is not merely the grammatical subject of logical predicates but the existential ground and dynamic center of activity that overflows to others. Through its actions, it establishes relations with other beings; it expresses itself through its powers or activities but cannot be identified with any or all of them. According to the moderate realism of Aristotle and Aquinas, substance can be really and reliably known—but not exhaustively, since the reality always exceeds our cognition: *individuum est ineffabile*. There is an echo of the incommunicable character of substance in the "Ithaca" episode: "What were Stephen's and Bloom's quasisimultaneous volitional quasisensations of concealed identities? Visually, Stephen's: The traditional figure of hypostasis" (*U* 17.781–83). We shall return to the meaning of the term "hypostasis."

John S. Rickard expresses the importance of entelechy for Joyce: "Entelechy is not simply Stephen's way of facing his debts but is an important way of thinking about many of the centripetal, holistic elements of *Ulysses* that work to provide the essential tension with the book's postmodernist and fragmentary tendencies."[110] That tension arises, I suggest, from a failure to recognize the difference between accidental and substantial change. If the author of *Ulysses* had grasped this distinction, many of the questions that enliven its pages would have ceased to perplex him. As already suggested, however, for that we may be grateful, since otherwise we would be deprived of the recurring dramatization of the enigma of self-identity that never ceases to preoccupy him.

The Aristotelian meaning of "entelechy," employed by Stephen in "Scylla and Charybdis," needs clarification in light of the explanations offered by Judith Ryan and John S. Rickard. They both seem to suggest that entelechy is a perfection awaiting achievement, whereas for Aristotle it is a basic perfection that is already complete. Ryan refers to Stephen's concept of "the self that moves towards a predetermined goal ('entelechy')."[111] Rickard recognizes three different meanings,[112] each of which calls for comment.

(1) "Aristotle," Rickard states, "used the word [entelechy] to denote the actualization of what is potential or possible in an organism."[113] This is, however, Aristotle's definition of movement or accidental change (*kinêsis*), rather than *entelecheia*. The activity that characterizes movement is the imperfect act of a substance as it acquires a perfection it lacks but for which it has potency and that it achieves through a gradual process or movement. With his newly minted term "*entelecheia*," Aristotle intended something much more profound, namely the primary, unconditional, first, and basic completion of the individual that determines its specific nature. Given the particular essence that an individual has, its specific actualization is already complete. If it is a human, it does not have the potential to be a dog or a butterfly; there is no actualization/attainment of further potential in respect of *what* it is. To be human is its actualized perfection, its *entelecheia*: it is either human or it is not; there is no change through which it can become *more* a human being. The only change to which an individual human is open, considered simply in its nature as human, is the substantial change through which it ceases to be, when its constitutive prime matter loses the substantial form and becomes a different substance, with the ensuing corruption of the individual. That to which the human substance is certainly open is the actualization of accidental potentialities that are enabled by the kind of substance that it is. This for Aristotle is *kinêsis*, movement or change; it is an imperfect act because it is a gradual and temporal process whereby a substance achieves a previously potential perfection. *Entelecheia*, by contrast, refers to the completed, perfect state of having been actualized from the outset as a definite essence.

A minor point needs to be made regarding Rickard's formula (understood as referring to change/*kinêsis*, rather than *entelecheia*). The word "possible" in the definition "actualization of what is potential or possible in an organism" should be removed; the correct term for Aristotle is "potential," which is distinctly different from "possible." "Possible" may simply denote whatever is logically possible insofar as it does not involve contradiction. An ontological chasm divides the potential from the possible.[114] Potency implies that there is in the individual an already-existing resource for further perfection, not merely absence of contradiction.[115]

(2) Rickard states that entelechy "has become identified in Roman Catholic theology with the soul."[116] It was in fact Aristotle's own definition of the soul, long before it was adopted by Christian theologians. He defines

the soul as "the first actuality (*entelechy*) of a natural body endowed with organs."[117]

(3) Rickard states that, based on its etymology (ἐντελέχεια derived from τέλος, "fulfillment or consummation"), entelechy signifies "a vital, motive, teleological, and unconscious force that drives ineluctably toward some form of completion, wholeness, or closure."[118] This is a misreading, related to Rickard's first assigned interpretation. Entelechy is not a driving force that is directed toward completion or wholeness: it is itself the state of completion whereby an individual substance (plant, animal, human) is determined to be what it is in its specific nature. One could equally say that "entelechy" is simply another word for "nature" or "essence." Needless to say (with reference to this and the first explanation), it is a thing's entelechy or nature that determines the range of potencies within a substance's capacity, which both enables and limits its perfectibility ("human life [as] infinitely perfectible," *U* 17.993). It is true, as Rickard indicates, that the word *entelechy* is related to *telos*, Greek for "goal"; *telos* is however at the root of a more developed concept, namely, ἐντελής, meaning "perfect." *Entelecheia* properly means "perfectedness" or "perfection"; this is the achieved condition conveyed by Aristotle in his newly coined term. It denotes the deepest sense of actuality, the perfection of a nature actualized as a complete substance, not a goal to be attained. *Entelecheia* (ἐντελέχεια) is the complete and perfected reality of substance or *ousia* (οὐσία).[119]

There are apparent parallels between Aristotle's *entelecheia* and Bergson's *élan vital* (*FW* 149.20: "Bitchson," *FW* 221.22: "Elanio Vitale"), insofar as they are the deepest principles of entities in their respective systems. Regarding the division between being and becoming, however, the two philosophers occupy opposing extremes. The entire thrust of the French thinker's philosophy is toward the primacy of change or flux. He declares: "If movement is not everything, it is nothing. [. . .] There are changes, but there are underneath the change no things which change: change has no need of a support. There are movements, but there is no inert or invariable object which moves: movement does not imply a mobile. [. . .] [Change] is the very substance of things."[120] In his stimulating book, *Bergson and the Stream of Consciousness Novel*, Shiv K. Kumar argues that *Finnegans Wake* is best interpreted in light of Bergsonian influence.[121] While Joyce may well have taken inspiration from Bergson in expressing the fluctuating nature of existence and human nature, it is not at all obvious that he opted for Bergson's primacy of becoming. This was for him one side of the divide between being and becoming; for Joyce the Aristotelian, this aspect of the universe is secondary. Nor is Bergson its greatest champion; Joyce had already found this emphasis in Heraclitus.

Michael Maher's Psychology Handbook

There can be little doubt but that Joyce acquired much of his knowledge of the Aristotelian-Thomist theory of personal identity from *Psychology: Empirical and Rational* by Michael Maher, S.J., published in the series Catholic Manuals of Philosophy.[122] Maher was the nephew of Fr. Delany, Jesuit president of University College during Joyce's student days, referred to in *Stephen Hero* as Fr. Dillon. As already explained, these manuals were the daily diet of many of Joyce's classmates at University College.[123] Joyce also had his personal copy of the book in Trieste and read it closely, as evidenced by his marginal marks. Rickard correctly states: "Joyce's reading in Maher's Psychology textbook provides a clear example of the ways in which his training in traditional Catholic philosophy influenced his ideas about memory and identity, creating a cultural unconscious in his writing that operated in a chaosmic tension with the more materialist prevailing discourses of the late nineteenth and early twentieth centuries."[124] Rickard has surveyed the importance of this volume, but its prominence as a source warrants repetition; it will also be profitable to cite extended passages to illustrate Maher's significance as a major source for Joyce's theory of self-identity.

Maher unequivocally rejects Locke's definition of a person in terms of memory or self-consciousness:

> Self-consciousness presupposes the abiding existence of the person who is self-conscious, but it does not constitute his personal identity: this has its basis in the persistence of the same individual soul throughout the life of each individual. [. . .] Locke's definition of a Person *as a self-conscious substance,* is therefore inaccurate. In this view a child or a sleeping man would not be a person at all, and an interruption of the continuity of consciousness should break up the personality of the individual. [. . .] Memory and self-consciousness *reveal,* but they do not *constitute* personal identity.[125]

Later in the volume, Maher writes:

> The true doctrine is the Peripatetic theory. This explanation was formulated by Aristotle, and later on adopted by St. Thomas and all the leading Scholastic philosophers. The soul is described by these

writers as the substantial form of the body. The living being is conceived as the resultant of two factors,—the one active and determining, the other passive and determinable. The first is called the Form, the second the Matter of the being.[126]

This is the concept of soul that is repeatedly articulated by Stephen Dedalus.

Maher recognizes the importance of memory for self-knowledge but emphasizes its ontological dependence on a prior principle:

> Through memory we are aware of our own abiding personal identity. We know with the most absolute certainty that we are the same persons who yesterday, last week, fifty years ago, had some very vivid experience. But this would be impossible were the mind constituted of successive states, or were the material organism the substantial principle in which these states inhere. The constituent elements of the latter, it is a generally admitted physiological fact, are completely changed in a comparatively short time; and fleeting mental acts which did not inhere in a permanent subject, could result no more in memory than could the disconnected cognitions of successive generations of men. It is only an indivisible principle, persisting unchanged amid transitory states, that is able to afford an adequate basis for the faculty of remembrance.[127]

Maher likewise rejects Hume's view of the self:

> If the mind were but a succession of transient states, then judgment, reasoning, self-conscious reflexion, and rational memory would be absolutely impossible; but this is not the case; therefore the mind is not merely such a series. Judgment requires the indivisible unity of the agent which compares the terms; reasoning cannot take place unless the premises successively apprehended are combined by one and the same simple energy; lastly, self-conscious reflexion and rational memory evidently imply the persistence of an abiding subject which can juxtapose the past with the present.[128]

Hume's theory of the self could not account for the unity of the "discrete succession of images" (*U* 17.108) or the "integral parts of the human whole" (*U* 17.996).

Joyce read a number of pages in Maher's *Psychology* attentively, underscoring significant passages. In the following sentence, his underlining of Maher's italicized phrases illustrates how well he grasped Aristotle's concept of form and substance: "A *substantial form* is accordingly defined as *a determining principle which by its union with the subject that it actuates constitutes a complete substance of a determinate species.*"[129] The words underlined are a precise definition of Aristotle's entelechy: the substantial form or determining principle of a complete substance of a determinate species. In the paragraph that follows, he marked with a marginal line the words after the dashes in the following sentence: "For, since *actio sequitur esse*—since every *action* of an agent flows from the *being* of that agent—*the principle which is the root of the natural activity of a substance must be the determinant of its being and nature.*"[130]

On page 519, Joyce drew a vertical line in the margin alongside the following passage, which anticipates Stephen's response to the question whether or not he still owes a pound to Russell: "It is on the permanence of the substantial form that the identity of the individual depends. The material constituents of the living body are nearly all changed, as we have before stated, in the course of a few years, yet we affirm that the man of sixty is identical with the boy of six: the soul has persisted unchanged." Substantial form is the core of the Aristotelian doctrine of permanent self-identity that underpins Stephen's recognition of self in "Scylla and Charybdis."

Joyce placed a star beside the second sentence in the following passage on page 520, which emphasizes the unity of soul and body as one person: "Moreover, the union of soul and body results in a single *nature*. *The nature of a being is simply its essence viewed as the source of its actions." The paragraph continues:

> But in the living animal the various processes of growth, sleep, motion, and sensation, are not operations of the soul or body alone, but of the being as a whole. They are activities of one nature. An individual nature conceived as a complete being subsisting in itself, and not communicated to or coalescing with another, is called by the Schoolmen a *suppositum* or *hypostasis*. The *suppositum* is, therefore, the entire and ultimate source of all operations. Hence the axiom: *Actiones sunt suppositorum*. When the *suppositum* is endowed with intelligence it is termed a person.

Maher concluded the paragraph with the following definition: "A *Person* may accordingly be defined in scholastic language as a *suppositum of a rational nature,* or *an individual and incommunicable substance of a rational nature.* The human person is thus neither the body nor the soul, but the rational being arising out of the substantial union of both principles."[131] Joyce

highlighted the latter sentence with a marginal mark and paid special attention to the associated footnote, in which he underlined certain key terms:

> The terms *substance, essence, nature,* severally denote the same ob-
> ject, but connote more especially different features. *Substance* points
> to the general fact of *existence per se; essence* points to the *reality of
> which the being is constituted; nature* signifies the *essence as principle
> of activity. Suppositum* implies that the substance, essence, or nature
> subsists in itself in possession of such *complete individuality* as to be
> incommunicable or incapable of being assumed into another being.
> The invention of the term is due to the dogma of the Incarnation.
> In Christ, the church teaches, there is *one Person, one rational "sup-
> positum,"* but two *natures.* The Human Nature of our Lord does not
> of itself constitute a *Person,* or subsist *in se,* but by the subsistence of
> the Divine Nature.

From the underlined word "reality," he drew a line to the words "acting
totality," which he added in the margin.

A word of explanation may be included here, regarding the term "hypostasis," which is referred to by Maher and which features twice in *Ulysses.*[132]
In "Proteus," Stephen ponders the theological implications of the simultaneous consecration of hosts into the body of Christ at celebrations of
the Mass in different locations. How can multiple quantities of bread be
transubstantiated into the undivided body of God-made-man? This question likewise taunted the English Franciscan theologian William of Ockham (1287–1347), who wrote extensively on the quantitative and corporeal
nature of Christ's body in the Eucharist. Stephen reflects: "Dan Occam
thought of that, invincible doctor. A misty English morning the imp hypostasis tickled his brain" (*U* 3.123–25). Joyce was possibly aware that Ockham
famously differed from St. Thomas in his theology of the Eucharist.

The word "hypostasis" also occurs in the "Ithaca" episode as that which
Stephen sensed lay hidden beneath the veil of concealed identity: "What
were Stephen's and Bloom's quasisimultaneous volitional quasisensations
of concealed identities? Visually, Stephen's: The traditional figure of hypostasis" (*U* 17.781–83). Stephen had gleaned that "hypostasis" was not only
central to the theological doctrine of the hypostatic union,[133] according
to which Christ's human and divine natures are united in one person or
hypostasis, but denotes also the hidden ground that guarantees autonomy
and identity. The word "hypostasis," Greek ὑπόστασις, (< ὑφίστημι < ὑπὸ
+ ἵστημι) signifies that which "stands under"; it was first translated into

Latin as substantia, subsequently with greater accuracy as subsistentia. As Maher explains in the paragraph cited above, the terms "suppositum" or "hypostasis" emphasize the radical autonomy of the individual in its exercise of existence, its possession of a specific essence, the radical ground of its own actions, and its incommunicable self-possession. For the passage of "Ithaca," Joyce adopted the term as synonymous with substance, attributing to Stephen an insight of profound philosophical seriousness.

Maher concludes his treatment of the union of soul and body with the following remarks, which summarize the doctrine implicit in Joyce's understanding of the human soul as the entelechy or primary actualization of the body, thus explaining its unity and endurance as a selfsame individual:

> Our present chapter ought to have rendered intelligible and justified Aristotle's celebrated definition: "The soul is the first entelechy of a natural organized body potentially having life," or "the first entelechy of a natural body capable of life." By *entelechy* is meant in the Peripatetic philosophy an actualizing or determining principle, as opposed to a recipient or determinable subject—*form* as contrasted with *matter.* The epithet, *first,* implies that the soul is the *primary* form by which the nature or specific substance of the creature receives its determination in the order of being. It is contrasted with *secondary* or *accidental* forms, e.g. heat, colour, motion, which may supervene when the *primum esse,* the first complete substantial being of the object, is constituted. A *natural* or *physical* body, signifies that the subject of the soul is not a mere *artificial* aggregate. The adjective, *organized,* expresses the fact that the body is composed of heterogeneous or dissimilar parts adapted for separate functions. The last words of the definition mean that the soul is united not with an *actually* living being, but with an organism capable of exercising vital activities when informed by the soul.[134]

A Portrait, Rickard observes, is a detailed account of "Stephen's attempts to construct a stable sense of himself as he experiments with the roles of sensualist, or religious devotee and so on, finally settling on the persona of the artist as the most appropriate."[135] Stephen's attempt, however, is not entirely successful; instead of a stable sense of himself and his place in the world, we are left with a series of selves. The enigma of the self thus lingers, to be resumed in *Ulysses,* as Rickard explains: "While *A Portrait* may seem superficially to validate the strong sense of self-presence and sureness of identity that Stephen feels at the end of the book, in *Ulysses* anxieties about the solidity of personal identity, about the possibility of positing and believing in a stable 'self' that underlies time and change, are more insistent and tenacious." The phrase *Tempora mutantur, nos et mutamur in illis* ("Times change, and we change with them"),[136] as Rickard notes, holds no urgency for the youth in *A Portrait*,[137] but with the realization "I am other I now" (*U* 9.215), it assumes existential significance for the protagonist of "Scylla and Charybdis." *Ulysses* is therefore a "transitional text" between *A Portrait*, in which the subject implicitly holds to the traditional principle of selfhood, and *Finnegans Wake* (*FW* 253.05: "I once was otherwise"), where subjectivity is dissolved into a multiplicity of "fluid personalities" and the "dissolution or multiplicity of subjectivity."[138] In *Ulysses*, Joyce confronted head-on the question of personal identity and permanence.

While Joyce experimented with various models of self-identity without explicitly endorsing any in particular, it would appear he favored Aristotle's theory of the soul, or entelechy.[139] Neither the Humean bundle theory nor Lockean memory identity can explain the unity amid the diversity of psychological phenomena or the permanence that underlies change. In a brilliant example of an "Irish bull," Oliver St. John Gogarty declared it to be a fact that "no Irishman can endure being himself for long."[140] He was most likely referring not to an Irish idiosyncrasy but to the universal itch in human nature for novelty (*novitatis cupiditas*)—"always something new" (*FW* 472.14). The paradox of the witticism plays upon a confusion of substantial and accidental change. Personality is renewed and enriched through continual change. To remain profoundly itself and become fully authentic, personality must unfurl its natural powers; this it can only do through change. There is literal truth in the apparent paradox: plus ça change plus c'est la même chose. Permanence and continuity of life require growth that springs from within the self. John Henry Newman remarked that "to live is to change, and to be perfect is to have changed often."[141]

Joyce was aware that character development is a requisite for the satisfactory depiction of personal identity. To the suggestion that he "give Bloom a rest" and pay more attention to Stephen, he declared: "Stephen no longer interests me to the same extent. He has a shape that can't be changed."[142] And while Buck Mulligan is "witty and entertaining," his wit "wears threadbare." Bloom, by contrast, "is like a battery that is being recharged. He will act with all the more vigour when he does reappear."[143]

5

Totality, Diversity, and Order

The Unity of Analogy

What makes Joyce unique in his Aristotelianism is that he reflectively made it his own, embracing it artistically—either as material content or as a principle of organization. In this chapter, I consider what I regard as the overall principle of unifying order, namely Aristotelian analogy, adopted by Joyce to discern similarity in difference and unity in diversity. It has been rightly suggested that the key to Aristotle's own mind was his early recognition that the causes of being are analogical in nature. Marie-Dominique Philippe suggested that Aristotle's use of analogy "best characterizes his philosophical approach."[1] An analogical outlook likewise marked Joyce's mind. Vincent J. Cheng has remarked: "James Joyce's mind is that of the essential poet: it works by analogy."[2] Joyce was aware of Aristotle's emphasis upon analogy as an organizing rule of order and adopted it as a principle of architectonic design in *Ulysses,* and to a lesser extent in his other works.

Analogy is the similarity of relations within and among a diversity of beings, the agreement of correspondent relations that are diversely realized in unrelated domains; it provides the widest possible framework for universal unity. Analogy is intrinsic to human cognition, discovery, and creativity. Most importantly, it allows us to unify disparate elements within the totality. Analogy was central to Aristotle's synoptic vision; it was also the most fruitful key for Joyce in conceiving and constructing his literary works. Aristotelian analogy was the key that provided Joyce with a universal optic, a unifying perspective that embraced the multitude within a single totality. Through its comprehensive power of reference, he perceived correspondences across widely diverse contexts.

Analogy for Aristotle

Analogy is the key to Aristotle's synthesizing mind, yielding rich results in many areas of his system, especially his biological works, poetics, and metaphysics. It is the organizing principle of his zoological investigations, allowing the discovery of order among disparate species on the basis of similarity of function or operation. Put simply: birds have wings, fish have fins;[3] the study of a function in one species casts light upon the corresponding function in another entirely different species, thus making for economy of research. In the *Poetics,* Aristotle understands metaphor as analogy of proportion. The most important element in poetry, the perception of likeness in the most unlikely places, it cannot be learned from another but is the true sign of natural genius. Most far-reaching is Aristotle's use of analogy in metaphysics. "There is," he declares, "analogy between all the categories of being."[4] He states: "In one sense, the causes and principles of distinct things are distinct, but in another sense, if one is to speak universally and analogically, they are all the same."[5]

Analogy or proportionality is not confined to thought and language but is manifest at a deeper level within the nature, action, and behavior of individual substances. Species are diversified, but across the wide range of manifold difference, there are underlying parallels between members of distinct groups. The similarity consists in the fitness of relation that binds the individual organically to its constituent elements, dynamically directs it toward its end-goal, and equips it with the appropriate means to achieve its perfection. For Aristotle, each substance is defined—made what it is—by its form (εἶδος / *eidos*); the form of living things is also called nature (φύσις / *phusis*); the animating form of intellectual things is *psuchê* (ψυχή). Each individual has its task (ἔργον / *ergon*) and goal (τέλος / *telos*). Its virtue (ἀρετή / *aretê*) is to satisfactorily attain its *telos* by appropriate means. Individuals differ in their end goals, but there is a similarity of relationship (ἀναλογία / *analogia*) among all things in how nature, means, and goal are appropriately linked in each case. Different goals require various tasks. Aristotle describes as niggardly the smiths of Delphi who manufacture only one kind of knife, instead of different ones for various tasks—they had no sense of analogy.[6] In his own way, Joyce grasped the analogical character of the universe: all things combining in unity, but each doing its own thing. In the phrase of "Aeolus," "Everything speaks in its own way" (*U* 7.177).

The notions of fitness to purpose and adequacy of means toward end pervade Aristotle's outlook. Nature, he states, provides every living thing with whatever it needs, to each according to its nature, providing all that is necessary and nothing that is without purpose. Proportionality and fitness may be observed in all areas of reality, or prescribed for human activity. Justice is defined as proportion and must take into account the circumstances of the individual situation.[7] Political life demands equitable harmony; in his *Rhetoric,* Aristotle draws a parallel between the balance required between leniency and severity in a democracy and the mean between aquiline and snub in a handsome nose.[8] There should be a certain proportion and fittingness between one's position in life and the possession of goods.[9] In friendship among unequals, love should be proportional, that is, analogously balanced by different levels of dedication and response.[10]

For a definition of proportion, we may consult the *Nicomachean Ethics,* where it is defined as "an equality of ratios, implying at least four terms."[11] In the *Poetics,* Aristotle prescribes the following formula: "Proportional metaphor is possible whenever there are four terms so related that the second is to the first, as the fourth to the third; for one may then put the fourth in place of the second, and the second in place of the fourth."[12] He illustrates this by the imagined parallel between the shield of Ares and the cup of Dionysus. Ares is the god of war, for whom the shield is essential equipment; Dionysus is the god of wine, whose indispensable implement is the drinking bowl. Thus, as the shield is to Ares, so is the drinking bowl to Dionysus. The cup is, as it were, "Dionysus's shield," and the shield "Ares's cup."[13] Another correspondence is between the duration of the day and the span of a lifetime. "Old age is to life as evening is to day." Thus old age is called the "evening of life" or "sunset of life."[14]

Aristotle worked out the framework for two different kinds of analogy, which later became known as the analogy of proportionality and analogy of attribution. He did not explicitly refer to the latter as analogy, but it was central to his search for a unified perspective of the cosmos. Analogy of proportion refers to the similarity of relation that exists between distinct pairs that, though different, are constituted by the same intrinsic relation, for example, the wing is to the bird as the fin is to the fish.[15] Analogy of attribution, on the other hand, is performed by the mind when in thought and language we group a variety of apparently disparate concepts or realities around a common primary focus. Aristotle's example is health: we say that climate, color, action, and food are all healthy because they have a common referent, namely, the body or organism, which is intrinsically and of itself healthy; the others are called healthy by reference to the primary analogue of body. Aristotle relies on the analogy of focal meaning to affirm the unity among the categories of being. The accidental modes of time, place, action, relation, and so on do not exist in themselves but are affirmed as real because they inhere in substance, which exists in itself. Analogy of attribution, allied with a Platonically inspired Thomist theory of participation, was later used to describe the relationship between God and creatures. Aristotle's unity of the categories has recently come to be known as predication by focal meaning: dependent variations of meaning converge upon a single focus. Both kinds of analogy, proportionality and focal unity, as we shall see, operate throughout *Ulysses,* especially the former, shaping the entire oeuvre into a vast conspectus and constellation of similarities within a magnificent overall scheme.

Analogy for Joyce

Philip Kitcher refers to James Joyce as "a man with a mind of almost unsurpassed breadth but one that was relatively shallow."[16] Given Joyce's reputation as one of the greatest literary geniuses of all time, this may strike the devotee as preposterous.[17] The assessment, however, is accurate. The question therefore is, in what does Joyce's genius consist? Shakespeare, with whom Joyce has been favorably compared, was gifted with both a profound mind and a creative imagination. Confessing that he lacked imagination, Joyce claimed his forte lay in memory. This is clearly obvious; over decades he accumulated a vast array of knowledge and detail from every branch of human knowledge. He trawled and sifted the mine of memory for the raw materials of his artistic work. Joyce's genius lay in the manner and method by which he mastered this vast material. His skill was the ability to order the great diversity of human detail into an orderly scheme. Joyce had a voracious mind, assembled myriad bric-a-brac, but in his writings ordered them to a definite scheme. By contrast with the ninth-century annalist Nennius, who in the preface to his *History of the Britons* announced his organizing principle, "I have made a heap of all I could find" (*ego autem coacervavi omne quod inveni*),[18] Joyce was the master of studied order and organization. In his systematic ordering, he was guided in large measure by Aristotle's rule of analogy.

Joyce was trained to forge unities, establish order, codify relations. This was a characteristic of his education, and it cohered with the twin Aristotelian methods of analysis and synthesis. Asked by the sculptor August Suter what he retained from his Jesuit education, he replied: "I have learnt to arrange things in such a way that they become easy to survey and to judge" (*JJII* 27).[19] Commenting on Aristotle, Aquinas defined wisdom as the discovery of order: *Sapientis est ordinare.*[20] The opening words of a translation of Aquinas that Joyce possessed, read: "According to established popular usage, which the Philosopher [Aristotle] considers should be our guide in the naming of things, they are called 'wise' who put things in their right order and control them well."[21] Curiously, AE remarked to the young Joyce: "I do not see in your beginnings enough chaos to make a world."[22] It was precisely this confrontation with chaos that spurred him on. In *Stephen Hero* we read: "And over all the chaos of history and legend, of fact and supposition, he strove to draw out a line of order, to reduce the abysses of the past to order by diagram" (*SH* 33).

Order was the hallmark of Aristotle's mind; his investigations were a comprehensive attempt not only to analyze and differentiate the entirety of given reality but also more importantly to integrate and unify.[23] This fixity upon order is formulated in the mind of Bloom: "The necessity of order, a place for everything and everything in its place" (*U* 17.1410). This is repeated in the essay title associated with Aristotle in "Night Lessons" in *Finnegans Wake:* "A Place for Everything and Everything in its Place" (*FW* 306.17–18). Joyce had occasionally (and obsessively), in Wallace Stevens's phrase, a "blessed rage for order." When Frank Budgen inquired of the progress of *Ulysses,* Joyce replied: "I have been working hard on it all day." "Does that mean that you have written a great deal?" Budgen asked. "Two sentences," said Joyce, in all seriousness. "You have been seeking the *mot juste?*" "No. I have the words already. What I am seeking is the perfect order of words in the sentence. There is an order in every way appropriate. I think I have it."[24] The words in question referred to the seductive effect of women's silk petticoats hanging in a shop window: "Perfume of embraces all him assailed. With hungered flesh obscurely, he mutely craved to adore" (*U* 8.38–39). "You can see for yourself," said Joyce, "in how many different ways they might be arranged." This is echoed in *Finnegans Wake:* "The ring man in the rong shop but the rite words by the rote order" (*FW* 167.32–33).

The profound analogies that for Joyce shape the orchestral harmony of the universe involve much more than the simple, superficial "significances of similitude" or the symbolism between the "squat stuffed easychair" and the "slender splayfoot chair of glossy cane curves" in Bloom's home (*U* 17.1292–300). Joyce himself uses the word "analogy" in a variety of contexts. In *Stephen Hero* we read: "The intelligent centres of the movement were so scantily supplied that the analogies they gave out as exact and potent were really analogies built haphazard upon very inexact knowledge" (*SH* 62). In "Ivy Day in the Committee Room," Mr. Henchy animatedly protests: "In the name of God, where's the analogy between the two cases?"[25] The concept occurs with frequency in *Ulysses*.[26] The most significant, though implicit, reference to analogy is the phrase "equality of relations" (*FW* 283.11), a perfect expression for the analogy of proportionality. Suggesting that Joyce borrowed the phrase from Herbert Spencer's essay "The Genesis of Science," Tim Conley equates the phrase with the expression "all things being equal" (ceteris paribus), which, he asserts, "smacks of some utopian project."[27] This is to overlook the real significance of the term for Spencer and Joyce, which is that of analogy, the recognition of parallel or similar relationships between diverse pairs.

In a paragraph strongly reminiscent of Aristotle's rhetorical and biological writings, Spencer illustrates the importance of analogy for scientific investigation, before suggesting its intrinsic role to reasoning in general.[28] Knowledge of organic forms gives rise to ideas not only of simple equality (i.e., equality of things) but also of equality of relations. Given the "similarity of two creatures of the same species but of different sizes," it follows for the zoologist that "any two parts of the one bear the same ratio to one another, as the homologous parts of the other."[29] On the basis of "equality of relations," the zoologist recognizes that "two things are intimately connected, remote as they at first seem."[30] All of this is pure Aristotle, who emphasizes the importance of analogy for biological investigation and who repeatedly declares that the clearest sign of genius is the recognition of similarity between unlike things.[31] Spencer, like Aristotle, goes further and declares that "the fundamental conception of similarity is *equality of relations*."[32] This insight has significance far beyond zoology: it is reflected in every sphere of speculation: "With this explanation we shall be understood when we say that the notion of equality of relations is the basis of all exact reasoning. Already it has been shown that reasoning in general is a recognition of *likeness* of relations; and here we further find that while the notion of likeness of things ultimately evolves the idea of simple equality, the notion of likeness of relations evolves the idea of equality of relations."[33] It is highly likely that Joyce was familiar with this essay of Spencer, which both chimes with Aristotle's deepest insights and is reflected in Joyce's own writings.

Although the phrase "equality of relations" occurs in a passage of *Finnegans Wake* that has no reference to analogy, the choice of words reveals something of how Joyce's mind works. The definition of equanimity given in "Ithaca," with the significant phrase "dissimilar similarity" (*U* 17.2180), likewise bears remarkable resemblance to Aristotelian analogy, grounded in appropriateness of function:

> Equanimity? As natural as any and every natural act of a nature expressed or understood executed in natured nature by natural creatures in accordance with his, her and their natured natures, of dissimilar similarity. [. . .] As not more abnormal than all other parallel processes of adaptation to altered conditions of existence, resulting in a reciprocal equilibrium between the bodily organism and its attendant circumstances, foods, beverages, acquired habits, indulged inclinations, significant disease. (*U* 17.2177–94)

While there is no evidence that Joyce read the *Politics,* this passage reflects Aristotle's statement: "Nature has differentiated their modes of life to suit their facilities and their predilection for those articles of food."[34] Phrases such as "parallel processes of adaptation," "altered conditions," and "reciprocal equilibrium" accurately convey Aristotle's grasp of the analogical workings of nature.

Almost certainly, the writings of John Henry Newman were another of Joyce's sources for Aristotelian analogy. James Pribek rightly observes that "Joyce and Newman perceived the world through analogy and correlation."[35] At the age of twenty-one, Newman read Bishop Joseph Butler's *Analogy of Religion* (1736) and adopted as a primary principle of his teaching the idea of "an analogy between the separate works of God."[36] He adopted the fundamental insight that "the relationship between all things physical and metaphysical was one of analogy and correspondence."[37] Writing of Aristotle, St. Thomas, Newton, and Goethe, Newman, who, as we have seen, held Aristotle in the highest regard, stated that "a truly great intellect [. . .] is one which takes a connected view of old and new, past and present, far and near, and which has an insight into the influence of all these one on another; without which there is no whole, and no centre. It possesses the knowledge, not only of things, but also of their mutual and true relations; knowledge, not merely considered as acquirement, but as philosophy."[38] These words might equally refer to James Joyce.

Analogy in *Ulysses*

Joyce consciously adopted Aristotelian analogy as the organizing principle of *Ulysses*. In a letter to Ezra Pound (April 9, 1917), he wrote: "I wonder if you will like the book I am writing? I am doing it, as Aristotle would say, by different means in different parts" (*LI* 101). In a critical essay on Joyce published five years later (June 1922), Pound wrote: "He expresses himself differently in different parts of his book (as even Aristotle permits), but this does not mean, as the distinguished Larbaud contends, that he abandons unity of style."[39] Surprisingly, Pound seems to have missed the significance of Joyce's reference to Aristotle, since diversity of means for distinct ends is exactly the unity of style demanded, not merely permitted, by Aristotle. It would appear that Pound likewise misunderstood Valery Larbaud, who had endorsed Joyce's method with enthusiasm in an article published two months earlier:

> It must be acknowledged that, although each of the eighteen parts differs from all of the others in form and language, the whole forms none the less an organism, a book. As we arrive at this conclusion, all sorts of coincidences, analogies, and correspondences between these different points come to light; just as, in looking fixedly at the sky at night, we find that the number of stars appears to increase. We begin to discover and to anticipate symbols, a design, a plan, in what appeared to us at first a brilliant but confused mass of notations, phrases, data, profound thoughts, fantasticalities, splendid images, absurdities, comic or dramatic situations; and we realise that we are before a much more complicated book than we had supposed, that everything which appeared arbitrary and sometimes extravagant is really deliberate and premeditated; in short, that we are before a book which has a key.[40]

Despite his misreading of Joyce and Larbaud, however, Pound correctly grasped the importance of Joyce's technique: "Each character not only speaks in his own manner, but thinks in his own manner, and that is no more abandoning unity of style than when the various characters of a novel in the so-called unified style speak in various ways: the quotation marks are left out, that's all."[41] Referring to the diversity of styles employed in *Ulysses*, Hermann Broch also notes "the extraordinary concentration with which all these instruments of style and forms of expression are gathered together into artistic unity." Broch refers to the "truly symphonic mastery (*wahrhaft symphonische Meisterschaft*)" of Joyce's achievement.[42]

The variety of stylistic composition contributed to an overall schematic unity, a unity similar to that of Aristotelian analogy. The *principium operis* is made explicit in another letter by Joyce:

> It is the epic of two races (Israel–Ireland) and at the same time the cycle of the human body as well as a little story of a day (life). [. . .] It is also a kind of encyclopaedia. My intention is not only to render the myth *sub specie temporis nostri* but also to allow each adventure (that is, every hour, every organ, every art being interconnected and interrelated in the somatic scheme of the whole) to condition and even to create its own technique. Each adventure is so to speak one person although it is composed of persons—as Aquinas relates of the heavenly hosts.[43]

Joyce shared Aristotle's recognition of analogy as fundamental to our understanding of nature. It is interesting to note that a question in Joyce's second-year logic examination at University College (set by Fr. Woodburn and Fr. Darlington) included the following question: "Distinguish clearly, with examples, between Aristotelian and ordinary analogy."[44]

In the final paragraph of his important essay "*Ulysses*: A Short History," Richard Ellmann has written: "*Ulysses* may be seen to conduct its affirmation by discovery of kinship among disparate things, whether these are mind and body, casual and important, contemporary and Homeric, or Bloom and Stephen. The universe is, if nothing else, irrevocably interpenetrating."[45] This all-universal interconnectedness of the universe is summed up in one of the phrases of Aristotle that Joyce copied by hand in the Bibliothèque Sainte-Geneviève in Paris: "Nature, it seems, is not a collection of unconnected episodes, like a bad tragedy."[46] This line from the *Metaphysics* is reechoed in Stephen's reference to the "playwright who wrote the folio of this world and wrote it badly" (*U* 9.1046–47). Shakespeare captured Aristotle's vision of the world as a unified whole in a line from *Troilus and Cressida,* which interestingly is spoken by the character Ulysses: "One touch of nature makes the whole world kin.[47] The insight is twice echoed by Joyce in *Finnegans Wake*: "with one touch of nature set a veiled world agrin" (*FW* 138.36–139.01); "one twitch, one nature makes us oldworld kin" (*FW* 463.16–17).[48] Gerty MacDowell, troubled by temptation, had been assured by her confessor in a similar vein that "that was only the voice of nature and we were all subject to nature's laws" (*U* 13.455–56).

Although explicitly about a small number of personalities, *Ulysses* dramatizes everything and everyone, employing a multitude of voices. Everything "speaks in its own way" (*U* 7.177)—"Everyone according to his needs or everyone according to his deeds (*U* 16.247) ("Dublin is such a small city: everyone knows everyone else's business").[49] In *Ulysses,* characters merge and mingle: "We walk through ourselves, meeting robbers, ghosts, giants, old men, young men, wives, widows, brothers-in-love, but always meeting ourselves." Even the Creator "is doubtless all in all in all of us" (*U* 9.1044–50).

For Aristotle, the universe was a "cosmos" in its original sense of an ordered unity. His sense of the universal interconnectedness of the universe, of unity amid diversity, is conveyed in *Metaphysics* 12: "All things are ordered together somehow, but not all alike—both fishes and fowl and plants; and the world is not such that one thing has nothing to do with another, but they are all connected. For all are ordered together to one end."[50] The perception of such pervasive unity that allows the convergence of relations between widely divergent realities and experiences is likewise one of the most fundamentally characteristic structures of Joyce's oeuvre. In words from "Proteus," "The cords of all link back, strandentwining cable of all flesh. [. . .] Gaze in your omphalos." The word "omphalos" further suggests the bond between all things as having the same center. A radical Thomist note is added with the words "Creation from nothing" (*U* 3.37–39).[51]

Joyce remarked to Frank Budgen: "Among other things my book is the epic of the human body. [. . .] In my book the body lives in and moves through space and is the home of a full human personality. The words I write are adapted to express first one of its functions then another. In *Lestrygonians* the stomach dominates and the rhythm of the episode is that of the peristaltic movement."[52] Something akin to the analogy of attribution is at work here, with the body as central focus. Theoharis Constantine Theoharis explains the parallel role of the soul, more importantly, as the principle of synthesis and unity:

[The] Aristotelian account of the soul supplies much of the logic for the encyclopedic, polysemous design of Bloomsday. By absorbing a foreign body's sensible or intelligible form, the soul identifies itself with that body. In this manner the soul is all that is: the mediating factor between individual consciousness and external objects, the substance continually transformed by other substances, but under all transformations changeless, undivided, permanently individual. This quality of soul, its integrity and its multiple transfigurations, is the most important Aristotelian idea in *Ulysses*. The idea has conceptual and technical applications in the novel.[53]

By plotting *Ulysses* against Homer's *Odyssey*, and plotting parallels between Bloom and the greatest character of ancient literature, Joyce enlisted the classic epic into service for his modern representation of universal human history. Adding to this broad framework a variety of techniques, perspectives, and styles, he achieved in miniature a tangible symbol of the universal. As Umberto Eco suggests, Joyce considered *Ulysses* a "*summa* of the universe."[54] The totality is embodied and reflected in the concrete. Analogies, parallels, similarities, symmetries, symbols, echoes, and resonances of varied registers: all are integral to the construction of *Ulysses*. By means of such literary devices, Joyce could introduce unity into the immense wealth of human experience that comprises the raw material of the novel. As Ezra Pound remarked, "The excuse for parts of *Ulysses* is the WHOLE of *Ulysses*."[55]

The principal unifying figure at the center of this great diversity is Leopold Bloom. Not only is Bloom a modern counterpart of Homer's Odysseus, but he also represents a uniting focus for the "accidental manners and humours," "whimsicalities and circumstances," of men and women, which the eighteen-year-old Joyce recognized as the realm of literature. In his lecture "Drama and Life," the aspiring writer also referred to human society as the "embodiment of changeless laws" (*CW* 40). The distinction between accidental circumstances and changeless elements may be readily translated into the Aristotelian concepts of substance and accident. Substance is the dynamic center and foundation for the unceasing activities by which individuals express themselves and through which they engage with others in the world. Bloom embodies and exemplifies Aristotle's individual concretely in all his variety. As Theoharis Constantine Theoharis states, Joyce "creates his representative man in *Ulysses* primarily by showing Bloom's senses and intellect at work. In those activities Joyce could continually show forms interchanging, the dynamic that he, following Aristotle, considered actuality's presence." Theoharis explains:

> There is a close correspondence between Aristotle's account of the relationship of the soul to the body and Joyce's construction of *Ulysses*. He made Bloom's story an epic of the body, by sustaining an allegorical schema throughout the novel in which chapters and details of

chapters are symbolically associated with various organs and organic systems (respiratory, nervous, and the like). The point of this analogical identification of character and culture with bodily functions is Aristotelian: the soul is not separable from the body; the reality of human experience, individual or social, always has an inalienable material basis; consciousness in any mode is, somehow, always in the flesh.[56]

Joyce created Bloom's character in accordance with Aristotle's theory of human nature.

Joyce's biographer Herbert S. Gorman remarked: "There is an Aristotelean leaning toward the unities in Joyce."[57] For Aristotle, as remarked already, the ability to perceive likeness within the most unlikely contexts is a true sign of genius. Joyce was most likely familiar with this declaration from the *Poetics,* and it is clear that he himself appreciated the importance of analogy—evidenced by the frequent references to analogy throughout *Ulysses.* In a phrase that rivals Johnson's celebrated description of metaphor as "two ideas for one,"[58] Joyce provides an analogy that conveys the essence of analogy itself: "Though they didn't see eye to eye in everything, a certain analogy there somehow was, as if both their minds were travelling, so to speak, in the one train of thought" (*U* 16.1579–81).

The perception of such pervasive unity that allows the convergence of relations between widely divergent realities and experiences is one of the most fundamentally characteristic structures of Joyce's work. For Aristotle, there is nothing random in the cosmos; coincidences are rooted in causality: action grounds relations among beings. There is nothing random in Joyce's *Ulysses.* Coincidence is not absence of purpose but the intersection of causal lines; it is anything but accidental or casual. Lionel Trilling referred to Joyce's "pervading sense of the interrelation and interpenetration of all things."[59] Consequences cascade, everything ramifies. Joyce found excitement in synchronicity and symmetry, in concurrences of time and place, in the conjunction of conditions.

In his essay "The Art of Fiction," published when Joyce was a two-year-old, Henry James advised the novice: "Write from experience, and experience only," adding: "Try to be one of the people on whom nothing is lost!"[60] Nothing was lost on Joyce: everything was retained in the vault of memory, to be recalled, transformed, transmuted, and reexpressed in artistic formulation. "Work in all you know," Stephen would reflect (*U* 9.158).[61] Robert

McAlmon (who estimated that Joyce read about a third of the book to him) commented: "It was impressive to observe how everything was grist to his mill."[62] Joyce worked it all in but fused his material into an organic whole.

Joyce envisaged *Ulysses,* arguably *Finnegans Wake* also, as a unified totality and proceeded to construct it organically from a central focal point from which the action radiated. It is the reader's task to rediscover the underlying unity. As Nabokov observed, "Joyce takes a complete and absolute character, God-known, Joyce-known, then breaks it up into fragments and scatters these fragments over the space-time of his book. The good reader gathers these puzzle pieces and gradually puts them together."[63]

Although Joyce was obsessed with collecting and collating vast amounts of detailed experience, he did not lose sight of the grand scheme. His mind's eye was on the majestic, the universal. As Ezra Pound remarked, "the author is quite capable of dealing with things about him, and dealing directly, yet these details do not engross him, he is capable of getting at the universal element beneath them."[64] By setting up correspondences between his own work and major works from the past, Joyce enlisted the latter as elements in a vast new whole. Pound has recognized this:

> In this super-novel our author has also poached on the epic, and has, for the first time since 1321,[65] resurrected the infernal figures; his furies are not stage figures; he has, by simple reversal, caught back the furies, his flagellant Castle ladies. Telemachus, Circe, the rest of the Odyssean company, the noisy cave of Aeolus gradually place themselves in the mind of the reader, rapidly or less rapidly according as he is familiar or unfamiliar with Homer. These correspondences are part of Joyce's mediaevalism and are chiefly his own affair, a scaffold, a means of construction, justified by the result, and justifiable by it only. The result is a triumph in form, in balance, a main schema, with continuous inweaving and arabesque.[66]

Stephen and Bloom, each in his own style, seek out the implications of a wider plan, Stephen at the metaphysical level ("All sides of life should be represented. He smiled on all sides equally," *U* 9.505–06), Bloom at the physical level. Chris Ackerley has referred to the "analogical cast" of Bloom's mind, evidenced by the latter's alertness to coincidences.[67] Derek Attridge makes the valuable observation: "Bloom is always on the lookout for connections across time and place, verbal echoes, patterns in the heap of fragments that characterize his consciousness and his surroundings. Stephen, by contrast, seems driven by the traditional (and I include here the modernist) artist's need to *make* connections, to fuse and shape them, rather than to find and celebrate them in passing."[68] Were we privy to all the forces operating in the universe ("Well, of course, if we knew all the things," *U* 8.50), we would recognize that so-called coincidences arise from preceding circumstances. Nothing is arbitrary or random. As Ackerley notes: "Bloom, caught in his own drama with Boylan and unable to appreciate the wider drama of events, does not understand the causality but notes only the affinity, which he calls 'coincidence.'"[69] Bloom would most likely believe in "cocoincidences" (*FW* 597.01).[70]

Bloom's appreciation of links and connections is illustrated by his relaxed and pensive mood when, relieved after his erotic admiration of Gerty MacDowell, he reflects upon the broader scheme: "It was all things combined. Excitement" (*U* 13.940–41). Bloom proceeds to reflect on the manner in which like finds like in a fitting union of marriage: "Still there's destiny in it, falling in love. [. . .] little chits of girls, height of a shilling in coppers, with little hubbies. As God made them he matched them" (*U* 13.973–76). He ponders presently the malfunctioning of wristwatches and the possible influence of magnetism. Everything is linked together: "Then if one thing stopped, the whole ghesabo would stop bit by bit. Because it's all arranged" (*U* 13.990). He continues to reflect on the connectedness of things: "Make their own use of everything" (*U* 13.1003); "Suppose there's some connection. [. . .] Mysterious thing too" (*U* 13.1014–15).

Joyce's remark that he had "a grocer's assistant's mind" (*LIII* 304) referred to his commercial instinct but might equally refer to his penchant for lists, labels, and disparate data. In June 1921, he wrote to Harriet Shaw Weaver: "My head is full of pebbles and rubbish and broken matches and lots of glass picked up 'most everywhere.' The task I set myself technically in writing a book from eighteen different points of view and in as many styles, all apparently unknown or undiscovered by my fellow tradesmen, that and the nature of the legend chosen would be enough to upset anyone's mental balance" (*LI* 167). Joyce, however, maintained his equipoise; besides the magpie's beak, which gathers the detritus and discarded debris, fragments of everyday living, Joyce had the eagle eye to grasp the grand majestic design. Wyndham Lewis referred to *Ulysses* as "an Aladdin's cave of incredible bric-à-brac."[71] Stuart Gilbert remarked: "*Ulysses* is like a great net let down from heaven including in the infinite variety of its take the magnificent and the petty, the holy and the obscene, interrelated, mutually symbolic. In this story of a Dublin day we read an epic of mankind."[72]

Ulysses has itself been cleverly described with a phrase from "Oxen of the Sun" as "this chaffering allincluding most farraginous chronicle" (*U* 14.1412). The work is crammed with a blindingly vast diversity of detail, but Joyce is always in control. The Greek poet Archilochus contrasted the wiles of the fox, who knows many things, with the single-mindedness of the hedgehog, who knows one big thing.[73] True genius discerns in unison both the singularity of the grand unity and the minutiae of multiplicity; for that reason, it is exceedingly rare. The brilliance of *Ulysses* is that of a universal panorama woven from the torn shreds and broken shards of multifarious living; its success derives from the writer's mastery of creative analogy. Joyce is proof of Aristotle's conviction that analogy is a sign of genius, a rare gift of nature that cannot be learned. He effected in art a fundamental insight gained from his study of Aristotle. Sartre's remark is apt: "The novelist's aesthetic always sends us back to his metaphysic."[74] This appreciation of analogy is one of the most profound affinities between Aristotle and James Joyce. Both would eagerly agree with the words of a modern critic: "Analogy—likeness between dissimilar things—holds within itself the very secret of the universe."[75]

Joyce set his ambitions high and was equal to the overwhelming challenge; his aim was to embrace through art the full amplitude of human existence. As Herbert S. Gorman notes, "*Ulysses* is the revelation of all life in a single day."[76] Joyce aimed to transpose the universal humanity personified by Odysseus to the Dublin of his day. The strategy adopted for this purpose was ingenious: the daily events of the modern citizen would resonate with the echoes of the greatest character from world literature. *Ulysses* follows loosely the structure of Homer's *Odyssey,* not slavishly but in cavalier fashion. As T. S. Eliot comments, Joyce's use of myth, "in manipulating a continuous parallel between contemporaneity and antiquity [. . .] is simply a way of controlling, of ordering, of giving a shape and a significance to the immense panorama of futility and anarchy which is contemporary history."[77] At times the parallel is tenuous and inventive; nonetheless, Joyce himself regarded it as crucial. He wrote to his aunt Josephine: "If you want to read *Ulysses* you had better first get or borrow from a library a translation in prose of the *Odyssey* of Homer" (*SL* 286).

Referring to the "inner simultaneity" that links the principal characters of *Ulysses,* Hermann Broch remarks:

> Soon, however, we become aware that all these persons are caught up in a single current, and that although, to be sure, each has his own life, they nevertheless belong together in a closely-knit whole. And

this whole is represented by Bloom, it is Bloom, and beyond Bloom it is mankind in general. It would be permissible to speak of Bloom's different selves, of selves which reflect each other reciprocally as in a dream, and if we were to attempt to explain this naturalistically, it might be said that intimate relations are only established between persons who partake each of the other's self. Thus Bloom's wife, Molly, whose life is one of bald instinct, embodies his most obscure, most brutish humanity, while his reason is manifested in Dedalus, who incarnates his spiritual son.[78]

Richard M. Kain rightly refers to *Ulysses* as "a metaphysical novel,"[79] citing Joyce's remark to Arthur Power: "For myself, I always write about Dublin, because if I can get to the heart of Dublin, I can get to the heart of all the cities of the world. In the particular is contained the universal."[80] As Broch notes, "a single concrete quotidian is chosen to represent the universal quotidian. [. . .] The commonplace quotidian of Mr. Bloom, the hero of *Ulysses*, became the 'universal quotidian' of the epoch of 1904."[81] The notion that the individual contains the universal is conveyed in an age-honored concept of human nature as a miniature or mirror image of the universe, man as microcosm ("microchasm," "nikrokosmikon," *FW* 229.24, 468.21). Throughout his works, Joyce depicts, as Richard Kearney observes, "the quintessential inimitable strangeness of each human person." In *Finnegans Wake,* he pivots brilliantly, according to Kearney, upon the bipolarity of the "thisness" of each (*ecce + haecceitas* = look at/behold + thisness) and the commonality of all (HCE–*Haec-Ecce*): "Each person is everyone. The particular is the universal. The concrete is the cosmic. The infinitesimal the infinite."[82] Some one in particular can summarize for the whole ("someone imparticular who will somewherise for the whole anyhow," *FW* 602.07–08). To quote from "Oxen of the Sun": "Any object, intensely regarded, may be a gate of access to the incorruptible eon of the gods" (*U* 14.1166–67).

Uncle Charles Principle

The essence of analogy is proportion, and this can be discerned in various applications in Joyce's writings. Apart from the symmetries and correspondences with which his works are replete, there is proportional fitness also in the literary styles and methods employed. Language is tailored to the material described, especially to the character represented; the language used is fitted to the person who is described. This technique has been labeled the "Uncle Charles Principle" by Hugh Kenner,[83] a term suggested by the language adopted at the start of chapter 2 of *A Portrait:* "Every morning, therefore, uncle Charles repaired to his outhouse" (*P* II.12–13). The word "repaired" represents the idiosyncratic language Uncle Charles himself would use. Kenner explains: "The Uncle Charles Principle entails writing about someone much as that someone would choose to be written about."[84] This stylistic technique is itself as ancient as Homer, as Plato observed in the *Republic:* "When he delivers a speech as if he were someone else, shall we not say that he then assimilates thereby his own diction as far as possible to that of the person whom he announces as about to speak?"[85] We might say of Homer: "how cutely to copy all their various styles of signature" (*FW* 181.15).

Aristotle in the *Rhetoric* prescribes a similar adaptation between style and content: "A different style suits each genre."[86] In the *Poetics,* he notes that the language of tragedy needs to be embellished by a variety of artistic ornament, "the several kinds being found in separate parts of the play."[87] He refers to it as ἀρετή λέξεως (*aretê lexeôs*), "virtue of the word": the appropriate trope must be found for the function at hand. Each character and each mood requires its own voice. "Every talk has his stay" (*FW* 597.19). The "Uncle Charles Principle" is thus no more than a time-honored literary strategy employed by Homer, endorsed by Plato and Aristotle, and recommended throughout the centuries. Coleridge expressed it in an unacknowledged borrowing, which he translated from August Wilhelm Schlegel: "No work of true genius dares want its appropriate form."[88] Something akin is affirmed in *Finnegans Wake:* "Now, to be on anew and basking again in the panaroma of all flores of speech" (*FW* 143.03–04).

Besides the idiosyncratic speech of Uncle Charles, the entire language of *A Portrait* follows the technique of fitting language to character. The inner life of Stephen Dedalus is recounted in language suited to his age and development. His earliest thoughts, though profound, are expressed with naive simplicity; as he matures, there is explicit use of advanced philosophical concepts. Likewise in *Ulysses,* Stephen's solitary reflections are voiced in the high-flown cerebrations of an overactive mind. In "Oxen of the Sun," the gestation of the child in the womb is reflected in parallel with the historical evolution of the English language.[89] The extraordinary soliloquy of "Penelope" corresponds to the mind and mental processes of Molly Bloom, as does the opening sentence of "The Dead": "Lily, the caretaker's daughter, was literally run off her feet."[90]

Eloise Knowlton remarks on the Aristotelian quality of this narrational strategy:

> If *A Portrait*'s matter is the acquisition and use of language, it is also its manner. Stephen and style emerge together, in a teleological trajectory that leads, in a familiar *ricorso,* back to the author of *A Portrait:* the mature author James Joyce. If the narrative voice is not quite Stephen's, it closely parallels his acquisition and mastery of language. This may be the crux of the book's believability: that style, in true Aristotelian fashion, conforms to its object, performing an impersonation that reproduces on the level of "author" something more like the discourse of the character than we are used to. This is one of Joyce's most effective tricks of verisimilitude: in a story about growth, about maturation, the prose and its object interact and grow together.[91]

"Word Known to All Men": Love the Analogical Center of *Ulysses*

The Turkish writer Orhan Pamuk suggests that as its deepest locus and focus, every novel has a "secret center" that animates the work in its entirety, a cohering principle that remains unspoken.[92] It inspires the author and unconsciously guides the reader: "The center of the novel is like a light whose source remains ambiguous but which nonetheless illuminates the whole forest—every tree, every path, the clearings we have left behind, the glades we are heading toward, the thorny bushes, and the darkest, most impenetrable undergrowth."[93] Such a center, it could be argued, functions as a radical and radial focus conferring a unifying depth similar to—analogous to—the focal point of attributive analogy in metaphysics. We have seen Joyce's penchant for unity and cohesion but may still ask if there is a deeper unitive core and motif in his works.

There is a clear unity in both *Dubliners* and *A Portrait*. Later, we shall discuss *Finnegans Wake.* Manifestly, there is unity in *Ulysses:* superficially that of the timespan between daybreak and nightfall, and more deeply in the intermingled actions and thoughts of its protagonists, as well as emblematic figures from earliest literature and human history. Is there a further "secret center" that inspires the work? If such a motif exists, the most likely hypothesis is that it is the "word known to all men." That word is "love," now confirmed by the restoration of a critical passage in "Scylla and

Charybdis." Brenda Maddox goes so far as to suggest that "the new lines offer grounds for reinterpreting the meaning of the book."[94] If we are to look for an overall principle of unity in Joyce's work as a whole, we might pursue the suggestion proposed by Richard Ellmann in his introduction to the Gabler edition of *Ulysses*, in which he emphasizes the centrality of love.[95]

This cryptic phrase occurs strategically on three occasions in *Ulysses*. In "Proteus," we read:

> Touch me. Soft eyes. Soft soft soft hand. I am lonely here. O, touch me soon, now. **What is that word known to all men**? I am quiet here alone. Sad too. Touch, touch me. (*U* 3.434–36)

In "Scylla and Charybdis," the phrase recurs in a dialogue concerning the love of father for daughter in Shakespeare's plays, a discussion that extends to granddaughters:

> Will any man love the daughter if he has not loved the mother?
> [. . .]
> **—Will he not see reborn in her, with the memory of his own youth added, another image?**
> **Do you know what you are talking about? Love, yes. Word known to all men.** *Amor vero aliquid alicui bonum vult unde et ea quae concupiscimus* . . . (*U* 9.427–31)

The words in bold were restored by Hans Walter Gabler; the emendation, while not universally accepted, has been unanimously recognized as the most important in the critical edition. It is significant that the motif is referred to Aquinas; it privileges him with an insight regarding the ultimate, most meaningful, and deepest universal desire of human nature. The phrase is an amalgam from two sentences in the *Contra Gentiles*. The full text reads:

> Sciendum itaque quod, cum aliae operationes animae sint circa unum solum obiectum, solus amor ad duo obiecta ferri videtur. Per hoc enim quod intelligimus vel gaudemus, ad aliquod obiectum aliqualiter nos habere oportet: **amor vero aliquid alicui vult**, hoc enim amare dicimur cui aliquod **bonum** volumus, secundum modum praedictum. **Unde et ea quae concupiscimus**, simpliciter quidem et proprie desiderare dicimur, non autem amare, sed potius nos ipsos,

quibus ea concupiscimus: et ex hoc ipsa per accidens et improprie dicuntur amari. (*CG* 1, 91)

The passage has been translated as follows:

> Accordingly it must be observed that while other operations of the soul are about one object only, love alone appears to be directed to a twofold object. For if we understand or rejoice, it follows that we are referred somehow to some object: whereas **love wills something to someone**, since we are said to love that to which we **will some good**, in the way aforesaid. Hence **when we want a thing**, we are said simply and properly to **desire it**, and not to love it, but rather to love ourselves for whom we want it: and in consequence we are said to love it accidentally and improperly.[96]

Joyce was familiar with the *Contra Gentiles* of Aquinas. A little later in "Scylla and Charybdis," we read another quotation from the work (to which I will presently return), followed by Stephen's reference to Saint Thomas "whose gorbellied works I enjoy reading in the original" (*U* 9.778–79). Joyce had in his library in Trieste not only a copy of the Latin text of the *Contra Gentiles* but also the impressive, large folio edition of an abridged translation by Joseph Rickaby, S.J., which he purchased between October 1, 1913, and May 9, 1914.[97]

Commenting on the borrowing in "Scylla and Charybdis," Ellmann refers to the "rather tortured Latin, which uses the vocabulary of Thomas Aquinas." The tortured character of the Latin results from Joyce's unsuitable juxtaposition of words rather than the Latin of Aquinas, which, as Joyce observed, was a model of lucidity. Ellmann translates the text as a complete sentence: "Love truly wishes some good to another and therefore we all desire it." I believe this is incorrect as it ignores the relative pronoun "*quae.*" Stephen's reflection is tentative and tails off as if he is uncertain of the words. The text is more accurately translated: "Love truly wishes some good to someone, and therefore the things we desire . . ."

The chapter of the *Contra Gentiles* from which Stephen's words are excerpted treats of divine love: *Quod in Deo sit amor.* Aquinas explains that to love is to will the good of the beloved. Love is a unitive power, since those who love are joined to that which they love. All things, he states, are united in their desire of the good as they strive instinctively to imitate divine goodness. "There is in God not only a true love, but also a most perfect and a most enduring love."[98] Pure and selfless love is proper to God alone; Aquinas distinguishes in the case of humans between the selfless love of friendship (*amor amicitiae*) and instrumental love, which desires things not for their own sake but for our benefit (*amor concupiscentiae*): this is the distinction referred to in Stephen's truncated quotation.[99]

In affirming the primacy of *amor amicitiae*, Aquinas adopted Aristotle's definition of friend as "one who wishes, and promotes by action, the real or apparent good of another for that other's sake; or one who wishes the existence and preservation of his friend for the friend's sake." Significant for our present context is Aristotle's comment: "This is the feeling of mothers towards their children."[100]

The third instance of the "word known to all men" occurs in "Circe," when Stephen encounters his mother's ghost (a reenactment of Ulysses's meeting with his mother in Hades). Stephen is reminded that he sang for his mother the song "Who goes with Fergus?" referring to the mystery of love that inevitably is pierced with pain:

THE MOTHER: (A green rill of bile trickling from a side of her mouth.) You sang that song to me. *Love's bitter mystery.*
STEPHEN: (Eagerly.) **Tell me the word, mother, if you know now. The word known to all men.**
THE MOTHER: Who saved you the night you jumped into the train at Dalkey with Paddy Lee? Who had pity for you when you were sad among the strangers? Prayer is all powerful. Prayer for the suffering souls in the Ursuline manual, and forty days' indulgence. Repent, Stephen.
[. . .]
THE MOTHER: I pray for you in my other world. Get Dilly to make you that boiled rice every night after your brain work. Years and years I loved you, O my son, my firstborn, when you lay in my womb. (*U* 15.4189–203)

This poignant meeting is foreshadowed in "Nestor," when Stephen reflects: "*Amor matris:* subjective and objective genitive" (*U* 2.165–66). Observing his awkward pupil, Cyril Sargent, he ponders the power of a mother's love for her child: "Ugly and futile: lean neck and thick hair and a stain of ink, a snail's bed. Yet someone had loved him, borne him in her arms and in her heart. But for her the race of the world would have trampled him underfoot, a squashed boneless snail. She had loved his weak watery blood drained from her own. Was that then real? The only true thing in life?" (*U*

2.139–43). The powerful statement that a mother's love is the one true reality is repeated in "Scylla and Charybdis," where paternal love is disparagingly dismissed: "*Amor matris,* subjective and objective genitive, may be the only true thing in life. Paternity may be a legal fiction. Who is the father of any son that any son should love him or he any son?" (*U* 9.842–45). Even the grammar of the double genitive, love by a mother, and love for a mother, emphasizes the contrast. A father's only link in nature is "an instant of blind rut" (*U* 9.859), a brutal contrast with the caring and tender love described by Stephen's mother in "Circe." The indubitable reality of maternal love was already affirmed in *A Portrait* by Stephen's friend Cranly: "Whatever else is unsure in this stinking dunghill of a world a mother's love is not. [. . .] whatever she feels, it, at least, must be real." (*P* V.2398–401)

The topic of love is raised a second time in "Scylla and Charybdis" (separately from the "word known to all men"), when Stephen reflects on one of Aquinas's arguments against marriage between close relatives: "*Amplius. In societate humana hoc est maxime necessarium ut sit amicitia inter multos*"[101] (*U* 9.770–71). Don Gifford states in *Ulysses Annotated* that the source of the quotation is unknown.[102] It is from *Contra Gentiles* (3, 125), the work of Aquinas that Stephen enjoyed reading in the original (*U* 9.778–79), In translation, the phrase reads: "Moreover, in human society it is most necessary that there be friendship among many people."[103] Stephen tells his friends with a smile that St. Thomas "likens [incest] in his wise and curious way to an avarice of the emotions" (*U* 9.780–81). The phrase "avarice of the emotions" seems to be Joyce's; avarice, in Aquinas's vocabulary, means greed or covetousness in general but can, in a general sense, refer to a wider variety of vices.

Not only Stephen but also Bloom also seems imbued with the spirit of love. In the unpleasant surroundings of Barney Kiernan's pub, he likewise affirms that love is the only real thing in life:

—But it's no use, says he. Force, hatred, history, all that. That's not life for men and women, insult and hatred. And everybody knows that it's the very opposite of that that is really life.
—What? says Alf.
—Love, says Bloom. I mean the opposite of hatred.
—[. . .]
—A new apostle to the gentiles, says the citizen. Universal love.
—Well, says John Wyse. Isn't that what we're told. Love your neighbour.

—That chap? says the citizen. Beggar my neighbour is his motto.
Love, moya! He's a nice pattern of a Romeo and Juliet.
Love loves to love. Nurse loves the new chemist. Constable 14 A loves
Mary Kelly. Gerty MacDowell loves the boy that has the bicycle. M.
B. loves a fair gentleman. Li Chi Han lovey up kissy Cha Pu Chow.
Jumbo, the elephant, loves Alice, the elephant. Old Mr Verschoyle
with the ear trumpet loves old Mrs Verschoyle with the turnedin eye.
The man in the brown macintosh loves a lady who is dead. His Maj-
esty the King loves Her Majesty the Queen. Mrs Norman W. Tupper
loves officer Taylor. You love a certain person. And this person loves
that other person because everybody loves somebody but God loves
everybody. (*U* 12.1481–501)

The last lines, reflections of one of the narrators, are an obvious parody
and mockery, which is somewhat puzzling. Ellmann refers to it as "twad-
dle," noting that "it parodies not only Bloom but Joyce's master Dante, and
Dante's master, Thomas Aquinas," and the latter's assertion in the *Summa
Theologiae* that "God is love and loves all things." Ellmann explains, however: "It is the kind of parody that protects seriousness by immediately going away from intensity. Love cannot be discussed without peril, but Bloom
has nobly named it."[104]

Ellmann suggests: "The larger implications of *Ulysses* follow from the
accord of Bloom and Stephen about love."[105] He points out Joyce's reticence
to make the theme fully explicit: "Joyce is of course wary of stating so distinctly as Virgil does to Dante in *The Divine Comedy* his conception of love
as the omnipresent force in the universe. [. . .] But allowing for the obliq-
uity necessary to preserve the novel from didacticism or sentimentality, we
perceive that the word known to the whole book is love in its various forms,
sexual, paternal, filial, brotherly, and by extension social. It is so glossed by
Stephen, Bloom, and Molly."[106] The theme of love in Dante, needless to say,
antedates Virgil, pointing to Aristotle's *Metaphysics* and the personification
of his Prime Mover as "*l'amor che move il sole e l'altre stelle,*" the final words
of the *Divina Commedia* so admired by Joyce.[107] The theme of divine love
was the *causa movens* of Aquinas's nine-million-word corpus.

In his action and adventure, Odysseus was polytropic, but he had a
single focus in mind: to return to Ithaca. In Aristotelian terms, his voyage
was *pros hen* (πρὸς ἕν), it had a solitary goal. Joyce's language is polytropic,
but just as "being is said in many ways (πολλαχῶς / *pollachôs*),"[108] there

is a commanding unity. Analogy provides the controlling and ordering principle.

I propose as a possible unifying motif the *idée mère,* a conceivable "secret center" of *Ulysses,* the instinct, emotion, and ideal of love in its multifarious, miscellaneous, multiple modes and manifestations. The following curious assertion by Joyce in his notes to *Exiles* perhaps belies this hypothesis: "Love (understood as the desire of good for another) is in fact so unnatural a phenomenon that it can scarcely repeat itself."[109] He recognizes that it is a high demand, a tall order.

The most explicit expression of universal love to be found in Joyce's writings is the universal panorama presented in *A Portrait:*

> But he could no longer disbelieve in the reality of love since God Himself had loved his individual soul with divine love from all eternity. Gradually, as his soul was enriched with spiritual knowledge, he saw the whole world forming one vast symmetrical expression of God's power and love. Life became a divine gift for every moment and sensation of which, were it even the sight of a single leaf hanging on the twig of a tree, his soul should praise and thank the Giver. The world for all its solid substance and complexity no longer existed for his soul save as a theorem of divine power and love and universality. (*P* IV.92–105)

In the previous paragraph, we are told that Stephen had found it difficult to accept "the simple fact that God had loved his soul from all eternity, for ages before the world itself had existed" (*P* IV.76–78). In the earlier part of the novel, we read that the sixteen-year-old Stephen, preparing for his confession, had made love the focus of his resolve to amend: "He would love his neighbour. He would love God Who had made and loved him. He would kneel and pray with others and be happy. God would look down on him and on them and would love them" (*P* III.1449–52). He later confesses: "I tried to love God. [. . .] It seems now I failed" (*P* V.2356).

Here we have the equivalent of a universal analogy of attribution, which was Aquinas's answer to the ancient question of the One and the Many. Aristotle limited the analogy of attribution to the categories of individual substances; at the universal level he perceived countless proportionalities but did not rise above a universal pluralism. Aquinas combined analogy of proportionality with the analogy of attribution and forged a synoptic, synthetic, and panoramic vision of universal reality that was both horizontally unified and vertically grounded. This was the Thomist worldview into which Joyce was initiated and to which implicitly he lent allegiance until he relinquished the Catholic faith. Its categories and perspectives, however, defined his mental outlook for good. The Aristotelian/Thomist perspective provides the reader with an invaluable key to understanding how he interpreted the world and reshaped it in his artistic (re-)creation.

Unity in Diversity: Totality and Analogy

The themes of order and chaos, unity and diversity, resurface at many points in the interpretation of Joyce's work. It was these same questions that gave the original impetus to Greek philosophy and sustained its development through the golden period of Plato and Aristotle. The need to unify the data of experience is embedded deeply in the human mind. Joyce was also concerned with the relation between art and reality: how life is transformed, transfigured, and transmuted through the creative process. He was fascinated by correspondences, the most fundamental of which is that between knowledge and reality. He confronted the question of order and reality: is the universe a cosmos, chaos, or "chaosmos"? All art deals somehow with order, either as it traces the patterns underlying the disparate data of experience or displaces and supplants given structures with newly arranged categories. Joyce at different periods practiced both. The tension, order *versus* disorder, was a tacit touchstone in all his writings.

The relationship of unity and diversity, order and chaos, is as crucial for literature as it is for philosophy. The literary response may be different, but it employs many of the same categories and concepts. Joyce, as Aristotle, believed in an ordered universe but sought to discover novel, unperceived levels of relationship—and, increasingly, anti-relationship. In his final masterpiece, *Finnegans Wake,* he remolded the universe by reconfiguring the grand order, controverting the inner structure of language, the vehicle that shuttles between thought and reality.

The unity of *Finnegans Wake* is not readily identified. It is a knotted totality operating at many layers blending reality, illusion, dream, and myth. It thrives in a multiplicity of meanings, complicated ambiguities, and multiple homonymies. The author, however, is always in control and the work never collapses in confusion. It is a multifarious cipher that hints at a totality somewhere beyond reason and imagination: "Time's Finist Joke. Putting Allspace in a Notshall" (*FW* 455.29). To a question from the editor of *Vanity Fair* regarding *Finnegans Wake,* "Are the sketches in it to be consecutive and interrelated?," Joyce replied: "It is all consecutive and interrelated" (*LIII*, 193n8). Behind the jocose and playful language ("hilariohoot windup"), he affirmed the "*isce et ille* equals of opposites, evolved by a onesame power of nature or of spirit, *iste*, as the sole condition and means of its himund-her manifestation and polarised for reunion by the symphysis [Gk '*sun*' + '*phusis*' = with + nature] of their antipathies" (*FW* 92.07–11).[110]

H. G. Wells described *A Portrait* as "a mosaic of jagged fragments that does altogether render with extreme completeness the growth of a rather secretive, imaginative boy in Dublin."[111] In *Ulysses*, Joyce expanded the jagged mosaic into a kaleidoscope of the entire city in its daily life composed of myriad concrete experiences and encounters. *Finnegans Wake* was the "collideorscape" (*FW* 143.28) that attempted the seeming impossible task of integrating the entire scope of human history.

Joyce had a deep impulse for totality, unity, and order; he aimed at "totalisating" all human reality and experience (*FW* 29.33). This triple impulse translates further into a passion for simultaneity: the desire to know, experience, and possess all things in the simplicity of a single moment. Joyce remarked to Jacques Mercanton that in *Ulysses* "there is no past, no future; everything flows in an eternal present."[112] This sense of simultaneity is a further reflection of the soul's universal capacity for all things, plenitude, totality. Such simplicity is beyond human experience: it is tantamount to eternity itself, defined classically by Boethius as "the whole, simultaneous and perfect possession of endless life" (*interminabilis vitae tota simul et perfecta possessio*), a definition cited by Aquinas and which Joyce may well have read or heard. T. S. Eliot adverts to this motif, as recorded in his notes for a class on Joyce at Harvard on April 18, 1933: "*The Synchronisation*. Several periods of time and several planes of reality at once. Strong historical sense, and of everything happening at once."[113] Joyce's mind had a touch of what Byron referred to as "altogethery."[114] Borrowing from Joyce's lecture on the Renaissance (*OCPW* 189–90), we may say that listening—rather than reading—to the ebb and flux of *Finnegans Wake*, we hear the tumult of voices reverberate as sounds of the sea that resonate in a shell against the ear.

The unity of *Finnegans Wake* is that of an inverted order but is nonetheless discernible. The goal of unity is not abandoned but assumes a different optic in which "the traits featuring the chiaroscuro coalesce, their contrarieties eliminated" (*FW* 107.29–30). The principle of noncontradiction is not so much abandoned as overcome; cognitive dissonance is sublimated in a cipher of higher harmony. In an attempt at wit, Buck Mulligan flippantly quotes Walt Whitman's "Song of Myself": "Contradiction. Do I contradict myself? Very well then, I contradict myself" (*U* 1.517). Buck's wit is threadbare and void of wisdom. A deeper and more authentic intuition, a desire for reconciliation—mildly reminiscent of Hegel—permeates *Finnegans Wake*. An appetite for new forms of discourse and dialectic, unity in contradiction, hangs in the air, aptly conveyed by Whitman's parenthetical assertion: "I am large, I contain multitudes." One commentator observes: "The directing principle of Hegel's thought as it was seen by Pater's contemporaries was the search for unity, for a principle of perception to which the differences and contradictions in experience might be reduced."[115] Joyce struggled to reconcile competing ingredients. He wrote to Harriet Shaw Weaver: "I work as much as I can because these are not fragments but active elements and when they are more and a little older they will begin to fuse of themselves" (*LI* 205).

Referring to "Work in Progress," Joyce confided in Adolf Hoffmeister: "I am thinking of a beautiful book where each occasion, each situation, and each word will choose its own language. In all the languages and dialects of the world there is only one word that exactly designates a given thing. I have actually tried it in *Ulysses,* although there it gives the impression of being a jumble of quotations and a superfluous stuffing of foreign words."[116] He stated that in his new work, he would use eighteen languages: "Each word has the charm of a living thing and each living thing is plastic."[117] In fact, he used many more than the projected eighteen.

As Bruce Stewart remarks, "Joyce kept in mind the possibility of 'totalisating' human history through literary art in such a way as to capture the 'whatness' of humanity in a multi-lingual, trans-temporal, cross-cultural, polysemous text constructed by means that fly in the face of 'cutanddry grammar and go-ahead plot,' as Joyce himself averred."[118] Writing in 1929, Thomas McGreevy already perceived in *Work in Progress* an integrity and order, a Thomistic "beauty and fitness" equal to that of *Ulysses*. He remarks:

> Mr. Joyce has created a language that is necessary precisely to give beauty and fitness to his new work. [. . .] Obviously, the book being still unfinished, one may not yet say that it is marked by beauty and fitness as a whole. But every chapter and passage that has appeared is so admirably realized and so related to every other chapter and passage that one has no doubts that when the end does come the author of *Ulysses* will have justified himself again as a prose writer who combines a wellnigh flawless sense of the significance of words with

a power to construct on a scale scarcely equalled in English literature since the Renaissance, not even by the author of *Paradise Lost*. The splendour of order, to use Saint Thomas's phrase, has not been the dominating characteristic of modern English prose and it is partly because the quality was demonstrated on a vast scale in *Ulysses* that that book marked a literary revolution. And signs are not absent that, in spite of the difficulty of having to invent a new language as he writes, Mr. Joyce in his latest work has lost nothing of his amazing power in this direction.[119]

Joyce himself observed the philosophic progression within his own work: "Each of my books is a book about Dublin. Dublin is a city of scarcely three hundred thousand population, but it has become the universal city of my work. *Portrait* was the picture of my spiritual self. *Ulysses* transformed individual impressions and emotions to give them general significance. "Work in Progress" has a significance completely above reality; transcending humans, things, senses, and entering the realm of complete abstraction. [. . .] It is a simultaneous action, represented by the novel's circular construction."[120] *Finnegans Wake* is a labyrinth of three dimensions that extends through diverging times and disparate space, yet it returns upon itself to recapture in ever-widening circles and deeper-running well-springs the whole, with "every person, place and thing in the chaosmos of Alle anyway connected" (*FW* 118.21–22). Joyce shared the insight of Coleridge: "*All* is an endless, fleeting abstraction; *the Whole* is a reality."[121]

Circularity and repeated allusion, with recurring echoes, had been applied by Joyce to effect the totalizing dynamic that carried *Ulysses* forward. The supporting scaffolding of circulation and recirculation, a concept adopted from Vico,[122] provides the "structuring principle" for *Finnegans Wake:* "The Vico road goes round and round to meet where terms begin. Still onappealed to by the cycles and unappalled by the recoursers we feel all serene, never you fret, as regards our dutyful cask" (*FW* 452.21–24). The "commodius vicus of recirculation" (*FW* 3.2) is not a vicious cycle but a fruitful projection from which can be metaphorically extrapolated, by synecdoche or metonymy, Mercator-like, the map of universal geography and the panorama of history as it synchronically unfolds.

Whereas *Ulysses* is the book that celebrates daytime life and existence, *Finnegans Wake* ponders the brooding world of nocturnal obscurity (*FW* 411.08: "nightmaze"). In *Ulysses,* what Mario Vargas Llosa calls the "metaphysical greyness of Dublin"[123] becomes lambent in the epiphanies of

Stephen, illuminated by the categories of Aristotle. In *Finnegans Wake*, the shadows of darkness prevail; the lucid grammar of existence is no longer valid. In a letter to Joyce, Harriet Shaw Weaver referred to the "darkness and unintelligibilities of your deliberately-entangled language system" (*JJII* 590). This was possibly in reply to what Joyce had written to her some weeks earlier: "One great part of every human existence is passed in a state which cannot be rendered sensible by the use of wideawake language, cutanddry grammar and goahead plot" (*LIII* 146). As Sheldon Brivic remarks, "Causality is carried beyond Aristotle in the *Wake*."[124] The logic of identity, of "either/or," ruled by the law of noncontradiction, is subsumed into a unity of opposites governed by the paradox of "both/and." Aristotle gives way to Nicholas of Cusa: "Now let the centuple celves of my egourge as Micholas de Cusack calls them, [. . .] by the coincidance of their contraries reamalgamerge in that indentity of indiscernibles" (*FW* 49.33–50.01) Florry Talbot, lady of Nighttown, proclaims the profound axiom of psychoanalytic theory: "Dreams go by contraries" (*U* 15.3928). Seamus Deane states: "In the *Wake*, the Greeks don't get a look-in,"[125] which accounts for its antinomical and paralogical language and style.

Joyce's philosophical inspiration for the scheme of *Finnegans Wake* comes not from Aristotle but from Giambattista Vico,[126] for whom human history is a recurring cycle of divine and human epochs, and from Giordano Bruno's emphasis upon "interdependent and mutually-generating opposites."[127] Motivated by a desire to mold an entirely new order, Joyce sought to invert the old certainties. The first of these is the principle of noncontradiction. His two guides in this enterprise, Vico and Bruno, offer different perspectives. With his theory of history as cyclic return, Vico sanctioned the identity of personality in change; this, it should be emphasized, is entirely consistent with Aristotle's view of the self, the diversity of whose accidents (especially action) is rooted in the unity of substance.[128]

Over a period of many years, Joyce seems to have been fascinated by Bruno's notion of the coincidence of contraries ("Them boys is so contrairy," *FW* 620.12–13). Reviewing a book on the Italian thinker in 1903, he wrote: "Is it not strange, then, that Coleridge should have set him down a dualist, a later Heraclitus, and should have represented him as saying in effect: 'Every power in nature or in spirit must evolve an opposite as the sole condition and means of its manifestation; and every opposition is, therefore, a tendency to reunion.'?" (*CW* 133–34).[129] Writing in April 1912, he noted: "Giordano Bruno himself says that all power, whether in nature or the spirit, must create an opposing power without which man cannot fulfil himself, and he adds that in every such separation there is a tendency towards a reunion."[130] In 1925, he adopted Coleridge's formula to describe Bruno's system: "His philosophy is a kind of dualism—every power in nature must evolve an opposite in order to realise itself and opposition brings reunion etc etc." (*LI* 226). The following year, in May 1926, while recommending the writings of Bruno and Vico to Harriet Shaw Weaver, he cautioned: "I would not pay overmuch attention to these theories, beyond using them for all they are worth, but they have gradually forced themselves on me through circumstances of my own life" (*LI* 241).

Of the theories of the two Italian philosophers, both of whom held great fascination for Joyce, Bruno's notion of identity in contrariety is especially problematic; he pushed to extremes Cusanus's notion of coinciding opposites, transferring it from the divine transcendence to the natural world. Bruno was almost unique in his attempt to prescribe for the possible unity of contradictory opposites.[131] For classical philosophy, the idea of opposites coinciding only made sense as a hypothetical, methodic strategy of human inquiry: the mind progresses dialectically, plotting counterpoints as it moves forward in discovery. In reality, analogy provides the only access to a harmonious synthesis. Analogical similarity enables the mind to transcend duality and diversity, to perceive unity in bipolar tension; opposites are not rescinded nor tension abandoned but provide instead mutual enrichment, allowing reciprocal comparisons and the exchange of attributes.

F. Scott Fitzgerald famously began his short story *The Crack-Up* (1936) with "the general observation—the test of a first-rate intelligence is the ability to hold two opposed ideas in the mind at the same time, and still retain the ability to function." He does not say "two contradictory ideas," since contradiction abolishes not only all discourse but also every action. Just as we cannot simultaneously affirm and deny, we cannot simultaneously perform opposing actions. We do not fill and empty the jug at the same time. It may be possible to accommodate two opposed ideas ("two thinks at a time," *FW* 583.07) and still function, but we cannot simultaneously perform contrary or opposed actions or assert contradictory statements. Tim Conley contends that "Joyce posits a 'world mind' capable of sustaining total contradictions and containing multitudes of meaning."[132] This might conceivably be "the Great Sommboddy within the Omniboss" (*FW* 415.16–17).

Although Joyce was not directly concerned with the unconscious, remarking that it was already a sufficient challenge to understand the conscious, he (unconsciously, as it were), delved into the unconscious world in *Finnegans Wake*. An early advertisement for the German translation of

Ulysses cited a "serious critic" on Joyce's approach: "He knows that the ultimate spiritual decision is metaphysical-religious by nature." It continues: "But what is absolutely new about Joyce is that he has given the interconnectedness and correspondence of our conscious and unconscious thinking the fullest artistic expression. In the process the last veil shrouding our natural instincts was dropped."[133]

*   *   *

Joyce's aspiration was to have the entire universe, culture, history, thought, and tradition refracted through the genius of a single mind. By his own declaration, this desire for wholeness motivated his master novel: "[*A Portrait*] was the book of my youth but *Ulysses* is the book of my maturity. Youth is a time of torment in which we can see nothing clearly, but in *Ulysses,* I have seen life clearly, I think, and as a whole."[134] The same impulse was the moving force behind *Finnegans Wake.* Many of Joyce's iterations reveal his deep aspiration for complete and total knowledge and the abolition of nondualistic thinking. Although we are rooted in a material world, there is no limitation to the human desire or capacity for knowledge. One particularly dense passage of *FW* conveys the tension and the duality at the core of the human self in its subconscious search for innermost spiritual selfhood. Seeking to innerly embrace the cosmic totality, it remains bound to the material division of the here and now while aspiring with rage to a higher level where knower and known are united in a single "allself": "eysolt of binnoculises memostinmust egotum sabcunsciously senses upers the deprofundity of multimathematical immaterialities wherebejubers in the pancosmic urge the allimmanence of that which Itself is Itself Alone [. . .] exteriorises on this ourherenow plane in disunited solod likeward and gushious bodies with (science, say!) perilwhitened passionpanting pugnoplangent intuitions of reunited selfdom (murky whey, abstrew adim!) in the higherdimissional selfless Allself" (*FW* 394.30–95.02). This is the impossible goal of human knowledge. With his assertion that "the soul is somehow all things," Aristotle sets the horizon, but our human condition sets the limit. Through symbol, metaphor, and projection alone can we attain a symbolic image of the totality in which all contradictions, contrarieties and limitations are sublimated, negated, and transcended. To the artist alone is it possible to metaphorically attain what cannot be achieved by reason. This was the achievement of *Finnegans Wake.*

Aristotle is punned in *Finnegans Wake* as "aristotaller." He was indeed a "totaller," and Joyce rightly recognizes the encyclopedic range of his investigations. As Donald Phillip Verene points out, Aristotle was "the first philosopher to write a treatise on every part of human knowledge to create the forms of all the sciences."[135] With his ambition to symbolically embrace in *Finnegans Wake* the vast comprehension of all reality, knowledge, and human experience, Joyce emulates Aristotle's totalizing spirit. Verene characterizes *Finnegans Wake* as a "book of wisdom," "one that [contains], in principle and to an extent in fact, all that there is, a truth of the whole."[136] The ambition is identical, the methods different. The impulse behind *Finnegans Wake,* as the inspiration also for *Ulysses,* was the Aristotelian insight that "the soul is in a sense all things" and the desire to grasp universal truth rationally or symbolically. Karl Jaspers's definition of the "great man" applies alike to Aristotle and James Joyce: "The great man is like a reflection of the whole of Being, infinitely interpretable. He is its mirror or its representative. Only what relates to the totality of existence, to the entirety of the world can acquire greatness. Greatness is there where the actuality through such reflection becomes a symbol of the whole."[137] To James Joyce may be attributed the accolade of "myriadminded man," said by Coleridge of William Shakespeare (*U* 9.768). Fred Higginson has remarked: "What makes *Finnegans Wake* a great book is that there is in it as much of these pleasurable workings of one man's mind—the whole of it, shoddy and magnificent both—as has ever been put between covers."[138] The pleasure is all the greater when Joyce's work is viewed as a whole and valued as a sustained attempt to engage with the great questions of human nature and reality.

6

Beauty

Joyce's Thomist Aesthetics

As an undergraduate, Joyce gleaned an elementary knowledge of Aquinas's theory of beauty in a variety of ways: by attending lectures at University College and meetings of the Academy of St. Thomas, by reading some basic texts of Aquinas and exposés in student manuals, and through discussion with classmates who studied philosophy. He was familiar with the definition "*pulchra sunt quae visa placent*" ("those things are beautiful which, when seen, are pleasing"), as well as the requisites *integritas, consonantia,* and *claritas.* His interpretation and application of these concepts was idiosyncratic, diverging significantly from Aquinas's understanding. The resulting theory might be described either as a careless distortion or an ingenious invention—a daring enterprise for a young author dealing with the subtle and elusive concepts of a domain between introspection and objectivity, an apparent "maze out of which we cannot escape" (*P* V.1229). But to suggest he "distorted" Aquinas's aesthetics assumes that Joyce intended his theory as a faithful elaboration of the definitions he had cited, whereas these were more likely a cue for his independent theorizing. To measure and evaluate this divergence, we must first examine the philosophical concepts inherent in Aquinas's definitions. It should be noted that the core of Thomist aesthetics is to be found in Plato, who already defined the beautiful as "that which is pleasing through hearing and sight"; Plato also emphasized the aspects of splendor and symmetry. For Aristotle, the central marks of beauty were order, symmetry, and a magnitude appropriate to the integrity of the object. These elements were transmitted to Aquinas through Cicero, Augustine, Pseudo-Dionysius, and his master, Albert the Great.[1]

*   *   *

On March 20, 1903, Joyce wrote to his mother from Paris: "My book of songs will be published in the spring of 1907. My first comedy about five

years later. My 'Esthetic' about five years later again."[2] In fact, Joyce made his
first serious attempt at an aesthetic theory within eighteen months of that
letter to his mother. He conceived the embryonic elements of his aesthetic
theory in November 1904, shortly after settling on the Adriatic coast. Over
a period of ten days, Joyce inscribed in his notebook three elaborate reflections on aspects of aesthetic experience, namely, goodness, beauty, and
apprehension. These formulations constitute his clearest attempt to codify
an aesthetic theory.[3] Joyce pursued his aesthetic program from the start of
his literary activity, which confirms how important it was that he elaborate
his own theory of beauty. We are told in *Stephen Hero* that, helped by his
younger brother Maurice, Stephen was actively engaged "in the building of
an entire science of esthetic" (*SH* 36).[4]

The aim of this chapter is to analyze, textually and philosophically, Joyce's
earliest reflections on beauty, penned at the age of twenty-two shortly after
his arrival in Pola. Joyce's entries in the celebrated "Early Commonplace
Book"[5]—three paragraphs and a quotation—go right to the heart of Aquinas's aesthetics. In the first paragraph, he discusses the relationship between the fundamental concepts of goodness, beauty, and truth, unaware
that he was considering the "transcendental" properties of reality, discussion of which dates back to Plato. In the second paragraph, he examines
Aquinas's definition of beauty, "Pulchra sunt quae visa placent."[6] In the
third paragraph, titled "The Act of Apprehension," he offers an original
and intelligent interpretation (albeit somewhat confused) of the activity of
aesthetic cognition. Two pages later, we read the following entry:

—Ad pulcritudinem [*sic*] tria requiruntur: integritas, consonantia et
claritas—
S. Thomas Aquinas.

For beauty there are three requisites: wholeness, symmetry and
radiance.[7]

In his personal reflections, two of which were headed by quotations from
Aquinas, Joyce set out, presumably to his own satisfaction, important principles—epistemological, philosophical, and psychological—of his aesthetic
theory. He subsequently incorporated these into his autobiographical novels, *Stephen Hero* and *A Portrait*. The fact that they are signed with the
flourish of the young author's initials indicates that, rather than attribute
a naive theory to Stephen Dedalus as part of a strategy to portray him
ironically (as some commentators have claimed), Joyce is ad idem with

his literary alter ego on fundamental matters of aesthetic theory. We may therefore assess Joyce's conclusions against Aquinas's own thought, since it was explicitly in response—perhaps in reaction—to the latter that he elaborated his aesthetic.

Joyce's explanation of his own aesthetics is significant—that is, if we take his account of Stephen as largely autobiographical. In *Stephen Hero,* we read: "His Esthetic was in the main 'applied Aquinas,' and he set it forth plainly with a naïf air of discovering novelties" (*SH* 77). This characterization is reaffirmed in *A Portrait:* "MacAlister, answered Stephen, would call my esthetic theory applied Aquinas" (*P* V.1267–68). Joyce's debt to Aquinas is confirmed in *Stephen Hero:* "But, during the formulation of his artistic creed, had he not found item after item upheld for him in advance by the greatest and most orthodox doctor of the Church [. . .] while the entire theory, in accordance with which his entire artistic life was shaped, arose most conveniently for his purpose out of the mass of Catholic theology?" (*SH* 205). This Thomistic inclination is further confirmed in *A Portrait,* where we are informed of Stephen's "search for the essence of beauty amid the spectral words of Aristotle and Aquinas" (*P* V.87–88). In *A Portrait,* we have a particularly emphatic confirmation of Stephen's attachment to Aquinas: "It wounded him to think that he would never be but a shy guest at the feast of the world's culture and that the monkish learning, in terms of which he was striving to forge out an esthetic philosophy, was held no higher by the age he lived in than the subtle and curious jargons of heraldry and falconry" (*P* V.206–11).

Aquinas nowhere expounds a theory of aesthetics as such. His remarks on beauty are spare, obiter dicta on the margin of other topics. St. Thomas would share the surprise of Father Butt, who "confessed that it was a new sensation for him to hear Thomas Aquinas quoted as an authority on esthetic philosophy" (*SH* 104).[8] Such an aesthetic must be constructed from elements drawn from his psychology, his theory of knowledge, as well as his metaphysics and theology. Joyce's elaboration of an aesthetic from the sparse pronouncements of Thomas Aquinas is testament either to his creativity or naiveté. At minimum, it evinces significant allegiance.

The clearest illustrations of Joyce's stated reliance upon Aquinas are the carefully honed declarations composed under the banner of two statements from St. Thomas on the nature of goodness and beauty. These are of primary importance for the investigation into Joyce's definition of beauty and their subsequent application in his creative writings. In particular, they are the basis for the doctrine later expounded in *Stephen Hero* and *A Portrait.*

The two phrases are: "*Bonum est in quod tendit appetitus*" ("The good is that towards which the appetite tends") and "*Pulchra sunt quae visa placent*" ("Beautiful things are those which please when seen"). A third reflection, titled "The Act of Apprehension," is Joyce's explication of the cognitive process involved in the aesthetic experience. These paragraphs will be presently examined.

In his reflections, Joyce not only considered Aquinas's definition of beauty by effect ("*quod visum placet*") and his causal-analytic definition ("*tria requiruntur*") but also discussed the relation between truth, goodness, and beauty. These latter three were first identified by Plato as the supreme properties of the transcendent cause, the universal principle of *Agathon* (the Good), which surpasses worldly existence;[9] his Neoplatonist follower Plotinus added unity. In medieval philosophy, the theory of "transcendentals" was developed, according to which these properties, together with "thing" and "something," were recognized as belonging to all beings simply by virtue of their existence. The characteristics of truth, goodness, beauty, unity, and thing are not restricted to any level or category of being; they "transcend" all boundaries and are affirmed of everything that is.

The definition of beauty as that which pleases, constituted by order and splendor, is already found in Plato, who at the transcendent level equates beauty with truth and goodness while concretely analyzing it in terms of symmetry and luster. In *A Portrait*, Stephen asserts: "Plato, I believe, said that beauty is the splendour of truth. I don't think that it has a meaning, but the true and the beautiful are akin." While the definition of beauty as *splendor veri* is in fact nowhere to be found in Plato, it captures one of his most profound intuitions.[10] And despite Stephen's hesitation, the notion had for Plato a valuable and significant meaning.

Aquinas on Beauty

St. Thomas never composed a treatise on beauty, but, as William Noon rightly remarks, "The concept of the beautiful is given generous and serious attention in the metaphysics of Aquinas."[11] His theory of beauty is well summed up in the statements quoted by Joyce: "*Pulchra sunt quae visa placent*," and "*Ad pulchritudinem tria requiruntur: integritas, consonantia, et claritas*." In the first statement, he notes how we empirically recognize and affirm things to be beautiful; in the second, he identifies the properties that constitute their beauty.

Despite the frequency with which it is quoted as the most complete statement of Aquinas's aesthetic theory, it is notable that in his entire oeuvre there is only a single occurrence of his famous tripartite definition of beauty as constituted by integrity, harmony, and splendor. The context may also be unexpected. Joyce was probably unaware that Aquinas's definition occurs in a discussion of the characteristics attributed specifically to each of the divine persons of the Blessed Trinity. In *ST* I 39, 8, Aquinas considers the statement of St. Hilary regarding the Trinity: "Nothing can be found lacking in that supreme union which embraces, in Father, Son and Holy Spirit: infinity in the eternal, his likeness in his image, our enjoyment in the gift."[12] Referring to the epithet "*species*," as applied to the second member of the Trinity, Aquinas comments:

> Species or beauty (*pulchritudo*) has a likeness to the property of the Son. For beauty includes three conditions, "integrity" or "perfection," since those things which are impaired are by the very fact ugly; due "proportion" or "harmony"; and lastly, "brightness" or "clarity," whence things are called beautiful which have a bright color.
>
> The first of these has a likeness to the property of the Son, inasmuch as he as Son has in himself truly and perfectly the nature of the Father (*habens in se vere et perfecte naturam patris*).
>
> The second agrees with the Son's property, inasmuch as he is the express image of the Father (*imago expressa patris*). Hence we see that an image is said to be beautiful, if it perfectly represents even an ugly thing (*aliqua imago dicitur esse pulchra, si perfecte repraesentat rem, quamvis turpem*). This is indicated by Augustine when he says "Where there exists wondrous proportion and primal equality" (*tanta convenientia, et prima aequalitas*).
>
> The third agrees with the property of the Son, as the Word, which is the light and splendor of the intellect (*quidem lux est, et splendor intellectus*), as Damascene says. Augustine alludes to the same when he says: "As the perfect Word, not wanting in anything, and, so to speak, the art of the omnipotent God."[13]

It is noteworthy that Aquinas at the outset introduces *pulchritudo* as the equivalent of *species*. With characteristic creative insight, Aquinas justifies Hilary's attribution of beauty to the second person of the Holy Trinity. Christ enjoys integrity or perfection because he "has in himself truly and perfectly the nature of the Father" (*habens in se vere et perfecte naturam patris*). He has due "proportion" or "harmony" because "he is the express image of the Father" (*imago expressa patris*) and has splendor or *claritas* because he is *Logos* or Word, signifying "light and splendor of the intellect" (*quidem lux est, et splendor intellectus*).

Since the discussion here is theological, the application of beauty is necessarily analogical; each of the three requisites is affirmed in a unique sense of the second divine person. Aquinas's concept of beauty is nevertheless grounded in sense experience. The empirical origin of the concept of integrity is clear when he states that "those things which are impaired are by the very fact ugly"; the sensible origin of harmony is illustrated by the statement that "an image is said to be beautiful, if it perfectly represents even an ugly thing." That *claritas* is a prerequisite is illustrated by an example from the sense recognition that "things are called beautiful which have a bright color." It has on occasion been suggested that Aquinas first conceived beauty a priori as a preeminent perfection of God and applied it derivatively to creatures. This would run counter to his epistemology and entire philosophical method; his writings abound with examples of perfection, harmony, and clarity perceived in the physical world. Beauty is analogous, to be recognized and affirmed variously in diverse contexts and at distinct levels.

Out of a total of twenty-six texts where he defines beauty, only on a single occasion does Aquinas list all of these three requirements. Most frequently, he specifies only harmony and splendor, characteristics emphasized by Pseudo-Dionysius. In one of his earliest works, a commentary on the *Sentences* of Peter Lombard, he omits integrity but includes magnitude as stipulated by Aristotle. He states:

> According to Dionysius, two things come together in the account of beauty, namely, consonance and luster. For he says that God is the cause of all beauty insofar as he is the cause of consonance and luster, just as we say that men are beautiful who have proportionate members and a resplendent color. To these two the Philosopher adds a third when he says that beauty does not exist except in a sizable body; so that small men can be called well-proportioned and pretty, but not beautiful.[14]

It has been suggested that magnitude is the equivalent of *integritas*,[15] but this is not convincing; the concepts of *magnitudo* and *integritas* are quite distinct. By *integritas,* Aquinas clearly means *perfectio*.[16]

Joyce's Interpretation of Thomist Beauty

One perceptive Thomist writer, Immanuel Chapman, has remarked:

> Joyce's depth as an artist made him aware of certain aspects of St
> Thomas' aesthetics missed by some of the philosophers, but unfor-
> tunately the truths which Joyce the artist saw were often marred by
> distortions introduced by Joyce the man, who was often in tragic con-
> flict with the artist in him. In interpreting St Thomas's three requisites
> of the beautiful, Stephen Dedalus, who images so perfectly Joyce, his
> artificer, glimpses certain truths which he obscures and combines in
> the wrong way. It is not surprising that the existential meanings of the
> requirements of the beautiful are missed altogether.[17]

Joyce's handling of Aquinas's texts was far from simple. In the following
pages, I will consider his treatment of the texts and his analysis of beauty in
A Portrait. I begin with his interpretation of the quotations from Aquinas,
which serve as mottos for two of his reflections, entered into his notebook
in 1904 and later incorporated into *A Portrait*. These reflections deal with
the transcendental properties of beauty, goodness, and truth. Joyce's interpretation of these passages is revealing of his own attempt to construct an
aesthetics and reveal also how well, or not so well, he understood Aquinas.
I will suggest that, although he alludes to supreme categories of being, Joyce
was not conversant with the theory of transcendentals.[18] He was aware of
pulchrum, bonum, and *verum* as higher values discussed in metaphysics
and aesthetics; he had also acquired the notions of "one" and "thing" (employed in his interpretation of *integritas* and *claritas*) but was not familiar
with Aquinas's theory of the convertibility of all five with being (*ens*).

At the start of his *Disputed Question on Truth (De Veritate)*, Aquinas examines the widest possible concepts that may be applied to things. The first
positive, absolute, concept we have of anything directly in itself, without
reference to anything else, is that it is a "thing" (*res*). Considered absolutely
in itself negatively, it is subsequently conceived as undivided, that is, as one
(*unum*). Aquinas then proceeds to examine how a being is conceived in
relation to what is other than itself. Firstly, it is affirmed to be distinct from
every other being—as "some other thing"; this is suitably conveyed in Latin
as "*aliquid,*" not so clearly when translated into English as "something."
Aquinas explains: "Just as a being is said to be *one* in so far as it is without
division in itself, so it is said to be *something* in so far as it is divided from
others."[19] Continuing his enumeration of transcendental concepts, Aquinas

considers the *correspondence* each being can have with what is other than itself—and here we arrive at two of the concepts that are of particular interest to Joyce's understanding of beauty. Correspondence with all things is possible only if there exists an entity with a capacity for such universal relationship, and this exactly is what Aristotle meant when he said that "the soul is in a way all things."[20] The universal openness of the soul (*anima*) was adopted by Aquinas as a fundamental axiom of his metaphysical psychology. The soul, through its twin powers of appetite and intellect, is the unique entity that relates to all things. Goodness is the correspondence of being to the will; truth is the correspondence of being to the intellect. Insofar as every being is a potential object of the will, it is called "good"; insofar as each being is affirmed as real, it is objectively true. Goodness is conformity of reality with the will; truth is conformity with the intellect.

There is much debate among Thomist scholars as to whether *pulchrum* is also a transcendental property of all things. Aquinas repeatedly states that beauty is convertible with being and goodness, but in his rationale for the origin of transcendental notions, beauty is not listed. He emphasizes, however, that *pulchrum* and *bonum* are identical, *pulchrum* having the additional quality of pleasure consequent upon cognition. Joyce's paragraphs of November 7 and 15 deal precisely with the relations between the notions of *bonum, verum,* and *pulchrum*. He was concerned with what he believed to be a false dichotomy between beauty and truth. The texts clearly show that for Aquinas, rather than a dichotomy, there is identity between truth and beauty.

Thematically, the three speculations of November 1904 are closely related, dealing as they do with beauty, goodness, and truth. It is significant, as it was unfortunate, that Joyce did not realize that in the two paragraphs of the *Summa* upon which he relies, Aquinas provides a comprehensive summary of the mutual and integral relationship between the three properties. He sets them in clear comparison and contrast, precisely in order to bring out their fundamental identity. Aquinas articulated a solution to the (nonexistent) problem raised by Joyce.

The motto for Joyce's first reflection (November 7, 1904)[21] reads: *Bonum est in quod tendit appetitus.* It is a slightly modified phrase from *ST* I, 16 regarding the desirability of goodness. Here is Aquinas's text, with significant words in bold:

As the good denotes that towards which the appetite tends, so the true denotes that towards which the intellect tends.' (*Sicut bonum* *nominat id in quod tendit appetitus, ita verum nominat id in quod tendit intellectus.*) Now there is this difference between the appetite and the intellect, or any knowledge whatsoever, that knowledge is according as the thing known is in the knower, whilst appetite is according as the desirer tends towards the thing desired. Thus the term of the appetite, namely good, is in the thing desirable, and the term of knowledge, namely true, is in the intellect itself.[22]

The epigraph for Joyce's second reflection—*Pulchra sunt quae visa placent*[23]—is a slight variation upon a phrase from Question 5 of *ST* I, in which Aquinas defines goodness and beauty in their mutual relation. Significant is that, immediately before the definition of beauty cited by Joyce, he gives his standard definition of the good:

> Beauty and good in a subject are the same, for they are based upon the same thing, namely, the form; and consequently good is praised as beauty. But they differ logically, for goodness properly relates to the appetite, since **the good is what all things desire (*est enim bonum quod omnia appetunt*)**, and therefore it has the aspect of an end, for the appetite is a kind of movement towards a thing. On the other hand, beauty relates to the knowing power; **for those things are called beautiful which please when seen** (*pulchrum autem respicit vim cognoscitivam, **pulchra enim dicuntur quae visa placent***). Hence beauty consists in due proportion, for the senses delight in things duly proportioned, as in what is after their own kind—because even sense is a sort of reason, just as is every cognitive faculty. Now since knowledge is by assimilation, and likeness relates to form, beauty properly belongs to the nature of a formal cause.[24]

Had Joyce been conversant with these passages, he would have recognized that Aquinas's purpose in *ST* I, 5, 4 ad 1 was precisely to define goodness and beauty in relation to one another and to explain their fundamental identity. The text clarifies those relationships that were uppermost in Joyce's mind. Instead of conflict or opposition, there was for Aquinas fundamental identity between goodness, truth, and beauty.

The fact that Joyce elaborates separately, at a distance of over a week, upon the phrases *Bonum est in quod tendit appetitus* and *Pulchra sunt quae visa placent* might suggest to the reader that they were also expounded separately by Aquinas, whereas in fact the two principles (one in a slightly different formula) occur in the same short paragraph, the point of which is precisely to distinguish notionally between the concepts of *bonum* and *pulchrum,* goodness and beauty, while emphasizing their identity in reality. In Question 5, Aquinas juxtaposes to the definition of beauty his standard definition of the good: *Bonum est quod omnia appetunt.* He does this for the purpose of mutual definition and to highlight the specific distinctions of goodness and beauty. Were he familiar with the text, Joyce would have immediately grasped the relevance of the contrast expressed by Aquinas: goodness refers to the will or appetite; beauty refers to the cognitive power (*Bonum proprie respicit appetitum* [. . .] *Pulchrum autem respicit vim cognoscitivam*).[25] Aquinas explicitly clarifies the very relation investigated by Joyce: goodness attracts the will that desires possession of the reality known; beauty is the attraction that is fulfilled simply by cognition.

Joyce's first reflection begins: "The good is that towards the possession of which an appetite tends: the good is the desirable. The true and the beautiful are the most persistent orders of the desirable." In Question 5 of *ST* I, St. Thomas situates the good vis-à-vis beauty; in Question 16, he situates goodness vis-à-vis truth.[26] He integrates the will's desire for the good, the intellect's tendency toward truth, and the beauty of things that please when known. Joyce viewed these as separate phenomena; for Aquinas, they were integrally linked. He defined goodness and beauty in their mutual relationship—goodness as goal of the will, truth as goal of the intellect, and beauty as the crowning delight of both.

Aquinas, like Joyce, was concerned with the relation between goodness, beauty, and truth. These three ultimates had been the focus of profound speculation as early as Plato and developed into the highly sophisticated theory of the so-called transcendentals, that is, those characteristics pertaining to all things simply by virtue of the fundamental richness of their existence. Because of their importance as pristine characteristics of divine being, Aquinas examines their relations in the early questions of the *Summa Theologiae.* Joyce was familiar with single phrases from Aquinas but did not grasp his overall perspective. It is evident that he had no first-hand knowledge of Aquinas's most important systematic work; otherwise, he would have recognized that these early pages treated precisely those fundamental notions—*bonum, pulchrum, verum*—with which he was so keenly preoccupied.

Two "errors" in Joyce's quotation from Aquinas on beauty confirm that he was working from memory rather than with the text. Instead of "*Pulchra **dicuntur** quae visa placent*" ("those things *are called beautiful* which please when seen"), he wrote "*Pulcra* [*sic*] **sunt** *quae visa placent*" ("those things *are beautiful* which please when seen"). The misspelling of "*pulchra*" is in itself unimportant—an "error" that persisted through later citations (*SH* 95, *P* V.420). The interpretive implications of the other error—substituting "*dicuntur*" for "*sunt*"—are not inconsiderable. Joyce's rendition, "*Pulchra sunt quae visa placent,*" implies that those things that please when seen are essentially beautiful; beauty would thus depend on subjective factors—on seeing and the pleasure of seeing. By defining beauty as that which is *called* beautiful, Aquinas assigns a role to the subjective element of experience but does not make beauty depend entirely on experience. As Hugh Bredin points out, "Aquinas is not talking here about the conditions of beauty in itself. What he says is that certain subjective factors induce us to *call* something beautiful, so that, essentially, he is talking about the experience of beauty, and about linguistic usage—but not about beauty itself."[27]

A further detail of considerable textual interest may be noted. The heading for Joyce's first reflection is a slight variation of the phrase from Question 16. Aquinas wrote: "*Bonum nominat id in quod tendit appetitus*"; Joyce cites: "*Bonum est in quod tendit appetitus.*" This formulation of the principle occurs only once in the entire corpus of Aquinas.[28] Joyce cites it almost verbatim, and probably from memory.[29] Apart from this single exception, St. Thomas always defines the good as "that which all things desire" (*bonum est quod omnia appetunt*); this is a simple translation of the definition from the start of Aristotle's *Nicomachean Ethics*. Aquinas refers to Aristotle's definition more than thirty times throughout his writings. Joyce may have encountered the expression in the *Summa Contra Gentiles,* which he read closely; it is twice cited in a chapter devoted to the allied principle that "every agent acts for a good" (*omne agens agit propter bonum*).[30] It is remarkable, therefore, that instead of the more common formulation, Joyce chose as his slogan the once-off formulation of *ST* I, q. 16: "*Bonum nominat id in quod tendit appetitus.*"[31] We may only speculate where Joyce encountered this single occurrence of the formula but can understand his preference for the more active meaning that it conveys, expressing the tendency of the individual appetite, rather than making a universal generalization.

An intriguing detail may also be observed in Joyce's second reflection on aesthetics (November 15, 1904), written under the heading "*Pulchra sunt quae visa placent.*" He begins by stating, "Those things are beautiful the *apprehension* of which pleases." This happens to be an almost exact translation of an alternative formulation of Aquinas's definition, given much later in the *Summa:* "*Pulchrum autem dicatur id cuius ipsa apprehensio placet*" ("Let that be called beauty, the very *apprehension* of which pleases").[32]

This confirms the surmise that Joyce was familiar with the most common phrases from Aquinas on beauty but appears not to have known any of his works other than the *Contra Gentiles*. I conjecture that he acquired these phrases in the conversations on aesthetics in which he frequently engaged with the professor of Italian at University College.

We may perhaps glimpse the motivation for Joyce's interest in goodness and beauty from the account in *Stephen Hero* of the young student's discussions on aesthetics with the Italian professor, named here as "Father Artifoni." We are told: "The Italian lessons often extended beyond the hour and much less grammar and literature was discussed than philosophy" (*SH* 169). It would be legitimate to suppose that the Italian Jesuit, educated with Latin manuals replete with appropriate citations, may have been the source for Joyce's telegrammatic knowledge of Aquinas's notions of beauty. The following passage is most relevant, as it reproduces verbatim a significant portion of Joyce's text from Pola; it suggests moreover the problem in Joyce/Stephen's mind to which it responds:

> They argued very acutely of the beautiful and the good. Stephen wished to amend or to clarify scholastic terminology: a contrast between the good and the beautiful was not necessary. Aquinas had defined the good as that towards the possession of which an appetite tended, the desirable. But the true and the beautiful were desirable, were the highest, most persistent orders of the desirable, truth being desired by the intellectual appetite which was appeased by the most satisfying relations of the intelligible, beauty being desired by the esthetic appetite which was appeased by the most satisfying relations of the sensible. (*SH* 170–71)

The distinction presented to the Italian professor in *Stephen Hero* between truth, which is beheld by the intellectual appetite, and beauty, beheld by the aesthetic appetite, is omitted from their conversation in *A Portrait*. It is included, however, in Stephen's conversation with Lynch, with significant changes:

> Plato, I believe, said that beauty is the splendour of truth. I don't think that it has a meaning, but the true and the beautiful are akin. Truth is beheld by the intellect which is appeased by the most satisfying relations of the intelligible; beauty is beheld by the imagination which is appeased by the most satisfying relations of the sensible. The first step in the direction of truth is to understand the frame and scope of the

intellect itself, to comprehend the act itself of intellection. Aristotle's entire system of philosophy rests upon his book of psychology and that, I think, rests on his statement that the same attribute cannot at the same time and in the same connexion belong to and not belong to the same subject. The first step in the direction of beauty is to understand the frame and scope of the imagination, to comprehend the act itself of esthetic apprehension. (*P* V.1207–21)[33]

Rather than the "esthetic appetite" (the term used in the Pola text), Stephen now states that beauty is beheld by the *imagination,* which is appeased by the most satisfying relations of the sensible. Another novelty in Stephen's explanation of the distinction between intellect and imagination is the assertion that each faculty must be investigated as a pre-requirement to the knowledge of their respective objects. This is an intriguing addition, one that is alien to the psychology and epistemology of both Aristotle and Aquinas, according to whom the faculty can only be observed in the activity of knowing its object. Their position is accurately stated in *Stephen Hero:* "The apprehensive faculty must be scrutinised in action" (*SH* 212). We discuss below Stephen's distinction between intellect and imagination or aesthetic appetite as apprehending separately beauty and truth.

We are told in *Stephen Hero* that "Father Artifoni admired very much the wholehearted manner in which Stephen vivified philosophic generalizations and encouraged the young man to write a treatise on esthetic" (*SH* 171). Joyce's real-life Italian teacher was Fr. [Charles] Ghezzi, S.J. His real name is given in *A Portrait,* in a greatly curtailed account of their conversation, which makes no reference to their discussion of aesthetics but which retains the rebellious riposte: "He said Bruno was a terrible heretic. I said he was terribly burned" (*P* V.2650–51).[34] If we are to believe the fictional account, Ghezzi's spirit of open debate and questioning suited the young artist.[35] We may infer that he was an important source for Joyce's philosophic and aesthetic ideas. While Joyce never formally studied Aquinas at University College, philosophy—those of Aristotle and St. Thomas—dominated Italian classes with Fr. Ghezzi. Eugene Sheehy depicts the scene: "Joyce and I both attended the same class for Italian. Our lecturer was an Italian Jesuit named Father Ghezzi. [. . .] My function in the class was to listen to Father Ghezzi and Joyce discuss philosophy and literature in Italian, and, for all I could understand of the dialogue, I would have been more profitably engaged in taking high dives from the spring-board at the Forty-foot Hole in Sandycove."[36]

It would be interesting to speculate what different conclusions Joyce might have reached, had he before him at Pola the full text from which he quoted. He would have seen that for Aquinas goodness and beauty are identical, responding to different faculties of the soul. Instead of contrast or dichotomy, there is fundamental unity in reality; they differ only in their relation to our spiritual capacities. As is obvious from this passage, for Aquinas more than for Joyce, "a contrast between the good and the beautiful was not necessary" (*SH* 170). In reality, they were identical; they differ only according to how we perceive and appreciate them.

Truth and Beauty as Desired

If Joyce's intention was to avoid a dichotomy between the beautiful and the good, it remains to be seen how successful was his attempt to harmonize them. Having defined the good as the desirable, he continues his first reflection: "The true and the beautiful are the most persistent orders of the desirable." He regards both truth and beauty as desirable goods. In a certain sense, he is stating the obvious. Aquinas quotes Aristotle as saying that truth is the good of the intellect.[37] (Aristotle begins his *Metaphysics* with the phrase "All men by nature desire to know.")[38] Superficially, this is adequate, but there is a deeper and more universal connection between goodness, truth, and beauty. According to Aquinas's doctrine of transcendentals, every being, precisely as real, has the property of truth insofar as it can be the object of knowledge; inasmuch as it can be the goal of desire, it has the quality of goodness; insofar as it can elicit pleasure when known, it has the character of beauty. It is *reality* that is desirable and therefore good; it is *reality* that is the goal of knowledge, and therefore true; it is *reality* that is beautiful because it gives pleasure when known.

In Joyce's Pola reflections, there is thus a confusion between reality, or being as such, as the primary datum of experience and the different aspects or points of view under which it is experienced. Having endorsed Aquinas's definition of the good as "that towards the possession of which an appetite tends" ("the desirable"), Joyce proceeds to list truth and beauty among the things that are desired as "good": "Truth is desired by the intellectual appetite which is appeased by the most satisfying relations of the intelligible; beauty is desired by the esthetic appetite which is appeased by the most satisfying relations of the sensible." There is here a confusion between the senses of "being" (*ens*), "goodness" (*bonum*), "truth" (*verum*), and "beauty" (*pulchrum*) in their basic meaning. It is true that beauty and truth may be labeled good, but only in a secondary or supervenient sense; ontologically, they do not subsist in themselves but abide in the relationship between concrete entities and the capacities of intellect and will. *Bonum* is reality as it satisfies the will; *verum* is the real in its agreement with intellect; *pulchrum* is the real insofar as it delights the intellect when cognized. Truth and beauty are without doubt desirable, but they are not what is primarily intended by Aquinas's definition of the good as that which is desired.

Aquinas's Theory of Cognition

To disentangle the somewhat confused terminology used by Joyce in elaborating the fundamental principles of Aquinas, it is necessary to outline the latter's interpretation of knowledge. As understood by Thomist epistemology, cognition involves a number of distinct stages: sensation, perception, imagination, the concept, and judgment. We might say it germinates in sensation, buds in perception, blossoms in the concept, and bears fruit in judgment. The first single complete act of knowledge, however, is the judgment in which the mind or intellect affirms or denies what is known. In judgment alone is cognition complete and truth attained, when the mind pronounces upon what it knows.

In the philosophical theory of knowledge, "judgment" is a mildly technical term for the pronouncement made by the mind upon what it knows. The earlier stages of sense perception and concept formation are necessary for knowledge but are not sufficient of themselves: they do not attain truth as such. In sense perception, an object in the external world stimulates one or more of the sense organs and impresses certain characteristics in a dematerialized manner upon the sense faculty. Elaborating upon what is thus given, the intellect forms a concept of what is experienced. But neither the percept nor the concept is knowledge properly speaking. Only when intellect reflectively affirms the identity of its knowledge with the object is the cognitive operation completed and truth attained. Aquinas states: "It is because the intellect reflects upon itself that it knows the truth."[39] The intellect knows truth insofar as it reflects upon itself and its affirmative commitment to what is known. Truth is therefore attained in recognition: the recognition of the relation between what I know and the manner in which I know it. To know that I know is to know that something really is as I assert it to be. In this recognition, the mind attains fulfillment. In that sense, Joyce is correct in suggesting that the most complete form of cognition (which he calls "apprehension," incorrectly, as we will see) involves satisfaction. This is confirmed by Aquinas in *ST* I 16, 1,[40] from which Joyce takes the epigraph to his first reflection. Discussing the nature of truth as it applies to God, Aquinas asks if truth resides in the thing known or the intellect. He states that whereas the good is that toward which the appetite tends, truth is that toward which the intellect tends: *sicut bonum nominat id in quod tendit appetitus, ita verum nominat id in quod tendit intellectus.* The intellect has an innate tendency toward the truth; it is the appetite for truth. Only in the moment of recognition does it achieve *quietas,* its quietude or satisfaction.

Divorce of Sense and Intellect, Beauty and Truth

It is interesting to observe the progress of Joyce's ideas and their articulation in the three consecutive Pola reflections on aesthetics. The first entry includes the following brief statement: "Beauty is desired by the esthetic appetite which is appeased by the most satisfying relations of the sensible." This is expanded in the second: "Those things are beautiful the apprehension of which pleases. Therefore beauty is that quality of a sensible object in virtue of which its apprehension pleases or satisfies the esthetic appetite which desires to apprehend the most satisfying relations of the sensible." Having, in the first entry, distinguished between truth and beauty as instances of the good (and hence as objects, respectively, of the intellectual appetite and the aesthetic appetite), Joyce proceeds, in the second entry, to consider beauty itself under the motto *"Pulchra sunt quae visa placent."* As already noted, his elaboration includes without acknowledgment Aquinas's alternative formulation of the same definition: *pulchrum dicatur id cuius ipsa apprehensio placet* ("Let that be called beautiful the very apprehension of which pleases").[41]

Retaining the plural of the phrase cited as his epigraph, Joyce translates: "Those things are beautiful the apprehension of which pleases." Aquinas's use of the word *apprehensio* perhaps explains Joyce's predilection for this term, which occurs fifteen times in the Pola paragraphs. Having defined beauty as that which pleases merely by its apprehension, the entire second entry is an attempt to explain the nature of this term, together with its attendant and constituent elements. In his second reflection, Joyce unambiguously restricts beauty to the domain of the sensible, making it the object of a supposedly unique and properly aesthetic appetite.

Joyce has his own strange ordering of the relation between truth and beauty. Confusion ensues when, pursuing his explanation of truth and beauty in terms of desire and goodness, he defines this distinction as one between intellect and sense: "Truth is desired by the intellectual appetite which is appeased by the most satisfying relations of the intelligible; beauty is desired by the esthetic appetite which is appeased by the most satisfying relations of the sensible." This arrangement inverts a number of items in the Thomist scheme, which Aquinas adopted from Aristotle. For Aquinas, there is no distinct "esthetic appetite," separate from the "intellectual appetite," "which is appeased by the most satisfying relations of the sensible." Beauty is always apprehended by intellect. While this occurs most frequently in cooperation with the imagination and senses, beauty in itself may also be exclusively intellectual and suprasensible. While human experience of beauty is always sensitivo-intellectual, we may analogically affirm the beauty of God.

In *A Portrait,* where the Pola reflections are reprised, the phrase "truth is beheld by the intellect" substitutes "truth is desired by the intellectual appetite"; the phrase "beauty is beheld by the imagination" replaces "beauty is desired by the esthetic appetite" (*P* V.1209–13). The first change is not greatly significant; the shift from the "esthetic appetite" to imagination, however, confirms that for Stephen beauty seems confined to sensible experience, since the imagination cannot grasp intellectual qualities.

For Aquinas, the intellect has a capacity for truth, which is fulfilled by the recognition of its agreement with affirmed reality. It is difficult to understand why Joyce limits truth to "the most satisfying relations of the intelligible," as distinct from the sensible. According to Aquinas, the real, precisely as real—including the sensible—is intelligible, although as mysterious, it may surpass our mental grasp. All being has the transcendental quality of truth (*verum*); the intellectual appetite is directed not simply toward intelligible relations but also toward reality itself, the ground of all intelligibility. Truth, as we have seen, is itself a relationship of agreement (*convenientia*) between intellect and reality; intellect affirms truth when it reflectively discerns a relationship of agreement between its knowledge and the thing itself: between how it conceives something and how the thing itself is.

Joyce's identification of the aesthetic appetite or imagination with the capacity for satisfactory sensible relations is perhaps to be explained by his recurrent reliance upon Aquinas's definition, which refers to things that are seen: *Pulchra sunt quae visa placent.* He elaborates, moreover, in words resemblant of Aquinas's alternative definition: "Those things are beautiful the apprehension of which pleases." While this would allow for beauty as something more than sensible, Joyce relates aesthetic pleasure to the grasp of sensible relations. We find an explanation of this misunderstanding in *A Portrait*. Referring to Aquinas, Stephen says: "He uses the word *visa* to cover esthetic apprehensions of all kinds, whether through sight or hearing or through any other avenue of apprehension" (*P* V.1197–98). He correctly assumes that *visa* is intended by Aquinas to embrace all sensible apprehension. Aquinas, however, goes further; using "*visa*" to refer to those things which please when known, he restricts beauty neither to the visible nor the sensible. To the question whether "light" is properly affirmed of spiritual realities, he quotes St. Ambrose, that "splendor" is one of those characteristics affirmed metaphorically of God.[42] Aquinas explains that while vision (*visio*) originally refers to the sensible act of sight, "since sight is the noblest and most trustworthy of the senses, the word is extended, in accordance with linguistic usage, to all cognition through the other senses [. . .] and ultimately to intellectual knowledge."[43]

Joyce contrasts the intellectual appetite, which seeks the most satisfying relations of the *intelligible,* with the aesthetic appetite, which aims to discern the most satisfying relations of the *sensible.* This contrast is open to multiple interpretations, and it is not clear what Joyce has in mind. Does he mean that the intellectual appetite is focused exclusively upon non-sensible realities and relationships? For Aquinas, however, the relations between physical beings and events are no less intelligible. My act of breaking a window, for example, establishes a physical relationship but is intelligible in terms of cause and effect, my free will, and my bad upbringing.

By contrasting the intellectual and aesthetic appetites by reference to the most satisfying relationships respectively of the intelligible and the sensible, Joyce introduces a false dualism between truth as the grasp of pleasing suprasensible relationships, and beauty as the apprehension of pleasing sensible relations. Why is this false? From the Thomist-Aristotelian point of view, the intellect grasps not only the suprasensible but also the sensible.[44] And beauty pertains not only to the most satisfying relations of the sensible but also to harmonious relations at every level of existence: Aquinas's primary interest is in beauty as a divine characteristic. It is true that our first experience of beauty comes through the senses, but our concept expands to apply to the nonphysical.[45] In the order of reality, spiritual beauty is primary, as it coincides with the intrinsic integrity, harmony, and splendor of divine being, which is the origin of the beauty of the created universe.

Joyce radically departs from his putative authority. Having cited two phrases from Aquinas (the explicit Latin quotation, and an unacknowledged translation of another Thomistic phrase), he states: "*Therefore* beauty is that quality of a sensible object in virtue of which its apprehension pleases or satisfies the esthetic appetite which desires to apprehend the most satisfying relations of the sensible." This conclusion is Joyce's inference, because it is far removed from Aquinas. For Thomas, there is no "intellectual appetite" or "sensible appetite"; there are intellectual and sensible capacities or powers to receive the realities that may be known. The will as a conjoined, but distinct, power of the individual motivates the person to seek knowledge, both sensible and intellectual. The pleasure that attends sensible and intellectual cognition is the blossom upon the actualization of the cognitive capacities.

Joyce distinguishes between the intellectual appetite, which has truth as its object, and the aesthetic appetite, which has beauty as its object. From the Thomist point of view this is a false contrast. The phrase in *ST* I 5, 4 that immediately precedes the words used by Joyce as the heading to his second reflection, reads: *Pulchrum autem respicit vim cognoscitivam.* Beauty relates to the knowing power; it thus must have some relationship with truth. There is no separate "esthetic appetite." A person may have a desire for beauty, but beauty is experienced through the selfsame faculty with which the person knows. Joyce's statement, "The true and the beautiful are spiritually possessed" is uncontroversial; for Aquinas, all experience, even that of sensation, is spiritual. In *A Portrait*, Joyce rejects as unaesthetic those emotions that are "not more than physical," since they are akin to the purely reflex action of the nervous system (*P* V.1139).

Apprehension

As already noted, the word "apprehension" and its cognates occur as many as fifteen times in the Pola reflections; in his second reflection, it occurs twelve times, while the third is titled "The Act of Apprehension." Why such importance and frequency? We can only speculate that Joyce may have encountered Aquinas's alternative definition of beauty, noted above, as that whose very apprehension pleases (*pulchrum dicatur id cuius ipsa apprehensio placet*).[46] Needless to say, for Aquinas, *apprehensio* is broader than *visio* and less obviously sense-related.

If Joyce had studied the required textbook for his second-year course in logic at University College, he would have been familiar with the philosophical meaning of the term "apprehension." In its widest sense, the word "apprehension" (from *ad,* to + *prehendere,* to seize) may denote any act of knowledge. Like its cognates "perception" and "conception," it depends upon the analogy between physically "taking hold of," or "seizing," an object and mentally "grasping" a thing's nature through intellectual intuition. In Scholastic philosophy, *apprehensio* received a particular meaning through the addition of the word *simplex*. In the definition of a textbook used in Joyce's student days, "Simple apprehension is the act of perceiving an object intellectually, without affirming or denying anything concerning it."[47] According to Aquinas, the intellect performs two distinct, successive, operations: apprehension and judgment. Through the first act, the intellect grasps a thing's nature, its essence or quiddity (*quidditas,* whatness).[48] In a second act of cognition, it affirms or denies something (*compositio et divisio*) about the object—its existence, or a particular characteristic. As already noted, this second act is termed "judgment," because the mind pronounces upon what is grasped through apprehension; in judgment, the act of cognition is completed and truth is achieved. Apprehension in itself is neither true nor false, since it makes no pronouncement; alternatively, we might say that it is always true, since the mind infallibly grasps at least some of the essential features of the object. Truth, however, in the strict sense, is attained when the intellect asserts its own acknowledged and self-reflected agreement with reality; this occurs in judgment.

Truth is more than spontaneous apprehension; it involves the further conscious affirmation of what has been apprehended. The sensation of beauty is the delight caused by that which pleases simply in its mere apprehension. This experience is direct, immediate, and spontaneous. It requires no reflection or analysis. We may of course investigate this experience and the objective and subjective conditions that make it possible. We may analyze the elements inherent in the object that stimulate the delight. We may conclude that it comports integrity, proportion, and clarity; this theoretical knowledge, however, is not itself a requisite for our enjoyment of the beautiful.

Aquinas frequently uses "apprehension" as synonymous with knowledge itself. He uses it on occasion to refer not only to intellectual knowledge but also to the initial activity of sense-perception and the intermediate stage of imagination. On one occasion, he remarks that "the apprehension of reason and imagination is of a higher order than the apprehension of the sense of touch."[49] Joyce also variously uses the word "apprehension" in a variety of senses, but without clarity or precision. His interpretations of apprehension in the second and third Pola reflections are particularly confused.

Joyce was clearly struggling to formulate his ideas—with some success, since the paragraph of November 16, 1904, is clearer and more succinct than the prolix deliberation of the previous day.[50] For the sake of both brevity and clarity, it is sufficient to consider this shorter text, which contains Joyce's essential conclusions. A continuing problem is that Joyce takes what are for Aristotle and Aquinas three related aspects of a single and dynamically progressive act of cognition to be separate activities: the initial act of simple perception, the moment of recognition, and the ensuing satisfaction.[51] We have seen that sense perception and the moment of intellection, in which the mind recognizes the nature of what is perceived, are distinct but inseparable stages in a single act of cognition. Joyce treats them not only as distinct but separate, and he posits yet another stage, namely, the activity of satisfaction. He proceeds to attribute to each activity its specific pleasure and degree of beauty. The confusion is multiple: the satisfaction of cognition is not distinct but rather identical with the act of recognition; moreover, beauty is grasped intellectually at the moment of recognition, rather than in the passivity of sensory experience. Recognition is at once the moment of aesthetic experience.[52] It is true that for Aristotle and Aquinas—here, Joyce has made their view his own—each activity is accompanied by its attendant pleasure.[53] But even though Aristotle states that since "the activities of the intellect differ from those of the senses, so also therefore do the pleasures that perfect them,"[54] he does not equate sensory pleasure with the experience of beauty.

The Language of Thomist Aesthetics

To formulate his aesthetics, Joyce made copious borrowings from Aquinas's terminology, which he reshaped to his own understanding. In his general definition of beauty, he deployed the concepts of goodness, beauty, and truth, unaware that these were the primary transcendental properties that may be affirmed interchangeably and universally of all beings. Expounding the requisites for beauty in the concrete (*integritas, consonantia, claritas*), he made reference to three further transcendentals, namely, "thing" (*res*) and its associated term "*quiddity*," "one" (*unum*), and "something" (*aliquid*).[55]

Aquinas regarded "thing" (*res*) as a transcendental concept that can be applied to all beings. Everything that exists has of necessity a definite content or mode of being; it embodies a particular kind. The first concept that we acquire when we cognitively respond to anything is "being," since what we first notice about anything is that it exists. Simultaneously, we register that it is a particular kind of "thing," with an individual determination. It is a firm or constant reality, possessing its own essence. While there are nu-anced differences between the two notions, *res* denotes an object's essence (*essentia*).[56] In his *General Metaphysics,* one of the philosophy textbooks in use at University College when Joyce was a student, John Rickaby cites Aquinas: "There is nothing affirmable of every being (*ens*) except its es-sence (*essentia*): and the latter is signified by the word *thing* (*res*), which differs from *being* (*ens*) in this, that *being* is a term derived from the act of existing (*ab actu essendi*), while *thing* expresses the quiddity or essence of being."[57] Rickaby cites Aquinas's early *Commentary on the Sentences:* "That is called simply a *thing* which has a definite, fixed nature (*habet esse ratum et firmum in natura*): but it is called *being* so far as it has existence."[58]

Having grasped the object positively as *res,* or "thing," possessing its own essence or quiddity, we may pronounce negatively in two ways on what is apprehended. This furnishes us with additional transcendental concepts. Affirming that it is undivided in itself, we form the transcendental concept of "one" (*unum*), which signifies that each thing is unified in itself. John Rickaby quotes Aquinas: "The 'one' is nothing but undivided being, for it adds to being only the negation of division."[59] Aquinas states: "'One' does not add any reality to being, only the negation of division, for 'one' means undivided being."[60] The transcendental *unum* denotes the absence of inter-nal division within a being, the undividedness that each being has through its act of existence. Proceeding further, by a second negative judgment, we may consider the object not as undivided in itself but as separate from every other being. This is the transcendental *aliquid—*"*aliud quid*"*—*"some other thing." It connotes a being as separate or divided off from other be-ings: it is "something else." As already observed, this is misleadingly ren-dered in conventional language as "something," which fails to convey the status of each being in its distinction from every other being. Aquinas sums up the distinction between *unum* and *aliquid:* "Just as a being is said to be *one* in so far as it is without division in itself, so it is said to be *something* in so far as it is divided from others."[61]

The transcendental terms *res, unum,* and *aliquid* are employed in Ste-phen's exposition of Aquinas's three specific requisites for beauty in *A Portrait.* Stephen also refers to an object's "quiddity," a term related to *res,* which is broadly synonymous with "essence." The term "*quidditas*" was coined in the twelfth century from the Latin particle *quid* ("what") to trans-late the awkward expression "*to ti ên einai*" ("what it was to be"), which Aristotle coined to designate the fundamental principle in virtue of which something is real (its *ousia* or "beingness"). In his earliest work, *On Being and Essence,* Aquinas wrote: "Since that by which a thing is constituted in its proper genus or species is what is signified by the definition expressing what the thing is, philosophers have taken to using the word *quiddity* for the word *essence.* The Philosopher frequently calls this the *what a thing was to be,* in other words, that by which a thing is a *what.*"[62] St. Thomas explained the nuances of the related terms "quiddity," "essence," "form," and "nature." Quiddity signifies the content of the definition, spontaneously apprehended when we initially experience an object. Essence is the being's deeper ontological principle, which is actualized by the act of being (*actus essendi*): "that through which and in which a being has its act or existing."[63] Closely related is form, the metaphysical principle that causes a thing to be what it is ("the determination of each thing"). Nature refers to an individual in its activity, "the essence of a thing as directed to its specific operation."

According to Aquinas, "the proper object of the human intellect, which is united to a body, is the quiddity or nature existing in corporeal matter (*quidditas sive natura in materia corporali*)."[64] Cognition is achieved through intellectual insight but is rooted in physical experience: "The object of our intellect in its present state is the quiddity of a material thing. . . . Quiddity is the primary and proper object of the intellect."[65] Reason is directed primarily to the universal forms of things, but it first grasps them as immersed in matter.[66] Quiddity is the first object of intellectual apprehension, and in this the intellect is infallible: "The proper object of the intellect is the quiddity of a material thing; and hence, properly speaking, the intellect is not at fault concerning this quiddity."[67] The proper objects of the intellect are the quiddities of material things (*quidditates rerum materialium*).[68] As Etienne Gilson summarizes, quiddity is "the essence apprehended by the intellect in the sensible datum."[69]

We can clarify the apprehension of beauty if we juxtapose the following statements by Aquinas: "The proper object of the human intellect is the quiddity of a material thing;"[70] and "Let that be called beautiful the very apprehension of which pleases."[71] Apprehension is the first act of the intellect, and when the apprehended object gives delight, we call it beautiful. According to Aquinas's understanding of aesthetic apprehension, the three aspects of *integritas, consonantia,* and *claritas* are given together and simultaneously with our grasp of what a thing is, its quiddity. The pleasure of beauty does not require that we first analyze the object, or consciously examine if it is complete, well-proportioned, and radiant. The intellect, presented with the sensible datum, spontaneously recognizes these qualities before analyzing them in detail. As Aquinas repeatedly affirms, the proper object of the intellect is the quiddity of individual sensible objects immersed in their material conditions. The abstractive power of intelligence (*intellectus*, "reading into") is one of insight, which figuratively "sees" if the sense-object is whole or deficient, if it is well composed or imbalanced, and if it presents itself clearly to the senses and hence is intelligible.

Having outlined Aquinas's theory regarding the apprehension of particular individual material objects (the first stage of knowledge), and the most universal concepts applied by the intellect to all things, we may proceed to evaluate Stephen's account of the cognition of beauty in the concrete. Stephen presents a lengthy analysis of beauty through his interpretation of the three characteristics contained in Aquinas's definition. It cannot be overstressed that the experience of beauty does not consist in analysis but rather in simple apprehension. Analysis does not replace or replicate the experience. According to Aquinas, those things are beautiful the mere apprehension of which gives delight. Nonetheless, it is possible to identify the elements that contribute to that experience.

Aesthetic Analysis in *A Portrait of the Artist as a Young Man*

We have already considered the more general aspects of the aesthetic theories presented in *A Portrait,* especially how the supreme concepts of beauty, truth, and goodness are related. When it comes to the experience of beautiful objects, Joyce makes heavy weather in his detailed analysis of the particular features that constitute beauty. His insights are, nevertheless, remarkably rich. We are now in a position to evaluate Stephen's analysis and application of Aquinas's famous statement "Ad pulchritudinem tria requiruntur, integritas, consonantia, claritas": "Three things are needed for beauty, wholeness, harmony and radiance."[72]

Having cited the definition, Stephen immediately suggests that wholeness, harmony, and radiance are "phases of apprehension" (*P* V.1348–49). As William J. Noon rightly points out, however, these "are conceived by Aquinas as qualities of things which the mind comes to know, not as 'stages' in the mind's own act of knowing."[73] As another commentator puts it, while Joyce makes the three things needed for beauty correspond to phases of aesthetic apprehension, "Aquinas, on the other hand, primarily considered the qualities of universal beauty as conditions for esthetic apprehension. Joyce misunderstood Aquinas; he mistook the preparation for the process, for the process itself. For Aquinas, integrity, consonance, and clarity were primarily existential qualities, stimulating the sense of the beholder. For

Joyce, integrity, consonance, and clarity exist primarily in the mind of the beholder as stages in the generation of the 'concept' of beauty."[74] Frank L. Kunkel expresses the Thomist point of view: "A beautiful being [. . .] presents within itself the concrescence of all three qualities only formally distinguished by reason."[75] For Aquinas, it is not a matter of phases but the instantaneous and simultaneous delight in the apprehension of three aspects in unison.

One might, however, suggest that in explaining the three aspects of beauty to Lynch as three successive phases, Joyce exhibits practical didactic insight. To reconfigure simultaneous and concurrent aspects as consecutive stages may be pedagogically helpful. Our aim, however, is to assess Stephen's analysis in light of St. Thomas, his cited authority. Here is the text to be discussed:

> Stephen pointed to a basket which a butcher's boy had slung inverted on his head.
> —Look at that basket, he said.
> —I see it, said Lynch.
> —In order to see that basket, said Stephen, your mind first of all separates the basket from the rest of the visible universe which is not the basket. The first phase of apprehension is a bounding line drawn about the object to be apprehended. An esthetic image is presented to us either in space or in time. What is audible is presented in time, what is visible is presented in space. But, temporal or spatial, the esthetic image is first luminously apprehended as selfbounded and selfcontained upon the immeasurable background of space or time which is not it. You apprehend it as *one* thing. You see it as one whole. You apprehend its wholeness. That is *integritas*. (*P* V.1353–67)

By separating the object out from everything that is not it, Stephen gives priority to *aliquid*, the object as something else. He next attributes to it the property of *unum*, which he views as the ground of wholeness or integrity. For Aquinas, however, integrity or wholeness belongs in the first place to the object as thing (*res*). As *res* it is indeed "selfbounded and selfcontained," but for it to be grasped as *res*, it is not necessary to first "separate the basket from the rest of the visible universe which is not the basket." It is as *res*, "thing," that I first apprehend the object. *Integritas* implies all three transcendental characteristics, *res* (thing), *unum* (thing), and *aliquid* (something); but of the three, *res* is primary.

Although Stephen employs Thomist language and claims to expound a

Thomistic analysis of beauty, his use of terms is at variance with Aquinas when he states that to apprehend the basket, the mind must first draw a line separating it from everything else. According to Aquinas, the intellect immediately grasps an object positively in itself, apprehending its quiddity, that is, its essence as present in material conditions. This is to grasp it as a thing (*res*). It is simultaneously grasped as one, although the explicit concept of unity requires the reflected confirmation that it is undivided in itself. Stephen's explanation of *integritas* is acceptable so far as it goes: "You apprehend it as *one* thing. You see it as one whole. You apprehend its wholeness. That is *integritas*." However, Stephen is mistaken in suggesting that this insight depends for Aquinas on first isolating the object from everything else. To regard the object as self-bounded and self-contained, distinct from everything else, is not to understand it as *unum* but to make a subsequent judgment corresponding to the transcendental *aliquid,* that is, that every thing universally is something other than all else.[76]

In the earlier version of the novel, in conversation with the less sympathetic Cranly, Stephen gave essentially the same explanation of the first apprehension of beauty:

> Consider the performance of your mind when confronted with any object, hypothetically beautiful. Your mind to apprehend that object divides the entire universe into two parts, the object, and the void which is not the object. To apprehend it you must lift it away from everything else: and then you perceive that it is one integral thing, that is *a* thing. You recognise its integrity. Isn't that so? (*SH* 212)

Here, priority is also given to *aliquid;* the object is first apprehended as "something other." Once perception has divided the universe between the object and everything else, it recognizes it as "one integral thing," as "*a* thing." The ensuant properties of "one" and "thing" (*unum* and *res*) contribute to its integrity, "the first quality of beauty: it is declared in a simple sudden synthesis of the faculty which apprehends" (*SH* 212).

While didactically it may be helpful to explain cognition as a process whereby the object is initially isolated from everything else, in Aristotelian or Thomist terms this is not what happens. It is not the case that to see the basket the mind must first separate it from everything else in the visible universe. For Aristotle and Aquinas, an object is directly and immediately perceived as an autonomous individual, as a thing (*res*) in itself with its individual quiddity; recognition of its unity and otherness is secondary and subsequent.

It is true that "An esthetic image is presented to us either in space or in time. What is audible is presented in time, what is visible is presented in space" (*P* V.1360–63). Stephen's observation anticipates in a less complicated expression the famous phrases of the "Proteus" episode of *Ulysses*, "ineluctable modality of the audible" and "ineluctable modality of the visible," and the accompanying distinction between *nacheinander* and *nebeneinander*.[77] Time and place are for Aristotle and Aquinas accidental aspects of the individual substance; otherness is an accident of relation. The recognition of an object's isolation in time or space from everything other than itself is subsequent to our apprehension of it as an individual identical with itself. The recognition that an individual is "selfbounded [. . .] upon the immeasurable background of space or time which it is not" is a secondary awareness consequent upon the primary act of perception.

Aquinas relates the notion of *integritas* to the concepts of "all," "whole," and "perfect," which he finds in Aristotle.[78] A thing is perfect in the first instance when it is complete as a substance: "this perfection is the form of the whole, which results from the integrity of its parts (*ex integritate partium*)."[79] Joyce's reading was praised by no less than Etienne Gilson, one of the greatest Thomist experts of the twentieth century: "James Joyce renders *integritas* 'wholeness,' which is a perfectly legitimate rendering, and he means by this word the property inherent in all being to constitute a self-sufficient whole, distinct from other beings. [. . .] This has been described as the separative power of the form."[80]

Integrity as the first requisite of beauty is clearly illustrated in *Ulysses*, when Bloom's admiration of Gerty MacDowell in "Nausicaa" comes to an abrupt halt as he suddenly discovers that she has a physical defect. This is made all the more shocking, given the manner in which she is initially described: "She was pronounced beautiful by all who knew her. [. . .] The waxen pallor of her face was almost spiritual in its ivorylike purity though her rosebud mouth was a genuine Cupid's bow, Greekly perfect." Her "threequarter skirt cut to the stride showed off her slim graceful figure to perfection," revealing the "perfect proportions"—the second requisite of beauty—of her wellturned ankle (*U* 13.81–82, 87–89, 154–55, 168). The description is so convincing and well-paced, that the shock is all the greater:

> She walked with a certain quiet dignity characteristic of her but with care and very slowly because—because Gerty MacDowell was . . .
> Tight boots? No. She's lame! O!

Mr Bloom watched her as she limped away. Poor girl! That's why she's left on the shelf and the others did a sprint. Thought something was wrong by the cut of her jib. Jilted beauty. A defect is ten times worse in a woman. (*U* 13.769–75)

It is revealing to compare Joyce's account of the "first phase of apprehension" in conversation with Lynch (*P* V.1359) with what Aquinas has to say about the first grasp of an object in sense perception: "The human intellect does not acquire perfect knowledge by the first act of apprehension; but it first apprehends something about its object, such as its quiddity, and this is its first and proper object; and then it understands the properties, accidents, and the various relations of the essence."[81] Aquinas repeatedly states that the proper object of the human intellect (in this life) is the "quiddity" or "whatness" of material objects. *Quidditas* is defined as a thing's nature or essence existing in corporeal matter (*quidditas sive natura in materia corporali*). The grasp of quiddity may be minimal and superficial, but for Aquinas, as for Aristotle, it is infallible; our immediate spontaneous grasp reveals something of what the object really is. Apprehension of a thing's *quidditas* does not mean that we have a knowledge of the inmost nature of a thing's essence; something can be identified as "what" it is by a superficial accidental quality. Fleeting glances at an elephant and a snail, for example, lead to distinct concepts that could never be confused, although our insight into their nature is minimal.

We pass to Stephen's explanation of the second aspect ("stage") of the experience of beauty, namely *consonantia*:

Then, said Stephen, you pass from point to point, led by its formal lines; you apprehend it as balanced part against part within its limits; you feel the rhythm of its structure. (*P* V.1369–71)

The lines that follow are not entirely consistent:

In other words the synthesis of immediate perception is followed by the analysis of apprehension. Having felt that it is *one* thing you feel now that it is a *thing*. You apprehend it as complex, multiple, divisible, separable, made up of its parts, the result of its parts and their sum, harmonious. That is *consonantia*. (*P* V.1371–76)

Here is the corresponding version in *Stephen Hero*, where Stephen contrasts the "simple sudden synthesis of the faculty" that apprehends *integri-*

tas ("the first quality of beauty") with an analysis that explores the relation between its parts:

> What then? Analysis then. The mind considers the object in whole and in part, in relation to itself and to other objects, examines the balance of its parts, contemplates the form of the object, traverses every cranny of the structure. So the mind receives the impression of the symmetry of the object. The mind recognises that the object is in the strict sense of the word, a *thing*, a definitely constituted entity. (*SH* 212)

Balance, structure, and symmetry belong to *consonantia* or harmony; mention of "thing," however, inverts the order. "Thing" (*res*) is the ground of integrity and clarity, as well as harmony: it is the object as first perceived. Recognition of harmony is consequent upon the apprehension of the object as thing, not vice versa.

The phrases "synthesis of perception" and "analysis of apprehension" are questionable. It would appear that for Stephen the initial act of perception is constituted by the activity of synthesizing, to be followed by a distinct act of apprehension, which is constituted by analysis. On this reading, perception and apprehension result respectively in recognition of the object as *one* thing and as a *thing*. Considering these aspects of cognition and their resulting concepts from a Thomist point of view, we should say that there is no distinction between perception and apprehension—the terms are interchangeable—and that the concepts of both "one" and "thing" express different aspects of the same entity.

In the analysis of the three constituents of beauty in *Stephen Hero*, although implied, *consonantia* is not in fact named. Stephen identifies it with symmetry, appreciation of which comes with recognition that "the object is in the strict sense of the word, a *thing*, a definitely constituted entity." Symmetry partly conveys the meaning of *consonantia* but is not a complete definition. Stephen is mistaken in equating *consonantia* with "*thing*," which is more accurately the ground of *integritas*. The phrase "definitely constituted entity" is a perfect definition of what is meant by the transcendental *res*.

Stephen's explanation in *A Portrait* of how we experience an object's *consonantia* as feeling the "rhythm of its structure" is an original and successful phrase. Earlier in the conversation with Lynch, he had referred to "the rhythm of beauty," explained as "the first formal esthetic relation of part to part in any esthetic whole or of an esthetic whole to its part or parts or of any part to the esthetic whole of which it is a part" (*P* V.1154–57).

Stephen's explanation of *consonantia* touches the perceptible level but not its ontological ground. He declares: "You apprehend it as complex, multiple, divisible, separable, made up of its parts, the result of its parts and their sum, harmonious. That is *consonantia*." However, as Immanuel Chapman comments, "*Consonantia* is qualitatively more than the sum of its parts, but more serious is the failure to recognize that it is the ontological good of a thing."[82] More important than the recognition by the observer of its visibly pleasing aspect is the deeper intrinsic, organic, mutual, and reciprocal arrangements of its constituent parts.

When Aquinas states that "beauty consists in due proportion,"[83] he is not referring just to a superficial symmetry, which suffices to please the eye; indeed, right proportion may at the deeper level require asymmetry. Correct proportion is determined by the intrinsic order of the individual as a whole.[84] By "due" (*debita*) proportion is meant the correct order and disposition of parts within the whole as required by its nature. A body is beautiful if its members (hands, feet, etc.) are so ordered as befits its nature.[85] Proportion refers to the inherent presence of the correct order of relationships between the parts of an individual. By the proportion that causes beauty, Aquinas is referring to the proper internal relationship between the parts of an individual.

Having expounded on the meaning of *consonantia*, Stephen responds to Lynch's challenge to complete his exposé of Aquinas's triple prescription for beauty by explaining the meaning of *claritas*:

The connotation of the word, Stephen said, is rather vague. Aquinas uses a term which seems to be inexact. It baffled me for a long time. It would lead you to believe that he had in mind symbolism or idealism, the supreme quality of beauty being a light from some other world, the idea of which the matter is but the shadow, the reality of which it is but the symbol. I thought he might mean that *claritas* is the artistic discovery and representation of the divine purpose in anything or a force of generalization which would make the esthetic image a universal one, make it outshine its proper conditions. But that is literary talk. I understand it so. When you have apprehended that basket as **one thing** and have then **analysed** it according to its **form** and apprehended it as **a thing** you make the only synthesis which is logically and esthetically permissible. You see that **it is that thing which it is and no other thing**. The radiance of which he speaks is the scholastic *quidditas,* the *whatness* of a thing. This supreme quality is felt by the artist when the esthetic image is first conceived in his imagination. (*P* V.1379–96)[86]

The corresponding explanation in *Stephen Hero* is as follows:

—Now for the third quality. For a long time I couldn't make out what Aquinas meant. He uses a figurative word (a very unusual thing for him) but I have solved it. *Claritas* is *quidditas.* After the analysis which discovers the second quality the mind makes the only logically possible synthesis and discovers the third quality. This is the moment which I call epiphany. First we recognise that the object is *one* integral thing, then we recognise that it is an organised composite structure, a *thing* in fact: finally, when the relation of the parts is exquisite, when the parts are adjusted to the special point, we recognise that it is *that* thing which it is. Its soul, its whatness, leaps to us from the vestment of its appearance. The soul of the commonest object, the structure of which is so adjusted, seems to us radiant. The object achieves its epiphany. (*SH* 213)[87]

In the proto-version, Stephen believed that he had solved the meaning of *claritas* in Aquinas: "*Claritas* is *quidditas.*" This is reformulated in *A Portrait*: "The radiance of which he speaks is the scholastic *quidditas,* the *whatness* of a thing."[88] It is true that in apprehension, there is an illuminative intuition ("luminously apprehended," *P* V.1365) of a thing's *quidditas*. Through its native light, the intellect illumines the sense datum so as to actualize its intelligible nature; in this sense, there is a link between *quidditas* and *claritas*.

To sum up Stephen's analysis of beauty in *A Portrait*: he substitutes *integritas* for *aliquid, res* for *consonantia,* and *quidditas* for *claritas*.

Despite what Stephen suggests, the connotation of the figurative term "*claritas*" was for Aquinas neither vague nor inexact. It refers to the self-manifestation by which an object presents itself to the human intellect, which, for its part, is also metaphorically viewed in the manner of a *lumen naturale* or natural light that illuminates the object of sense knowledge. The metaphor of light to convey the subtle mystery of knowledge had an established history in philosophy and theology when dealing with spiritual and divine matters.

Joyce was right not to attribute to Aquinas an idealist and symbolist view of beauty.[89] Aquinas would also reject the view that beauty is caused by an otherworldly light within material beings, where matter is but the shadow and the reality a symbol. Material things are illumined by their determining form: matter and form together constitute the individual, which in itself is complete and intrinsically intelligible.

Although in their origin things are infused with the transcendent light of their divine origin, the immanent forms of material beings are the source of their intrinsic and autonomous light. Immanuel Chapman remarks: "In a way hardly suspected by Joyce and others, which brings out even more sharply the radiance of each being's own form, St. Thomas spoke of *claritas* as a resplendent ray of light irradiating a being from within and belonging to it by its very nature, the 'beautifying' givenness making things beautiful, really given to these participated likenesses by the Source of all light."[90]

As a committed Aristotelian in matters of epistemology, Aquinas attributed to the intellect a *lumen naturale,* which actualizes the intelligibility of form immersed in matter. There is an element of truth in the interpretation rejected by Joyce, insofar as in his theory of participation adapted from Plato, Aquinas sees the light of reason as partaking of divine intellect, and he regards the intelligibility of material things as ultimately caused by divine intelligence. Methodically, however, his explanation of human cognition is entirely Aristotelian in viewing material beings as latently luminous (intelligible) in themselves, and the intellect as naturally capable of educing their intelligibility through its *lumen naturale.*

The clarity required for beauty is that an object have a vivid presence to sensation; it may not be dull or obscure. Of itself, matter is dark and unintelligible, since it is a principle of potency. A quality or form immersed in matter remains potentially intelligible; its intelligibility must be actualized through the illuminative and abstractive act of the intellect. As Thomas Gilby remarks, the mind is powerful enough to "light up and isolate the spiritual meaning of material things."[91]

In concluding his analysis of the experience of beauty, Joyce correctly makes the connection between form and *quidditas.* It is "form" that is at the origin of the three characteristics of *integritas, consonantia,* and *claritas:* not as distinct stages but as a single source that simultaneously governs and causes all three. The assertion "The radiance of which he speaks is the scholastic *quidditas,* the *whatness* of a thing," however, is hasty. *Quidditas* is correctly translated as *whatness,* but it is not quite identical with the luminous element whereby an object becomes manifest or shines forth.

The following lines from *Stephen Hero* merit further comment, as they substitute *unum* for *aliquid* to explain *integritas* and introduce another term, "that," to explain *claritas*:

> First we recognise that the object is *one* integral thing, then we recognise that it is an organised composite structure, a *thing* in fact: finally, when the relation of the parts is exquisite, when the parts are adjusted to the special point, we recognise that it is *that* thing which it is. (*SH* 213)

This is Stephen's summary for Cranly of the three "stages" in which we discern the three marks of beauty. Having two paragraphs earlier explained the object's integrity by separating it mentally from everything else (*aliquid*), he now grounds it in the fact that it is *one*. This is a silent but significant shift. Secondly, we grasp its "organised composite structure" as a *thing*; finally, in its *claritas*, we recognize it as "*that* thing." We have thus respectively the three characteristics of "one," "thing," and "that." Stephen's attention on the object as "that thing" resonates with the medieval term *haecceitas* ("thisness"), which he takes as synonymous with the quite distinct term "*quidditas*" ("whatness"). Quiddity or "whatness" ("what something is") was contrasted by the Scholastics with the *haecceitas* or "thisness" of a thing. *Haecceitas* was coined by Duns Scotus (1266–1308) to denote the unique particularity of the individual (what makes it *this* singular numerically unique individual), as distinct from the *kind* of thing whereby it resembles other members of its class (its whatness or *quidditas*). *Haecceitas* denotes the unique individual that can only be known and sense-intuited here and now. This was for Scotus the primary focus of cognitive attention. According to Aquinas, on the other hand, we do not have a concept of the individual as a *this* (*individuum est ineffabile*); it can only be understood in light of a general concept expressing *what* it is. William T. Noon explains further: "The Thomist would argue too that the Scotist *haecceitas*, in any case, presupposes the specifying *quidditas,* and that the *haecceitas* of itself is ineffable and incommunicable, capable of intuition but in no way capable of conceptualization, whereas the *quidditas* of the singular is utterable, intelligible in one's own mind, and communicable to the minds of others."[92]

Stephen's use of *quidditas* is inexact when he states: "Its soul, its whatness, leaps to us from the vestment of its appearance" (*SH* 213). There is indeed a profound insight here, although it is partially lost by the equation of soul with "whatness." "Soul" is the term reserved for the animating form of living substances; it denotes the profound principle by which an individual possesses itself. It is identical with "nature," which Aristotle defines as the principle of rest and movement within the individual. Soul is the principle of actuality determining the potential co-principle of matter within the individual. The important difference is that *quidditas* refers to the nature or soul of the individual as immersed within matter. Soul is defined in its distinction from matter. Omitting from Stephen's assertion the word "whatness" we could, speaking metaphorically, say that the soul of the object "leaps to us from the vestment of its appearance," meaning that in aesthetic insight we intuitively grasp the form liberated from its material vesture. We perceive the individual's beauty by divesting the form of its material conditions. A Thomist reading would readily accept the ensuing sentence, on condition that we take "soul" in a weak, metaphorical, sense as referring to the innermost principle of the commonest object: "The soul of the commonest object, the structure of which is so adjusted, seems to us radiant. The object achieves its epiphany" (*SH* 213).

One might well regret that by the time he came to write *A Portrait,* Joyce had dropped the notion of epiphany in his explanation of *claritas.* His use of the term in *Stephen Hero* expresses perfectly the profound experience of aesthetic insight and illumination. In saying that "the object achieves its epiphany," Stephen accurately conveys the cognitive union of object and observer. The experience (simultaneous manifestation of itself by the object and its illumination by the knowing subject) is fittingly conveyed in one of the most compelling passages of *A Portrait,* where Stephen describes the moment of aesthetic delight:

> The mind in that mysterious instant Shelley likened beautifully to a fading coal. The instant wherein that supreme quality of beauty, the clear radiance of the esthetic image, is apprehended luminously by the mind which has been arrested by its wholeness and fascinated by its harmony is the luminous silent stasis of esthetic pleasure, a spiritual state very like to that cardiac condition which the Italian physiologist Luigi Galvani, using a phrase almost as beautiful as Shelley's, called the enchantment of the heart. (*P* V.1397–405)

Shelley's comparison of the mind with a fading coal is reminiscent of Sextus Empiricus, who remarked that as it draws near the divine Logos, the human soul is like a cinder that glows when placed beside the fire and darkens when removed.[93] The chiaroscuro in Stephen's mind as he struggles to define his artistic identity is conveyed in similar mode: "His thinking was a dusk of doubt and self-mistrust, lit up at moments by the lightnings of intuition, but lightnings of so clear a splendour that in those moments the world perished about his feet as if it had been fire-consumed" (*P* V.100–103).

In his "novel" *As I was Going Down Sackville Street,* Oliver St. John Gogarty makes a gratuitous suggestion about how Joyce became acquainted with the term "epiphany": "Probably Father Darlington had taught him, as an aside in his Latin class—for Joyce knew no Greek—that 'Epiphany' meant 'a showing forth.'"[94] Apart from the fact that neither Darlington taught, nor Joyce studied, Latin at university, it is strange that Gogarty could have forgotten how Catholic children the world over, when old enough to listen to a sermon, receive an annual lesson in etymology with the explanation that the feast of the Epiphany (January 6) celebrates the "manifestation" or "showing forth" of the Christ child to the world, represented by the three Magi who had followed the star to Bethlehem. Joyce's use of the word to describe the moment of revelation in which the observer is receptive to the "manifestation" or "showing forth" of beauty—the irradiation or resplendence of form—could not be more appropriate. It expresses *claritas* in its very activity. Stephen puts it perfectly in the proto-novel: "It is just in this epiphany that I find the third, the supreme quality of beauty" (*SH* 211).

Once theological revelation had lost its meaning for Joyce, he applied the word to those random but privileged moments when we grasp the revelation of what a thing really is, when "its soul, its whatness, leaps to us from the vestment of its appearance," when "the soul of the commonest object . . . seems to us radiant" (*SH* 213). "By epiphany he meant a sudden spiritual manifestation, whether in the vulgarity of speech or of gesture or in a memorable phase of the mind itself" (*SH* 211). Joyce expanded the term "epiphany" to describe his practice of capturing special moments of insight and revelation, not only of special aesthetic beauty but also of any "sudden spiritual manifestation, whether in the vulgarity of speech or of gesture or in a memorable phase of the mind itself" (*SH* 211). William T. Noon describes Joycean epiphany as "a formulation through metaphor or symbol of some luminous aspect of individual human experience, some highly significant facet of most intimate and personal reality, some particularly radiant point of the meaning of existence."[95] An epiphany is a cipher of transcendence, a sign revealing a dimension beyond the ordinary. Joyce's epiphany resembles Pound's "method of luminous detail" whereby an apparently trivial incident or moment is used to illustrate an essential truth.[96] Epiphanies can be attained in the humblest of actions, "an old woman praying, or a young man fastening his shoe"; the point is "to see what is there well done and how much it signifies" (*OCPW* 54). Epiphany is recognition of the value of such actions. They are not inventions but factual experiences. Joyce had an intense sense of the concrete richness of the ordinary, and this is precisely what he turned into his epiphanic pen pictures. A sense of his keen gift for observation and intuitional insight was noticed by those to whom he opened up most intimately.

In his volume, *The First Principles of Knowledge,* in the Stonyhurst series, John Rickaby defines evidence as "the manifestation or shining forth" of a thing's "ontological truth."[97] He explains that the word *evidentia* is Cicero's translation of the Greek word ἐνάργεια, the root of which is found also in *argentum* (silver) and *argumentum.* Joyce's epiphanies are perhaps no more than those experiences described by Chesterton, in which a window in a character's mind "lets in that strange light of surprise in which we see for the first time things we have known all along."[98] Too much, I suggest, has been made of Joyce's use of "epiphany." Perhaps, like Stephen, Joyce's mind "had from the first been only too submissive to the infant sense of wonder [. . .] hypnotised by the most commonplace conversation" (*SH* 26).

Hegelian Joyce?

The most detailed commentary to date on Joyce's aesthetics is Jacques Aubert's influential book *The Aesthetics of James Joyce.*[99] The indispensable hypothesis of Aubert's study is that the primary source for Joyce's aesthetic was Bernard Bosanquet's *History of Aesthetic* and consequently that his approach was predominantly Hegelian. However, no hard evidence is presented to support this premise. While Joyce entered the bibliographic details of Bosanquet's *History* in his notebook in Paris,[100] there is no indication that he consulted it; nor is there any evidence he ever read Hegel. It seems to me that on the basis of tenuous associations Aubert attributes to the young Joyce a Hegelian influence. From the statement in Joyce's early autobiographical essay "A Portrait of the Artist" (January 7, 1904)—"He had interpreted for orthodox Greek scholarship the living doctrine of the *Poetics*"[101]—Aubert draws the following conclusion:

> "Interpreted" and "living" strangely echo "applied" in "applied Aquinas" and add another dimension to it. The words suggest both a historical perspective of impermanence and decay compensated for by rebirth and the necessity to reread ("interpret") the text of past doctrine: a dialectic that the use of the word "applied" tends to specify as Hegelian, in the spirit if not in orthodox doctrinal terms.[102]

I believe this interpretation to be ungrounded; there is no evidence for direct Hegelian influence. As a possible interpretation of Joyce's reference to the "living doctrine of the *Poetics*," Aubert suggests: "Butcher and Bosanquet were making exciting intellectual news exactly at the time when Joyce was being exposed to the Aristotelian teaching of his English Literature professors."[103] While this may be true, temporal coincidence does not amount to causal influence.

According to Jacques Aubert, it was Hegel, and not Aquinas, who provided the main inspiration for Joyce's aesthetics. Despite the corruption of the printed text, Aubert's position is clear: "Here again we are threatened by hasty oversimplifications and may be misled. A couple red herrings [*sic*] are, if I may say so, a particularly bright red, one involving Thomas Aquinas more than any other."[104] I have argued in an earlier chapter that the most likely source for Joyce's Thomist aesthetics were the philosophical handbooks written by the Jesuits of Stonyhurst, which were the prescribed texts at University College. This opinion had already been expressed with emphatic conviction by Joyce's classmate Constantine Curran. Joyce had no need to depend upon Bosanquet for his knowledge of Aquinas. Aubert's suggestion that Joyce, as a sixteen-year-old schoolboy, "enlists Hegel's help" in writing the essay "Force" is difficult to credit.[105] Joyce entered the bibliographic details of Bosanquet's book in his notebook during his stay in Paris in 1903, which possibly suggests that he had previously been unfamiliar with it. We may be confident that he had elaborated the kernel of his aesthetics while still an undergraduate, namely, before his visit to Paris. According to Aubert, Joyce's talk of "the great things that are hidden . . . in the leaves of the trees and in the flowers" (*CW* 21) "seems but a commentary on the Hegelian conception of nature."[106] The surmise is gratuitous: the facts of nature are common to all; the poetic and youthful Joyce did not need to read the German idealist to be moved by the power of Nature.

Aubert remarks that from the 1860s until the end of the century, due to an accelerating rate of translations, "Hegel's philosophy was the major influence in English philosophy."[107] In fact, there was relatively little of Hegel available in English; his influence within the Catholic philosophical circles of Ireland was certainly minimal. Central to the channel of influence upon Joyce, as Aubert would have it, is not only Bosanquet's *History of Aesthetic* (1892) but also his partial translation of Hegel's *Philosophy of Fine Art* (1887). As a Neo-Hegelian, Bosanquet viewed the development of aesthetics as "a dialectical history of aesthetic consciousness."[108] There is, moreover, a relationship of dialectical influence between Bosanquet and

S. H. Butcher, editor of Aristotle's *Poetics*. According to Aubert, Bosanquet's influence may be observed in the preface to Butcher's book *Aristotle's
Theory of Poetry and Fine Art*.[109] The only explanation I can find in favor
of such a suggestion is that Butcher equates Aristotle's insight into "the
essential quality of Poetry, as a concrete expression of the universal" with
Hegel's notion of the "concrete universal." The two notions, however, could
not be further apart.

For Aristotle, the notion of the "concrete universal" is a contradiction
in terms. It must be noted that the term is indeed open to ambiguity. From
Latin *con* and *crescere* (with+grow), "concrete" refers to an entity composed
of more basic principles. In Aristotelian terms, it refers to a particular "this"
(*tode ti*), a composite (*suntheton*) of primary matter and substantial form.
In *Metaphysics* 7, Aristotle considers the composite as one of the candidates
for the primacy of being (*ousia* = "beingness," or substance), but since it derives from its constituent principles, it cannot itself be ultimate.[110] Another
candidate for the ultimacy of existence is the universal character shared by
a multiplicity of individuals and grasped by the general concept. As such,
however, this exists only in the intellect albeit with a foundation in the
physical world. In the Aristotelian scheme, the concrete individual and the
universal belong to distinct orders of knowledge and reality. Only in the
worlds of Parmenides and Hegel—for whom fundamentally only a single
self-existent individual exists and reality and thought are identical—can
one speak meaningfully of the "concrete universal."[111]

From his repeated references to Bosanquet, the reader of Aubert might
expect to find on pages 147–48 of *A History of Aesthetic* the full range of
Aquinas's pronouncements on aesthetics and that the book provided everything needed for Joyce's Pola reflections and Stephen's theories in *Stephen Hero* and *A Portrait*. One might even assume that, in formulating his
aesthetic theory, Joyce was *vir unius libri*. In fact, Bosanquet simply gives
the references to some important passages of the *Summa Theologiae* (*ST*
II-II 145, 2; *ST* I 39, 8; *ST* I, 5, 4); he cites some phrases[112] but not a single
complete sentence. Joyce would have had to trace these texts for himself;
apart from the fact that such was not his practice, there was no copy of
the *Summa Theologiae* in the National Library of Ireland. Furthermore,
as I have argued above, had he consulted the relevant text of *ST* I 5, 4, he
would have immediately recognized that the question was concerned with
the relation between goodness and beauty. Moreover, the epigraph to one
of his passages, the unique phrase "*Bonum nominat id in quod tendit appetitus*" from *ST* I 16, was not referred to by Bosanquet.[113] Conspicuous also

by its absence from Bosanquet's treatment of Aquinas is the quotation "*Ad pulchritudinem tria requiruntur: integritas, consonantia, et claritas.*"

Aubert has presented interesting affinities between Joyce, Hegel and Bosanquet; this is, I suggest, an indication both of the universal and perennial outlook of Aristotle and Hegel and of Joyce's unlimited curiosity and philosophical interest. It does not provide convincing evidence that Joyce himself consulted these authors. The supposed influence of Hegel upon Joyce is more likely a case of their common admiration for Aristotle. Butcher rightly remarked of Aristotle's perennial importance: "His philosophy has in it the germs of so much modern thought that we may, almost without knowing it, find ourselves putting into his mouth not his own language but that of Hegel."[114] Jacques Aubert quotes this passage in support of his claim of Hegelian influence in Joyce; perhaps he has fallen prey to the temptation. Joyce draws from the Aristotelian source and not the Hegelian repository; what has been taken as Hegelian influence points instead to a common inspiration. Hegel's own admiration for Aristotle was unbounded. In his *Lectures on the History of Philosophy,* we read: "He penetrated into the whole universe of things, and subjected its scattered wealth to intelligence; and to him the greater number of philosophical sciences owe their origin and distinction."[115] He would have agreed with Joyce's opinion that Aristotle was the greatest philosopher of all time. Indeed it is significant that Joyce seemed to regard Kant rather than Hegel as the greatest modern philosopher.[116]

It is also significant that none of Hegel's books is listed in the catalogue of Joyce's Trieste library. In all of his available writings, we find but a single serious reference to Hegel, one of little importance; otherwise, there are a jocose reference and a few parodied variations upon his name.[117] There is no mention of Hegel as a source of inspiration. Nor, apart from the bibliographic entry in Joyce's commonplace book, are there any references to Bosanquet's *History of Aesthetic;* there is no indication that Joyce ever consulted or owned a copy. It has been suggested that Joyce never had an unpublished thought: had Hegel been so important, this would be evident from his writings. Richard M. Kain commented aptly: "Always restlessly curious, he put everything he knew, everything he remembered, into his two great works."[118] Joyce left us in no doubt about the sources that influenced him. For sure we can find ideas and phrases resembling Hegelian terms, but the more obvious explanation is that Hegel, like Joyce, was a great admirer of Aristotle. Hegel and Bosanquet are, it would appear, the red herrings that distract from the pursuit of Joyce's aesthetic.[119]

Aubert's comments on Joyce's Pola texts include a radical misconception stated at the outset. The epigraph for the first text (*Bonum est in quod tendit appetitus*, i.e., "The good is that toward which the appetite tends") is adapted from the start of Aristotle's *Nicomachean Ethics*. Aubert concludes: "This sets the key for the whole Pola Notebook, whose line of investigation is definitely *ethical*."[120] The same mistake is found in the introduction by Mason and Ellmann to their chapter "Aesthetics" in *The Critical Writings*.[121] Aristotle's concept of goodness is not confined to ethical value but is associated with the wider notion of end in whatever domain. To say that grass is good for horses is not to make a moral judgment but to recognize grass as suitable nourishment, allowing a horse to function properly in accordance with its nature. The horse instinctively responds to it as good without any moral awareness; Aristotle's definition applies equally to the appetite of the horse. Inversely, if I say that grass is bad for humans, I am likewise asserting a functional fact rather than pronouncing moral censure. For both Aristotle and Aquinas, goodness is predicated of function in relation to goal. For Aristotle, goodness is ultimately founded upon being: "It is better to be than not to be."[122]

Aubert's assumption is not only that Joyce was entirely indebted to Bosanquet for his knowledge of Aquinas's aesthetics but also that Bosanquet's Hegelianism was the decisive influence in shaping Joyce's own aesthetic theorizing. He argues that "by giving chapter and verse for the Aquinian texts on beauty," Bosanquet may have been the decisive stimulation for Joyce's interest in Thomist aesthetics.[123] This is an unwarranted assumption, one that is moreover unnecessary since the most likely source were the philosophical handbooks published by the Jesuits of Stonyhurst, which, as has been pointed out, were the daily fare of Joyce's fellow students at University College.[124] We have the following convincing testimony of Constantine Curran regarding the source of Joyce's aesthetics: "These Stonyhurst manuals would have escaped the attention of no intelligent student in the College; Joyce could have got what he wanted from them in half an hour."[125] Joyce himself mentions these volumes in *Stephen Hero*, referring to Cranly's friend, O'Neill, in the National Library: "He was very busy all the summer reading philosophical handbooks" (*SH* 148).

One may note in conclusion that while there is no evidence that Joyce was directly influenced by Hegel, it would be foolish to deny that he was influenced by the neo-Hegelian spirit that was in the air at the time. Pater, for example, was a definite influence; such influence, however, is nowhere evident in the Pola reflections.[126]

Jacques Aubert's book has for decades enjoyed unquestioned authority resulting, I believe, in various misreadings of Joyce's aesthetics. His conclusions have been accepted by such leading Joyceans as Jean-Michel Rabaté[127] and Michael Patrick Gillespie. James Walter Caufield, in a carefully argued study of the influence of Schopenhauer on Joyce's aesthetics,[128] draws the following conclusion from the research of Robert Spoo, who, he suggests, "has argued persuasively that Stephen's conception of history was distinctly anti-Hegelian in tenor, an attitude that makes Stephen's reliance on Hegel's aesthetic ideas much less likely." Caufield tellingly remarks: "While it is true, as Aubert states, that 'Butcher and Bosanquet were making exciting intellectual news exactly at the time when Joyce was being exposed to the Aristotelian teachings of his English Literature professors,' yet Schopenhauer's popularity was eclipsing Hegel's by the end of the nineteenth century."[129] A further, albeit superficial, argument in favor of the stronger influence of Schopenhauer is that his writings were translated into English before those of Hegel.

The majority consensus among Joyce scholars is that Aristotelian Aquinas is the primary source for Joyce's aesthetics. According to Mark Patrick Hederman, "Joyce's aesthetic was far nearer to that of Thomas Aquinas than is generally allowed by most commentators. This is not because the words he uses are directly borrowed from 'the bulldog of Aquin,' but because the context in which he uses them implies a similar preoccupation."[130] Eloise Knowlton remarks: "Ransacking Catholic theology, the young Joyce transforms Thomas Aquinas, the central figure in the ethical structure of Catholicism, into an aesthete."[131] Andrew Gibson concludes: "The chief sources of the aesthetic theory which he developed, and which is so significant a marker of Stephen's intellectual calibre, are Aquinas and Aristotle, the second, in large part, because of the Aristotelianism of the first."[132] Thomas E. Connolly remarks: "It is the height of the novel's irony that the theory of aesthetics which drove him from the Church is derived from Aquinas."[133] Referring to Joyce's "fondness for Aristotle," Richard Ellmann rightly observes: "If he liked a writer he tried to read everything by him—a compliment he paid to Flaubert, Dante, Ibsen, and a few others." None of the idealist writers is included in the list. The reason is obvious from Ellmann's explanation of Aristotle's attraction:

> The special relevance of this philosophy to Joyce in Dublin in the year 1904 was that he saw around him an idealism as rampant as Plato's. What he liked about Aristotle was that he demoted Plato's

Ideas, had denied that universals could be detached from particulars, and in short had set himself against mysticism. In Dublin Joyce observed his contemporaries bemused by the "fairyland" which in his essay "Drama and Life" he had already rejected. They saw a folk not a people, fairies not forces, folklore not engaged art. For philosophy they turned to occultism, to theosophy, to magic, all purporting to commandeer Private Matter by Sergeant Mind. Their metaphysics was linked to a belated aestheticism, in which beauty was sought as if it had being apart from material entanglement. To their eyes, it *floated*.[134]

7

Joyce's Quotations from Aristotle

Among the extraordinary collection of James Joyce manuscripts acquired by the National Library of Ireland in 2002,[1] one of the most fascinating is the notebook used by the author in Paris and Pola in 1903/04.[2] Long believed to have been lost, this jotter, its cover damp-stained and well-worn, was for the aspiring writer something of a pocket atelier or ambulant workshop. Filled with a variety of notes, reflections, accounts,[3] booklists, poems, and quotations, it affords precious insights into both his daily concerns and artistic interests during that formative period. Scholars previously referred separately to the "Paris Notebook" and the "Pola Notebook"; it is now referred to as Joyce's "Early Commonplace Book." While the most important contents were known through the transcriptions of Joyce's biographer Herbert S. Gorman, the original allows us a privileged position as bystanders at Joyce's literary workbench.

Of special value is the evidence that the notebook provides for Joyce's study of Aristotle.[4] Particularly revealing are the thirty-one quotations that he copied into his notebook and upon which he drew during the decades that followed. Joyce's choice is testimony to what he himself regarded as important in Aristotle; the act of selecting a text and transcribing it in careful longhand into his cahier is significant of itself.

Joyce was a sympathetic reader of Aristotle, capturing with remarkable incisiveness and insight, in scant phrase, much of the profundity of the philosopher. While not all of the passages that he copied into his notebook resurface in his work, many recur verbatim, sometimes in the most unlikely locations; for others one can only suspect an oblique allusion, while for a few there appears to be no reference whatsoever. Instead of rigidly adhering to any set of received ideas or principles, Joyce adapted materials to his own mold. Regardless of any putative relevance to his writings, however, the quotations provide a cross-section of Aristotle's system in itself. There is a certain connectedness in the choice; most of them touch upon

Aristotle's basic interpretation of the world, the nature of human reality, and the operations of knowledge.

Herbert S. Gorman gives the following account of Joyce's evening routine in the early months of 1903: "After his meagre dinner he would saunter across the Boulevard Saint-Michel to the Bibliothèque Sainte-Geneviève and forget his loneliness in a perusal of Victor Cousin's translation of Aristotle."[5] Ellmann simply repeats Joyce's dependence on Cousin's translations, (*JJII* 120), but, as Jacques Aubert has pointed out, Joyce relied for the most part upon the translations of J. Barthélemy-Saint-Hilaire. Victor Cousin, a Plato specialist, translated only books 1 and 12 of Aristotle's *Metaphysics;* these were also used by Joyce, to a greater extent than was recognized by Aubert.[6]

The purpose of this chapter is to reproduce accurately the phrases copied by Joyce into his Paris notebook, to elucidate their original context, and to assess their assimilation into Joyce's literary works. The quotations fall into two groups: the first is taken from what may loosely be described as Aristotle's psychological treatises, the second from his *Metaphysics.*[7] Of the first group, fifteen are from the strictly psychological work, *On the Soul* (*De Anima*), which Joyce read in Barthélemy-Saint-Hilaire's translation, titled *Psychologie d'Aristote: Traité de l'âme.* The remaining three are drawn from *Psychologie d'Aristote: Opuscules (Parva Naturalia),* a collection of less philosophical writings traditionally appended to *De Anima.*[8] The title *Psychologie d'Aristote* is somewhat misleading and probably explains why Joyce was drawn to it in the first place. He soon lost interest in the second volume, having quoted only from the first two of the nine treatises. There was a time gap between the quotations on psychology and metaphysics. The eighteen quotations from the volumes *Psychologie d'Aristote* appear on pages 3 and 4; the remaining thirteen, from *Métaphysique d'Aristote,* are to be found on page 12 of the notebook.[9]

In the following presentation of Joyce's quotations from Aristotle, I have introduced numbers to facilitate identification and reference. They follow the order in which the texts appear in Joyce's notebook. Where it seemed helpful, I have included some extra lines from the French text to illustrate Joyce's selective use of his sources. To present the wider context of Aristotle's thought, and to allow comparison between the ancient philosopher and the aspiring author, I have quoted in English as much of the surrounding text as seemed useful. To facilitate the reader who wishes to make the ultimate comparison, I include also the Greek text, more or less extensively as appeared helpful. (Joyce himself knew no Greek at the time; he later acquired an amateur's knowledge of ancient Greek and made serious efforts, with some success, to learn modern Greek.)

Quotation 1. "The soul is the first entelechy of a naturally organic body."

> *Psychologie d'Aristote: Traité de l'âme* (J. Barthélemy-Saint-Hilaire), 165: "Si donc on veut quelque définition commune à toute espèce d'âme, il faut dire que l'âme est l'entéléchie première d'un corps naturel organique."[10]
>
> *On the Soul* 2, 1, 412b4–6: "If then it is necessary to give a definition common to all souls, it will be that it is the first actuality (entelechy) of a naturally organic body."[11]
>
> *De Anima* 2, 1, 412b4–6: εἰ δή τι κοινὸν ἐπὶ πάσης ψυχῆς δεῖ λέγειν, εἴη ἂν ἐντελέχεια ἡ πρώτη σώματος φυσικοῦ ὀργανικοῦ.[12]

As we have seen, Aristotle ingeniously appeals to the primacy of actuality to formulate his definition of soul as the most fundamental determining principle of the living body. "Entelechy" is the newly invented term he applies to the soul as the actualization of the body. It provides for Stephen in "Scylla and Charybdis" the solution for the question of self-identity. See 19–20, 92, 105.

Quotation 2. "The most natural act for living beings which are complete is to produce other beings like themselves and thereby to participate as far as they may in the eternal and divine."

> *Psychologie d'Aristote: Traité de l'âme*, 187–88: "L'acte le plus naturel aux êtres vivants qui sont complets, et qui ne sont ni avortés ni produits par génération spontanée, c'est de produire un autre être pareil à eux, l'animal un animal, la plante une plante, afin de participer de l'éternel et du divin autant qu'ils le peuvent."
>
> *On the Soul,* 2, 4, 415a22–415b1: "It follows that first of all we must treat of nutrition and reproduction, for the nutritive soul is found along with all the others and is the most primitive and widely distributed power of soul, being indeed that one in virtue of which all are said to have life. The acts in which it manifests itself are reproduction and the use of food, because for any living thing that has reached its normal development and which is unmutilated, and whose mode of generation is not spontaneous, the most natural act is the production of another like itself, an animal producing an

animal, a plant a plant, in order that, as far as its nature allows, it
may partake in the eternal and divine." (*CW*1 61)

De Anima 2, 4, 415a25–415b1: ἧς ἐστιν ἔργα γεννῆσαι καὶ τροφῇ
χρῆσθαι· φυσικώτατον γὰρ τῶν ἔργων τοῖς ζῶσιν, ὅσα τέλεια καὶ
μὴ πηρώματα ἢ τὴν γένεσιν αὐτομάτην ἔχει, τὸ ποιῆσαι ἕτερον
οἷον αὐτό, ζῷον μὲν ζῷον, φυτὸν δὲ φυτόν, ἵνα τοῦ ἀεὶ καὶ τοῦ
θείου μετέχωσιν ᾗ δύνανται.

Aristotle examines the powers that are common to all living beings, plants,
animals, and men; nutrition is a basic need for survival, and reproduction
is a fundamental impulse in all living things. For Joyce, this passage not
only conveys an important truth but also reflects a deep personal conviction, for which we have ample testimony. His brother Stanislaus recalled:
"In spite of his struggle with poverty, he believed in fatherhood and considered it a form of cowardice, 'too great a fear of fate,' not to have children."[13]
Joyce remarked to Louis Gillet: "I can't understand households without
children. I see some with dogs, gimcracks. Why are they alive? To leave
nothing behind, not to survive yourself—how sad!" (*JJII* 204). To his sister
Eva he declared: "The most important thing that can happen to a man is
the birth of a child."[14]

Robert McAlmon records Joyce's earnest wish for a large family:

One night he wept in his cups when telling of his forefathers. His
father had parented a large family, and his grandfathers before him
had been parents of families of from twelve to eighteen children.
Joyce would sigh, and then pull himself together and swear that by
the grace of God he was still a young man and he would have more
children before the end. He didn't detect that I, the youngest of ten
children of a poor minister, did not fancy his idea. He would not listen when I suggested that if one is to produce children one had better
have money to educate and care for them in the childhood years.[15]

Writing to Frank Budgen about the composition of "Oxen of the Sun," Joyce
referred to "the crime committed against fecundity by sterilizing the act of
coition" (*LI* 39). Theodore Purefoy refers in "Circe" to "a mechanical device to frustrate the sacred ends of nature" (*U* 15.1740–41). It would appear,
however, that Joyce's concern went beyond the frustration of the coital act:
he despised also those who did not engage in that act. Mary Lowe-Evans
comments: "A close examination of the episode reveals that the crime is

impossibly complex, and in fact surfaces in a myriad of forms. Contraceptive devices, abortion, onanism, and permanent celibacy are the obvious subjects of discussion in the anteroom of the Holles Street Maternity Hospital."[16] An example of the celibate is Bob Doran in Joyce's story "The Boarding House." He is endowed, as Lowe-Evans notes, with "good qualifications for marriage—a steady job, a savings account, and a depleted supply of wild oats."[17] Selfishness, however, restrains him: "His instinct urged him to remain free, not to marry. Once you are married you are done for, it said. [. . .] The instinct of the celibate warned him to hold back."[18] Hélène Cixous speaks of "Joyce's satire against bachelors," notably Robert Hand (*Exiles*), Blazes Boylan, and Buck Mulligan. She refers to

> a small group of men for whom Joyce feels the profoundest antipathy;
> he takes pleasure in plotting their downfall. [. . .] These men, who
> share between them all the faults Joyce detests, are bachelors. [. . .]
> The typical portrait which emerges from a comparison and study of
> these men shows that Joyce associates the defensive egoism of the
> man who wants to enjoy life without paying the price with a complete lack of humanity, which is manifest in all their behaviour: they
> are brutal, their intelligence is without warmth or scruples, they are
> athletic and proud of their physical and fleshly accomplishments.[19]

Such characters, depicted by Joyce, clearly do not measure up to Aristotle's model of the naturally complete individual.

Quotation 3: "A voice is a sound which expresses something."

> *Psychologie d'Aristote: Traité de l'âme*, 226: "La voix, en effet, est un
> son exprimant quelque chose."
> *On the Soul* 2, 8, 420b29–33: "Not every sound, as we said, made
> by an animal is voice (even with the tongue we may merely make
> a sound which is not voice, or without the tongue as in coughing); what produces the impact must have soul in it and must be
> accompanied by an act of imagination, for voice is a sound with
> a meaning, and is not the result of any impact of the breath as in
> coughing."[20]
> *De Anima* 2, 8, 420b32–33: σημαντικὸς γὰρ δή τις ψόφος ἐστὶν ἡ
> φωνή.

Joyce's interest in the voice was well noted. To say that music and song were integral to his art is an understatement. Music was for Joyce a manner of being and living, of knowing the world, and reenacting it in his writing; in this, song was paramount. He read in Aristotle's *Politics* (part of which was included in a compilation that he reviewed)[21] the words of Musaeus, the Orphic poet: "Sweetest to mortals is song." He himself would later write: "The human voice, two tiny silky chords. Wonderful, more than all the others" (*U* 11.791–92).

Quotation 4: "In the sense of touch man is far above all other animals and hence he is the most intelligent animal."

Quotation 5: "Men who have tough flesh have not much intelligence."

Both of these quotations are from the same paragraph, which is here reproduced in full. Since Quotation 6 also refers to the faculty of touch and the role of flesh, they may be commented on together.

> *Psychologie d'Aristote: Traité de l'âme*, 228–29: "Pour les autres, il est fort au-dessous de bien des animaux; mais pour le toucher, il est fort au-dessus d'eux tous, ce qui fait aussi qu'il est le plus intelligent des animaux. La preuve, c'est que, même parmi les hommes, les uns sont naturellement bien doués pour ce sens, et que les autres le sont mal, tandis qu'il n'y a rien de pareil pour les espèces inférieures: et ainsi les hommes qui ont la chair dure sont mal doués pour l'intelligence; ceux qui ont la chair douce sont au contraire bien doués."

> *On the Soul* 2, 9, 421a16–26: "It seems that there is an analogy between smell and taste, and that the species of tastes correspond to those of smells, but that we have a more accurate sense of taste, because it is itself a kind of touch, and man has this sense most accurately. In the other senses he is at a loss compared to many kinds of animals, but **in the sense of touch he is by far much more accurate and discriminating. That is why he is the most intelligent of animals.** Proof of this is that in the human race, individuals are well or poorly endowed by nature in proportion to their sense of touch, and none other. **Men who have tough flesh are ill endowed with intellect, men of soft flesh are well endowed.**"[22]

> *De Anima* 2, 9, 421a16–26: ἔοικε μὲν γὰρ ἀνάλογον ἔχειν πρὸς τὴν γεῦσιν, καὶ ὁμοίως τὰ εἴδη τῶν χυμῶν τοῖς τῆς ὀσμῆς, ἀλλ' ἀκριβεστέραν ἔχομεν τὴν γεῦσιν διὰ τὸ εἶναι αὐτὴν ἁφήν τινα, ταύτην δ' ἔχειν τὴν αἴσθησιν τὸν ἄνθρωπον ἀκριβεστάτην· ἐν μὲν γὰρ ταῖς ἄλλαις λείπεται πολλῶν τῶν ζῴων, κατὰ δὲ τὴν ἁφὴν

πολλῷ τῶν ἄλλων διαφερόντως ἀκριβοῖ· διὸ καὶ φρονιμώτατόν
ἐστι τῶν ζῴων. σημεῖον δὲ τὸ καὶ ἐν τῷ γένει τῶν ἀνθρώπων παρὰ
τὸ αἰσθητήριον τοῦτο εἶναι εὐφυεῖς καὶ ἀφυεῖς, παρ' ἄλλο δὲ μηδέν·
οἱ μὲν γὰρ σκληρόσαρκοι ἀφυεῖς τὴν διάνοιαν, οἱ δὲ μαλακόσαρκοι
εὐφυεῖς.

Quotation 6: "The flesh is the intermediary for the sense of touch."

> **Psychologie d'Aristote: Traité de l'âme**, 245: "On en peut conclure
> que c'est la chair qui est l'intermédiaire pour l'organe qui touche."
> **On the Soul** 2, 11, 423b26: "Flesh is the medium for the sense of touch."
> **De Anima** 2, 11, 423b26: ὥστε τὸ μεταξὺ τοῦ ἁπτικοῦ ἡ σάρξ.[23]

One may only speculate regarding the reasons for Joyce's interest in these
passages on touch and the role of flesh in sensation. In "Lestrygonians,"
Bloom reflects on the blind stripling's heightened sense of touch, which
compensates for his lack of sight (U 8.1128–29). We later read of Bloom's
sensory equilibrium as he shaves: "Why did absence of light disturb him
less than presence of noise? Because of the surety of the sense of touch in
his firm full masculine feminine passive active hand" (U 17.289).

Aristotle's teaching on touch is intriguing. As Aquinas explains it, Aristotle regards touch as the basis for all the other senses: "For it is clear that
the organ of touch is spread throughout the whole body, that each instrument of sense is also an instrument of touch, and that something is called
sensory as a result of the sense of touch. Thus it follows from something's
having a better sense of touch that it unconditionally has a better sensory
nature and consequently a better intellect. For having a good sense disposes
one for having a good intellect."[24]

The suggestion that individuals with hard skin are of lesser intelligence
seems preposterous. Aristotle's elitist views on free men and slaves are perhaps at work here. By nature, some are destined for a life of toil and labor
in the service of those citizens who are privileged through free birth to
pursue loftier ideals. It was of course empirically evident that slaves had
calloused hands and weathered skin—perhaps the basis for Aristotle's conclusion. Aquinas finds philosophical clarification of Aristotle's position by
suggesting that a refined sense of touch results from a good constitution or
harmony among the elements. He concludes: "Now the soul's lofty stature
results from the body's good constitution, because every form is propor-
tioned to its matter. It follows then, that those who have a good sense of
touch have a loftier soul and an acuter mind."[25]

Quotation 7: "A sense receives the form without the matter."

> **Psychologie d'Aristote: Traité de l'âme**, 247: "Il faut admettre, pour tous les sens en général, que le sens est ce qui reçoit les formes sensibles sans la matière, comme la cire reçoit l'empreinte de l'anneau sans le fer ou l'or dont l'anneau est composé, et garde cette empreinte d'airain ou d'or, mais non pas en tant qu'or ou airain."

> **On the Soul** 2, 12, 424a17–21: "In general we must assume of all sensation, that a sense is that which receives sensible forms without the matter, as the wax takes on the impression of the signet-ring without the iron or gold, and receives the impression of the gold or bronze, but not as gold or bronze."

> **De Anima** 2, 12, 424a17–21: καθόλου δὲ περὶ πάσης αἰσθήσεως δεῖ λαβεῖν ὅτι ἡ μὲν αἴσθησίς ἐστι τὸ δεκτικὸν τῶν αἰσθητῶν εἰδῶν ἄνευ τῆς ὕλης, οἷον ὁ κηρὸς τοῦ δακτυλίου ἄνευ τοῦ σιδήρου καὶ τοῦ χρυσοῦ δέχεται τὸ σημεῖον, λαμβάνει δὲ τὸ χρυσοῦν ἢ τὸ χαλκοῦν σημεῖον, ἀλλ' οὐχ ᾗ χρυσὸς ἢ χαλκός.

Aristotle's simile of wax receiving the impression of the signet-ring to illustrate the abstractive nature of sensation is strengthened by its clear imagery.

Bloom muses on the experience of the blind stripling in "Lestrygonians": "And with a woman, for instance. More shameless not seeing. That girl passing the Stewart institution, head in the air. Look at me. I have them all on. Must be strange not to see her. Kind of a form in his mind's eye" (*U* 8.1125–27).

Quotation 8: "The sensation of particular things is always true."

> **Psychologie d'Aristote: Traité de l'âme**, 278: "La sensation des choses particulières est toujours vraie, même dans tous les animaux; mais on peut faire aussi un usage erroné de la pensée, et cette faculté n'appartient à aucun être qui n'ait en même temps la raison."[26]

> **On the Soul** 3, 3, 427b11–14: "For the perception of the proper objects is always true, and this is found in all animals; it is possible to think erroneously, however, but this occurs only in beings which have reason."

> **De Anima** 3, 3, 427b11–14: ἡ μὲν γὰρ αἴσθησις τῶν ἰδίων ἀεὶ ἀληθής, καὶ πᾶσιν ὑπάρχει τοῖς ζῴοις, διανοεῖσθαι δ' ἐνδέχεται καὶ ψευδῶς, καὶ οὐδενὶ ὑπάρχει ᾧ μὴ καὶ λόγος.

Barthélemy-Saint-Hilaire mistranslates the text, thereby missing the entire point of Aristotle's distinction. "*Aisthêsis tôn idiôn*" does not refer to the perception of particular things but to the sensation of the special or proper objects of each particular sense faculty: sound is grasped only by the ear, color only by the eye. For Aristotle, it is by nature impossible for the eye to err with regard to the color of which it has a sensation; the perceiver, however, is open to err in his interpretation of what he perceives. Error in the perception of particular things is most definitely possible; Joyce's quotation misrepresents Aristotle in this regard.

Despite the inaccuracy of this quotation, Joyce nevertheless captures the kernel of Aristotle's theory of sensation, expressing it admirably with two of the most famous phrases from the entire work: "ineluctable modality of the visible" and "ineluctable modality of the audible." See 52–56 above.

Quotation 9: "That which acts is superior to that which suffers."

> **Psychologie d'Aristote: Traité de l'âme**, 303. See Quotation 10.
> **On the Soul** 3, 5, 430a18–19. See Quotation 10.
> **De Anima** 3, 5, 430a18–19. See Quotation 10.

This refers to the distinction between cause and effect. The cause is superior to the effect; the cause is actual, the effect takes place in the subject undergoing change, which has the potency for that determination but does not possess it in actuality. What is potential can be brought to actuality only through the action of a cause, which is actual. That which acts must be actual; potency is acted upon.

There is no clear allusion to this passage in Joyce. In "Scylla and Charybdis," we read: "The boy of act one is the mature man of act five. All in all. In *Cymbeline,* in *Othello* he is bawd and cuckold. He acts and is acted on" (*U* 9.1021–22).

Quotation 10: "Only when it is separate from all things is the intellect really itself and this intellect separate from all things is immortal and divine."

> **Psychologie d'Aristote: Traité de l'âme**, 303–04: "Telle est, en effet, l'intelligence, qui, d'une part, peut devenir toutes choses, et qui, d'autre part, peut tout faire. C'est en quelque sorte une virtualité pareille à la lumière; car la lumière, en un certain sens, fait, des couleurs qui ne sont qu'en puissance, des couleurs en réalité. Et telle est l'intelligence qui est séparée, impassible, sans mélange avec quoi que ce soit, et qui par son essence est en acte. **C'est que toujours ce qui agit est supérieur à ce qui souffre l'action, et que le principe est supérieur à la matière.** La science en acte se confond

avec l'objet auquel elle s'applique. Mais la science en puissance est pour l'individu seul antérieure dans le temps. Absolument parlant, elle n'est point antérieure dans le temps. Mais ce n'est point lorsque tantôt elle pense et tantôt ne pense pas, **c'est seulement quand elle est séparée que l'intelligence seule est immortelle et** éternelle."

On the Soul 3, 5, 430a14–23: "Intellect as described is such because it becomes all things; but there is another kind of intellect, which is what it is because it makes all things: this is a kind of positive state like light, for in a certain manner light makes potential colours into actual colours. Intellect in this sense is separable, impassive and un-mixed, since it is essentially an activity; **for the agent [that which acts] is always superior to the patient [that which undergoes action]**, and the originating cause to the matter. Actual knowledge is identical with its object. [. . .] The intellect does not sometimes think and sometimes not think. **Only when separated is it what it really is itself, and this alone is immortal and eternal.'** [27]

De Anima 3, 5, 430a14–23: καὶ ἔστιν ὁ μὲν τοιοῦτος νοῦς τῷ πάντα γίνεσθαι, ὁ δὲ τῷ πάντα ποιεῖν, ὡς ἕξις τις, οἷον τὸ φῶς· τρόπον γάρ τινα καὶ τὸ φῶς ποιεῖ τὰ δυνάμει ὄντα χρώματα ἐνεργείᾳ χρώματα. καὶ οὗτος ὁ νοῦς χωριστὸς καὶ ἀπαθὴς καὶ ἀμιγής, τῇ οὐσίᾳ ὢν ἐνέργεια. ἀεὶ γὰρ τιμιώτερον τὸ ποιοῦν τοῦ πάσχοντος καὶ ἡ ἀρχὴ τῆς ὕλης. τὸ δ' αὐτό ἐστιν ἡ κατ' ἐνέργειαν ἐπιστήμη τῷ πράγματι· ἡ δὲ κατὰ δύναμιν χρόνῳ προτέρα ἐν τῷ ἑνί, ὅλως δὲ οὐδὲ χρόνῳ, ἀλλ' οὐχ ὁτὲ μὲν νοεῖ ὁτὲ δ' οὐ νοεῖ. χωρισθεὶς δ' ἐστὶ μόνον τοῦθ' ὅπερ ἐστί, καὶ τοῦτο μόνον ἀθάνατον καὶ ἀΐδιον.

Quotations 9 and 10 are from the same paragraph of *De Anima* 3, which presents two of Aristotle's most important doctrines on soul and intellect. He makes use again of the theory of act and potency to distinguish between the active and passive functions of the intellect. Potentially, the intellect can know all things. In that sense, it passively *becomes* all things (Quotation 15); however, this knowledge must first be made actual, and this is the function of the active or agent intellect. Aristotle compares its function to that of light, which brings to actuality colors that would otherwise remain poten-tial or latent. It is in this connection that Aristotle declares that the agent is superior to that which undergoes the action. (Joyce's quotation truncates the meaning of the passage, by leaving out the word *l'action* after *souffre*.)

Aristotle's suggestion of the "separated intellect" is among the most acutely disputed topics in the history of Aristotelian philosophy. It was interpreted by the Arab philosopher Averroes (1126–1198) to mean that there was only a single intellect, separate from individuals but common to all mankind, that makes it possible for humans to think. Aquinas, on the other hand, found in these words of Aristotle a proof for the immortality of the individual soul.

Aristotle's text states that the separated intellect is "immortal and eternal." For a possible explanation as to why Joyce wrote "immortal and divine," see 243n50 below.

Quotation 11: "Error is not found apart from combination."

> *Psychologie d'Aristote: Traité de l'âme,* 307: "C'est que l'erreur, ici non plus, ne se trouve jamais que dans la combinaison."
> *On the Soul* 3, 6, 430b1–2: "Error is always found in a combination."
> *De Anima* 3, 6, 430b1–2: τὸ γὰρ ψεῦδος ἐν συνθέσει ἀεί.

As already explained (Quotation 8), Aristotle maintains that the senses do not err in the grasp of their proper object; nor does the intellect err in its intuition of some intelligible aspect of the object. Error occurs only at the level of judgment, when intellect combines diverse data and mentally forms the wrong combination. Whereas sensations of particular sense qualities are always infallible, combinations are open to error when judgment is made without proper care. See 55 above.

Quotation 12: "The principle which hates is not different from the principle which loves."

> *Psychologie d'Aristote: Traité de l'âme,* 315: "[E]t avoir du plaisir ou de la douleur, c'est, pour la moyenne sensible, agir à l'égard du bien ou du mal, en tant que les choses sont l'un ou l'autre. La haine en acte pour l'un, et le désir en acte pour l'autre, ne sont que la douleur et le plaisir; le principe qui, dans l'âme, désire, et celui qui hait, ne sont pas différents entre eux, pas plus qu'ils ne le sont du principe qui sent; la façon d'être est seule diverse."
> *On the Soul* 3, 7, 431a10–14: "To feel pleasure or pain is to act with the sensitive mean towards what is good or bad as such. Both avoidance and appetite when actual are identical with this: the faculty of appetite and avoidance are not different, either from one another or from the faculty of sense-perception; although their manner of being is different." (*CW*1 685)

De Anima 3, 7, 431a10–14: καὶ ἔστι τὸ ἥδεσθαι καὶ λυπεῖσθαι τὸ ἐνεργεῖν τῇ αἰσθητικῇ μεσότητι πρὸς τὸ ἀγαθὸν ἢ κακόν, ᾗ τοιαῦτα. καὶ ἡ φυγὴ δὲ καὶ ἡ ὄρεξις ταὐτό, ἡ κατ' ἐνέργειαν, καὶ οὐχ ἕτερον τὸ ὀρεκτικὸν καὶ τὸ φευκτικόν, οὔτ' ἀλλήλων οὔτε τοῦ αἰσθητικοῦ· ἀλλὰ τὸ εἶναι ἄλλο.

Joyce is somewhat misled by the French translation; the words *orektikon* and *pheuktikon* should be translated as "attraction" and "aversion," rather than "love" and "hate." Aristotle's statement concerns neither cosmic origins nor metaphysical principles of love or hate nor the moral dilemma of odium or devotion; rather, it concerns the spontaneous response of pleasure and pain, which naturally accompanies simple sensation. Instead of love or hate, it is more accurate to speak of appeal and repulsion, appetite and avoidance. Aristotle's point is that not only do we seek or avoid objects in virtue of the same capacity but that this response is rooted in sensation itself. Aquinas suggests a reason for this clarification: "He says this in opposition to Plato, who located the organ of appetitive capacity in one part of the body and the organ of the sensory capacity in another."[28] I have been unable to identify any allusion to this quotation in Joyce's work.

Quotation 13: "The intellect conceives the forms of the images presented to it."

> *Psychologie d'Aristote: Traité de l'âme*, 317–18: "Ainsi donc, l'âme intelligente pense les formes dans les images qu'elle perçoit."
> *On the Soul* 3, 7, 431b2: "The faculty of thinking then thinks the forms in the images."[29]
> *De Anima* 3, 7, 431b2: τὰ μὲν οὖν εἴδη τὸ νοητικὸν ἐν τοῖς φαντάσμασι νοεῖ.

This is a basic doctrine of Aristotle's theory of the soul and his interpretation of how knowledge operates. The mind cannot think without recourse to images or phantasms. Joyce's reading of the passage is not quite complete; it is not enough to state that the intellect conceives the forms of the images presented to it: the fact is that without images, the intellect cannot think at all.

The lines immediately following Quotation 12 are very similar to the text quoted here: "For the intellective soul, images are like sense objects. [...] Hence the soul never thinks without images" (*On the Soul* 3, 7, 431a14–17. Barthélemy-Saint-Hilaire's translation: "Quant à l'âme intelligente, les images remplissent pour elle le rôle des sensations. [. . .] Voilà pourquoi cette âme ne pense jamais sans images").

I have not been able to identify any passage that bears resemblance to this quotation. The nature and function of the imagination, and its role in artistic creation, were of great interest to Joyce. He was from early on intrigued by the working of the mind.

Quotation 14: "The intellectual soul is the form of forms." (*On the Soul* 3, 8, 432a2).

Quotation 15: "The soul is in a manner all that is." (*On the Soul* 3, 8, 431b21).

Both of these quotations are from the same paragraph, although Joyce reverses the order in which they occur. It will be helpful to cite the passage in full, adding emphasis to the phrases used by Joyce.

> *Psychologie d'Aristote: Traité de l'âme*, 320–22: "Maintenant, en ré-capitulant ce qui a été dit de l'âme, nous répéterons que *l'âme est en quelque sorte toutes les choses qui sont*. En effet, les choses sont ou sensibles ou intelligibles, et la science est en quelque façon les choses qu'elle sait, de même que la sensation est les choses sen-sibles. Comment cela est-il possible, c'est ce qu'il faut rechercher, et le voici: la science et la sensation sont divisées, selon les cho-ses mêmes qu'elles embrassent: celle qui est en puissance, selon les choses en puissance; celle qui est en toute réalité, en entéléchie, selon les choses en entéléchie. Le principe qui sent et le principe qui sait dans l'âme sont en puissance les objets mêmes: ici, l'objet qui est su, et là, l'objet qui est senti. Mais nécessairement, ou il s'agit ici des objets eux-mêmes, ou seulement de leurs formes; et ce ne sont certainement pas les objets; car ce n'est pas la pierre qui est dans l'âme, c'est seulement sa forme. Ainsi donc, l'âme est comme la main: si la main est l'instrument des instruments, *l'intelligence est la forme des formes*; et la sensation est la forme des choses sensibles."

> *On the Soul* 3, 8, 431b20–432a2: "Now summarizing what we have said about the soul, let us repeat that **the soul is in a manner all that is**. The things which exist are either sensible or intelligible; knowledge is in a way what is knowable, and sensation in a way the sensible—how this is so, we must inquire. Knowledge and sensa-tion are divided according to their objects: potential knowledge to

what is potential, actual knowledge to what is actual. The sensible and the cognitive faculties of the soul are potentially these objects: the one cognitively, the other sensibly. They must be either these things themselves, or their forms; but they are not the things themselves, since the stone does not exist in the soul, but rather its form. The soul is thus like the hand; for as the hand is the instrument of instruments, so **the intellect is the form of forms**, and sensation the form of sensible objects."

De Anima 3, 8, 431b20–432a2: νῦν δέ, περὶ ψυχῆς τὰ λεχθέντα συγκεφαλαιώσαντες, εἴπωμεν πάλιν ὅτι ἡ ψυχὴ τὰ ὄντα πώς ἐστι πάντα . . . ὥστε ἡ ψυχὴ ὥσπερ ἡ χείρ ἐστιν· καὶ γὰρ ἡ χεὶρ ὄργανόν ἐστιν ὀργάνων, καὶ ὁ νοῦς εἶδος εἰδῶν.

Both quotations are to be found in "Nestor," in a paragraph that is replete with Aristotelian allusion: "The soul is in a manner all that is: the soul is the form of forms. Tranquillity sudden, vast, candescent: form of forms" (*U* 2.75. See Quotation 28 below). In "Proteus," this double allusion is repeated: "Take all, keep all. My soul walks with me, form of forms" (*U* 3.79–80). And in "Scylla and Charybdis," Stephen enlists Aristotle to resolve the problem of personal identity: "But I, entelechy, form of forms, am I by memory because under everchanging forms" (*U* 9.208–09. See commentary on Quotation 1 above).

Quotation 16: "Colour is the limit of the diaphane in any determined body."

> ***Psychologie d'Aristote. Opuscules, De la sensation et des choses sensibles*** (J. Barthélemy-Saint-Hilaire), 39–40: "Mais comme la couleur est dans une limite, elle doit être aussi à la limite du diaphane; et par conséquent, on pourrait définir la couleur: la limite du diaphane dans un corps déterminé."
>
> ***On Sense and Sensible Objects*** 3, 439b10–12: "But since the colour is at the extremity of the body, it must be at the extremity of the transparent in the body. Whence it follows that we may define colour as the limit of the transparent in a determinately bounded body."[30]
>
> *De Sensu* 3, 439b11–12: ὥστε χρῶμα ἂν εἴη τὸ τοῦ διαφανοῦς ἐν σώματι ὡρισμένῳ πέρας.

For an explanation of color, the diaphanous, and bodies, see 57–60 above.

Quotation 17: "Nature always acts in the view of some end."

Quotation 18: "The end of every being is its greatest good."

Both quotations derive from the same paragraph of Aristotle's work *On Sleep*. Aubert gives a correct reference to Aristotle but cites as Joyce's French source a paraphrase from the "plan du traité" (140): "La nature fait toujours toutes choses en vue de quelque fin." Joyce's version corresponds more accurately to the phrase in the treatise itself. I will cite the paragraph in its entirety, since it conveniently outlines Aristotle's theory of the four causes, depicted graphically in Joyce's notebook. (See 223 below.)

> ***Psychologie d'Aristote. Opuscules, Du sommeil et de la veille*** (J. Barthélemy-Saint-Hilaire), 156–57: "Il faut expliquer maintenant la cause qui détermine le sommeil, et la nature de cette affection. Mais, d'abord, on distingue plusieurs espèces de causes. Ainsi, la fin en vue de laquelle se fait une chose, puis le principe d'où part le mouvement, en troisième lieu, la matière, et enfin l'essence, sont pour nous autant de causes distinctes. Nous disons donc d'abord **que la nature agit toujours en vue de quelque fin**, et que cette fin est toujours un bien. Mais pour tout ce qui a naturellement un mouvement, sans d'ailleurs pouvoir conserver ce mouvement toujours et continuellement, le repos est nécessairement agréable et utile; et c'est avec toute vérité que l'on applique cette métaphore au sommeil qu'on regarde comme un repos et un délassement. Par conséquent, le sommeil est donné aux animaux en vue de leur conservation. Mais la fin en vue de laquelle le sommeil a lieu, c'est la veille; car sentir et penser est la fin véritable de tous les êtres qui ont l'une ou l'autre de ces facultés, parce qu'elles sont leur plus grand bien, et que **la fin de chaque être est toujours son bien le plus grand**. Ainsi il faut nécessairement que la fonction du sommeil appartienne à tout animal sans exception."
>
> ***On Sleep and Waking*** 2, 455b13–26: "We have next to consider the cause of sleep, and what sort of affection it is. Now there are several causes—we recognize as such the final, the efficient, the material and the formal cause. First of all then, since we hold that **nature acts with some end in view** and that this end is a good, and that to everything which naturally moves, but cannot with pleasure move always and continuously, rest is necessary and beneficial; and since sleep is accurately called 'rest' by metaphor: it follows that the object of sleep is to preserve animal life. But its goal is the waking

state; for perception or thinking is the proper end of all creatures which have either of these capacities, inasmuch as these are best, and **the end is what is best**. Hence sleep belongs necessarily to every animal."[31]

De Somno 2, 455b17: λέγομεν τὴν φύσιν ἕνεκά του ποιεῖν.

De Somno 2, 455b24–25: τὸ δὲ τέλος βέλτιστον.

Both quotations surface in *Stephen Hero,* spoken by Cranly: "Most people have some purpose or other in their lives. Aristotle says that the end of every being is its greatest good. We all act in view of some good" (*SH* 220).

As a convinced Aristotelian, Joyce perhaps recognized the fundamental importance of Aristotle's teleology and his unbending optimism in the goodness of nature. It is a fundamental evidence for Aristotle that "Nature does nothing in vain, but always does the best possible for the substance of each kind of animal; therefore, if one way is better than another, this is also the way of nature."[32] He repeats in a variety of formulations this attitude, which imbues his entire approach in biology and philosophy.

Quotation 19: "Speculation is above practice."

Métaphysique d'Aristote (J. Barthélemy-Saint-Hilaire) I, 11–12: "[D] ans l'opinion de tout le monde, la science que l'on décore du nom de Sagesse, la Philosophie, a pour objet les causes et les principes des choses. Je le répète donc, en résumant ce qui précède: l'expérience, à ce qu'il semble, est un degré de science plus relevé que la sensation, sous quelque forme que la sensation s'exerce; l'homme qui se guide par les données de l'art est supérieur à ceux qui suivent exclusivement l'expérience; l'architecte est au-dessus des manoeuvres; et **les sciences de théorie sont au-dessus des sciences purement pratiques**."

De la Métaphysique d'Aristote (Victor Cousin), 125–26: "[L]'expérience est supérieure à la sensation, l'art à l'expérience, l'architecte au manœuvre et la théorie à la pratique."

Metaphysics 1, 1, 981b28–982a3: "It is presumed by everyone that what is called 'wisdom' is concerned with primary causes and principles; so that, as has been already stated, the man of experience seems wiser than one who simply has sensations, the artist is wiser than the man of experience, the master craftsman than the artisan; and **the theoretical sciences than the productive sciences**. It is clear that wisdom is a knowledge of certain principles and causes."[33]

Metaphysics 1, 1, 981b28–982a3: τὴν ὀνομαζομένην σοφίαν περὶ τὰ πρῶτα αἴτια καὶ τὰς ἀρχὰς ὑπολαμβάνουσι πάντες· ὥστε, καθάπερ εἴρηται πρότερον, ὁ μὲν ἔμπειρος τῶν ὁποιανοῦν ἐχόντων αἴσθησιν εἶναι δοκεῖ σοφώτερος, ὁ δὲ τεχνίτης τῶν ἐμπείρων, χειροτέχνου δὲ ἀρχιτέκτων, αἱ δὲ θεωρητικαὶ τῶν ποιητικῶν μᾶλλον. ὅτι μὲν οὖν ἡ σοφία περί τινας ἀρχὰς καὶ αἰτίας ἐστὶν ἐπιστήμη, δῆλον.

This quotation summarizes Aristotle's position regarding the superior value of the speculative inquiry of philosophy, which seeks wisdom for its own sake without any practical motivation. His *Metaphysics* begins with the assertion "All men by nature desire to know" and proceeds to explain that this desire reaches its highest expression in the speculative inquiry into the most fundamental causes and principles of all things. It is possible that, rather than render here a single phrase (that does not entirely correspond), Joyce is summarizing Aristotle's general attitude, as clearly stated in the following paragraph, which should be consulted in toto.[34]

There is a clear reference to the start of the *Metaphysics* in Joyce's review of Lady Gregory's *Poets and Dreamers,* where the merits of speculation over practice are made clear. See 15 above.

Quotation 20: "The wood does not make the bed nor the bronze the statue."

Métaphysique d'Aristote I, 33: "Ce n'est pas le bois apparemment qui fait le lit; ce n'est pas l'airain qui fait la statue."[35]

Metaphysics 1, 3, 984a24–25: "The wood does not make a bed, nor the bronze a statue."

Metaphysics 1, 3, 984a24–25: οὐδὲ ποιεῖ τὸ μὲν ξύλον κλίνην ὁ δὲ χαλκὸς ἀνδριάντα.

According to Aristotle, scientific knowledge is knowledge through causes; an individual is known only when its causes are disclosed. (Unexpectedly, perhaps, it is Bloom who declares: "Every phenomenon has a natural cause," *U* 15.2795–96.) In this quotation, Aristotle refers to the need for an efficient cause in order to explain how an individual comes to be. Matter or the material cause is insufficient of itself to explain the process whereby a living substance or artifact originates; it requires the action of an agent cause, which determines it according to a definite form. Joyce was familiar with Aristotle's famous theory of the four causes: material, efficient, formal, and final. On page 11 of his Paris notebook, Joyce depicted their relationship by means of the cruciform sketch reproduced below. At the center stands the imagined individual (substance or artifact). The arrow indicates

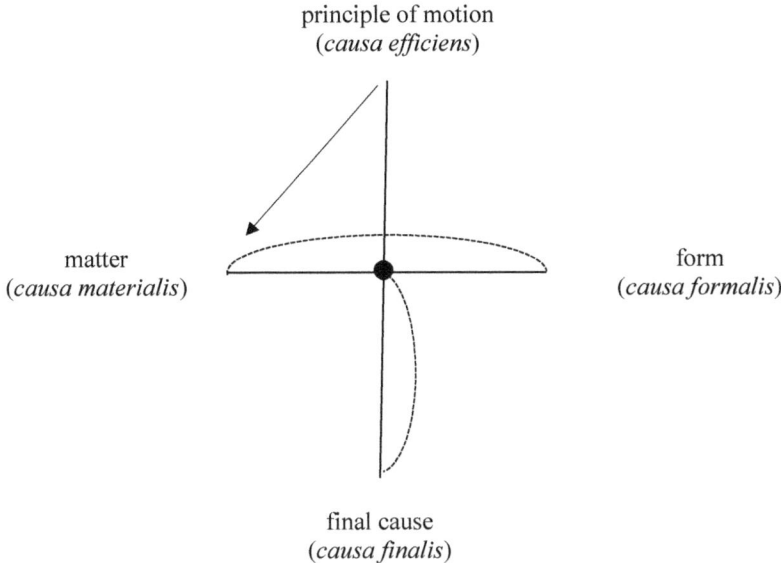

Figure 1. Cruciform illustration of Aristotle's four causes.

the action of the agent-cause upon the matter, which, for its part, stands in a binary, intrinsic, co-relationship vis-à-vis the form (formal cause); the efficient cause acts through an impetus directed toward the final cause—the ultimate explanation and reference point for the individual in its totality. Joyce could read the Latin terms for the four causes in footnotes to Cousin's translation (132): *causa formalis* (identified by Cousin as "la *quidditas* des scholastiques"), *causa materialis, causa efficiens,* and *causa finalis.*

In *Finnegans Wake,* Joyce refers obliquely—to say the least!—to Aristotle's four causes: "Gives there not too amongst us after all events (or so grunts a leading hebdromadary) some togethergush of stillandbutall-youknow that, insofarforth as, all up and down the whole concreation say, **efficient** first gets there **finally** every time, as a complex **matter** of pure **form**." (*FW* 581.26–30)

Quotation 21. "One who has only opinion is, compared with one who knows, in a state of sickness with regard to truth."

> *Métaphysique d'Aristote* II, 49: "En effet, comparativement à l'homme qui sait les choses, celui qui ne s'en forme qu'une vague opinion n'est pas dans une santé parfaite par rapport à la vérité."

Metaphysics 4, 4, 1008b30–31: "By contrast with someone who knows, the one who has mere opinion is not in a healthy disposition towards the truth."

Metaphysics 4, 4, 1008b30–31: καὶ γὰρ ὁ δοξάζων πρὸς τὸν ἐπιστάμενον οὐχ ὑγιεινῶς διάκειται πρὸς τὴν ἀλήθειαν.

I am unaware of any allusion to this quotation. Quotations 21, 22, 23, 24, and 26 share a common motif and indicate a fundamental Aristotelian attitude, which is characteristic of Joyce's mind—his belief in the objectivity and reliable nature of knowledge.

Quotation 22: "The same attribute cannot at the same time and in the same connection belong and not belong to the same subject."

Métaphysique d'Aristote II, 25: "Il est impossible qu'une seule et même chose soit, et tout à la fois ne soit pas, à une même autre chose, sous un même rapport."

Metaphysics 4, 3, 1005b19–20: "The same attribute cannot at the same time belong and not belong to the same subject and in the same respect."[36]

Metaphysics 4, 3, 1005b19–20: τὸ γὰρ αὐτὸ ἅμα ὑπάρχειν τε καὶ μὴ ὑπάρχειν ἀδύνατον τῷ αὐτῷ καὶ κατὰ τὸ αὐτό.

In *A Portrait of the Artist as a Young Man*, Stephen explains: "Aristotle's entire system of philosophy rests upon his book of psychology and that, I think, rests on his statement that the same attribute cannot at the same time and in the same connection belong and not belong to the same subject" (*P* V.1215–19). For a discussion see 16–17 above.

Joyce's rendition of the principle differs noticeably from the French translation. We can be certain however that, having taken logic as a second-year subject at University College, he was already familiar with this fundamental law of thought.

Quotation 23: "There cannot be a middle term between two contrary propositions."

Métaphysique d'Aristote II, 73: "Il n'est pas possible davantage qu'entre deux propositions contradictoires, il y ait jamais un terme moyen; mais il y a nécessité absolue, ou d'affirmer, ou de nier une chose d'une chose."[37]

Metaphysics 4, 7, 1011b23–24: "Nor indeed can there be any intermediate between contrary statements, but of one thing we must either assert or deny one thing, whatever it may be."[38]

Metaphysics 4, 7, 1011b23–24: ἀλλὰ μὴν οὐδὲ μεταξὺ ἀντιφάσεως ἐνδέχεται εἶναι οὐθέν, ἀλλ' ἀνάγκη ἢ φάναι ἢ ἀποφάναι ἓν καθ' ἑνὸς ὁτιοῦν.

This is the principle of excluded middle, the complement to the principle of noncontradiction. The latter states that of two contrary statements, both cannot be true; the former states that of two contrary statements, at least one must be true. There does not seem to be any reference to this principle in Joyce's works.

Quotation 24: "Necessity is that in virtue of which it is impossible that a thing should be otherwise."

Métaphysique d'Aristote II, 109–10: "Quand une chose ne peut pas être autrement qu'elle n'est, nous déclarons qu'il est nécessaire qu'elle soit ce qu'elle est; et, à dire vrai, c'est d'après le Nécessaire pris en ce sens qu'on qualifie tout le reste de nécessaire."

Metaphysics 5, 5, 1015a33–36: "We say that what cannot be otherwise, is necessarily as it is; and all other kinds of necessary are affirmed according to this meaning of necessary."

Metaphysics 5, 5, 1015a33–36: ἔτι τὸ μὴ ἐνδεχόμενον ἄλλως ἔχειν ἀναγκαῖόν φαμεν οὕτως ἔχειν· καὶ κατὰ τοῦτο τὸ ἀναγκαῖον καὶ τἆλλα λέγεταί πως ἅπαντα ἀναγκαῖα.

Joyce's rendition captures admirably and accurately the essence of Aristotle's meaning. His quotation appears almost verbatim in "Scylla and Charybdis": "Stephen looked down on a wide headless caubeen, hung on his ashplanthandle over his knee. My casque and sword. Touch lightly with two index fingers. Aristotle's experiment. One or two? Necessity is that in virtue of which it is impossible that one can be otherwise. Argal, one hat is one hat" (*U* 9.295–99).

Joyce's quotation is taken from *Metaphysics* 5, a lexicon of philosophical terms, in which Aristotle provides a comprehensive survey of the various kinds of "necessity."[39] There is the hypothetical necessity of a condition needed for an effect to occur; the—unnatural—necessity of violence or compulsion; the logical necessity proper to demonstration; and the absolute necessity of that which cannot be otherwise than it is: this is the primary meaning of necessity, implicit in all of the others. These are, in Aristotle's terms, the "ineluctable modalities" of the world.

Aristotle's so-called experiment, mentioned in *Ulysses,* refers to an intriguing tactile illusion noted in two of the works studied by Joyce in Paris, the *Metaphysics* and *On Dreams,* which forms part of the *Parva Naturalia.* In the latter, Aristotle states: "When the fingers are crossed, one object seems to be two; but yet we deny that it is two; for sight is more authoritative than touch. Yet, if touch stood alone, we should actually have pronounced the one object to be two."[40] In the *Metaphysics,* he says: "Touch says there are two objects when we cross our fingers, while sight says there is one."[41] A slightly more comprehensive account is given in *Problems:* "Why is it that an object which is held between two crossed fingers appears to be two? Is it because we touch it with two sense-organs? For when we hold the hand in its natural position we cannot touch it with the outer sides of the two fingers."[42]

The tactile illusion known as "Aristotle's experiment" is the impression of touching two objects when one places a single object between two crossed fingers.[43] The illusory perceptual disjunction (known as "tactile diplesthesia") does not arise, as Stephen supposes, with the two index fingers, but with adjacent fingers from the same hand, preferably the ring and middle finger. The classic example is a sphere such as a pea placed between crossed fingers, or crossed fingers placed on either side of the nose. Stephen's mention of necessity in this context is strange, since a tactile illusion does not yield reliable knowledge. The definition of necessity, however, is accurate. Stephen's mind is obviously sequencing incompatible ideas.

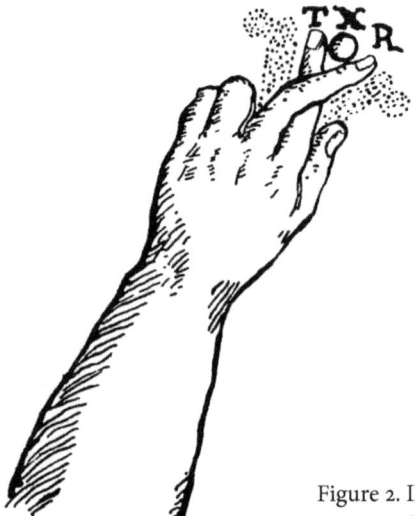

Figure 2. Illustration of "Aristotle's Experiment" from Descartes's *Traité de l'Homme,* 1662.

Quotation 25: "The hand is not (absolutely) part of the body."

> *Métaphysique d'Aristote* II, 327–28: "Ainsi, la main, absolument par-
> lant, n'est pas une partie de l'homme; elle est uniquement la main
> tant qu'elle est animé, et qu'elle peut remplir la fonction qui lui est
> propre; si elle n'est pas animée et vivante, ce n'est plus une partie de
> l'homme."
>
> *Metaphysics* 7, 11, 1036b30–32: "For it is not the hand in any condition
> which is a part of man, but only when it can fulfil its function, and
> so is alive; without life, it is not a part."[44]
>
> *Metaphysics* 7, 11, 1036b30–32: οὐ γὰρ πάντως τοῦ ἀνθρώπου μέρος
> ἡ χείρ, ἀλλ' ἡ δυναμένη τὸ ἔργον ἀποτελεῖν, ὥστε ἔμψυχος οὖσα·
> μὴ ἔμψυχος δὲ οὐ μέρος.

This statement occurs in *Metaphysics* 7, where Aristotle—in a notoriously
difficult series of discussions—seeks to identify the basic principle of substance: what is it that accounts for the "beingness" of something? Concluding that it is to be identified primarily as form (*eidos*), he emphasizes
that in the case of living things, this cannot exist apart from their material
parts. Saint-Hilaire's phrase "absolutely speaking" does not clearly transmit
the sense of the original. Jacques Aubert has suggested an allusion to this
quotation in the following passage from *A Portrait*:[45] "He was in mortal
sin. Even once was a mortal sin. It could happen in an instant. But how so
quickly? By seeing or by thinking of seeing. The eyes see the thing, without
having wished first to see. Then in an instant it happens. But does that part
of the body understand or what?" (*P* III, 1331–36).

Quotation 26: "It is in beings that are always the same and are not susceptible of change that we must seek for (the) truth."

> *Métaphysique d'Aristote* III, 101: "On ne doit chercher à trouver la
> vérité que dans les choses qui sont éternellement les mêmes, et qui
> ne subissent jamais le moindre changement."
>
> *Metaphysics* 11, 6, 1063a13–15: "We should pursue truth by reference
> to those things which are always the same, and which undergo no
> change."[46]
>
> *Metaphysics* 11, 6, 1063a13–15: δεῖ γὰρ ἐκ τῶν ἀεὶ κατὰ ταὐτὸ ἐχόντων
> καὶ μηδεμίαν μεταβολὴν ποιουμένων τἀληθὲς θηρεύειν.

This quotation is one of those that indicate Joyce's interest in affirming the
stability of knowledge; it is closely related to Quotation 24, which defines

necessity. Against Parmenides, Aristotle accepted the evidence of change, yet maintained that the object of knowledge requires a measure of necessity or permanence;[47] against Plato, he believed that it is possible to attain stable knowledge about changing realities. There is an element of necessity even in mutable, sensible, things that allows them to be known scientifically, but this must ultimately be traced back to eternal beings, which are utterly necessary and cannot be otherwise than as they are. As well as the Prime Mover, according to Aristotle, the heavenly bodies are also necessary and eternal.

Quotation 27: "Movement is the actuality of the possible as possible."

> *Métaphysique d'Aristote* III, 120–21: "L'Être se divisant dans chacun de ses genres, ici en puissance, et là en acte parfait, en Entéléchie, j'appelle mouvement l'acte du possible en tant que possible."[48]
>
> *Metaphysics* 11, 9, 1065b14–16: "Since every kind of reality is divided into the potential and the actual (*entelecheia*), I call movement the actualization of the potential as such."
>
> *Metaphysics* 11, 9, 1065b16: τὴν τοῦ δυνάμει ᾗ τοιοῦτόν ἐστιν ἐνέργειαν λέγω κίνησιν.

For a discussion of this important quotation, see 23–24 above. In "Scylla and Charybdis," Stephen reflects upon the imponderable reality of unfulfilled contingencies of the past, and the status of unrealized possibilities: "Here he ponders things that were not: what Caesar would have lived to do had he believed the soothsayer: what might have been: possibilities of the possible as possible: things not known: what name Achilles bore when he lived among women" (*U* 9.348–51).

Quotation 28: "Thought is the thought of thought."

> *De la Métaphysique d'Aristote* (Victor Cousin), 214: "Dieu donc se pense lui-même, s'il est ce qu'il y a de plus puissant, et sa pensée est la pensée de la pensée."
>
> *Metaphysics* 12, 9, 1074b33–35: "Therefore it must be itself that thought thinks, since it is the most excellent of things, and its thinking is a thinking of thinking."[49]
>
> *Metaphysics* 12, 9, 1074b33–35: αὐτὸν ἄρα νοεῖ, εἴπερ ἐστὶ τὸ κράτιστον, καὶ ἔστιν ἡ νόησις νοήσεως.[50]

For a discussion of this quotation see 24 above. It is possible that Joyce's reading of this passage was influenced by the following passage from Victor

Cousin's book on Aristotle's *Metaphysics:* "Ce n'est pas la virtualité de la pensée, mais sa manifestation active qui fait sa beauté et son caractère divin. De là, cette formule d'Aristote: la vraie pensée est la pensée de la pensée, ἔστιν ἡ νόησις νοήσεως νόησις."[51]

There is an audible echo of this quotation in Bloom's musings on the advantages of shaving: "With thought of aught he sought though fraught with nought" (*U* 17.284–85).

Quotation 29: "God is the eternal perfect animal."

> *De la Métaphysique d'Aristote* (Victor Cousin), 200–201: "Aussi nous disons que Dieu est un animal éternel et parfait."
>
> *Metaphysics* 12, 7, 1072b28–29: "We say therefore that God is a living being, eternal, most good."[52]
>
> *Metaphysics* 12, 7, 1072b28–29: φαμὲν δὴ τὸν θεὸν εἶναι ζῷον ἀΐδιον ἄριστον.

This statement might be seen as the logical finale to those quotations from Aristotle cited by Joyce in response to what he viewed as the shyness of the modern era, which "discountenances the absolute." I am not familiar with any reference by Joyce in his creative works to this line from Aristotle.

Joyce's cousin Kathleen Murray recalled a conversation he had with his aunt Josephine: "I remember him saying that he envied her faith. 'Do you believe in a Supreme Being?' she once asked. 'Yes,' he answered, and she left it at that."[53] Aristotle's eternal, perfect, God was perhaps the object of his belief.

Quotation 30: "The object of desire is that which appears to us <u>beautiful</u> . . . We desire a thing because it appears to us <u>good</u> . . . . (?)"

> *De la Métaphysique d'Aristote* (Cousin), 197: "**En effet, l'objet du désir est ce qui paraît beau**; et l'objet premier de la volonté est le bien lui-même; car **nous désirons une chose parce que nous la jugeons bonne**, plutôt que nous la jugeons telle parce que nous la désirons."
>
> *Métaphysique d'Aristote* (J. Barthélemy-Saint-Hilaire) III, 181–82: "L'objet désiré est ce que nous paraît être bien; et le primitif de la volonté, c'est le bien même. Nous le souhaitons, parce qu'il nous paraît souhaitable, bien plutôt qu'il ne nous paraît souhaitable parce que nous le souhaitons."
>
> *Metaphysics* 12, 7, 1072a27–29: "The primary objects of desire and thought are the same. For the apparent good is the object of

appetite, and the real good is the object of the will. Desire is the result of opinion rather than opinion that of desire."[54]

Metaphysics 12, 7, 1072a27–29: ἐπιθυμητὸν μὲν γὰρ τὸ φαινόμενον καλόν [. . .] ὀρεγόμεθα δὲ διότι δοκεῖ μᾶλλον ἢ δοκεῖ διότι ὀρεγόμεθα.

Joyce follows Cousin's translation. Aristotle is here concerned with the distinction between that which appears to be good or beautiful and moves the appetite and that which is really beautiful and motivates the rational will. Cousin's translation perhaps suggests that the distinction in question is between the good and the beautiful; Aristotle, however, refers only to the beautiful (to *kalon*). Joyce's question mark suggests that he is unsure of the sense of the passage. He translates this uncertainty into one of the questions written elsewhere in his notebook: "I desire to see the Mona Lisa. Is it therefore beautiful or is it good?" While Joyce's question is understandable in light of the translation, it is not Aristotle's intention here to distinguish between good and beauty but rather between the distinct value that something has for the appetite and the will.

Quotation 31. "Nature, it seems, is not a collection of unconnected episodes, like a bad tragedy."

Métaphysique d'Aristote III, 355: "Cependant, d'après tout ce que nous voyons, la nature ne montre pas à nos yeux une succession de vains épisodes, comme on en trouve dans une mauvaise tragédie."[55]

Metaphysics 14, 3, 1090b19–20: "From what we observe it does not appear that nature is a series of episodes, like a bad tragedy."

Metaphysics 14, 3, 1090b19–20: οὐκ ἔοικε δ' ἡ φύσις ἐπεισοδιώδης οὖσα ἐκ τῶν φαινομένων, ὥσπερ μοχθηρὰ τραγῳδία.

This passage is more than likely behind Stephen's reference to "The playwright who wrote the folio of this world and wrote it badly" (*U* 9.1046–47).[56] The theme of Aristotle's view of the universe as "cosmos," an ordered unity, was discussed in chapter 5.

Afterword

It remains to summarize briefly the results of the foregoing investigation into the importance of Aristotle and Aquinas in the writings of James Joyce. The survey confirms that both thinkers exerted decisive and extensive influence: the question remains how profound was that effect and whether Joyce stayed faithful to his sources.

The concrete influences of Aristotle and Aquinas have been charted by referring to circumstances external to Joyce's writings and by identifying copious references in his literary works. The biographical facts of Joyce's education and his initiation into the intellectual world of Aristotle and Aquinas have been catalogued in detail. Besides the semi-autobiographical information that may be recognized in *Stephen Hero, A Portrait,* and *Ulysses,* I have referred to a wide variety of sources, such as letters, lectures, book reviews, recorded remarks, reminiscences of acquaintances, and academic syllabi. Joyce's Catholic upbringing and Jesuit education were shown to be of great importance in nurturing a commitment toward Aristotelian Thomism. The quotations that Joyce transcribed in Paris are especially significant for his knowledge of Aristotle, even those not incorporated into his writings, since these also are confirmation of the philosophical position to which he was attracted. I have frequently extracted from their original context various phrases that I believe disclose Joyce's Aristotelian mentality when applied to particular philosophical themes. Theoharis's remark applies not only to *Ulysses:* "Joyce, at crucial moments in the novel, flashes Aristotelian spotlights, thereby suggesting, with the cunning he trusted more than frankness, a way that leads attention successfully to the truth in the Dedalian labyrinth."[1]

A remote historical factor of great importance for Joyce's philosophical formation was the revival of interest in St. Thomas prompted by the encyclical *Aeterni Patris.* This sufficiently transformed a moribund Thomism that would within a decade determine the intellectual atmosphere at Dublin's

University College. A consequence of this revival were the philosophical handbooks that, on the testimony of one of Joyce's classmates, were an important source for his knowledge of both Aristotle and Aquinas.

The philosophies of Aristotle and Aquinas had much in common, sharing central and fundamental principles. Joyce did not in any significant way advert to this commonality but had recourse to each for distinct purposes. Aristotle equipped him with fundamental principles regarding knowledge and reality. Without his careful study of Aristotle's *Metaphysics* and *On the Soul,* Joyce could not have created the intellectual character of Stephen portrayed in the early chapters of *Ulysses;* the debate in "Scylla and Charybdis" between Stephen, Eglinton, and Russell would likewise have been impossible. The basic concepts of act and potency, form and entelechy, are indispensable for Stephen's reading of the world and his sense of selfhood. The presentation of Aristotelian ideas in *Ulysses* is largely faithful and accurate. An exception is the definition of movement as the "actuality of the possible as possible," which was due to the faulty translation used by Joyce.

Apart from relying on Aquinas in a general way as an authority for his realist outlook, Joyce borrowed a number of slogans and concepts with which to elaborate his own aesthetic theory. These he adapted and reordered; in *A Portrait,* Stephen substitutes *integritas* for *aliquid, res* for *consonantia,* and *quidditas* for *claritas.* Joyce's interpretation diverged greatly from his acknowledged source. There would be nothing inconsistent in this, were the aesthetic theory not presented under the aegis of St. Thomas. The most significant departure from Aquinas was to divorce imagination and intellect as separate capacities, respectively, for beauty as sensible and for truth as intellectual. Such a view is not only alien to Aquinas but makes little sense in any comprehensive aesthetic theory that must accommodate both the sensible and the intellectual in a perspective that recognizes the continuity between sense and intellect.

Joyce had a natural philosophical penchant; he was interested in basic problems. His writings have a recognizable philosophical tenor, with recurrent questions and enigmas. This sensitivity allowed Joyce to maintain a sense of mystery and marvel at the big questions, finding new ways to articulate and express his feelings and experience in their presence. We may take as autobiographical the reflection Joyce attributes to Stephen in *A Portrait:* "By thinking about things you could understand them" (*P* I.1269). I have dealt in detail with major philosophical themes as they occur in Joyce's writings. I emphasized that he was preoccupied with traditional questions of stability and permanence of knowledge and of identity of the self over time. He was motivated to find a scheme that would embrace the totality.

In his proclivity toward Aristotelian realism, Joyce was no different from the majority of mankind; as Henri Bergson remarked, Aristotle's philosophy is the natural metaphysics of the human intellect. Despite this native philosophical sensitivity and stated loyalty to Aristotle and Aquinas, Joyce was, however, an amateur philosopher whose philosophical disposition remained largely undeveloped. He had a potentially profound mind, but his naturally philosophical mind was left untrained. The influence of Aristotle and Aquinas, while extensive, was shallow. Educated in an atmosphere permeated by Aristotelian realism, Joyce acquired some elementary notions that served him well. Aristotle provided him with a number of categories and certainties. He learned enough to provide answers to some basic questions but not enough to fully articulate and understand them.

Joyce had doubtless the Wordsworthian gifts of "clearest insight," and "amplitude of mind" but exercised these in the service of the literary imagination. George Santayana commented that had Locke's mind been more profound, it might have been less influential.[2] Had Joyce been a more skilled philosopher, his writings would have been greatly different: not necessarily better, but definitely not the same. Had he developed the philosophical habits of reasoning and analysis, he would have explored more deeply the topics that continued to interest him. Joyce's attitude to philosophical questions was that of the amateur: fascinated, wondering, but still puzzled. Gifted with a naturally philosophical mind, he lacked the training necessary to contemplate and articulate the mysteries he had perceived. Had he carefully studied, for example, Aristotle's *Organon,* he would have understood how it is possible for an individual to retain his identity while acquiring new determinations. The question of identity throughout change preoccupied Joyce in *A Portrait* and *Ulysses* because he was not familiar with Aristotle's theory of substance and accidents. *Finnegans Wake* thrives on ambiguity and apparent contradiction, but, as Aristotle points out, while one may utter contradictory statements, it is impossible to believe them and still make sense—even to oneself.

The question of the relationship between philosophy and literature has exercised philosophers since the time of Plato (whose own philosophical works were also exquisite works of literature—thereby adding to the irony that he would banish poets from his republic). A work of literature may spring from a secret truth, but it is better literature if that truth remains hidden, left for the reader to imagine and decipher. The writer who overtly uses his medium to convey a philosophical message will damage his art; his rational methods will intrude and vie with his literary tropes. Better to hint by metaphor and symbol at philosophical notions than to expound them. *Ars celare veritatem.* James Joyce achieved this, the amateur philosopher in him served the artist well.

Appendix

Texts on Aesthetics from James Joyce's "Early Commonplace Book" (MS 36,639/02/A)

[15r]

Bonum est in quod tendit appetitus.

S. Thomas Aquinas

The good is that towards the possession of which an appetite tends: the good is the desirable. The true and the beautiful are the most persistent orders of the desirable. Truth is desired by the intellectual appetite which is appeased by the most satisfying relations of the intelligible; beauty is desired by the esthetic appetite which is appeased by the most satisfying relations of the sensible. The true and the beautiful are spiritually possessed; the true by intellection, the beautiful by apprehension, and the appetites which desire to possess them, the intellectual and esthetic appetites, are therefore spiritual appetites . . .

JAJ

Pola. 7. XI. 04.

[16r]

Pulcra sunt quae visa placent —

S. Thomas Aquinas.

Those things are beautiful the apprehension of which pleases. Therefore beauty is that quality of a sensible object in virtue of which its apprehension pleases or satisfies the esthetic appetite which desires to apprehend the most satisfying relations of the sensible. Now the act of apprehension involves at least two activities, the activity of cognition or simple perception and the activity of recognition [original: "consequent satisfaction"]. If the activity of simple perception is like every other activity itself pleasant every sensible object that has been apprehended can be said in the first place to have been and to be beautiful [sic] in a measure beautiful; and even the most hideous object can be said to have been and to be beautiful in so far as it has been apprehended. In regard then to that part of the act of apprehension which is called the activity of simple perception there is no sensible object which cannot be said to be in a measure beautiful.

With regard to the second part of the act of apprehension which is called the activity of recognition [original: "satisfaction"] it may further be said that there is no activity of simple perception to which there does not succeed in whatsoever measure the activity of recognition ["satisfaction"]. For by the activity of recognition ["satisfaction"] is meant an activity of decision; and in accordance with this activity in all conceivable cases a sensible object is said to be satisfying or dissatisfying. But the activity of recognition ["satisfaction or decision"] is, like every other activity, itself pleasant and therefore every object that has been apprehended is secondly in whatsoever measure beautiful. Consequently even the most hideous object may be [16v] said to [be] beautiful for this reason as it is a priori said to be beautiful in so far as it encounters the activity of simple perception.

Sensible objects, however, are said conventionally to be beautiful or not for neither of the foregoing reasons but rather by reason of the nature, degree and duration of the satisfaction resulting from the apprehension of them and it is in accordance with these latter merely that the words "beautiful" and "ugly" are used in practical esthetic philosophy. It remains then to be said that these words indicate only a greater or less measure of resultant satisfaction and that any sensible object, to which the word "ugly" is practically applied, an object, that is, the apprehension of which results in a small measure of aesthetic satisfaction is, in so far as its apprehension results in any measure of satisfaction whatsoever, said to be for the third time beautiful. . . .

JAJ

Pola. 15. XI. 04

[17r]

The Act of Apprehension

It has been said that the act of apprehension involves at least two ac-tivities—the activity of cognition or simple perception and the activity of recognition. The act of apprehension, however, in its most complete form involves three activities—the third being the activity of satisfaction. By rea-son of the fact that these three activities are all pleasant themselves every sensible object that has been apprehended must be doubly and may be trebly beautiful. In practical aesthetic philosophy the epithets "beautiful" and "ugly" are applied with regard chiefly to the third activity, with regard, that is, to the nature, degree and duration of the satisfaction resultant from the apprehension of any sensible object and therefore any sensible object to which in practical aesthetic philosophy the epithet "beautiful" is applied must be trebly beautiful, must have encountered, that is, the three activities which are involved in the act of apprehension in its most complete form. Practically then the quality of beauty in itself must involve three constitu-ents to encounter each of these three activities . . .

JAJ

Pola. 16 . XI. 04.

Notes

Introduction

1. See among others Boyle, Bredin, Damon, Donoghue, Duncan, Eco, Ellmann, Gorman, Hedermann, Hibbs, Kain, Kenner, Killham, Kunkel, Levin, Levy, Livorni, Morse, Noon, Rickard, Smidt, Steinberg, Stewart, Sullivan, Theoharis, Tindall.

2. John Locke, *An Essay Concerning Human Understanding*, 10.

3. See Philip Kitcher, "Introduction," *Joyce's* Ulysses: *Philosophical Perspectives*, 2–3. See also 5n7.

4. Frank Budgen, *James Joyce and the Making of* Ulysses *and Other Writings*, 17–18.

5. Budgen, 16, 19.

6. See Georges Borach, "Conversations with James Joyce," 325.

7. Vincent J. Cheng, *Inauthentic: The Anxiety over Culture and Identity*, 14.

8. Emer Nolan, *James Joyce and Nationalism*, 148.

9. Cheng, 15.

10. Nolan, 17.

11. For an excellent treatment of this, see W. Norris Clarke, S.J., *Person and Being*, 27–28, 43. The *Index Thomisticus* (ed. Roberto Busa) gives thirty-four references for the phrase "*dominus sui*" referring to man's free and deliberative action. Two sample passages: *ST* II-II, q. 64 a. 5 ad 3: Ad tertium dicendum quod homo constituitur dominus sui ipsius per liberum arbitrium. *CG* 3, 155, 3283: Licet homo per voluntatem et liberum arbitrium sit dominus sui actus. Aristotle had expounded the thought at length in *EN* 3, 5, 1113b17–21. See *EN* 3, 3, 1112b31–32: ἄνθρωπος εἶναι ἀρχὴ τῶν πράξεων ("A man is the origin of his actions").

12. See W. K. C. Guthrie, *The Greek Philosophers from Thales to Aristotle*, 23–24.

13. It is worth noting that Joyce has been seen as worthy of commentary by some prominent philosophers, including Philip Kitcher, Martha C. Nussbaum, and Donald Davidson. See Philip Kitcher, "Something Rich and Strange: Joyce's Perspectivism"; Martha C. Nussbaum, "Between Detachment and Disgust: Bloom in Hades"; Donald Davidson, "James Joyce and Humpty Dumpty." Philip Kitcher is author also of *Joyce's Kaleidoscope: An Invitation to* Finnegans Wake.

14. Jean-Paul Sartre, "Time in Faulkner: *The Sound and the Fury*," 226.

15. Richard M. Kain, "Fifty Years of *Ulysses*: 1934–1984," 79.

16. Letter to Ezra Pound, July 27, 1922: "Some passages have great beauty, lyric beauty, even in the fashion of my generation, and the whole book incites to philosophy." Cited by R. F. Foster, *W. B. Yeats: A Life II,* 260. Yeats could write with such praise, although he never read all of *Ulysses.* Denis Donoghue, in "Joyce's Landscapes," remarks: "*Ulysses* is full of invitations to judgment: the landscape of the writing is metaphysical and moral rather than picturesque" (79).

17. Cheryl Temple Herr, *Joyce and the Art of Shaving,* 3–4.

18. Denis Donoghue, "Joyce and the Finite Order," 256.

Chapter 1. Aristotelian Joyce

1. Unless stated otherwise, translations of Aristotle are from the Loeb Classical Library published by Harvard University Press (Cambridge, Mass.) and Heinemann (London) with line references according to Bekker (Berlin, 1831–1870). Translations from the *Complete Works of Aristotle,* ed. Jonathan Barnes (Princeton University Press, 1995, are indicated by *CW1* and *CW2.* Unless stated otherwise, translations from Aquinas's *Summa Theologiae* are from *The Summa Theologica* (Chicago: Encyclopaedia Britannica, 1984) with occasional modifications. Unless stated otherwise, quotations from Aquinas are from the Marietti (Turin) editions.

2. Aristotle, *Fragmenta,* 420.

3. Jonathan Swift, *The Works of Jonathan Swift,* 180.

4. Georges Borach, "Conversations with James Joyce," *College English,* 325 (trans. modified). See Georges Borach, "Gespräche mit James Joyce," 331.

5. J. G. Kohl, *Travels in Ireland,* 70–71. See Michael Patrick Gillespie, *James Joyce's Trieste Library,* 139.

6. *Scribbledehobble, the Ur-Workbook for "Finnegans Wake,"* 99. Joyce copied this from Thomas F O'Rahilly, *A Miscellany of Irish Proverbs,* 73. He does not include it in *FW;* there is, however, the following scene in *Stephen Hero:* "The nights before the examination were spent sitting outside under the porch of the Library. The two young men gazed up into the tranquil sky and discussed how it was possible to live with the least amount of labour. Cranly suggested bees: he seemed to know the entire economy of bee-life and he did not seem as intolerant towards bees as towards men. Stephen said it would be a good arrangement if Cranly were to live on the labour of the bees and allow him (Stephen) to live on the united labour of bees and of their keeper" (*SH* 128).

7. Thomas Merton, *The Seven Storey Mountain,* 212.

8. Martin Luther, *Letters* I, 37.

9. Preserved Smith, ed., *Life and Letters of Martin Luther,* 26.

10. Saint Ignatius of Loyola, *Constitutions of the Society of Jesus,* 219–20, §§ 464, 470.

11. For an engaging account of Joyce's student days, see *Joyce the Student: University College, Dublin 1898–1902* by John Kelly, former Registrar, University College Dublin.

12. John Henry Newman, *The Idea of a University,* 109–10.

13. Herbert S. Gorman, *James Joyce: A Definitive Biography,* 94.

14. C. P. Curran, *James Joyce Remembered,* 3. Joyce had entered University College the previous year.

15. William Dawson, "The Society Restored (1897–1908)," 39.

16. For the original ("L'influenza letteraria universale del rinascimento"), see page 286: "All' epoca del rinascimento lo spirito umano lottava contro l'assolutismo scolastico, contro quell'immenso (ed in molti riguardi mirabile) sistema filosofico che ha le sue ime fondamenta nel pensiero aristotelico, freddo, chiaro ed imperterrito, mentre la sua cima sorge alla luce vaga e misteriosa dell' ideologia cristiana." Also in *James Joyce in Padua,* ed. Louis Berrone, 14.

17. Felix Hackett, "The Society Restored (1897–1908)," 42.

18. Stanislaus Joyce, *The Complete Dublin Diary of Stanislaus Joyce,* 53.

19. What were previously believed to have been two separate notebooks ("The Paris Notebook" and "The Pola Notebook") is now more accurately referred to as Joyce's "Early Commonplace Book," preserved in the National Library of Ireland. See Luca Crispi's comprehensive survey, "A Commentary on James Joyce's National Library of Ireland 'Early Commonplace Book.'" See 289n2 below.

20. In his 1912 Padua lecture, "The Universal Literary Influence of the Renaissance," having detailed the "much trumpeted progress" of the early twentieth century, Joyce remarks: "But in the midst of this complex and many-sided civilization the human mind, almost terrorized by materialistic greatness, becomes lost, denies itself and grows weaker. Should we then conclude that present-day materialism [. . .] atrophies the spiritual faculties of man, impedes his development, blunts his keenness?" (*OCPW* 187). Joyce's assessment of the consequences of the Renaissance is informative: "Untiring creative power, heated, strong passion, the intense desire to see and feel, unfettered and prolix curiosity have after three centuries degenerated into frenetic sensationalism. Indeed, one might say of modern man that he has an epidermis rather than a soul. The sensory power of his organism has developed enormously, but it has developed to the detriment of the spiritual faculty. We lack moral sense and perhaps also strength of imagination." *OCPW* 188–89.

21. Hugh Kenner, "Joyce and the 19th Century Linguistics Explosion," 48.

22. See 9 above.

23. Richard M. Kain, *Fabulous Voyager: A Study of James Joyce's* Ulysses, 4.

24. The editors of the volume remark in a footnote: "Here again Joyce shows his devotion to Aristotle's aesthetic."

25. See Joyce's letter to Stanislaus, February 8, 1903: "I am feeling very intellectual these times and up to my eyes in Aristotle's Psychology. If the editor of the 'Speaker' put in my review of 'Catalina' you will see some of the fruits thereof." *LII* 28. Richard Ellmann comments: "Aristotle's *De Anima* is not mentioned in the review of *Catalina,* but some phrases are perhaps indebted to it. Joyce later used this work as the basis of much of the *Proteus* episode of *Ulysses." LII* 28n2.

26. Cited *CW* 135n1.

27. *Met.* 4, 3, 1005b19–21.

28. Stanislaus Joyce, *The Complete Dublin Diary of Stanislaus Joyce,* 100.

29. Joyce had read the following statement in Burnet's book, which he had reviewed: "What we do find is that Theophrastos, Aristotle's immediate successor, founded scientific Botany, as he himself had founded scientific Zoology, and that it was either in

such branches of inquiry or in historical research that Aristotle's followers chiefly distinguished themselves." John Burnet, *Aristotle on Education*, 135.

30. *EN* 1, 3, 1094b.

31. *CG* 1, 3. Trans. Joseph Rickaby, *Of God and His Creatures*, 2.

32. Richard Ellmann, *Ulysses on the Liffey*, 16.

33. Henri Bergson, *Creative Evolution*, 344.

34. Harry Levin, *James Joyce: A Critical Introduction*, 35.

35. See Arthur Koestler, *The Act of Creation*, 176.

36. *Met.* 7, 1, 1028a10.

37. Hugh Kenner, "The Cubist Portrait," 107.

38. The Greek word *entelês* means "complete" or "full" (it derives from the word *telos*, goal or end).

39. *De An.* 2, 1, 412b5–6. See also *U* 15.106–07: "the first entelechy, the structural rhythm."

40. *De An.* 2, 1, 414a12–14, my trans. For a comprehensive account, see *De An.* 2, 4, 415a14–415b28.

41. *De An.* 2, 1, 412a31–32.

42. Edmund Spenser, "A Hymn in Honour of Beautie," *Shorter Poems of Edmund Spenser*, 712.

43. Isaac Newton, *Mathematical Principles of Natural Philosophy*, xvii.

44. See 213–14, 217–19 above.

45. *De An.* 2, 8, 432a2.

46. *De An.* 3, 8, 431b20–21.

47. For another important reference to Aristotelian entelechy in modern literature, see the account in Thomas Mann's *Doctor Faustus*: "We were delighted by Aristotle's theory of content and form—with content as the potential, the possible, urgently seeking form in order to realize itself; and form as that which moves but is unmoved, which is intellect and soul, the soul of what exists striving for self-realization, self-perfection as phenomenon—and thus were also delighted by his theory of entelechy, which as a piece of eternity penetrates and animates the body, manifesting itself in and giving shape to the organic, guides the body's mechanism, knows its goal, watches over its fate. Nonnenmacher had spoken of these intuitions very beautifully and eloquently, and Adrian proved to be extraordinarily moved by the concept. 'When,' he said, 'theology declares the soul is from God, that is philosophically correct, for as the principle that forms each individual manifestation it is a part of the pure form of being-in-general, arising out of the thought that eternally thinks itself, which we call "God." . . . I think I understand what Aristotle meant with his "entelechy." It is the angel of each single creature, the genius of its life, whose knowledgeable guidance it gladly trusts. What one calls prayer is actually that trust announcing itself in admonition and entreaty. It is properly called prayer, however, because ultimately it is God whom we thereby address.'" Thomas Mann, *Doctor Faustus*, 103.

48. Aristotle defines sensation as the power to receive a sensible form without the matter, as wax takes on the shape of a signet-ring without the gold; it "takes the figure

of the gold or bronze but not as bronze or gold" See *De An.* 2, 12, 424a17–21, quoted by Joyce in his Paris notebook. Is it possible that Joyce took the celebrated phrase "bronze by gold," central to "Sirens," from Aristotle's psychology? An alternative explanation might be Joyce's memory, aurally internalized, that he took the bronze medal for singing, and missed the gold, at the 1904 Feis Ceoil.

49. *De An.* 3, 5, 430a23.

50. A possible explanation for this misquotation is that Joyce was distracted by the line of one of his favorite Irish songs, *An Cruiscín Lán,* a line of which runs: "Immortal and divine great Bacchus god of wine." This song is included on the CD *JoyceSong: Irish Songs of James Joyce,* Fran O'Rourke and John Feeley. See www.joycesong.info.

51. Theoharis Constantine Theoharis, *Joyce's Ulysses: An Anatomy of the Soul,* 2. See pages 16–17: "For a spiritual firebrand like Stephen, who has rejected religious faith to pursue a free artistic devotion but still believes that the rightful inheritance of his artist's soul is the full radiance of truth, Aristotle was the perfect new authority, the mind that gave Catholicism much of its intellectual mettle without being itself touched by the church's religious falsehoods and absurdity. Stephen, recalling the intellectual labors he undertook for the creation of the conscience of his race, first suggests the great importance of Aristotle to his goal by retracing in 'Nestor' his mind's progress toward luminescent insight into *De Anima.* The other appearances of this work in *Ulysses* further reveal the great extent of Stephen's intellectual debt to Aristotle. Since Joyce's intellectual development was the model for Stephen's, there is some reason to think that Joyce himself owed a similar debt to the Greek philosopher."

52. *Poet.* 9, 1451b4–5.

53. Aristotle quotes the poet Agathon: "Of this alone even God is deprived, the power of making things that are past never to have been." See *EN* 6, 2, 1139b8–11.

54. See also *U* 9.1041–42: "He found in the world without as actual what was in his world within as possible."

55. See 228 above.

56. *Métaphysique d'Aristote,* trans. J. Barthélemy-Saint-Hilaire (Paris: Librairie Germer-Baillière, 1879), 3 vols.

57. J. Tricot, *Aristote: La Métaphysique* I, x. Tricot correctly translates the relevant passages from the *Metaphysics:* "Etant donné la distinction, en chaque genre, de ce qui est en puissance et de ce qui est en entéléchie, l'acte de ce qui est en puissance en tant que tel, je l'appelle mouvement" (11, 9, 1065b16); "C'est l'entéléchie de l'être en puissance, en tant qu'il est en puissance, qui constitue le mouvement" (11, 9, 1065b33). While Barthélemy-Sainte-Hilaire translated many of Aristotle's writings, they are generally ignored in the scholarly literature on Aristotle.

58. Sheldon Brivic, *Joyce the Creator,* 46.

59. Seamus Deane, introduction, *Finnegans Wake,* by James Joyce, xii.

60. *Poet.* 1461b11–12, Butcher's translation, which was used by Joyce.

61. *Notebooks of Samuel Taylor Coleridge* I, § 1770.

62. Anthony Burgess, *Joysprick,* 48.

Chapter 2. Thomist Joyce

1. Cited in Robert Scholes and Richard M. Kain, eds., *The Workshop of Daedalus: James Joyce and the Raw Materials for* A Portrait of the Artist as a Young Man, 101.

2. S. Foster Damon, "The Odyssey in Dublin," 222.

3. Herbert S. Gorman, *James Joyce: His First Forty Years,* 216.

4. Gorman, 7.

5. Anthony Burgess, *Re Joyce,* 31.

6. Richard F. Peterson, "More Aristotelian Grist for the Joycean Mill," 216.

7. Harry Levin, *James Joyce: A Critical Introduction,* 193.

8. Padraic Colum, "With James Joyce in Ireland," 52.

9. Frank O'Connor, "Joyce and Dissociated Metaphor," 374. See Hugh Kenner, *Dublin's Joyce,* 114: "An Aristotelian catalogue of senses, faculties, and mental activities is played against the unfolding of infant conscience."

10. Scholes and Kain, eds., *The Workshop of Daedalus,* 52.

11. Stanislaus Joyce, *My Brother's Keeper,* 108, 130.

12. Joyce was familiar with Sheehan and took part in a discussion of Arthur Clery's paper on *My New Curate* to the Library Conference of the College Sodality on June 16, 1901. In 1902, Sheehan published a paper in St. Stephen's titled "Certain Elements of Character." Joyce included his name in a long list of Irish fiction writers in his commonplace book.

13. P. A. Sheehan, *Under the Cedars and the Stars,* 1–2.

14. See Fran O'Rourke, "Aquinas and Platonism," 247–79.

15. Pope Leo XIII, *Aeterni Patris,* 1879, § 31.

16. In "Grace," Leo XIII is referred to as "one of the lights of the age" (*D* "Grace," 144.560–61).

17. Letter to J. D. Dalgairns, *Letters and Diaries of John Henry Newman,* 279.

18. Kristian Smidt, *James Joyce and the Cultic Use of Fiction,* 26.

19. Jacques Aubert, *The Aesthetics of James Joyce,* 4: "Thomism did not appear in the school curriculum or even, more surprisingly, in that of University College, St Stephen's Green, because of the special status in relation to the state." See Aubert, *Introduction à l'esthétique de James Joyce,* 17: "L'enseignement du thomisme ne figurait nullement au programme d'études des élèves de l'établissement: chose plus curieuse encore, il en allait de même à University College, pour des raisons tenant au statut de l'Université." Nothing could be further from the truth.

20. William T. Noon, S.J., *Joyce and Aquinas,* 3.

21. William T. Noon, S.J., Thesis, vol. 1, 7–8. There is no mention of Fr. McGrath in *Joyce and Aquinas.*

22. As might be expected, Noon's account is viewed as authoritative. Referring to Joyce's interest in Aristotle and Aquinas, Kevin Sullivan suggests that "it would seem natural to assume that so persistent an interest in scholastic thought and method began with his courses in philosophy under Jesuit guidance at University College." Sullivan rightly points out that while the assumption is natural, "unfortunately it is not borne out by the facts." Kevin Sullivan, *Joyce among the Jesuits,* 165.

23. See Thomas J. Morrissey, S.J., *Towards a National University*. Also, Aubrey Gwynn, S.J., "The Jesuit Fathers and University College," 25–26.

24. Thomas J. Morrissey, S.J., *Thomas A. Finlay SJ, 1848–1940*, 24.

25. Morrissey, *Finlay*, 24.

26. Morrissey, *Finlay*, 24.

27. Morrissey, *Finlay*, 24.

28. Morrissey, *Towards a National University*, 99.

29. Morrissey, *Finlay*, 25.

30. Morrissey, *Finlay*, 25.

31. C. P. Curran, *Under the Receding Wave*, 79; "Memories of University College, Dublin: The Jesuit Tenure. 1883–1908," 226.

32. Morrissey, *Finlay*, 26.

33. Michael Maher, *Psychology*.

34. Albert Stöckl, *Handbook of the History of Philosophy* I: *Pre-Scholastic Philosophy*.

35. J. F. Byrne, *Silent Years*, 38.

36. C. P. Curran, "Memories of University College, Dublin: The Jesuit Tenure 1883–1908," 226.

37. Morrissey, *Finlay*, 45.

38. *A Page of Irish History: Story of University College, Dublin 1883–1909*, compiled by Fathers of the Society of Jesus, 219.

39. *A Page of Irish History*, 351.

40. *A Page of Irish History*, 109.

41. *A Page of Irish History*, 349–50.

42. Sullivan, *Joyce among the Jesuits*, 169.

43. Noon, *Joyce and Aquinas*, 4.

44. Sullivan, 169.

45. William G. Fallon, "The Joyce I Knew," 51.

46. *A Page of Irish History*, 442.

47. C. P. Curran, *James Joyce Remembered*, 11.

48. Seanad Éireann debate, November 18, 1942. Accessed May 1, 2021: https://www.oireachtas.ie/en/debates/debate/seanad/1942-11-18/6/.

49. J. F. Byrne, *Silent Years*, 165.

50. Vivian Mercier, "Dublin under the Joyces," 296–97.

51. William Kirkpatrick Magee, *Irish Literary Portraits*, 132.

52. Jacques Mercanton, "The Hours of James Joyce," 228.

53. They were written "with studious regard to the mind of the Catholic Church and to the teaching of St Thomas." Joseph Rickaby, *Moral Philosophy or Ethics and Natural Law*, v.

54. Curran, *James Joyce Remembered*, 37.

55. John Rickaby, *General Metaphysics*, 152. Rickaby also borrows from Victor Cousin the example of a flower.

56. Curran, *James Joyce Remembered*, 36–37. It appears the same handbook was also used in literature classes. Referring to the English literature course, Curran wrote in his later memoir: "The regular textbook in this course was Boedder's *Natural Theology*, one

of the Stonyhurst series in Catholic philosophy. These manuals were in general circulation in the College, and very accessible. I retain still my Boedder and a copy of John Rickaby's *General Metaphysics*. Neither my class-fellow Joyce nor myself followed any course in philosophy, but turning over their pages I read again with a new interest certain familiar Thomistic dicta; in Boedder a page of aesthetics enshrining *Pulchra dicuntur quae visa placent,* and in Rickaby a more extended treatment of the beautiful, turning upon definitions of Aquinas and the significance of the *integritas, consonantia* and *claritas,* which were presently to occupy the mind of Stephen Daedalus [*sic*]. These books were in the hands of Joyce's class-fellows. He himself keener than the rest on his special objective and quicker to claim his property where he found it, found here the starting point of his aesthetics." C. P. Curran, *Under the Receding Wave,* 80–81.

57. Curran, *James Joyce Remembered,* 36–37.

58. Eugene Sheehy, *May It Please the Court,* 9.

59. See Mary Colum and Padraic Colum, *Our Friend James Joyce,* 43: "Kettle was regarded as the rising young man of the country. Like Joyce, he had been through the Jesuit school at Clongowes Wood and, also like Joyce, was a University College man. I remember an afternoon he and I and Joyce and Gogarty spent together by the beach at Sandymount. Kettle's Catholicism was reinforced by the neo-Thomism (though it was not called that then), and Joyce's dialectics and Gogarty's jokes were competently and good-humoredly dealt with by him."

60. A review of Boedder's book appeared in *The Lyceum* 5/56, 165–66; it concluded, "We cordially recommend this book to our university students."

61. The first edition had 560 pages; later editions were expanded to 610. The copy in Joyce's Trieste library was an American printing of the second edition (n.d., with original pagination), in which he made copious markings. Stanislaus notes in his diary that Joyce bought it in May 1908. For an account of Joyce's use of Maher's handbook, see 126–30 above. Also Michael Patrick Gillespie, *James Joyce's Trieste Library,* 158–59.

62. Maher, *Psychology,* 523 (560 in later editions).

63. Ellmann, *JJII* 756n65, reproduces Joyce's examination results from the archive of the Royal University, now held by the National University of Ireland.

64. *An. Post.* 2, 7, 92a34–92b38.

65. *An. Post.* 2, 7, 92a34–92b38. Clarke's *Logic* volume finds in Aristotle and St. Thomas "the solution of every difficulty and the treatment—at least, the incidental treatment—of every question that Logic can propose." Richard F. Clarke, S.J., *Logic,* x.

66. Mary Colum and Padraic Colum, *Our Friend James Joyce,* 131–32.

67. See *JJII* 779n30.

68. *ST* I-II, 27, art. 1 ad 3. See Joseph Rickaby, *Aquinas Ethicus,* 95.

69. John Rickaby, *General Metaphysics,* 147–51. Rickaby presents the following lines as a quotation from Aquinas, *ST* I, 4 ad 1: "When an object is such that it offers several elements at least virtually distinct, and these elements conspire to give to the whole a unity, each part bearing a proportion to the total nature of the thing; then there is offered to the mind an object which delights the gaze, and is called *beautiful.*" The passage is however a loose summary of Aquinas's approach, with little resemblance to his text. Rickaby then offers a definition: "Hence the beautiful lies in proportion, in unity amid variety, or in

the combination of the three elements, completeness of the whole (*integritas, perfectio*), harmonious relation of parts (*debita proportio, consonantia*), and, shed over all, a certain definiteness, clearness, lustre or splendour (*claritas*)" (149). Rickaby refers to *ST* I, 39, 8 as his source.

70. Bernard Boedder, S.J., *Natural Theology,* 340.

71. Boedder, 340; John Rickaby, *General Metaphysics,* 151. Rickaby significantly makes reference to beauty as the splendour of the good: "Hence with Plato and others the beautiful is not merely the true or the good, but the splendour of the true or the good, or the splendour of order." In a footnote, he cites the following definition, attributed to Aquinas by Matteo Liberatore, *Ontologia* (Naples: Gemelli, 1949): "The universal character of the beautiful is the splendour of form as shown either in different parts of matter, or in different powers and activities."

72. Rickaby, 283–93.

73. Rickaby, 222.

74. John Rickaby, *First Principles of Knowledge,* 7.

75. De Wulf originally published two separate articles "Les théories esthétiques propres à saint Thomas," *Revue néo-scolastique* 2 (1895) 188–205, 341–57, subsequently published in book form in Paris.

76. Curran, *James Joyce Remembered,* 37. As another possible source, Curran suggests Maurice De Wulf's *Introduction à la philosophie néo-scholastique,* published in 1904, followed by an English translation in 1907. By this time, however, Joyce had worked out the essentials of his aesthetic theory. His biographer Herbert S. Gorman states: "During this last year of his impatient existence in Ireland Joyce laboured fitfully at his literary conceptions. He had practically perfected in his own mind the long-pondered aesthetic based on the teachings of Aristotle and Aquinas and with it as master he was determined to create an art in letters that had never existed in his native country." Herbert S. Gorman, *James Joyce: A Definitive Biography,* 115.

77. Curran, 37.

78. Richard Ellmann, introduction, *My Brother's Keeper,* by Stanislaus Joyce, xv.

79. Oliver St. John Gogarty, "James Joyce: A Portrait of the Artist," 27.

80. Thomas Aquinas, *Summa Philosophica seu De Veritate Catholicae Fidei Contra Gentiles* (Paris: Lethielleux), 1906.

81. Stanislaus Joyce, *My Brother's Keeper,* 242–43.

82. Stanislaus Joyce, 128.

83. Thomas Aquinas, *Of God and His Creatures,* 288. A more complete translation: "Moreover, in human society it is most necessary that there be friendship among many people."

84. Robert McAlmon, *Being Geniuses Together,* 26. Joyce was not averse to adopting a contrary position—in both senses of the word, as stressed separately on the first and second syllables. Padraic Colum recalled: "The talk at dinner the talk turned to other saints, but Joyce would have none of them. He dismissed Saint Francis. He declared he took little interest in Augustine. Aquinas, then, whose aesthetic the young hero of *Portrait of the Artist* promoted? Joyce would have none of the great Doctor either, or of Saint Ignatius, despite his Jesuit training. The only saint he would praise was Saint Patrick." Colum

and Colum, *Our Friend James Joyce,* 183. Although he clearly recognized Aquinas's lucidity and rigor, there was also a certain ambivalence in his attitude. In conversation with Jacques Mercanton, he once compared him to Newman, whose prose he admired above all other authors: "But he bores me when he tries to make his reader believe the impossible. Saint Thomas is more entertaining: he proves far too much to convince anyone." Jacques Mercanton, "The Hours of James Joyce," 239.

85. Aubert, *The Aesthetics of James Joyce,* 100.

86. See https://portail.centreculturelirlandais.com/index.php?lvl=notice_display&id=6904. Accessed May 1, 2021.

87. Aubert, 3–4.

88. Roger Bede Vaughan, OSB, *The Life and Labours of Saint Thomas of Aquin,* 7.

89. Peter Costello, *James Joyce: The Years of Growth, 1882–1915,* 63. See also page 64: "Danby was a Protestant, and Mrs Conway's millennial fears owed more to the hectic fevers of the Evangelical Protestant tradition than to anything particular to Catholicism as a whole or to its peculiar Irish form."

90. McAlmon, *Being Geniuses Together,* 25–26.

91. Cited by Richard Ellmann, *The Identity of Yeats,* 87, from the manuscript intended as a preface to *Ideas of Good and Evil* (1903). The interview took place in 1902.

92. In 1913, Gilson published two books, *Index scolastico-cartésien* and *La liberté chez Descartes et la théologie.*

93. Mary Colum and Padraic Colum, *Our Friend James Joyce,* 134.

94. *LI* 147: "Ogni avventura è per cosi dire una persona benchè composita di persone—come favella l'Aquinate degli angelici eserciti" (*SL* 270, trans. *SL* 271). See 273n43 below.

95. Kenner, *Dublin's Joyce,* 3.

96. Kenner, 136.

97. Donald Phillip Verene, *James Joyce and the Philosophers at* Finnegans Wake, 43.

98. Verene, 42.

99. See also *FW* 245.12: "feriaquintaism"; *FW* 299.08: "Quoint a quincidence!"; *FW* 417.08: "aquinatance of the Ondt."

Chapter 3. Knowledge and Permanence

1. Portions of this chapter were adapted by permission from Springer Nature Customer Service Centre GmbH: Springer Nature, *Knowledge and Identity in Joyce* by Fran O'Rourke, © 2018. https://link.springer.com/chapter/10.1007/978-3-319-71994-8_2.

2. Alfred North Whitehead, *Science and the Modern World,* 174.

3. See references to Descartes in *Finnegans Wake:* "birthday cards" (*FW* 127.25); "If she can't follow suit Renée goes to the pack" [René goes back to the pack (of cards)] (*FW* 269n2); "Sink deep or touch not the Cartesian spring!" (*FW* 301.24–25); "a reborn of the cards [*rené des cartes*] [. . .] cog it out, here goes a sum [*cogito ergo sum*]" (*FW* 304: 27–31); "renations [. . .] motu propprior [. . .] I am" (*FW* 358.3, 9, 15); "No, before your corselage rib is decartilaged" (*FW* 437.8).

4. John Locke, *An Essay Concerning Human Understanding,* 25. Also: "It is evident the mind knows not things immediately, but only by the intervention of the ideas it has of

them. [. . .] the mind [. . .] perceives nothing but its own ideas." *An Essay Concerning Human Understanding,* 563. Professor William Magennis, who had significant influence on Joyce as a student, stressed the negative consequences of this doctrine, which was shared by major modern philosophers. He set the following question in the Honours BA degree examination in metaphysics in Autumn 1924: "Examine critically: 'With Kant, as with Locke, our ideas instead of bringing us into connexion with things, really shut us off from them.'"

Common to the idealist and empiricist views of knowledge is the recognition—indeed a truism—that what is known must somehow be "in" the mind or consciousness. Descartes, Locke, and Hume failed, however, to recognize the analogical use of the preposition when referring to cognition: whereas a physical object can only be in a single location, the object of knowledge—while enjoying an independent autonomous existence—is also, as known, somehow mysteriously present within the mind. In this sense, Joyce could remark to his brother Stanislaus: "What can a man know but what passes inside his own head?" (*JJII* 265).

5. We may confidently assume that Joyce did not share the materialism attributed to Buck Mulligan. In *Stephen Hero,* the young Daedalus is referred to as "this heaven-ascending essayist," and we read the following significant remarks concerning "the truth of the being of the visible world and [. . .] beauty, the splendour of truth": "The age, though it bury itself fathoms deep in formulas and machinery, has need of these realities which alone give and sustain life and it must await from those chosen centres of vivification the force to live, the security for life which can come to it only from them. Thus the spirit of man makes a continual affirmation" (*SH* 80). The young Stephen is also wary of Cranly's company: "He had begun to consider Cranly a bad influence. Cranly's method in argument was to reduce all things to their food values," a test that Stephen held to be "an extreme one and one which in its utter materialism suggested a declination from the heights of romanticism." Cautious about his friend's company, he was able to evaluate it properly: "He knew that Cranly's materialism was only skin-deep" (*SH* 208). See also *SH* 124: "He was fond of leading a philosophical argument back to the machinery of the intellectual faculty itself and in mundane matters he did likewise, testing everything by its food value."

6. See Locke, 134–35.

7. Locke and Boyle studied together at Oxford in the late 1650s and early 1660s and corresponded on scientific matters.

8. Robert Boyle, *Selected Philosophical Papers,* 41.

9. Henry Oldenburg, *Correspondence of Henry Oldenburg,* 61, 67.

10. Frank Delaney, "Matters of Measurement."

11. Declan Kiberd, *Ulysses and Us,* 64–65. On "Proteus," see Erwin R. Steinberg, "The Proteus Episode," 187–98; and James Cappio, "Aristotle, Berkeley, and Proteus," 21–32.

12. Kiberd, *Ulysses and Us,* 65, emphasis in original.

13. Hugh Kenner, *Dublin's Joyce,* 109–33.

14. The phrase "Signatures of all things I am here to read" at the start of "Proteus" indicates that Joyce was familiar with at least the title of Jakob Boehme's treatise *De Signatura Rerum* (1621). He had a copy of the work in his Trieste library. However, it

would not be unreasonable to also find in John Rickaby's reference to Jakob Boehme and *De Signatura Rerum* a possible source for Joyce's phrase within an otherwise very Aristotelian paragraph. As Rickaby describes it, Boehme had an epiphanic experience: "We may read of a mystic like Boehme, that walking one day near Görlitz, he had suddenly revealed to him the essences, the properties, and the uses of herbs, so that he was able to write his book *De Signatura Rerum:* yet even so it was from the outer appearances of plants that he argued what their curative powers must be." John Rickaby, *General Metaphysics,* 80–81. According to Rickaby, what seems to be portrayed as a direct and immediate intuition of essences is really an inductive knowledge from the appearance of the effect to the nature of the cause, which is precisely the doctrine of Aristotle: we infer what a thing *is* from what it *does.*

15. For Joyce's notebook materials, see Wim Van Mierlo, "The Subject Notebook: A Nexus in the Composition History of *Ulysses*—A Preliminary Analysis." See James Joyce, "The Subject Notebook."

16. J. Mitchell Morse suggests that "bald he was and a millionaire" refers not to Aristotle but to [the third earl of] Shaftesbury, criticized in Berkeley's *Alciphron.* J. Mitchell Morse, "Proteus," 37–38.

17. See also *U* 3.446–47: 'His gaze brooded on his broadtoed boots, a buck's castoffs, *nebeneinander.*'

18. *Sens.* 1, 436b10–11, trans. *CW1,* 693. *De An.* 2, 2, 413b4: "The primary form of sense is touch which belongs to all animals." Trans. *CW1,* 658.

19. *De An.* 3, 13, 435a13–14.

20. *De An.* 2, 9, 421a21–23. See Aquinas, *ST* I, 76, 5: "Now all the other senses are based on the sense of touch . . . Among animals man has the best sense of touch. [. . .] and among men, those who have the best sense of touch have the best intelligence. A sign of which is that we observe 'those who are refined in body are well endowed in mind,' as stated in *De Anima* 2, 9."

21. *U* 3.434–36: "Touch me. Soft eyes. Soft soft soft hand. I am lonely here. O, touch me soon, now. What is that word known to all men? I am quiet here alone. Sad too. Touch, touch me."

22. *Met.* 1, 1, 980b25–26. See *EN* 10, 4, 1174a14. "The act of sight appears to be perfect at any moment of its duration." Shakespeare referred to the eye as the "most pure spirit of sense." (*Troilus and Cressida,* 3, 3, 111).

23. *Sens.* 1, 437a4–16.

24. See also *U* 3.424–26: "She trusts me, her hand gentle, the longlashed eyes. Now where the blue hell am I bringing her beyond the veil? Into the ineluctable modality of the ineluctable visuality. She, she, she. What she?"

25. Robert McAlmon, *Being Geniuses Together,* 26.

26. This is the assumption of John Killham. See "'Ineluctable Modality' in Joyce's *Ulysses,*" 269–70.

27. I believe that Killham (269) is mistaken when he suggests that "Stephen's reflection on the 'ineluctable modality' of what he sees as he walks on Sandymount strand is obviously not to be taken as the beginning of a serious and sequential argument. He is in a somewhat jocose mood."

28. *Sens.* 4, 442b5–10: "Size, shape, rough and smooth, besides sharp and blunt, as found in solid bodies, are common, if not to all the senses, at least to sight and touch. So the senses are liable to error in dealing with common sensibles, but they are not mistaken about the objects of special senses; for instance vision is not in error about colour, nor hearing about sound." The reason Aristotle speaks here of rough and smooth is that he is criticizing Democritus's theory of sensation, which regards all sensible objects as objects of touch.

29. *De An.* 3, 3, 427b11–14, my trans. See also *De An.* 3, 3, 428b18–19: "The perception of proper objects is true, or is only capable of error to the least possible degree." *De An.* 3, 3, 428a12: "All sensations are true, but most imaginations are false." For a discussion of Joyce's quotation from Aristotle, see 213–14 above.

30. "Proteus," paragraph 1, University of Buffalo MSS (Slocum and Cahoon 5, b, ii), quoted by Robert Martin Adams, *Surface and Symbol*, 257.

31. Robert S. Ball, *The Story of the Heavens*, 151–52. See *U* 8.110: "Fascinating little book that is of sir Robert Ball's. Parallax," *U* 15.1010–12: "I was just chatting this afternoon at the viceregal lodge to my old pals, sir Robert and lady Ball, astronomer royal at the levee. Sir Bob, I said. . . . . ." See *U* 14.1089–90: "Parallax stalks behind and goads them, the lancinating lightnings of whose brow are scorpions."

32. In his story "The Amethyst Ring" ("*L'anneau d'améthyste*"), Anatole France expresses a similar phenomenon as perceived by Riquet, M. Bergeret's dog: "Men, animals, and stones grow larger as they approach me, and become enormous when they are quite close. It is not so with me. I remain the same size wherever I am." ("Les hommes, les animaux, les pierres grandissent en s'approchant et deviennent énormes quand ils sont sur moi. Moi non. Je demeure toujours aussi grand partout où je suis.") Anatole France, *Oeuvres complètes illustrées*, 87.

33. Michael Doran, *Conversations with Cézanne*, 113.

34. See 219 above.

35. *Sens.* 3, 439b10–12, *CW1*, 698. As a translation of διαφανὲς, Jonathan Barnes substituted "transparent" for "translucent" in his revision of the original Oxford version by J. I. Beare. The Loeb translation reads: "But since colour exists in the limit, it must lie in the limit of transparence. So that colour would prove to be the limit of transparence in a limited body."

36. *Sens.* 3, 439a18–30. My translation, drawing on Beare (*CW1*, 697) and Hett (Loeb).

37. James Boswell, *Boswell's Life of Johnson*, vol. 3, 471. A note by Michael Kearney (1733–1814) in John Wilson Croker's edition of Boswell's *Life* (1831), and frequently reprinted, correctly states: "Dr. Johnson seems to have been imperfectly acquainted with Berkeley's doctrine; as his experiment only proves that we have the sensation of solidity, which Berkeley did not deny. He admitted that we had sensations or ideas that are usually called sensible qualities, one of which is solidity: he only denied the existence of matter, i.e. an inert senseless substance, in which they are supposed to subsist. Johnson's exemplification concurs with the vulgar notion, that solidity is matter."

38. Don Gifford, Ulysses *Annotated*, 45.

39. Frank Budgen, *James Joyce and the Making of* Ulysses *and Other Writings*, 50.

40. *Phys.* 4, 4, 212a8, trans. *CW1*, 360.

41. *Phys.* 4, 4, 212a20–21: τὸ τοῦ περιέχοντος πέρας ἀκίνητον πρῶτον.

42. John Rickaby, *General Metaphysics,* 367–68.

43. *CW1,* 361.

44. John Rickaby, *General Metaphysics,* 368.

45. See John Rickaby, *General Metaphysics,* 368.

46. *Phys.* 4, 11, 219b1.

47. *Phys.* 4, 11, 220b14–16, trans. *CW1,* 373.

48. *Phys.* 4, 14, 223a16–22.

49. *Phys.* 4, 14, 223a25–26.

50. *Phys.* 4, 11, 219a3–8.

51. See Luca Crispi, "A First Foray into the National Library of Ireland's Joyce Manuscripts: Bloomsday 2011," *Genetic Joyce Studies* 11 (Spring 2011).

52. Joyce's handwritten selection may be viewed on the penultimate page (15r) of the "Subject Notebook." He began compiling the Subject Notebook in October 1917. See Wim Van Mierlo's excellent exhaustive study, "The Subject Notebook: A Nexus in the Composition History of *Ulysses*—A Preliminary Analysis," *Genetic Joyce Studies* 7 (Spring 2007).

53. Otto Weininger, *Über die Letzten Dinge: Mit einem biographischen Vorwort von Moriz Rappaport,* 107.

54. My trans. The published English translation reads: "Space is thus a projection of the ego (out of the realm of freedom into the realm of necessity). It contains, one beside the other, what can only be experienced temporally, one after the other." Otto Weininger, *On Last Things,* 92.

55. Immanuel Kant wrote in his *Critique of Pure Reason* (1781): "Different times are not simultaneous (*zugleich*) but successive (*nacheinander*) (just as different spaces are not successive (*nacheinander*) but simultaneous (*zugleich*)." *Critique of Pure Reason,* 75. See Immanuel Kant, *Kritik der reinen Vernunft,* 74: "Verschiedene Zeiten sind nicht zugleich, sondern nacheinander (so wie verschiedene Räume nicht nacheinander, sondern zugleich sind)."

56. Joyce had access to an English translation of Lessing's *Laocoön* in the National Library of Ireland: *Laocoön: An Essay on the Limits of Painting and Poetry,* trans. William Ross (London: Ridgeway, 1836). E. C. Beasley's translation was published in 1853 and reissued in 1888 in Bohn's Library; another translation by William Boss was published in 1886.

57. Gotthold Ephraim Lessing, *Laocoön: An Essay on the Limits of Painting and Poetry,* 99–101. For the original text see Gotthold Ephraim Lessing, *Werke* 2, 90–91: "[S]o findet sich doch dieser wesentliche Unterschied unter ihnen, daß jener eine sichtbare fortschreitende Handlung ist, deren verschiedene Teile sich **nach und nach**, in der Folge der Zeit, eräugnen, dieser hingegen eine sichtbare stehende Handlung, deren verschiedene Teile sich **nebeneinander** im Raume entwickeln. [. . .] Wenn es wahr ist, daß die Malerei zu ihren Nachahmungen ganz andere Mittel, oder Zeichen gebrauchet, als die Poesie; jene nämlich Figuren und Farben in dem Raume, diese aber artikulierte Töne in der Zeit; wenn unstreitig die Zeichen ein bequemes Verhältnis zu dem Bezeichneten haben müssen: so können **nebeneinander** geordnete Zeichen auch nur Gegenstände, die **nebeneinander**, oder deren Teile **nebeneinander** existieren, **aufeinander**folgende

Zeichen aber, auch nur Gegenstände ausdrücken, die **aufeinander,** oder deren Teile **aufeinander** folgen. Gegenstände, die **nebeneinander** oder deren Teile **nebeneinander** existieren, heißen Körper. Folglich sind Körper mit ihren sichtbaren Eigenschaften, die eigentlichen Gegenstände der Malerei. Gegenstände, die **aufeinander,** oder deren Teile **aufeinander** folgen, heißen überhaupt Handlungen. Folglich sind Handlungen der eigentliche Gegenstand der Poesie." See Fritz Senn, "Esthetic Theories," 134–35.

58. Joseph E. Duncan, "The Modality of the Audible in Joyce's *Ulysses*," 288–90.

59. John Killham, "'Ineluctable Modality' in Joyce's *Ulysses*," 270. It is an exaggeration, however, to describe Duncan's portrayal as "a travesty of Aristotle" (270); it is rather a confusion of the fluctuating appearances in the world as experienced with the epistemological and metaphysical consistencies that Aristotle nonetheless affirms. I agree with Killham's assessment that "to take Stephen's 'ineluctable modality of the visible' to mean (by a very forced construction) that the things we see are uncertain and unpredictable (in contrast to the necessity in the realm of the universal) is mistaken" (273–74).

60. Killham, "'Ineluctable Modality' in Joyce's *Ulysses*," 271.

61. Theoharis Constantine Theoharis, *Joyce's* Ulysses, 19.

62. Killham, "'Ineluctable Modality' in Joyce's *Ulysses*," 271–72.

63. *De An.* 2, 5, 417b20–22.

64. *De An.* 2, 11, 424a1.

65. *De An.* 3, 7, 431a1–2: "Knowledge when actively operative is identical with its object" *De An.* 3, 2, 426a9–12: "For just as acting and being acted upon resides in that which is acted upon, and not that which acts, so also the activity of the object perceived and of the percipient lies in the percipient."

66. *De An.* 3, 2, 425b26–27.

67. Budgen, *James Joyce and the Making of* Ulysses *and Other Writings,* 49.

68. Budgen, 55.

69. *EN* 7, 14, 1154b27–28.

70. When absorbed by the human body, food undergoes substantial change. See Aquinas, *ST* I, 119, 1.

71. Joyce's tangential reference to the "Materia Prima of Aquinas" suggests that he had a proper grasp of the concept. *CW* 134, also *OCPW* 94.

72. *Part. An.* 1, 1, 640b33–35.

73. *The Tempest* 2, 2, 396–401.

74. *Hamlet*, 4, 3, 27–29.

75. See *Odyssey* 4, 351–569. Proteus's flock or herd represents the diversity of minerals, plants, and animals into which matter is wrought and diffused. Matter is itself continually fluid.

76. See Shakespeare's *Henry VI*, Part 3, 3, 2, 191–92: "I can add colours to the chameleon, / Change shapes with Proteus for advantages."

77. Daniel R. Schwarz, *Reading Joyce's* Ulysses, 98. See J. Mitchell Morse, "Proteus," 29: "The essential thing about the ever-living Proteus is that he doesn't imitate fire, water, animals, etc., but is and by turns manifests himself as fire, water, animals, etc. He is all nature, potent, latent; through changing forms he manifests the rolling heaving neverchanging everchanging all. His name signifies Primal or Elemental."

78. Cited by James A. Weisheipl, *St. Thomas Aquinas, Commentary on the Gospel of Saint John* I, 464.

79. Stuart Gilbert, *James Joyce's* Ulysses, 111. This passage is taken from Welsh philosopher Thomas Vaughan's *Coelum Terrae* (*The Magician's Heavenly Chaos*) written in 1650.

80. The BA syllabus followed by Joyce included Bacon's *Advancement of Learning* II, chapters 1–21. The BA examination in English in Autumn 1902 included the following question: "Consider Bacon's attitude towards Poetry, as seen in *The Advancement of Learning* II."

81. Francis Bacon, *Works*, vol. 6, 725. For Latin original, see Bacon, *Works*, vol. 6, 651.

82. Ralph Waldo Emerson, *The Complete Essays and Other Writings of Ralph Waldo Emerson*, 138–39.

83. Plato, *Theaetetus* 182a, 183b. Trans. modified.

84. *Theaetetus* 183a–183b: "I used the words 'so' and 'not so,' whereas we have no right to use this word 'so'—what is 'so' would cease to be in change—nor yet 'not so'; there is no change in that either. Some new dialect will have to be instituted for the exponents of this theory, since, as it is, they have no phrases to fit their fundamental proposition—unless indeed it were 'not even nohow.' That might be an expression indefinite enough to suit them." *Collected Dialogues*, 888. A similar account of pervasive change is described at *FW* 118: 21–28: "every person, place and thing in the chaosmos of Alle anyway connected with the gobblydumped turkery was moving and changing every part of the time: the travelling inkhorn (possibly pot), the hare and turtle pen and paper, the continually more and less intermisunderstanding minds of the anticollaborators, the as time went on as it will variously inflected, differently pronounced, otherwise spelled, changeably meaning vocable scriptsigns."

85. In "Eumaeus," as he listens to Leopold discourse about the history of the Jews, religion, and patriotism, Stephen also finds that words are losing their stability, as their meaning fluctuates: "listening to this synopsis of things in general, Stephen [. . .] could hear, of course, all kinds of words changing colour like those crabs about Ringsend in the morning, burrowing quickly into all colours of different sorts of the same sand where they had a home somewhere beneath or seemed to" (*U* 16.1142–43).

86. There is an Aristotelian flavor to the comment in "Nestor," "Time surely would scatter all." Aristotle remarks at *Physics* 4, 221a30–221b3: "We are wont to say that time crumbles things, and that everything grows old under the power of time and is forgotten through the lapse of time. But we do not say that we have learnt, or that anything is made new or beautiful, by the mere lapse of time; for we regard time in itself as destroying rather than producing, for what is counted in time is movement, and movement dislodges whatever it affects from its present state."

87. Stuart Gilbert, *James Joyce's* Ulysses, 111.

88. Joseph E. Duncan, "The Modality of the Audible in Joyce's *Ulysses*," 287.

89. Killham, "'Ineluctable Modality' in Joyce's *Ulysses*," 269.

90. See George Berkeley, *Philosophical Commentaries*, 124, § 392. Berkeley's (perhaps playful) assertion that the Irish mind can reconcile being and nonbeing fits well with the dialectical harmonies that permeate *FW*: "There are men who say there are insensible extensions. There are others who say the wall is not white, the fire is not hot etc. We

Irishmen cannot attain to these truths. The mathematicians think there are insensible lines. About these they harangue—these cut in a point at all angles—these are divisible ad infinitum. We Irishmen can conceive no such lines. The mathematicians talk of what they call a point. This, they say, is not altogether nothing nor is it downright something. Now we Irishmen are apt to think something and nothing are next neighbours." Alexander Campbell Fraser, *Life and Letters of George Berkeley,* 500–501.

91. J. Mitchell Morse, "Proteus," 44.

92. George Berkeley, *The Works of George Berkeley Bishop of Cloyne,* vol. 1, 171, § 1.

93. George Berkeley, *A New Theory of Vision,* in *The Works of George Berkeley Bishop of Cloyne:* "I find it also acknowledged that the estimate we make of the distance of objects considerably remote is rather an act of judgment grounded on experience than of sense. For example, when I perceive a great number of intermediate objects, such as houses, fields, rivers, and the like, which I have experienced to take up a considerable space, I thence form a judgment or conclusion that the object I see beyond them is at a great distance. Again, when an object appears faint and small, which at a near distance I have experienced to make a vigorous and large appearance, I instantly conclude it to be far off: And this, 'tis evident, is the result of experience; without which, from the faintness and littleness I should not have inferred anything concerning the distance of objects." Works, vol. 1, 171, § 3.

94. A. A. Luce, introduction, *The Works of George Berkeley Bishop of Cloyne,* vol. 1, 147–48.

95. Berkeley, *The Theory of Vision Vindicated and Explained,* in *The Works of George Berkeley Bishop of Cloyne,* vol. 1, 266, § 44.

96. Berkeley, *A New Theory of Vision,* in *The Works of George Berkeley Bishop of Cloyne,* vol. 1, 231, § 147.

97. The opposition between Scylla and Charybdis, allegorized in the Library episode, should not be over-simplified as that between "the steadfast rock of Scylla and the whirlpool of Charybdis" (e.g., Hederman, 258). In Greek mythology, Scylla and Charybdis both dwell in mounds or rocks. The word used by Homer, σκόπελον, originally referred to a look-out or vantage point, a meaning extended to lofty "crag" or "rock" (as translated by Chapman). Scylla inhabited the higher rock and with each of her six heads could snatch and devour a passing sailor. In a cave on the other side of the strait dwelt the monster Charybdis, who three times daily sucked down the black water. Circe advised Odysseus to sail close to Scylla, thus losing six sailors, rather than lose his entire ship in the whirlpool. As Joyce's source for the Scylla and Charybdis parallel Vivian Mercier has suggested Francis Bacon's *Of the Wisdom of the Ancients,* two copies of which Joyce possessed (Vivian Mercier, "John Eglinton as Socrates: A Study of Scylla and Charybdis," 72). Bacon interpreted Scylla and Charybdis, respectively, as "the rocks of Distinction and the Gulfs of Universalities." According to Mercier, distinctions or definitions suggest Aristotle, while "universalities" or universals suggest Plato. Stephen accordingly, suggests Mercier, "mentally outlines his own Aristotelianism, in opposition to the Neo-Platonism of A.E. and the theosophists" in the reflection: "Unsheathe your dagger definitions. Horseness is the whatness of allhorse. Streams of tendency and eons they worship. God: noise in the street: very peripatetic. Space: what you damn well have

to see." The maritime image of the Platonic vortex, consuming everything it absorbs, recurs in a later reference to AE: "Gulfer of souls, engulfer. Hesouls, shesouls, shoals of souls. Engulfed with wailing creecries, whirled, whirling, they bewail. *In quintessential triviality / For years in this fleshcase a shesoul dwelt*" (*U* 9.285–88).

98. See Geoffrey Wagner, *Wyndham Lewis: A Portrait of the Artist as the Enemy,* 178: "Joyce's own notations from Aristotle, as well as the library scene in *Ulysses,* show how much store Joyce set on intellect from the first. [. . .] this scene, with Aristotle representing the rock of dogma facing Plato the whirlpool. But although Stephen well knows which of the two, Aristotle or Plato, would have banished him from his commonwealth, Bloom of course steers neatly between this Scylla and Charybdis."

99. Frank Budgen, *James Joyce and the Making of* Ulysses *and Other Writings,* 109.

100. Also *U* 9.61: "Formless spiritual." Anthony Burgess refers to the "wishy-washy, mystical, theosophical insubstantiality of Irish art, with George Russell (AE) burbling about the universals of Plato, against which whirlpool Stephen sets the solidity of his own art and the Scyllan rock of Aristotelian logic." Burgess, *Joysprick,* 110.

101. *SH* 171: "It must have been a surprise for him to find in such latitudes a young man who could not conceive a divorce between art and nature and that not for reasons of climate or temperament but for intellectual reasons. For Stephen art was neither a copy nor an imitation of nature: the artistic process was a natural process." This passage reproduces the key concept of Joyce's notebook entry of March 27, 1903: "*E tekhne mimeitai ten physin*—This phrase is falsely rendered as 'Art is an imitation of Nature.' Aristotle does not here define art: he says only, 'Art imitates Nature' and means that the artistic process is like the natural process . . . (James Joyce, March 27, 1903, Paris)" (*CW* 145). For Aristotle, see *Phys.* 2. 2, 194a. 21–22: ἡ τέχνη μιμεῖται τὴν φύσιν. For Aquinas's commentary on the definition, see *In Phys.* Lect. 4, 170–71. *Ars imitatur naturam* (*CG* 2, 75; 3, 10; *In 4 Sent.* 42. 2. 1 c; *De Ver.* 11. 1 c). *Ars imitatur naturam, inquantum potest* (1 *Anal.* 1 a). *CG* 2. 75, 1558; *CG* 3. 10, 1943: *Ars enim in sua operatione imitatur naturam.* On the metaphysics paper for the Honours BA in Autumn 1919, Professor Magennis, who greatly influenced Joyce at University College, called for the explanation of the following statement: "In the *Poetics* Aristotle says that Fine Art *imitates* Nature. To appreciate this properly we must note carefully what *Nature* means in this context, and the precise type of *imitation* contemplated." In "Circe," there is a bizarre reprise of Stephen's conversation with Lynch on art: "(*points*) The mirror up to nature. (*he laughs*) Hu hu hu hu hu!" (*U* 15.3820).

102. *Poet.* 9, 1451b4–7.

103. *Met.* 7, 13,1038b11–12.

104. Simplicius, *in Arist. Cat.* 208, 28–32.

105. *De An.* 2, 5, 417b22–23.

106. There are, needless to say, intermediary stages in the passage from sense to intellect; however, these are not thematized as such by Joyce—apart from one brief mention of the so-called internal faculties in *A Portrait.* Aristotle's theory of sensation is dramatized in the opening pages of *A Portrait,* where the child Stephen's awakening to the world is specified according to the different senses through which he first perceives his surroundings. One of the questions raised by Aristotle in his treatise *On the Soul* was that of the unity among the diverse sense faculties; he solved it by affirming the existence of

an internal common sense. Other internal senses—also relevant for Joyce—are memory and imagination. We may observe in passing that Stephen, in his practice of spiritual self-mortification, systematically disciplines each of the five senses (*P* IV.122–54). It is also worth noting that in the famous sermon in *A Portrait,* the preacher states that the internal faculties are more perfect than the external and therefore more susceptible to greater torment (*P* III.1007–08).

107. Hugh Kenner, *Dublin's Joyce,* 3.

108. *De An.* 3, 6, 430a26–28.

109. *De An.* 3, 6, 430b27–29: "The thinking of the definition in the sense of the essence is always true."

110. *De An.* 3, 10, 433a26.

111. *De An.* 3, 6, 430b1–2. See 216 above.

112. Richard Beckman, *Joyce's Rare View: The Nature of Things in* Finnegans Wake, 164.

113. See *FW* 452.29–31: "We only wish everyone was as sure of anything in this watery world as we are of everything in the newlywet fellow that's bound to follow."

114. William York Tindall, *A Reader's Guide to "Finnegans Wake,"* 319.

115. According to Joseph Campbell and Henry Morton Robinson, *FW* "may be said to be all compact of *mutually supplementary antagonisms.*" Joseph Campbell and Henry Morton Robinson, *A Skeleton Key to* Finnegans Wake, 14.

116. Beckman, *Joyce's Rare View,* 73–74.

117. Beckman, 169–70: "The druid veers towards the subjectivist pole; Patrick kneels at the objectivist. The druid arrogates the phenomenon of 'Roygbiv' making it his to pontificate upon, his to display on his mantle; his mind is full of ideas, his garment full of color. The saint, leaving color to God, empties his mind and wears only an alb."

118. Interestingly, one of the lectures that Joyce delivered at the Università Populare in Trieste was titled "Irlanda, Isola dei Santi e dei Savi," "Ireland, Island of Saints and Sages." See *CW* 153–74.

119. Beckman puts it well: "The rivals for our hearts and minds are a transcendental idealist who does not really understand Kant and an empiricist who is innocent of the main points made by Locke." *Joyce's Rare View,* 172.

120. Beckman, 176.

121. Joyce explained to Frank Budgen in a letter: "Much more is intended in the colloquy between Berkeley the archdruid and his pidgin speech and Patrick the [archpriest] and his Nippon English. It is also the defence and indictment of the book itself, B's theory of colours and Patrick's practical solution of the problem. Hence the phrase in the preceding Mutt and Jeff banter 'Dies is Dorminus master,' = Deus est Dominus noster plus the day is Lord over sleep, i.e. when it days" (*LI* 406).

122. Susan Shaw Sailer, *On the Void of to Be: Incoherence and Trope in* Finnegans Wake, 149–50, quoted by Beckman, *Joyce's Rare View,* 164.

123. Beckman refers to the "contrast between the narrow thinking of the practical St. Patrick and the enormous reasonings of the head-in-the-clouds archdruid" (79). The archdruid is "overly intellectual," Patrick "overly practical" (167). Again, "The archdruid is the man of involuted thought, the saint the simple man who knows what he

wants. [. . .] looking at objects in the most anticommonsensical and apparently wrong-headed way. [. . .] Patrick's approach is simple and sensible" (168). Whereas the druid has "subjective-idealist tendencies," the saint's "path to wisdom is untroubled by any analytic tendency. For him 'fear of the Lord is the beginning of wisdom' (Psalms 3:10), which settles the matter and helps him forget the druid's Celtic nonsense about a 'seventh degree of wisdom.'" (170) Bernard Benstock writes: "The Archdruid, strongly resembling the Irish metaphysician George Berkeley, represents profound philosophic thought, while Patrick is a simple-minded, hard-headed man of action." Benstock, *Joyce-Again's Wake*, 97.

124. See *U* 13.1075–6: "Roygbiv Vance taught us: red, orange, yellow, green, blue, in-digo, violet."

125. The druid's "heptachromatic sevenhued septicoloured roranyellgreenlindigan mantle" with the seven colors of the rainbow hints at Berkeley's episcopal vestments and his theory of color, on which Joyce already discoursed in "Proteus." A less complicated version of the archdruid's theory is given in earlier drafts of the passage. The first draft, June–July 1923, reads:

The archdruid then explained the illusions of the colourful world, its furniture, animal, vegetable and mineral, appearing to fallen man under but one reflection of the several iridal gradations of solar light, that one which it had been unable to absorb, while for the seer beholding reality, the thing as in itself it is, all objects showed themselves in their true colours, resplendent with the sextuple glory of the light actually retained within them.

The second draft, July 1923, reads:

Topside joss pidgin fella Berkeley, archdruid of the Irish josspidgin, in his hepta-chromatic sevenhued roranyellgreeblindigan mantle then explained to Patrick the albed, the illusiones of hueful world of joss its furniture mineral through vegetable to animal appearing to fallen men under but one reflectione of the several iridal gradationes of solar light that one which that part of it had shown itself unable to absorbere whereas for the seer beholding interiorly the true inwardness of reality, the thing as in itself it is, all objects showed themselves in their true coloribus re-splendent with the sextuple gloria of light actually retained within them.

The fourth draft, August 1923, reads:

Bymby topside joss pidgin fella Luchru Berkeley, archdruid of Irish chinchinjoss, in the his heptachromatic sevenhued septicoloured roranyellgreenblindigan mantle finish he show along the his mister guest Patrick with alb the whose throat he fast all time what time all him Italyman monkfellas with Patrick he drink up words belongahim all too much illusiones of hueful panepiphanal world of lord Joss the of which zoantholithic furniture from mineral through vegetal to animal not appear to full up together fallen man than under but one photoreflection of the several iridals gradationes of solar light that one which that part of it (furnit of huepanepi world) had shown itself (part of fur of huepanwor) unable to absorbere whereas for numpa one seer in seventh degree of wisdom of Entis-Onton he savvy inside true inwardness of reality, tha Ding hvad in idself id ist, all damfool objects (of panepi-wor) alloside showed themselves in trues coloribus resplendent with sextuple gloria of light actually retained inside them (goddam obs of epiwo).

126. George Berkeley, *Treatise Concerning the Principles of Human Knowledge,* 43. See also: "Upon shutting my eyes all the furniture in the room is reduced to nothing, and barely upon opening them is again created" (x).

127. Isaac Newton, *Opticks or A Treatise of the Reflections, Refractions, Inflections and Colours of Light,* 179. [Prop. X. Prob. V.]

128. Newton, *Opticks or A Treatise of the Reflections, Refractions, Inflections and Colours of Light,* 184. [Prop. X. Prob. V.]

129. See Dante, *The Divine Comedy,* vol. III: *Paradise,* XXXIII.85–90: "Nel suo profondo vidi che s'interna, / legato con amore in un volume, / ciò che per l'universo si squaderna: / sustanze e accidenti e lor costume, / quasi conflati insieme, per tal modo / che ciò ch'i' dico è un semplice lume" ("I saw how it contains within its depths / all things bound in a single book by love / of which creation is the scattered leaves: / how substance, accident, and their relation / were fused in such a way that what I now / describe is but a glimmer of that Light"), trans. Mark Musa, 392–93.

130. Beckman, *Joyce's Rare View,* 63.

131. Beckman, 64–65.

132. The words may also be taken to refer to Einstein, founder of the theory of relativity, and Newton, whose theory of colors influenced Berkeley.

133. *Met.* 7, 1, 1028b3–4, *CW2,* 1624.

134. Anthony Burgess, *Here Comes Everybody,* 260. In *A Shorter* Finnegans Wake, 259, Burgess refers to "St. Patrick refuting the philosophical gibberish of the archdruid Berkeley-Bulkily-Buckley in the presence of King Leary." Beckman refers in *Joyce's Rare View* to the druid's "intellectual muddle" (169).

135. See *FW* 611.34–35: "niggerblonker."

136. *FW* 83.10–12 refers to the "Nichtian [Nietzschean] glossery which purveys **apri-oric** roots for aposteriorious tongues this is nat language at any sinse of the world." See *FW* 343.16–19: "explaining **aposteriorly** how awstooloo was valdesombre sombre belowes hero and he was in a greak esthate phophiar an erixtion on the soseptuple side of him made spoil **apriori** his popoporportiums."

137. There is a tacit allusion here to Kant's distinction between analytic/synthetic and a priori/a posteriori knowledge. According to Kant, scientific knowledge must be synthetic *a priori,* that is, exhibit the necessity of strict mental categories as well as confer additional new content.

138. "Viritude" may also refer to green, "eruberuption" to the reddening of St. Patrick.

139. Suggestions referring to "whale" (Latin *balena*) are, I suggest, mistaken.

140. Hebrews 1:3. In the Old Testament, the rainbow was a symbol of the covenant God made to Noah that never again would there be a flood to destroy the earth (Genesis 9:9–17). See *FW* 1.13–14: "arclight and rory end to the regginbrow was to be seen ringsome on the aquaface."

141. Genesis 9:13: τὸ τόξον μου τίθημι ἐν τῇ νεφέλῃ καὶ ἔσται εἰς σημεῖον διαθήκης ἀνὰ μέσον ἐμοῦ καὶ τῆς γῆς.

142. Robert Boyle, S.J., believes that "Good safe firelamp!" (*FW* 613.01) refers to the celebration of Patrick's lighting the Paschal Fire celebrated on Holy Saturday. "Worshipper of the Word," 118.

143. Beckman, in *Joyce's Rare View* (9), suggests that "Joyce exaggerates Kant's idea of the unknowability of the material world; it becomes a 'spoof of visibility in a freakfog'" (48.01–02).

144. Alistair Cormack, *Yeats and Joyce: Cyclical History and the Reprobate Tradition,* 178–79.

145. Michael Patrick Gillespie, *Reading the Book of Himself,* 207.

146. See his reference, *LIII 166,* to the "scholastic machinery of the process of thought," quoted above, 41.

147. Harry Levin, *James Joyce: A Critical Introduction,* 35.

148. Beckman, *Joyce's Rare View,* 82–83. Beckman even suggests (68) that Kant's *Critique of Pure Reason* sometimes sounds like a commentary on *Finnegans Wake,* citing as an example the following statement: "[Reason] falls into obscurity and contradictions, from which it can indeed surmise that it must somewhere be proceeding on the ground of hidden errors, but it cannot discover them [on the basis of] experience" (*CPR* 99).

149. Beckman, 71.

Chapter 4. Identity, Soul, and Substance

1. "Rhythm" is used by Joyce as an alternative word for "form." See *U* 15.106–07: "the first entelechy, the structural rhythm." Ellmann is correct in stating, "What we are to look for is not a fixed character but an 'individuating rhythm,'" but mistaken, I believe, in suggesting that Joyce conceives personality "as river rather than statue" (*JJII,* 145). The image of a river conveys the fact of accidental change, while a statue suggests stability. The challenge is to affirm simultaneously the permanence and dynamism of self.

2. *JJII* 78.

3. Mary Lowe-Evans points out, moreover: "There are at least sixty variants of 'soul' in *The Wake,* indicating, at the very least, that quite late in his life, Joyce still attributed some kind of meaning to the concept and expected that his readers would too." Lowe-Evans, *Catholic Nostalgia in Joyce and Company,* 82. Lowe-Evans refers to "a fascinating though unsubstantial entity called the soul" (27). For Aquinas, and presumably for Joyce, the soul is anything but unsubstantial. On the soul as central to Joyce's concerns, see Sidney Feshbach, "A Slow and Dark Birth," 289.

4. See 19–21 above.

5. *In De An.* 3, 7, 699, trans. Foster and Humphries, 410.

6. See 111 above.

7. Addressing Theodore Purefoy in "Oxen of the Sun," Stephen uses the remarkable phrase "Godframed Godgiven preformed possibility": "Thou art, I vow, the remarkablest progenitor barring none in this chaffering allincluding most farraginous chronicle. Astounding! In her lay a Godframed Godgiven preformed possibility which thou hast fructified with thy modicum of man's work" (*U* 14.1411–14).

8. Hippocrates, *Nature of the Child,* 500 (7, 18 L).

9. Hippocrates, 511 (10, 21 L). In another work, *On Nutriment* (42), Hippocrates gives different time periods.

10. *Gen. An.* 2, 3, 736b2–5.

11. *Hist. An.* 7, 3, 583b3–5.

12. *Gen. An.* 2, 3, 736b27–29.

13. *Gen. An.* 2, 3, 736b5–29.

14. *ST* I 76, 3, obj. 3. See *CG* 2, 88. See Aristotle *Gen. An.* 2, 3.

15. *ST* I 76, 3 ad 3. See *CG* 2, 89, 9; *De Spir. Creat.* 3, ad 13.

16. *In 3 Sent.*, dist. 3, art. 2. David Albert Jones argues that in his reading of Aristotle, Aquinas mistakenly conflated the completion of form at forty days with the acquisition of a rational soul. David Albert Jones, *The Soul of the Embryo: An Enquiry into the Status of the Human Embryo in the Christian Tradition,* 123.

17. Jones, 122.

18. *ST* I, 76, 3.

19. *ST* I, 76, 4.

20. *ST* I, 118, 2 ad 2.

21. Cited in Roger Ariew, *Descartes and the Last Scholastics,* 15.

22. *D* "Sisters," 4. 43; 10. 268.

23. *D* "Ivy Day in the Committee Room," 104.172. See also *D* 111. 403.

24. See *U* 2.146: "A poor soul gone to heaven."

25. See *U* 9.147–49: "What is a ghost? Stephen said with tingling energy. One who has faded into impalpability through death, through absence, through change of manners."

26. *Phys.* 2, 1, 192b21–22.

27. Owens, *Aristotle: The Collected Papers of Joseph Owens,* 173. See Ralph Waldo Emerson's *The Complete Essays and Other Writings of Ralph Waldo Emerson:* "Nature is a mutable cloud, which is always and never the same" (129).

28. Patrick Kavanagh, whose two favorite books were *Ulysses* and *Moby Dick,* maintained that *Ulysses* "is only incidentally about Dublin and fundamentally the history of a soul." See Brendan Lynch, *Parsons Bookshop: At the Heart of Bohemian Dublin, 1949–1989,* 56.

29. The words are repeated verbatim, referring first to the peasant woman standing at the door in Clane ("a type of her race and his own," *P* V.326–34) and later to the girl of Stephen's affections ("a figure of the womanhood of her country," *P* V.1666–67). This bizarre repetition—in the same chapter—could never escape the attention of a careful editor!

30. *In I Cor.*, 15, lect. 2. Also *ST* I, 75, 4: "Homo non est anima tantum, sed est aliquid compositum ex anima et corpore."

31. *EN* 9, 8, 1168b28–30.

32. *De An.* 2, 1, 414a12–14. For a comprehensive account, see *De An.* 2, 4, 415a14–415b28.

33. *EN* 9, 8, 1168b35–1169a1.

34. *EN* 9, 4, 1166a16–17, trans. *CW2.*

35. Locke, *An Essay Concerning Human Understanding,* 305. Locke's view of substance is summed up by saying that it is a "something, I know not what," 295–97.

36. Locke, 175.

37. David Hume, *A Treatise of Human Nature*, 251.

38. Hume, 252.

39. See Joyce's review of *Humanism: Philosophical Essays,* by F. C. S. Schiller, "the leading European exponent of William James's philosophy," *CW* 135–36.

40. William James, *The Principles of Psychology,* vol. 1, xi. See page 342: "The passing Thought then seems to be the Thinker."

41. Daniel Dennett, *Consciousness Explained,* 225–26, 275.

42. Cited by William McDougall in *Body and Mind: A History and a Defense of Animism,* xii.

43. Virginia Woolf, *The Essays of Virginia Woolf,* vol. 3, 421.

44. Richard Rorty, *Philosophy and Social Hope,* 168.

45. St. Augustine, *Enarrationes in Psalmos,* XLI, 13, 470: "Tantamne profunditatem creditis esse in homine, quae lateat ipsum hominem in quo est?" See *Confessions* 10.33.50: "I have become a question to myself" (*Mihi quaestio factus sum*). Each one is a question to oneself, the question being precisely: What is it to be a self? What does it mean for me to exist uniquely as the irreplaceable individual who I am?

46. Fragment 45: Diels & Kranz, *Fragmente der Vorsokratiker* 1, 161.

47. Finn Fordham points out that Joyce had from early on a sharp interest in the phenomenon of multiple personality—"a hot topic in the early years of the twentieth century"—and experimented with it in *Ulysses,* especially in the "Circe" episode. "Joyce's interest would eventually blossom into the darkly coloured comedy of multiplicity, of multiple and split selves that is *Finnegans Wake.*" See Fordham, *I Do I Undo I Redo,* 213. See page 214: "Joyce had a sophisticated sense of the potential relations between multiple personality and the destabilization of identity in the early stages of *Ulysses.* That sense is present, for instance, in the concept of metempsychosis that is floated in 'Calypso.' Metempsychosis is an inverse version of the concept of multiples: rather than multiple discrete identities existing within one body, one soul moves between and through multiple bodies."

48. *EN* 10, 7, 1178a2–4.

49. *EN* 9, 7, 1168a8–9.

50. Philip Kitcher, *Joyce's Kaleidoscope,* 18. See also 53–54, 58, 63, 66.

51. Plato, *Republic* 443de, trans. Paul Shorey (Loeb); and Desmond Lee, ed., *Republic,* by Plato.

52. Robert McAlmon, *Being Geniuses Together,* 12. The enigma and challenge of self-identity was plainly expressed by Nobel Prize winner Bob Dylan, who, in response to the question why he would not discuss his "born again" Christianity, replied: "It's not tangible to me. I don't think I'm tangible to myself. I mean, I think one thing today and I think another thing tomorrow. I change during the course of a day. I wake and I'm one person, and when I go to sleep I know for certain I'm somebody else. I don't know who I am most of the time. It doesn't even matter to me." "Dylan Revisited," interview with David Gates, *Newsweek,* October 5, 1997.

53. For an excellent analysis, see Finn Fordham, *I Do I Undo I Redo,* 213–16. See page 215: "For the rest of the chapter Stephen steers between these alternative views of

personal identity: the whirlpool of Charybdis where identity is plural, multiple, and continuously changing, and Scylla, the all-too-hard rock of an identity that endures because memory has become history."

54. Joyce almost certainly borrowed this phrase from the conclusion to Walter Pater's *The Renaissance* (which has as its slogan Heraclitus's declaration of universal flux): "It is with this movement, with the passage and dissolution of impressions, images, sensations, that analysis leaves off—that continual vanishing away, that strange, perpetual, weaving and unweaving of ourselves." See Pater, *The Renaissance*, 236.

55. See *U* 9.407–08: "The leaning of sophists towards the bypaths of apocrypha is a constant quantity, John Eglinton detected."

56. Michael Groden, "The Complex Simplicity of *Ulysses*," 114. See page 117: "[H]is inner life is extraordinarily rich, as is evident both in his responses to people and objects and in his ideas, preoccupations and memories."

57. Stephen's reflections in *A Portrait* are conveyed in the language of sea change: "How foolish his aim had been! He had tried to build a breakwater of order and elegance against the sordid tide of life without him and to dam up, by rules of conduct and active interest and new filial relations, the powerful recurrence of the tides within him. Useless. From without as from within the waters had flowed over his barriers: their tides began once more to jostle fiercely above the crumbled mole" (*P* II.1347–53). On the beach at Sandymount, he is aware of the movements of the sea: "Vehement breath of waters amid seasnakes, rearing horses, rocks. In cups of rocks it slops: flop, slop, slap: bounded in barrels. And, spent, its speech ceases. It flows purling, widely flowing, floating foampool, flower unfurling" (*U* 3.457–60). See *U* 17.188–90: "the restlessness of its waves . . . the variability of states of sea."

58. *EN* 9, 4, 1166a19–23.

59. The word is repeated to describe HCE (*FW* 590.07).

60. Stephen stands for the Hellenic, intellectual, and artistic, as against Bloom, the Hebraist, sensualist, and scientific. They merge at the end of the work (Blephen and Stoom). See Geoffrey Wagner, *Wyndham Lewis: A Portrait of the Artist as the Enemy*, 178.

61. See also *U* 12.502, 503, 518, for repetition of "phenomenon."

62. See *U* 9.9–10: "The beautiful ineffectual dreamer who comes to grief against the hard facts."

63. As Declan Kiberd remarks in *Ulysses and Us*, Stephen seeks the inner meaning of things, "the soul which animates the exterior form" (64).

64. See Robert Burns: "O wad some Power the giftie gie us / To see oursels as ithers see us!" ("To A Louse, On Seeing one on a Lady's Bonnet at Church").

65. We might contrast the healthy, inquisitive, self-awareness of Stephen and Bloom with the strange self-alienation of Mr. Duffy in "A Painful Case": "He lived at a little distance from his body, regarding his own acts with doubtful side-glances. He had an odd autobiographical habit which led him to compose in his mind from time to time a short sentence about himself containing a subject in the third person and a predicate in the past tense" (*D*, 108). With a fractured self-reflection, Duffy was unable to take possession of himself or recognize his actions as his own. He could not distinguish selfhood from otherness.

66. In the *Contra Gentiles*, with which Joyce was very familiar, Aquinas states: "Omnis quod corrumpitur vel corrumpitur per se, vel corrumpitur per accidens" (*CG* 2, 55, 1303). The distinction between *corruptio per se* and *corruptio per accidens* was also explained in Maher's *Psychology*, which Joyce studied closely. The impossibility of annihilation by God had already been expressed by Stephen on Sandymount Strand: "From before the ages He willed me and now may not will me away or ever. A *lex eterna* stays about Him" (*U* 3.47–49). Aquinas distinguished between *lex aeterna, lex naturalis, lex divina,* and *lex humana. Lex aeterna* is identical with divine reason (*divina ratio*). See *ST* I-II, 91, art. 1: "Et ideo ipsa ratio gubernationis rerum in Deo sicut in principe universitatis existens, legis habet rationem. Et quia divina ratio nihil concipit ex tempore, sed habet aeternum conceptum, ut dicitur Prov. VIII; inde est quod huiusmodi legem oportet dicere aeternam." Lynch expresses a different view on immortality in "Oxen of the Sun": "Modern science has conclusively shown that only the plasmic substance can be said to be immortal" (*U* 14.1280–81).

67. Margot Norris, *The Decentered Universe of* Finnegans Wake, 92.

68. The question of unity and diversity in human nature, of simplicity and multiplicity, recurs throughout *Finnegans Wake*. A complete analysis lies outside the scope of the present study. A sample of passages will suffice to illustrate Joyce's abiding fascination with the question of permanence and change, identity, selfhood, unicity and diversity, and transmutation of identities. I cite first a selection of quotations referring to the unity of personality, followed by those highlighting the multiplicity and diversity of personality. The following quotations refer to the unity of personhood:

FW 32.9–21: An imposing everybody he always indeed looked, constantly the same as and equal to himself and magnificently well worthy of any and all such universalisation.

FW 57.30: Yet certes one is.

FW 62.26–27: We seem to us (the real Us!) to be reading our Amenti in the sixth sealed chapter of the going forth by black.

FW 114.33–35: establishing the identities in the writer complexus (for if the hand was one, the minds of active and agitated were more than so).

FW 123.30–31: The unmistaken identity of the persons in the Tiberiast duplex came to light in the most devious of ways.

FW 147.08–09: And you'll see if I'm selfthought.

FW 178.30–32: with an eachway hope in his shivering soul, as he prayed to the cloud Incertitude, of finding out for himself.

FW 185.27–186.9: this Esuan Menschavik and the first till last alshemist wrote over every square inch of the only foolscap available, his own body, till by its corrosive sublimation one continuous present tense integument slowly unfolded all marryvoising moodmoulded cyclewheeling history (thereby, he said, reflecting from his own individual person life unlivable, transaccidentated through the slow fires of consciousness into a dividual chaos, perilous, potent, common to allflesh, human only, mortal) but with each word that would not pass away the squidself which he had squirtscreened from the crystalline world waned chagreenold and doriangrayer in its dudhud. This exists that isits after having been said we know.

FW 193.35–36: haunted by a convulsionary sense of not having been or being all that I might have been or you meant to becoming.

FW 215.22–30: Teems of times and happy returns. The seim anew. Ordovico or viricordo. Anna was, Livia is, Plurabelle's to be. Northmen's thing made southfolk's place but howmulty plurators made eachone in person? Latin me that, my trinity scholard, out of eure sanscreed into oure eryan. *Hircus Civis Eblanensis!* He had buckgoat paps on him, soft ones for orphans. Ho, Lord! Twins of his bosom. Lord save us! And ho! Hey? What all men. Hot? His tittering daughters of. Whawk?

FW 248.31–32: the approaches to my intimast innermost.

FW 293.02–05: in truth, as a poor soul is between shift and shift ere the death he has lived through becomes the life he is to die into.

FW 329.18–19: The soul of everyelsesbody rolled into its olesoleself.

FW 343.26: the itch in his egondoom.

FW 354.08: now one and the same person.

FW 357.33: entrenched up contemplating of myself, wiz my naked I.

FW 358.15–16: I, my good grief, I am, I am big altoogooder.

FW 364.16–17: papertreated him into captivities with his inside man.

FW 365.02–03: as was I a locally person of caves until I got my purchase on her firmforhold I am, I like to think.

FW 373.29–30: now he canseels under veerious persons but is always that Rorke relly!

FW 394.30–33: eysolt of binnoculises memostinmust egotum sabcunsciously senses upers the deprofundity of multimathematical immaterialities wherebejubers in the pancosmic urge the allimmanence of that which Itself is Itself Alone.

FW 410.12: isolate i from my multiple Mes.

FW 411.12–14: But believe me in my simplicity I am awful good, I believe, so I am, at the root of me, praised be right cheek Discipline!

FW 425.25: in my mine's I.

FW 446.36–447.01: Let us, the real Us, all ignite in our prepurgatory grade as aposcals and be instrumental to utensilise.

FW 462.15–16: I'm not for forgetting me innerman mo nophone.

FW 463.07: me altar's ego in miniature.

FW 468.08–09: Thou the first person shingeller.

FW 472.26: the nucleus of a glow of a zeal of soul.

FW 472.30–31: humble indivisibles in this grand continuum, overlorded by fate and interlarded with accidence.

FW 484.05: What I (the person whomin I now am).

FW 485.05: And, Mind praisegad, is the first praisonal Egoname.

FW 490.09–10: By hearing his thing about a person one begins to place him for a certain in true.

FW 525.10: Wait now, leixlip, I scent eggoarchicism.

FW 597.07–09: The untireties of livesliving being the one substance of a streamsbecoming. Totalled in toldteld and teldtold in tittletell tattle.

FW 606.25–28: What will not arky paper, anticidingly inked with penmark, push, per sample prof, kuvertly falted, when style, stink and stigmataphoron are of one sum in the same person?

FW 614.27–615.11: Our wholemole millwheeling vicociclometer, a tetradomational gazebocroticon (the "Mamma Lujah" known to every schoolboy scandaller, be he Matty, Marky, Lukey or John-a-Donk), autokinatonetically preprovided with a clappercoupling smeltingworks exprogressive process, (for the farmer, his son and their homely codes, known as eggburst, eggblend, eggburial and hatch-as-hatch can) receives through a portal vein the dialytically separated elements of precedent decomposition for the verypetpurpose of subsequent recombination so that the heroticisms, catastrophes and eccentricities transmitted by the ancient legacy of the past; type by tope, letter from litter, word at ward, with sendence of sundance, since the days of Plooney and Columcellas when Giacinta, Pervenche and Margaret swayed over the all-too-ghoulish and illyrical and innumantic in our mutter nation, all, anastomosically assimilated and preteridentified paraidiotically, in fact, the sameold gamebold adomic structure of our Finnius the old One, as highly charged with electrons as hophazards can effective it, may be there for you, Cockalooralooraloomenos, when cup, platter and pot come piping hot, as sure as herself pits hen to paper and there's scribings scrawled on eggs. Of cause, so! And in effect, as?

FW 623.28–29: Ourselves, oursouls alone.

FW 620.27–32: The way I too. [. . .] I'll wait. And I'll wait. And then if all goes. What will be is. Is is.

FW 628.14: mememormee [= Me, me, more me].

The following texts refer to the multiplicity and diversity of persons:

FW 49.33–50.2: Now let the centuple celves of my egourge as Micholas de Cusack calls them,—of all of whose I in my hereinafter of course by recourse demission me—by the coincidance of their contraries reamalgamerge in that indentity of undiscernibles where the Baxters and the Fleshmans may they cease to bidivil uns.

FW 50.35–51.03: It is nebuless an autodidact fact of the commonest that the shape of the average human cloudyphiz, whereas sallow has long daze faded, frequently altered its ego with the possing of the showers (Not original!).

FW 54.01–06: Oilbeam they're lost we've fount rerembrandtsers, their hours to date link these heirs to here but wowhere are those yours of Yesterdays?

FW 104.01–05: In the name of Annah the Allmaziful, the Everliving, the Bringer of Plurabilities, haloed be her eve, her singtime sung, her rill be run, unhemmed as it is uneven! Her untitled mamafesta memorialising the Mosthighest has gone by many names at disjointed times.

FW 104.12: In the name of Annah the Allmaziful, the Everliving, the Bringer of Plurabilities.

FW 107.23–35: Closer inspection of the bordereau would reveal a multiplicity of personalities inflicted on the documents or document and some prevision of virtual crime or crimes might be made by anyone unwary enough before any suitable occasion for it or them had so far managed to happen along. In fact, under the closed eyes of the inspectors the traits featuring the chiaroscuro coalesce, their contrarieties eliminated, in one stable somebody similarly as by the providential warring of heartshaker with housebreaker and of dramdrinker against freethinker our social something bowls along bumpily, experiencing a jolting series of prearranged disappointments, down the long lane of (it's as semper as oxhousehumper!) generations, more generations and still more generations.

FW 113.14–15: There were three men in him (schwrites).

FW 118.21–28: every person, place and thing in the chaosmos of Alle anyway connected with the gobblydumped turkery was moving and changing every part of the time: the travelling inkhorn (possibly pot), the hare and turtle pen and paper, the continually more and less intermisunderstanding minds of the anticollaborators, the as time went on as it will variously inflected, differently pronounced, otherwise spelled, changeably meaning vocable scriptsigns.

FW 136.06–07: he is exalted and depressed, assembled and assundered.

FW 159.07: myriads of drifting minds in one.

FW 188.14–17: you have become of twosome twiminds . . . you have reared your disunited kingdom on the vacuum of your own most intensely doubtful soul.

FW 253.05: I once was otherwise.

FW 322.10: cuttered up and misfutthered in the most multiplest manner.

FW 336.15–18: And then. Be old. The next thing is. We are once amore as babes awondering in a wold made fresh where with the hen in the storyaboot we start from scratch.

FW 487.17–19: I indicate out to myself and I swear my gots how that I'm not meself at all, no jolly fear, when I realise bimiselves how becomingly I to be going to become.

FW 487.32–34: You knew me once but you won't know me twice. I am *simpliciter arduus,* ars of the schoo, Freeday's child in loving and thieving.

FW 576.32–3: guide them through the labyrinth of their samilikes and the alteregoases of their pseudoselves.

FW 584.34–05: O I you O you me! Well, we all unite thoughtfully in rendering gratias.

FW 613.13–14: Yet is no body present here which was not there before. Only is order othered. Nought is nulled. *Fuitfiat!*

FW 613.11–12: Hence we lived in two worlds. He is another he what stays under the himp of holth.

69. Norris, *The Decentered Universe of* Finnegans Wake, 11.

70. Patrick A. McCarthy, *Finnegans Wake,* 5.

71. Adeline Glasheen, *Who Is Who When Everybody Is Somebody Else: Third Census of "Finnegans Wake."*

72. See *CW* 154, 165.

73. C. H. Peake, *Joyce: The Citizen and the Artist,* 351.

74. Sigmund Freud, *The Interpretation of Dreams,* 630.

75. Joyce in an interview with Danish journalist Ole Vinding, *JJII* 696.

76. Ellmann, *Ulysses on the Liffey,* 16–17.

77. *Phys.* 2, 1, 193a29–30, my trans. See *Phys.* 2, 1, 192b13–14.

78. Don Gifford, Ulysses *Annotated,* 573.

79. Council of Nicaea (325 AD).

80. Catechism of the Catholic Church, paragraph 242.

81. Catechism of the Catholic Church, paragraph 467. The *New Catholic Encyclopedia* states: "Consubstantiality says identity of substance (nature, essence) between really distinct equals. The three Divine Persons, really distinct from one another, possess equally the one divine substance, or essence, that is, divinity. Because of the absolute unicity, unity, and simplicity of God, the identity of the substance is not merely specific but absolute, or numerical." *New Catholic Encyclopedia* 4, 252.

82. See John Simpson's elaborate note on the history of this tongue-twister at James Joyce Online Notes: http://www.jjon.org/joyce-s-words/c (accessed May 1, 2021).

83. Ellmann, *Ulysses on the Liffey,* 28.

84. *ST* I, 31, 2. The reference in Gifford, Ulysses *Annotated* (241), to *ST* I-II is incorrect.

85. *U* 16. 887–88, where Aquinas is referred to as "san Tomasso Mastino," Saint Thomas the Mastiff.

86. *U* 17.534–9. Gifford, Ulysses *Annotated,* 573.

87. John S. Rickard, *Joyce's Book of Memory,* 3.

88. Rickard, 4.

89. Rickard, 7.

90. See William James, *The Principles of Psychology,* vol. 1, 336. See, however, my remarks on page 102 above.

91. "Das Ich ist unrettbar." See Ernst Mach, *Die Analyse der Empfindungen und das Verhältnis des Physischen zum Psychischen,* 20.

92. Along with Hugo von Hofmannsthal, Arthur Schnitzler, Alfred Döblin, and Hermann Broch.

93. Judith Ryan, *The Vanishing Subject,* 149.

94. Locke, *An Essay Concerning Human Understanding,* 335.

95. Locke, 335.

96. Locke, 295.

97. Hume, *A Treatise of Human Nature,* 252–53. See 102 above.

98. Hume, 261.

99. Hume, 636.

100. See *ST* I, 14, 2 ad 3.

101. *ST* I, 77, 1, ad 7.

102. *CG* 2, 79.

103. *CG* 2, 94.

104. Professor William Magennis set the following question in the Honours BA degree examination in Metaphysics in Autumn 1920: "'Substance, with Locke, is the unknown and unknowable *substrate of attributes.*' Is this permanence under varying accidents the central note in the Scholastic conception of Substance?"

105. W. Norris Clarke, S.J., *Explorations in Metaphysics: Being-God-Person,* 55. Par-

ticularly relevant to our theme are chapter 3, "Action as the Self-Revelation of Being: A Central Theme in the Thought of St. Thomas" (45–64), and chapter 6, "To Be Is to Be Substance-in-Relation" (102–22).

106. A former professor of Psychology at University College Dublin, E. F. O'Doherty described Hume's self as "a hank of self-supporting onions on a non-existent rope." He asks: "If the mind is simply the succession of its own states, then how can it become conscious of itself as a succession of states? For all earlier states have ceased to exist before this present state of my mind. The series does not exist, but only the momentary term in the series. And it is not profitable to appeal to memory; since by definition mind is only the succession of its states, it must be the present state which remembers all the others." E. F. O'Doherty, "Russell and the Great Mystery," 31.

107. Hume, *A Treatise of Human Nature,* 262.

108. Ellmann, *Ulysses on the Liffey,* 95.

109. *ST* I, 87, 3.

110. Rickard, *Joyce's Book of Memory,* 29.

111. Ryan, *The Vanishing Subject,* 149.

112. Rickard, *Joyce's Book of Memory,* 28.

113. Rickard, 28.

114. See 23 above.

115. See 23 above.

116. Rickard, *Joyce's Book of Memory,* 28.

117. *De An.* 2, 1, 412b5–6. See Maher, *Psychology,* 523: "The soul is the first entelechy of a natural organized body potentially having life," or "the first entelechy of a natural body capable of life."

118. Rickard, *Joyce's Book of Memory,* 28.

119. Although he does not refer to it, Rickard's interpretation hints at an outdated etymology that would derive the word "entelechy" directly from *telos,* Greek for "goal" or "end." Charles H. Kahn states: "The standard etymology of ἐντελέχεια [coined from ἐν (in), τέλος (end/goal) and ἔχειν (have)], which dates from the Renaissance, is linguistically impossible: ἔχεια has nothing to do with ἔχειν, to have. The term seems to be an abstract noun derived from the adjective, ἐντελής 'perfected' or 'completed.'" Charles H. Kahn in *Aristotle's Vision of Nature,* 36.

120. Henri Bergson, *The Creative Mind,* 171, 173, 184.

121. In his book *Bergson and the Stream of Consciousness Novel,* Shiv K. Kumar, exclusively on the strength of a letter from Stuart Gilbert, claims that Joyce was directly acquainted with Bergson's thought but concedes that this "does not necessarily imply that his literary experiments show the influence of the philosopher's theories" (106): "Unlike Proust, Joyce makes no reference to Bergson in his *Letters,* nor did he ever acknowledge any such affiliations with the French philosopher. An attempt to trace Bergson's influence on his work would, therefore, be rather far-fetched and even misleading. What is of real importance to note is that Bergson and Joyce, together with all other stream of consciousness novelists, were, as suggested earlier, manifestations of the same *Zeitgeist.* Like Dorothy Richardson's, his acquaintance with Bergson was, in fact, in the nature of a self-realization. If, therefore, an interpretation of his work in terms of Bergsonian *durée,*

mémoire par excellence and fluid language reveals meanings hitherto unrealized, it is because there exists a marked parallelism between the Bergsonian flux and the stream of consciousness technique as employed by James Joyce" (Kumar, 106–7).

122. See Sheldon Brivic, *Joyce the Creator,* 6.

123. See 39 above.

124. Rickard, *Joyce's Book of Memory,* 27–28.

125. Maher, *Psychology,* 343.

126. Maher, 515–16, original emphasis. The corresponding text, with some variations, is found on page 555 of later editions. A digital version is available at https://maritain. nd.edu/jmc/etext/psycho25.htm. (Accessed May 1, 2021).

127. Maher, 447–48.

128. Maher, 345.

129. Maher, 518. The entire sentence is marked in the margin by a double vertical line, intersected by another double line. Interestingly, on the inside of the back cover, Joyce wrote: "Compenetrated: 518." The word is used by Maher on page 520 to indicate the role of the soul/substantial form in the domination of its subject/body. Joyce paid special attention to the associated footnote, marking it with three sets of double strokes: "Both Matter and Form are sometimes called *substances* by the Schoolmen, inasmuch as their coalescence results in a *substantial being.* Except the human soul, however, no *forma* or *materia prima* can exist *per se* apart. The epithet *incomplete* is occasionally used of inferior forms to express this circumstance; this adjective more properly, however, connotes the fact that the union of these factors gives rise to *one complete* composite substance. Even the human soul, though capable of subsisting in itself apart from the body, is styled an *incomplete substance,* since it possesses a natural aptitude to form with the body a single *complete* substance. An *integral part* of one complete being, *e.g.,* a man's hand, is also spoken of as an *incomplete substance.* The terms *constituent principle,* or *substantial principle,* seem less likely to mislead now-a-days than the word *substance* if employed to designate the essential coefficients of composite substances."

130. Maher, 518.

131. Maher, 521. Emphasis in original.

132. Joyce may have also encountered the term in John Rickaby's *General Metaphysics* handbook, the volume that contained the essentials of Aquinas's aesthetics. In his chapter titled "Substance as Hypostasis and Personality," Rickaby states: "When an individual substance is complete in itself, forming an entire nature, and remaining intrinsically independent, incommunicable, or *sui juris,* it is called a *suppositum* or *hypostasis,* because to it are attributed all the activities and passivities of the thing. [. . .] Hypostasis, though it has other senses in other connexions, is defined in the present connexion, as *any single substance which is of itself something complete, is not part of another thing, and cannot be regarded as a part.* [. . .] Furthermore, the hypostasis, if intelligent, is called a person." John Rickaby, *General Metaphysics,* 280–81. Italics in original. Subsequent sections in the same chapter are headed: "The wrong and dangerous doctrine of Locke in regard to personality," and "Hume goes still further astray" (279).

133. See *P* IV.69–74, for Stephen's reflections on the Blessed Trinity.

134. Maher, *Psychology,* 523. Emphasis in original. In a footnote, he supplies slight

variations on two texts of Aristotle: ἡ ψυχή ἐστιν ἐντελέχεια ἡ πρώτη σώματος φυσικοῦ ζωὴν ἔχοντος δυνάμει, or ἡ πρώτη ἐντελέχεια σώματος φυσικοῦ ὀργανικοῦ (De An. 2, 1, 412a, 412b).

135. Rickard, Joyce's Book of Memory, 19.

136. Rickard, 19. The Aristotelian Thomist would reply with Horace: Caelum, non animum, mutant, qui trans mare currunt: "They change their sky, not their soul, who rush across the sea" (Epistulae, I, 11, 27).

137. P II.1199–1201.

138. Rickard, 16, 17.

139. Theoharis Constantine Theoharis remarks: "To date there has been no detailed critical account of the presence of ideas of the soul from De Anima in Ulysses." He refers to "Joyce's expertise in the Aristotelian definition of the soul, which is explicitly presented repeatedly, and often prominently, in Ulysses." Joyce's Ulysses, 211n4.

140. W. R. Rodgers, Irish Literary Portraits, 142.

141. John Henry Newman, An Essay on the Development of Christian Doctrine, 40.

142. Frank Budgen, James Joyce and the Making of Ulysses and Other Writings, 107.

143. Budgen, 118.

Chapter 5. Totality, Diversity, and Order: The Unity of Analogy

1. M.-D. Philippe, "Analogon and Analogia in the Philosophy of Aristotle," 1.

2. Vincent J. Cheng, "History and Possibility: Shakespeare and the Stage in Finnegans Wake," 141.

3. Part. An. 1, 4, 644a21–22.

4. Met. 14, 6, 1093b18–19.

5. Met. 12, 4, 1070a31.

6. Pol. 1, 2, 1252b1–5.

7. EN 6, 10, 1137b30–32.

8. Rhet. 1, 4,1360a25–30.

9. Rhet. 2, 9, 1387a27–1387b2.

10. See EN 8, 7, 1158b23–28.

11. EN 5, 3, 1131a 31–32.

12. Poet. 21, 1457b16–19, CW2, 2332, modified.

13. Rhet. 3, 4, 1407a15–17. See Poet. 21, 1457b20–22.

14. Poet. 21, 1457b22–25.

15. William P. Alston puts it well: "Analogy of proportionality is found where there is likeness of two relationships. (A proportion is a relation; proportionality is a similarity between two proportions.)" Alston, "Aquinas on Theological Predication: A Look Backward and a Look Forward," 153. Analogy is a similarity of relationship, a correspondence of proportion. Both Alasdair MacIntyre and Martin Heidegger refer to analogy as a "relation of relations." MacIntyre, "Analogy in Metaphysics," 45; Heidegger, Wegmarken, 348.

16. Philip Kitcher, Joyce's Kaleidoscope: An Invitation to Finnegans Wake, 46.

17. T. S. Eliot is reported to have said that Joyce was the "greatest master of the English

language since Milton." See F. O. Matthiessen, *The Achievement of T.S. Eliot: An Essay on the Nature of Poetry,* 135.

18. J. A. Giles, ed., *History of the Ancient Britons* II, 303.

19. Frank Budgen quotes this as follows: "How to gather, how to order, and how to present a given material." *James Joyce and the Making of* Ulysses *and Other Writings,* 352.

20. *CG* 1, 1: A Philosopho ponitur quod sapientis est ordinare. See also *ST* I, 1, 6: Cum enim sapientis sit ordinare et iudicare.

21. Aquinas, *Of God and His Creatures,* 1.

22. Padraic Colum, *The Road Round Ireland* (New York: Macmillan, 1926), 316.

23. John Henry Newman remarked that "the function of philosophy is to view all things in their mutual relations, and its object is truth." Newman, *Essays Critical and Historical,* vol. 1, 29.

24. Budgen, *James Joyce and the Making of* Ulysses *and Other Writings,* 20.

25. *D* "Ivy Day in the Committee Room," 113, 470–71.

26. See *U* 15.2446, *U* 16.849, *U* 16.1579, *U* 16.1728, *U* 17.686, *U* 17.709, *U* 17.1155. For "metaphorical" and "metaphor," see *U* 7.889, *U* 16.1597, *FW* 070.32, *FW* 466.10.

27. Tim Conley, "Waking 'for an equality of relations,'" 156. Conley refers to Joyce's borrowing of the phrase from Spencer as "a compelling possibility." Joyce included two quotations from Spencer on page 10 of his Early Commonplace Book. See Luca Crispi, "A Commentary on James Joyce's National Library of Ireland 'Early Commonplace Book,'" 7. Joyce had his own copy of Spencer's *The Study of Sociology,* a work parodied in "Oxen of the Sun." See Richard Ellmann, *The Consciousness of Joyce,* 128. He was familiar with the phrase "survival of the fittest," coined by Spencer and used with frequency in *The Principles of Biology* (1864). See *U* 16.1602: "destruction of the fittest"; *FW* 145.27: "so-wiveall of the prettiest."

28. Herbert Spencer, "The Genesis of Science," 116–93.

29. Spencer, 153.

30. Spencer, 153.

31. On the importance of analogy, see Spencer, 150: "And the expressions we use in our arguments—'*analogy* implies,' 'the cases are not *parallel*,' 'by *parity* of reasoning,' 'there is no *similarity*,'—show how constantly the idea of likeness underlies our ratiocinative processes." Commenting on the indirect relationship between the sciences, Spencer remarks: "Where there is no dependence, there is yet analogy—*equality of relations; and the discovery of the relations subsisting among one set of phenomena, constantly suggests a search for the same relations among another set" (181). Spencer deals at length with metaphor in his essay "Philosophy of Style," published in *Essays: Scientific, Political, & Speculative* II, 30–33.

32. Spencer, "The Genesis of Science," 153–54.

33. Spencer, 154.

34. *Pol.* 1, 8, 1256a20.

35. James Pribek, "Joyce and Newman," 189.

36. John Henry Newman, *Apologia Pro Vita Sua,* 36.

37. Pribek, 189.

38. John Henry Newman, *The Idea of a University,* 134.

39. Ezra Pound, "Pound on *Ulysses* and Flaubert," 264. The French original is printed in *Pound/Joyce*, 206: "Il s'exprime différemment dans les differentes parties de son livre (comme le permet même Aristote), mais ce n'est pas, comme le dit le distingué Larbaud, qu'il abandonne l'unité de style."

40. Valery Larbaud, "Larbaud on Joyce," 259–60. Joyce was very pleased with Larbaud's judgment, as he told the Czech artist Adolf Hoffmeister: "You know the admirable Mr Valery Larbaud praised *Ulysses* exaggeratedly by a beautiful metaphor, likening it to the stars of the sky, whose beauty is increased when we study them for a long time, by the discovery of innumerable new stars." Adolf Hoffmeister, "Portrait of Joyce," 130.

41. Pound, "Pound on *Ulysses* and Flaubert," 264. For the original, see *Pound/Joyce*, 206: "Chaque personnage, non seulement parle à sa propre guise, mais il pense à sa propre guise, ce n'est pas plus abandonner l'unité de style que quand les divers personnages d'un roman dit de style uni parlent de manière diverses: on omet les guillemets, voilà tout." In a separate essay, Pound repeats the remark and provides examples of different dialects: "Joyce's characters not only speak their own language, but they think their own language. Thus Master Dignam stood looking at the poster: 'two puckers stripped to their pelts and putting up their props . . . Gob, that'd be a good pucking match to see. Myler Keogh, that's the chap sparring out to him with the green sash. Two bar entrance, soldiers half price. I could easy do a bunk on ma. When is it? May the twentysecond. Sure, the blooming thing is all over'" (*U* 10.1131–39). Pound remarks: "Joyce speaks [. . .] with a many-tongued and multiple language, of small boys, street preachers, of genteel and ungenteel, of bowsers and undertakers, of Gertie McDowell and Mr Deasy." He comments: "This variegation of dialects allows Joyce to present his matter, his tones of mind, very rapidly." See Ezra Pound, *Literary Essays*, 404–5.

42. Hermann Broch, *Geist and Zeitgeist*, 74. Also *Schriften zur Literatur* I. *Kritik*, 70. Broch refers to the deep unconscious desire of every art to portray "the totality of the universe," *Geist and Zeitgeist*, 161. He cites Joyce's *Ulysses* and Mann's *Joseph* as twentieth-century exemplars of the "great epic" (161). In a letter to his publisher, Daniel Brody, Broch wrote: "The claim to totality is surely the same for both Joyce and Mann. Joyce's solution lies in an extreme Platonism and subjectivism." *Briefe* I, 299–300, trans. Robert K. Weninger, *The German Joyce*, 46–47.

43. *SL* 271. I am using this translation in preference to that of *LI* 146–47. Joyce's allusion to "heavenly hosts" is a reference to Aquinas's theory that since all angels are infinitely perfect according to its appropriate essence, each one constitutes a species in itself; this contrasts with the human species, of which each member is a limited imperfect instantiation.

44. Eileen MacCarvill, *The Collection of Joyce Exam Papers and University Calendars*.

45. Richard Ellmann, "*Ulysses*: A Short History," 719.

46. *Met.* 14, 3, 1090b19–20. See 230 above.

47. *Troilus and Cressida* 3, 3. 175.

48. There is a reference to *Troilus and Cressida* in "Scylla and Charybdis," when John Eglinton remarks that Shakespeare "makes Ulysses quote Aristotle" (*U* 9.999). It was Hector, and not Ulysses, who anachronistically refers to Aristotle's view that young men were unfit to hear moral philosophy (*Troilus and Cressida* 2, 2, 166–67).

49. "The Boarding House," *D* 53.156–57.

50. *Met.* 12, 10, 1075a16–19. *CW2*, 1699.

51. See also *U* 1.176: "To ourselves. . . . new paganism. . . . *omphalos*"; *U* 1.544: "But ours is the *omphalos*."

52. Frank Budgen, *James Joyce and the Making of* Ulysses *and Other Writings,* 21.

53. Theoharis Constantine Theoharis, *Joyce's Ulysses,* 26.

54. Umberto Eco, *The Middle Ages of James Joyce,* 33.

55. *Pound/Joyce,* 185.

56. Theoharis, *Joyce's Ulysses,* 4, 25.

57. Herbert S. Gorman, *James Joyce: His First Forty Years,* 115.

58. James Boswell, *Boswell's Life of Johnson,* vol. 3, 174.

59. Lionel Trilling, "Freud and Literature," 99.

60. Henry James, "The Art of Fiction," 389–90.

61. *U* 13.1003: "Make their own use of everything."

62. Robert McAlmon, *Being Geniuses Together,* 26.

63. Vladimir Nabokov, *Lectures on Literature,* 217.

64. Ezra Pound, *Literary Essays,* 401. Pound was referrring to *Dubliners,* but his remark applies equally to *Ulysses:* "He gives us Dublin as it presumably is. [. . .] He gives us things as they are, not only for Dublin, but for every city. Erase the local names and a few specifically local allusions, and a few historic events of the past, and substitute a few different local names, allusions and events, and these stories could be retold of any town."

65. 1321 was the year of Dante's death.

66. Pound, *Literary Essays,* 406. On Joyce's use of Homer's *Odyssey* as a scaffold, Pound remarked: "Joyce uses a scaffold taken from Homer, and the remains of a medieval allegorical culture; it matters little, it is a question of cooking, which does not restrict the action, nor inconvenience it, nor harm the realism, nor the contemporaneity of the action. It is a means of regulating the form." "Pound on Ulysses and Flaubert," 264. French original in *Pound/Joyce,* 206.

67. Chris Ackerley, "'Well, of course if we knew all the things': Coincidence and Design in *Ulysses* and *Under the Volcano,*" 45. As examples of coincidences observed by Bloom, the following sample selection will suffice: *U* 4.415: "Fifteen yesterday. Curious, fifteenth of the month too"; *U* 8.502–04: "There he is: the brother. Image of him. Haunting face. Now that's a coincidence. Course hundreds of times you think of a person and don't meet him"; *U* 8.525–27: "And there he is too. Now that's really a coincidence: second time. Coming events cast their shadows before"; *U* 11.713: "Martha it is. Coincidence. Just going to write"; *U* 13.1270–72: "The stick fell in silted sand, stuck. Now if you were trying to do that for a week on end you couldn't. Chance. We'll never meet again"; *U* 11.302–3: "It is. Again. Third time. Coincidence"; *U* 15.593: "Coincidence too. They think it funny." See Derek Attridge: "In 'Eumaeus,' he remarks on no less than four 'coincidences' in the course of his unsuccessful attempts to engage Stephen in conversation (*U* 16.414, 890, 1222, 1776)—though, caught up as they are in the web of misinformation and bathos that characterizes the chapter, they don't qualify very obviously for the label. In 'Ithaca' [. . .] he recalls the coincidences that might have led him to predict the result of the Gold Cup that afternoon (*U* 17.322)." Derek Attridge, *Joyce Effects,* 123.

68. Attridge, 123.

69. Ackerley, "'Well, of course if we knew all the things,'" 46.

70. Joyce himself seems to have been obsessed with numerical coincidences. See Hoffmeister, "Portrait of Joyce," 129–30.

71. Wyndham Lewis, *Time and Western Man,* 91.

72. Stuart Gilbert, *James Joyce's* Ulysses, 53.

73. Ernestus Diehl, ed., *Anthologia Lyrica Graeca* III, Frag. 103.

74. Jean-Paul Sartre, "Time in Faulkner: *The Sound and the Fury,*" 226.

75. Caroline Spurgeon, *Shakespeare's Imagery and What It Tells Us,* 6.

76. Herbert S. Gorman, *James Joyce: His First Forty Years,* 116.

77. Eliot, "*Ulysses,* Order, and Myth," 201. Eliot emphasized "the significance of the method employed—the parallel to the Odyssey, and the use of appropriate styles and symbols to each division." He strongly rejected the charge that Joyce was "a prophet of chaos." Joyce's parallel use of the *Odyssey,* he suggested, "has the importance of a scientific discovery. No one else has built a novel upon such a foundation before: it has never been necessary." It is worth noting that almost two decades later, Eliot wrote: "The later books, *Ulysses* and *Finnegans Wake,* are too closely constructed, and depend too much upon cumulative effect, for any extracts to be more than those parts easiest to grasp in isolation." *Introducing James Joyce,* 5. Indeed, Joyce himself remarked to Beckett: "I may have oversystematized *Ulysses*" (*JJII* 702). See *FW* 179.26–27: "his usylessly unreadable Blue Book of Eccles." In a letter to Carlo Linati (September 21, 1920), Joyce referred to *Ulysses* as his "damned monster-novel" (*SL* 271).

78. Broch, *Geist and Zeitgeist,* 77–78. *Schriften zur Literatur I. Kritik,* 74–75.

79. Richard M. Kain, "Fifty Years of *Ulysses:* 1934–1984," 79.

80. Arthur Power, *From the Old Waterford House,* 63–64.

81. Broch, *Geist and Zeitgeist,* 69–70; *Schriften zur Literatur I. Kritik,* 66–67.

82. Richard Kearney, *Debating Otherness with Richard Kearney: Perspectives form South Africa,* 40–41.

83. Hugh Kenner, *Joyce's Voices,* 15–38. As Michael Groden puts it, the technique "goes so far as to let the vocabulary of the character being described permeate the narration." Michael Groden, "The Complex Simplicity of *Ulysses,*" 128–29, n13.

84. Kenner, 21.

85. Plato, *Rep.* 393c. Plato understands this as an imitation, *mimêsis.*

86. *Rhet.* 3, 12, 1413b3–4.

87. *Poet.* 1449b 25–26, trans. Butcher.

88. Samuel Taylor Coleridge, *Complete Works* vol. 4, 54. See August Wilhelm von Schlegel, *Vorlesungen über dramatische Kunst und Literatur,* 157: "Formlos zu sein darf also den Werken des Genius auf keine Weise gestattet werden."

89. T. S. Eliot wrote in a letter to Robert McAlmon: "But Joyce has form—immensely careful. And as for literary style—one of the last things he sent me contains a marvellous parody of nearly every style in English prose from 1600 to the Daily Mail. One needs a pretty considerable knowledge of English literature to understand it." McAlmon, *Being Geniuses Together,* 8.

90. "The Dead," *D* 151.1. As Fritz Senn rightly comments, "it has become a cliché that

Ulysses contains different styles." *Joycean Murmoirs,* 106. On Joyce's diversity of styles, Senn writes: "polytropy suffuses all of *Ulysses,* not just a few characters. It manifests itself in changing styles suitable for the situation at hand, and, above all, it infuses the very language. In *Finnegans Wake* almost every item is polytropic, turning in different ways" (74). Senn expands on Joyce's polytropic style in an essay on "Nausicaa": "Scenic changes implicit in the stylistic and metaphorical potential of this chapter's language will be taken literally in 'Circe,' where they are grotesquely staged. Stylistic guises adapted to the current themes are, of course, the distinctive mark of *Ulysses;* in the later chapters the method is intensified by formal intricacy, and the adaptability of the style, corresponding to the mercurial assumption of expedient roles, may perhaps be understood as a reflection of Odyssean tactics. Odysseus is known for his versatility: he cunningly suits his language, form of address, and guise to the immediate purpose and has on occasion recourse to impersonation (at times divine agencies help along with a touch of transfiguration)." See Senn, "Nausicaa," 308. See also Senn, "Book of Many Turns," 129: "Homer's Odysseus appealed to Joyce because of his universality and his encyclopaedic turns. In him the two opposites, the individual and the universe are combined. I cannot help but think that Joyce was conscious of a translation of *polytropos* into Latin, which would yield *multi-versus,* the exact anthetical correspondence to *uni-versus.*" Again: "Like Odysseus, Joyce chooses his speech, his role, and his narrative stance carefully and ruthlessly. Every style is a role adapted for some purpose. [. . .] *Ulysses* is Homerically polytropical. Voices change, characters are not fixed, language is versatile and polymorphous" (131). Also: "English must be one of the most Odyssean languages; resourceful, pliant, homophonous, versatile, it allows Joyce to assume the voice appropriate for the occasion, multiple guises, mercurial transformations" (132).

91. Eloise Knowlton, *Joyce, Joyceans, and the Rhetoric of Citation,* 58. See page 59: "Kenner recognizes style is meant to define the authorial self, and that Joyce's prose can flicker between different styles, different speaking selves."

92. Ellmann writes: "Joyce's theme in *Ulysses* was simple. He invoked the most elaborate means to present it" (preface, James Joyce, *Ulysses,* ix). He was thus echoing Joyce's remark that his thought was simple. See Michael Groden, "The Complex Simplicity of *Ulysses,*" 129.

93. Orhan Pamuk, *The Naive and the Sentimental Novelist,* 159. See also 153: "The center of a novel is a profound opinion or insight about life, a deeply embedded point of mystery, whether real or imagined. Novelists write in order to investigate this locus, to discover its implications, and we are aware that novels are read in the same spirit. When we first imagine a novel, we may consciously think of this secret center and know that we are writing for its sake—but sometimes we may be unaware of it." The center must remain veiled because "if the centre is too obvious and the light too strong, the meaning of the novel is immediately revealed and the act of reading feels repetitive."

94. Brenda Maddox, "Love Makes the Joycean World Go Round," 85.

95. Ellmann, preface, *Ulysses,* xii–iv. Also "The Big Word in *Ulysses,*" 30–31. See the following by Jean Kimball: "St. Augustine and Love in Bloom," 375–78; "Love and Death in 'Ulysses': 'Word Known to All Men,'" 143–60; "Love in the Kidd Era: An Afterword," 369–77.

96. *Summa Contra Gentiles,* trans. English Dominican Fathers, 193. A more recent translation, that of Anton C. Pegis, renders the passage as follows: "We must therefore observe that, although the other operations of the soul deal with only one object, love alone seems to be directed to two objects. For by the fact that we understand and rejoice, we must be somehow related to some object. **Love, however, wills something for someone,** for we are said to love the thing to which we **wish some good,** as explained above. Hence, the **things that we want,** absolutely and properly we are said to **desire,** but not to love; rather, we love ourselves for whom we want those things: whence it is by accident and improperly that such things are said to be loved." Aquinas, *On the Truth of the Catholic Faith,* 279–80.

97. *JJII* 779n30. The text as translated by Rickaby is abridged, failing to translate the crucial word "bonum": "In answer to this difficulty we must observe that whereas other activities of the soul are concerned with one object only, love alone seems to tend to two. For **love wishes something to somebody: hence the things that we desire,** we are properly said to 'desire,' not to 'love,' but in them we rather love ourselves for whom we desire them." Joseph Rickaby, *Of God and His Creatures,* 67.

98. *CG* 1, 91, trans. Pegis.

99. *ST* I-II, 26, 4, ad 1: "Love is not divided into friendship and concupiscence, but into love of friendship and love of concupiscence. For a friend is, properly speaking, one to whom we wish good, while we are said to desire what we wish for ourselves."

100. *EN* 9, 4, 1166a2–6.

101. *CG* 3, 125.

102. Don Gifford, Ulysses *Annotated,* 237.

103. The complete paragraph: Amplius. "In societate humana hoc est maxime necessarium ut sit amicitia inter multos. Multiplicatur autem amicitia inter homines dum personae extraneae per matrimonia colligantur. Conveniens igitur fuit legibus ordinari quod matrimonia contraherentur cum extraneis personis, et non cum propinquis." Trans. Vernon J. Bourke, *Summa Contra Gentiles,* 154: "Moreover, in human society it is most necessary that there be friendship among many people. But friendship is increased among men when unrelated persons are bound together by matrimony. Therefore, it was proper for it to be prescribed by laws that matrimony should be contracted with persons outside one's family and not with relatives."

104. Ellmann, preface, *Ulysses,* xiii.

105. Ellmann, xiii.

106. Ellmann, xiv. See also "The Big Word in 'Ulysses.'"

107. Dante, *The Divine Comedy,* vol. III: *Paradise* XXXIII.145. See also *Inferno* I, 38–39: "ch'eran con lui l'amor divino / mosse di prima quelle cose belle," and *The Divine Comedy,* vol. III: *Paradise* I.74: "amor che 'l ciel governi."

108. *Met.* 4, 1, 1003a33.

109. James Joyce, *Exiles,* 113.

110. Denis Donoghue contends: "Literally, there is no organic unity in *Finnegans Wake,* because many of the 'organs' have been dissolved into a glutinous literary mass." "Joyce's Landscapes," 88.

111. H. G. Wells, Review of *A Portrait of the Artist as a Young Man.*

112. Jacques Mercanton, "The Hours of James Joyce," 207.

113. T. S. Eliot, *Collected and Uncollected Poems,* 596–97. Eliot wrote to Jack P. Dalton (September 26, 1963): "It is true that I was responsible for the publication of *Finnegans Wake* but I never felt any warm enthusiasm for the work. [. . .] No one admires Joyce more than I do—but all one can say is that after *Ulysses* there was nothing else for him to do" (597).

114. Lord Byron, *Selected Letters and Journals,* 117.

115. Anthony Ward, *Walter Pater: The Idea in Nature,* 67.

116. Adolf Hoffmeister, "James Joyce," 126.

117. Adolf Hoffmeister, "Portrait of Joyce," 131.

118. Bruce Stewart, *A Short Life of James Joyce.*

119. Thomas McGreevy, "The Catholic Element in *Work in Progress,*" 58.

120. Hoffmeister, "Portrait of Joyce," 132.

121. Samuel Taylor Coleridge, *Table Talk* I. See also *The Notebooks of Samuel Taylor Coleridge* I, § 1725: "The dim Intellect *sees* an absolute Oneness, the perfectly clear intellect *knowingly perceives* it. Distinction and Plurality lie in the Betwixt."

122. Joyce remarked to Padraic Colum: "Of course I don't take Vico's speculations literally; I use his cycles as a trellis." Colum and Colum, *Our Friend James Joyce,* 123.

123. Mario Vargas Llosa, *Bloom,* 17.

124. Sheldon Brivic, *Joyce the Creator,* 50.

125. Seamus Deane, introduction, *Finnegans Wake,* by James Joyce, xii.

126. "My imagination grows when I read Vico as it doesn't when I read Freud or Jung" (*JJII* 340).

127. Bruce Stewart, "Joyce, James Augustine Aloysius," 795.

128. It is noteworthy that, having sketched the motley history of Giordano Bruno, Joyce explains in the language of Aristotle's metaphysics: "Bruno, through all these modes and accidents (as he would have called them) of being, remains a consistent spiritual unity"; *CW* 133.

129. Also *OPCW* 94. See Samuel Taylor Coleridge, *The Friend* I, 94n. Joyce seems to quote from memory, since he departs slightly from the original.

130. *OCPW* 188. From "L'influenza letteraria universale del rinascimento," an examination essay written for the University of Padua, April 1912.

131. Mark Patrick Hederman, "The 'Mind' of Joyce: From Paternalism to Paternity," 256.

132. Tim Conley, "*Finnegans Wake*: Some Assembly Required," 134. The reference is to *FW* 19.35–36: "But the world, mind, is, was and will be writing its own wrunes for ever."

133. Robert K. Weninger, *The German Joyce,* 33.

134. Power, *Conversations with James Joyce,* 45.

135. Donald Phillip Verene, *James Joyce and the Philosophers at* Finnegans Wake, 39. Verene refers to Goethe's famous comparison of Aristotle with Plato: "Plato seems to behave as a spirit descended from heaven, who has chosen to dwell a space on earth. [. . .] He aspires to rise and regain the heavenly abode from which he came down. The aim of all his discourse is to awaken in his hearers the notion of a single eternal being, of the good, of truth, of beauty. [. . .] Aristotle's attitude towards the world is, on the other

hand, entirely human. He behaves like an architect in charge of a building. [. . .] He gives his edifice an ample foundation, seeks his materials in every direction, sorts them, and builds gradually. He therefore rises like a regular pyramid, whereas Plato ascends rapidly heavenward like an obelisk or a sharp tongue of flame." I cite the translation given in Jacques Maritain, *An Introduction to Philosophy*, 68n1. See Johann Wolfgang von Goethe, *Naturwissenschaftliche Schriften* II/3, 141–42.

136. Verene, xiv.

137. Karl Jaspers, introduction to *The Great Philosophers*, 14.

138. Fred Higginson, *Anna Livia Plurabelle: The Making of a Chapter*, 14.

Chapter 6. Beauty: Joyce's Thomist Aesthetics

1. See Fran O'Rourke, "Beauty from Plato to Aquinas."

2. *LII* 38. From the start of his career, Joyce used the spelling "esthetic." When the typesetter at the *Egoist* substituted "aesthetic" in the serialized publication of *A Portrait* (1913) Joyce reversed in each case the printer's "correction." *James Joyce Archive* 7, 415–17, 426–32. I retain Joyce's spelling in quotations but otherwise use the standard spelling. "Esthetic" is not entirely unusual.

3. For the text of Joyce's paragraphs, see 235–37 above.

4. The introductory note by Ellsworth Mason and Richard Ellmann to the "Aesthetics" chapter in *The Critical Writings* provides an excellent survey of the trajectory of Joyce's aesthetic project: "Impelled in part by his ambition to establish the relation of drama to other genres, Joyce went heroically on to compound his own aesthetic. He inevitably began with Aristotle, then turned, surprisingly, to Flaubert. His earliest formulations were made during his second trip to Paris, in February and March 1903; he wrote them down in a notebook and signed his name and the date to every observation as if to guarantee its importance as well as to identify its authorship. He continued his speculations in Pola [. . .] in November 1904. [. . .] Between March and July of the following year he brought together his early essays and his notebook statements for *Stephen Hero*. The discussion of aesthetics in the *Portrait* was written several years later. He moves, then, from bald statement in the Paris and Pola notebooks to a mixture of narrative essay and dramatic presentation of his theories in *Stephen Hero*, and finally to the sheerly dramatic presentation in the *Portrait*" (*CW* 141). What Mason and Ellmann refer to as two separate notebooks are now more accurately referred to as Joyce's "Early Commonplace Book." See 241n19 above.

5. For Joyce's texts (including his revisions) see 235–37 above. These paragraphs were reproduced in Gorman, *James Joyce: A Definitive Biography*, 133–35, and reprinted in *CW* 146–48; *OCPW* 105–7; Aubert, *The Aesthetics of James Joyce*, 138–40; and Scholes and Kain, eds., *The Workshop of Daedalus*, 81–83. A slightly modified version of the first paragraph, also dated "7. XI. 04," is included in the Joyce MSS at Yale and reproduced in the *James Joyce Archive* 7, 108.

6. Kevin Barry, *OCPW* 105, renders the text as "Pulcera [*sic*] quae visa placent." This is incorrect: the manuscript clearly reads "pulcra"; the normal spelling is "pulchra," but it is not unusual to omit the "h."

7. *SH* 212: "You know what Aquinas says: The three things requisite for beauty are,

integrity, a wholeness, symmetry and radiance. Some day I will expand that sentence into a treatise."

8. William T. Noon, S.J., refers to "Saint Thomas's slight, incidental aesthetics." *Joyce and Aquinas,* 78.

9. See O'Rourke, "Beauty from Plato to Aquinas," 65–68.

10. It has been suggested that Joyce acquired the term from Flaubert's letter to Mlle Le-royer de Chantepie, March 18, 1857, in which Flaubert referred to "la beau indéfinissable résultant de la conception même et qui est la splendeur du vrai, comme disait Platon." Quoted *CW* 141n1. See Joyce's essay on James Clarence Mangan: "Beauty, the splendour of truth, is a gracious presence when the imagination contemplates intensely the truth of its own being or the visible world, and the spirit which proceeds out of truth and beauty is the holy spirit of joy" (*CW* 83). This is incorporated into *Stephen Hero:* "It is time for [the critics] to acknowledge that here the imagination has contemplated intensely the truth of the being of the visible world and that beauty, the splendour of truth, has been born" (*SH* 80). The attribution of the definition to Plato was not universally accepted. See Charles Lahr, *Cours de Philosophie,* 458: "On connaît la définition faussement attribuée à Platon: *le beau est la splendeur du vrai.*" Despite his frequent invocation of the reputedly Platonic definition of beauty as *splendor veri,* Joyce divorces truth and beauty, relating them, respectively, to the intellectual appetite for satisfactory intelligible relations and to the aesthetic appetite for satisfactory sensible relations.

11. Noon, *Joyce and Aquinas,* 21.

12. Hilary of Poitiers, *De Trinitate* 2, 1 (*PL* 10, 51): "Nec deesse quidquam consummationi tantae reperietur, intra quam sit, in Patre et Filio et Spiritu sancto, infinitas in aeterno, species in imagine, usus in munere." Trans., *Nicene and Post-Nicene Fathers,* 52 (modified). Aquinas cites "*Aeternitas est in Patre, species in Imagine, usus in Munere* (Eternity is in the Father, the species in the Image, and use is in the Gift)." *ST* I 39, 8 obj. 1.

13. *ST* I 39, 8: "Species autem, sive pulchritudo, habet similitudinem cum propriis filii. Nam ad pulchritudinem tria requiruntur. Primo quidem, integritas sive perfectio, quae enim diminuta sunt, hoc ipso turpia sunt. Et debita proportio sive consonantia. Et iterum claritas, unde quae habent colorem nitidum, pulchra esse dicuntur. Quantum igitur ad primum, similitudinem habet cum proprio filii, inquantum est filius habens in se vere et perfecte naturam patris. Unde, ad hoc innuendum, Augustinus in sua expositione dicit, ubi, scilicet in filio, summa et prima vita est, et cetera. Quantum vero ad secundum, convenit cum proprio filii, inquantum est imago expressa patris. Unde videmus quod aliqua imago dicitur esse pulchra, si perfecte repraesentat rem, quamvis turpem. Et hoc tetigit Augustinus cum dicit, ubi est tanta convenientia, et prima aequalitas, et cetera. Quantum vero ad tertium, convenit cum proprio filii, inquantum est verbum, quod quidem lux est, et splendor intellectus, ut Damascenus dicit. Et hoc tangit Augustinus cum dicit, 'tanquam verbum perfectum cui non desit aliquid, et ars quaedam omnipotentis Dei,' et cetera."

14. *In 1 Sent.,* dist. 31.

15. Cyril Barrett, "The Aesthetics of St Thomas Re-Examined," 111.

16. See *ST* I 39, 8: "integritas sive perfectio."

17. Immanuel Chapman, "The Perennial Theme of Beauty and Art," 340. Thomas

Hibbs comments: "One of the problems with appraising the use of Aquinas is that there are so many errors of interpretation interspersed with the insights that it is difficult to know what to attribute to whom." Thomas S. Hibbs, "Portraits of the Artist: Joyce, Nietzsche, and Aquinas," 130–31.

18. See also "The Day of the Rabblement," which refers to *verum* and *bonum*: "No man, said the Nolan, can be a lover of the true or the good unless he abhors the multitude" (*OCPW* 50).

19. *De Ver.*, 1, 1: Sicut ens dicitur unum, in quantum est indivisum in se, ita dicitur aliquid, in quantum est ab aliis divisum. Trans., Aquinas, *Truth* vol. I, 6.

20. *De An.* 3, 8, 431b21: ἡ ψυχὴ τὰ ὄντα πώς ἐστι πάντα.

21. For the text see 235 above.

22. *ST* I 16, 1: "Sicut bonum nominat id in quod tendit appetitus, ita verum nominat id in quod tendit intellectus. Hoc autem distat inter appetitum et intellectum, sive quamcumque cognitionem, quia cognitio est secundum quod cognitum est in cognoscente, appetitus autem est secundum quod appetens inclinatur in ipsam rem appetitam."

23. For the text see 235–36 above.

24. *ST* I 5, 4 ad 1: "Ad primum ergo dicendum quod *pulchrum et bonum in subiecto quidem sunt idem,* quia super eandem rem fundantur, scilicet super formam, et propter hoc, bonum laudatur ut pulchrum. Sed ratione differunt. Nam bonum proprie respicit appetitum, *est enim bonum quod omnia appetunt.* Et ideo habet rationem finis, nam appetitus est quasi quidam motus ad rem. Pulchrum autem respicit vim cognoscitivam, *pulchra enim dicuntur quae visa placent.* Unde pulchrum in debita proportione consistit, quia sensus delectatur in rebus debite proportionatis, sicut in sibi similibus; nam et sensus ratio quaedam est, et omnis virtus cognoscitiva. Et quia cognitio fit per assimilationem, similitudo autem respicit formam, pulchrum proprie pertinet ad rationem causae formalis (my emphases)."

In *ST* I 5, Aquinas treats goodness as pertaining to the nature of God. Article 4 asks whether God's goodness functions as final, formal, or efficient cause. At the start of his *Nicomachean Ethics,* Aristotle had given the classic definition of goodness in terms of final causality: the good is that which all things desire (*EN* 1, 1, 1094a). This is also Aquinas's view but, following the didactic style of his *Summa,* he first considers a number of contrary positions. The first objection cites Pseudo-Dionysius's declaration that "Goodness is praised as beauty" (*Bonum laudatur ut pulchrum*). But since beauty has the nature of a formal cause—so the objection—goodness must be a formal rather than final cause. In his reply to this objection, Aquinas is obliged to distinguish between beauty and goodness.

25. *ST* I 5, 4 ad 1.

26. Referring to this passage, John Rickaby states that "as truth is what intellect tends to, so goodness is what the will tends or appetite tends to; yet with this difference, that whereas the true is so determined primarily from the intellect, the good is so denominated primarily from the thing." John Rickaby, *General Metaphysics,* 129.

27. Hugh T. Bredin, "Applied Aquinas: James Joyce's Aesthetics," 61. See Antoine Levy OP, "Great Misinterpretations: Umberto Eco on Joyce and Aquinas," 131.

28. A variation occurs in Aquinas's *Commentary on Aristotle's Ethics:* "Consideran-

dum est quod finale bonum in quod tendit appetitus uniuscuiusque est ultima perfectio eius" (*In EN* 1, lect. 1, n12): "The final good to which the appetite of each thing tends is its ultimate perfection." My trans.

29. We can be quite sure that Joyce felt no obligation to consult Aquinas's works while formulating his aesthetic theories. My inquiries into library facilities in Pola at the time indicate that they were not in fact available in the academic or public libraries of the city. The first public library in Pola, the Biblioteca Civica or Biblioteca Comunale (1903), was closed in 1930 and succeeded by the Biblioteca Provinciale, with most of its collections eventually passing to the university (some books ending up in Venice). The present university library of Pula has no works of Aquinas that were in its collections in 1904. I am grateful to Adriana Gri Štorga of the Archaeological Museum of Istria, and to Tijana Barbić-Domazet of the University Library in Pula for their gracious and efficient correspondence.

30. *CG* 3, 3. Jacques Aubert, *The Aesthetics of James Joyce,* 101, incorrectly gives this as the reference for the epigraph to Joyce's reflections of November 7, 1904; the correct location is *ST* I 16, a. 1.

31. *ST* I 16, 1: "Respondeo dicendum quod, sicut bonum nominat id in quod tendit appetitus, ita verum nominat id in quod tendit intellectus" ("I reply that, as the good denotes that towards which the appetite tends, so the true denotes that towards which the intellect tends"). My trans.

32. *ST* I-II 27, 1 ad 3, my trans.

33. On Stephen's mistaken reference to Aristotle's *De Anima,* see 16 above.

34. In *A Portrait,* Joyce's Pola reflections are repeated not in Fr. Ghezzi's Italian class but in Stephen's conversations with the Dean of Studies and with his friend Lynch.

35. The author shows a sharp self-awareness of the relationship between student and professor: "The teacher probably knew the doubtful reputation of his pupil but for this very reason he adopted a language of ingenuous piety, not that he was himself Jesuit enough to lack ingenuousness but that he was Italian enough to enjoy a game of belief and unbelief" (*SH* 169–70).

36. Eugene Sheehy, *May It Please the Court,* 14.

37. Aquinas, *In Periherm.* 1, 3, 29 [7]: "Verum enim, ut Philosophus dicit in 5 Ethicorum, est bonum intellectus" ("Truth, as the Philosopher says in *Ethics* 5, is the good of the intellect"). The reference is to *EN* 6, 2, 1139a 28–30. See also *CG* 1, 59, 498: "But truth is the good of the intellect as is clear from the philosopher" (Sed verum est bonum intellectus, ut patet per Philosophum). Also *CG* 1, 61, 513; *CG* 1, 71, 604; *CG* 2, 84, 1688: "verum est bonum intellectus et finis ipsius"; *De Ver.* 1, 10 ad 4; *Q. Disp. De An.* 3, 1.

38. *Met.* 1, 1, 980a22.

39. *De Ver.* 1, 9: "Secundum hoc cognoscit veritatem intellectus quod supra seipsum reflectitur."

40. *ST* I 16, 1.

41. *ST* I-II 27, 1 ad 3.

42. *ST* I 67, 1, Sed Contra: "Ambrosius ponit splendorem inter ea quae de Deo metaphorice dicuntur" ("Ambrose includes splendour among those things which are said of God metaphorically"). My trans.

43. *ST* I 67, 1: "Sicut patet in nomine visionis, quod primo impositum est ad significandum actum sensus visus; sed propter dignitatem et certitudinem huius sensus, extensum est hoc nomen, secundum usum loquentium, ad omnem cognitionem aliorum sensuum [. . .] et ulterius etiam ad cognitionem intellectus."

44. See Thomas S. Hibbs: "There are a number of problems with Stephen's purported fidelity to Aquinas, not the least of which is his couching the theory in epistemological terms. What is more important, the theory embodies a set of dualisms alien to Aquinas. The split between soul and body, intellect and sensation, reason and desire runs through the entire discussion." Hibbs, "Portraits of the Artist: Joyce, Nietzsche, and Aquinas," 130–31.

45. See *ST* II-II 180, 2 ad 3; *ST* II-II, 145, 2; *ST* II-II, 145, 2 ad 1.

46. *ST* I-II 27, 1 ad 3.

47. Charles Coppens, S.J., *A Brief Text-Book of Logic and Mental Philosophy*, 11.

48. See John Rickaby, *General Metaphysics*, 75: "Simple apprehension is, as Aquinas calls it, *intelligentia indivisibilium et incomplexorum*, 'the perception of what is indivisible and without complexity.'" See Aquinas, *In Anal. Post. Prooem.*, 4.

49. *ST* I-II 35, 7: Nam apprehensio rationis et imaginationis altior est quam apprehensio sensus tactus.

50. For the text see 237 above.

51. In the longer version of November 15, Joyce had initially written "satisfaction" in three sentences, which he subsequently replaced with "recognition." The sentence "Now the act of apprehension involves at least two activities, the activity of simple perception and the activity of consequent satisfaction" was revised as follows: "Now the act of apprehension involves at least two activities, the activity of cognition or simple perception and the activity of recognition."

52. Intellectual insight or recognition is the first single completed act of human knowledge achieved by the human psyche. For its basic meaning, there is no need to refer to the dramatic *anagnorisis* of the *Poetics,* as suggested by Aubert, *The Aesthetics of James Joyce,* 103.

53. For Aristotle, pleasure is simply the natural feeling that accompanies any unimpeded activity, perfecting the exercise of a faculty. See *EN* 10, 4, 1174b21–23: "Each sense has a corresponding pleasure, as also have thought and speculation, and its activity is pleasantest when it is most perfect, and most perfect when the organ is in good condition and when it is directed to the most excellent of its objects; and the pleasure perfects the activity." Aristotle emphasizes the relation between activity and pleasure: "They appear to be inseparably united; for there is no pleasure without activity, and also no perfect activity without its pleasure" (*EN* 10, 4, 1175a19–22). See Aquinas's comment: "Pleasure perfects activity not as a habit that is inherent, i.e., not as a form intrinsic to the essence of the thing, but as a kind of end or supervenient perfection, like the bloom of health comes to young people." *In EN* 10, lect. 6, n2031.

54. *EN* 10, 4, 1175a27–28.

55. See 170 above.

56. Aquinas elsewhere distinguishes between *res* as concrete reality, *res* as the content of a concept, and *res* as the essence of individual beings. See *In I Sent.* 25, 1, a. 1.

57. Aquinas, *De Ver.* 1, 1: "Non autem invenitur aliquid affirmative dictum absolute quod possit accipi in omni ente, nisi essentia eius, secundum quam esse dicitur; et sic imponitur hoc nomen res, quod in hoc differt ab ente, secundum Avicennam in principio Metaphys., quod ens sumitur ab actu essendi, sed nomen rei exprimit quidditatem vel essentiam entis." See John Rickaby, *General Metaphysics,* 22.

58. *In II Sent.* 37, 1, 1: "Simpliciter enim dicitur res quod habet esse ratum et firmum in natura; et dicitur res hoc modo, accepto nomine rei secundum quod habet quidditatem vel essentiam quamdam; ens vero, secundum quod habet esse; ut dicit Avicenna distinguens entis et rei significationem." See also *In I Sent.,* 8, 1 a. 1; *ST* I 39, 3 ad 3; *In IV Met.,* 2, 553.

59. John Rickaby, *General Metaphysics,* 95. The quotation seems to be a paraphrase. The reference to *De Potentia* 9, 1, is incorrect. See *De Potentia* 9, 7: "Patet ergo quod unum quod convertitur cum ente, ponit quidem ipsum ens, sed nihil superaddit nisi negationem divisionis" ("It is clear then that *one* which is convertible with *being,* posits *being* but adds nothing except the negation of division").

60. *ST* I, 11, 1: "Unum non addit supra ens rem aliquam, sed tantum negationem divisionis; unum enim nihil aliud significat quam ens indivisum."

61. *De Ver.* 1, 1: "Sicut ens dicitur unum, in quantum est indivisum in se, ita dicitur aliquid, in quantum est ab aliis divisum."

62. Aquinas, *De Ente et Essentia* 2: "Et quia illud, per quod res constituitur in proprio genere vel specie, est hoc quod significatur per diffinitionem indicantem quid est res, inde est quod nomen essentiae a philosophis in nomen quidditatis mutatur. Et hoc est quod philosophus frequenter nominat *quod quid erat esse,* id est hoc per quod aliquid habet esse quid." *On Being and Essence,* 27–28.

63. Aquinas, *De Ente.*: "Quidditatis vero nomen sumitur ex hoc, quod per diffinitionem significatur. Sed essentia dicitur secundum quod per eam et in ea ens habet esse." (Trans. 28)

64. *ST* I 84, 7.

65. *ST* I 85, 8: "Obiectum intellectus nostri, secundum praesentem statum, est quidditas rei materialis [. . .] cuius quidditatem primo et per se intellectus accipit." See also *ST* I 85, 5 ad 3 (quoted in footnote 61 below); *ST* I 85, 6: "Obiectum autem proprium intellectus est quidditas rei." *CG* 1, 59: The proper object of our reason is the formal nature of a material thing. A clear statement is also found in the treatise *De Principio Individuationis,* the authenticity of which has been questioned: "Quidditas autem rei sensibilis est obiectum intellectus proprium, ut dicitur in tertio de anima."

66. Aquinas, *De Ver.* 10, 5: "The cognition of the human mind is directed, first, to material things according to their form, and, second, to matter in so far as it is correlative to form" ("Cognitio enim mentis humanae fertur ad res naturales primo secundum formam, et secundario ad materiam prout habet habitudinem ad formam").

67. *ST* I 85, 6. See also *ST* I 85, 6 ad 3.

68. Aquinas, *Q. Disp. De An.* 16, c.

69. Etienne Gilson, *Thomist Realism and the Critique of Knowledge,* 199.

70. *ST* I 85, 5 ad 3: Intellectus enim humani proprium obiectum est quidditas rei materialis. See *In I Sent.,* 19, 5, 1 ad 7: "Cum sit duplex operatio intellectus: una quarum dicitur

a quibusdam imaginatio intellectus, quam philosophus nominat intelligentiam indivisibilium, quae consistit in apprehensione quidditatis simplicis, quae alio etiam nomine formatio dicitur; alia est quam dicunt fidem, quae consistit in compositione vel divisione propositionis: prima operatio respicit quidditatem rei; secunda respicit esse ipsius. . . . intellectus habet verum judicium de proprio objecto, in quod naturaliter tendit, quod est *quidditas rei,* sicut et visus de colore."

71. *ST* I-II 27, 1 ad 3. "Pulchrum dicatur id cuius ipsa apprehensio placet."

72. Instead of *"pulchritudinem,"* Joyce writes *"pulcritudinem,"* which is unusual but not unknown.

73. Noon, *Joyce and Aquinas,* 22. Noon perceptively remarks: "Furthermore Aquinas does not bear down on these qualities in the same way as Stephen does, though in his effort to keep the objective-subjective scale in a delicate balance he gives in the final *Summa* an increasingly serious attention to the experience of beauty as an act of apprehension: 'pulchrum autem dicitur id cuius ipsa apprehensio placet,' or 'pulchra enim dicuntur ea quae visa placent.' This situation of the experience of beauty as much in the psychological order as in the ontological is in an important sense a clean break with the teaching of Aquinas' master, Albert. Albert was much more inclined to ally beauty with goodness as a reality which satisfies the longings and desires of man's will, of his heart. Aquinas speaks of beauty as satisfying the desire of the mind *to know.*"

74. Frank L. Kunkel, "Beauty in Aquinas and Joyce," 267.

75. Kunkel, 267.

76. See Chapman, "The Perennial Theme of Beauty and Art," 340–41.

77. See 52–53, 63–65 above.

78. *In de Caelo,* lib. 1, lect. 2, n 15: "Et dicit quod haec tria, *omne* et *totum* et *perfectum,* non differunt ab invicem *secundum speciem,* idest secundum formalem rationem, quia omnia important integritatem quandam."

79. *ST* I 73, 1: "Prima quidem perfectio est, secundum quod res in sua substantia est perfecta. Quae quidem perfectio est forma totius, quae ex integritate partium consurgit."

80. Etienne Gilson, *Painting and Reality,* 191n24.

81. *ST* I 85, 5: "Et similiter intellectus humanus non statim in prima apprehensione capit perfectam rei cognitionem; sed primo apprehendit aliquid de ipsa, puta quidditatem ipsius rei, quae est primum et proprium obiectum intellectus; et deinde intelligit proprietates et accidentia et habitudines circumstantes rei essentiam."

82. Chapman, 341.

83. *ST* I, 5, 4, ad 1: "Pulchrum in debita proportione consistit."

84. See Kunkel, "Beauty in Aquinas and Joyce," 264.

85. *ST* I-II 54, 1: "Si vero accipiantur membra, ut manus et pes et huiusmodi, earum dispositio naturae conveniens, est pulchritudo."

86. For a discussion of this passage, see A. D. Hope, "The Esthetic Theory of James Joyce," 200.

87. Italics in original.

88. *P* V.1394–95.

89. Hugh Kenner suggests that Joyce was reacting "against the sort of neo-platonism represented by Yeats' 'Dreams alone are certain good.'" *Dublin's Joyce,* 137–38.

90. Chapman, "The Perennial Theme of Beauty and Art," 341. See Aquinas, *In DN* 4, v, 339–40.

91. Gilby, *Poetic Experience*, 67.

92. Noon, *Joyce and Aquinas*, 72.

93. Sextus Empiricus, *Against the Logicians*, 70.

94. Oliver St. John Gogarty, *As I Was Going Down Sackville Street*, 295.

95. Noon, 70. See page 62n3: "From Stephen's remarks . . . it is clear that he claims St Thomas Aquinas as his source."

96. Ezra Pound, *Selected Prose 1909–1965*, 21.

97. John Rickaby, *The First Principles of Knowledge*, 221.

98. G. K. Chesterton, *The Innocence of Father Brown*, 214. Chesterton referred to the "real power of seeing things suddenly, not apparently reached by any process." *The Victorian Age in Literature*, 50.

99. The original French version appeared as *Introduction à l'esthétique de James Joyce*.

100. This is not part of Aubert's argument, since the notebook was not available to him at the time.

101. Robert Scholes and Richard M. Kain, eds., *The Workshop of Daedalus*, 67.

102. Aubert, *The Aesthetics of James Joyce*, 7.

103. Aubert, 8.

104. Aubert, 4–5.

105. Aubert, 12.

106. Aubert, 13.

107. Aubert, 7.

108. Aubert, 8.

109. S. H. Butcher, *Aristotle's Theory of Poetry and Fine Art*, 142n28.

110. *Met.* 7, 3, 1029a29–32.

111. I offer here a historical interpretation of Hegel: in Joyce's time, Hegel was understood as a monist. While more recent interpretations have viewed him in less Spinozist terms—the immanent whole is internally differentiated—there is finally only one individual for Hegel.

112. Bernard Bosanquet, *A History of Aesthetic*, 147: "Claritas et debita proportio," "Integritas sive perfectio," "Debita proportio sive consonantia," "Claritas—i.e., color nitidus," "Sicut in sibi similibus."

113. Bosanquet explains that in writing his *History of Aesthetic*, he has drawn on Johann Eduard Erdman's *History of Philosophy*, and the *Encyclopaedia Britannica*. He states: "In the case of Thomas Aquinas in particular, I profess no original knowledge at all." He thanks Dr. Gildea for having provided "very full quotations" from St. Thomas (xiii).

114. S. H. Butcher, *Aristotle's Theory of Poetry and Fine Art*, 114, in 1895 edition, 108.

115. See *Vorlesungen über die Geschichte der Philosophie* 2, 132: "Aristoteles ist in die ganze Masse und alle Seiten des realen Universums eingedrungen und hat ihren Reichtum und Zerstreuung dem Begriffe unterjocht; und die meisten philosophischen Wissenschaften haben ihm ihre Unterscheidung, ihren Anfang zu verdanken." Trans. George Henry Lewes, *Aristotle: A Chapter from the History of Science*, 18.

116. See 10 above.

117. See Joyce's letter of October 9, 1923, to Harriet Shaw Weaver: "I am sorry that Patrick and [?] [*sic*] Berkeley are unsuccessful in explaining themselves. The answer, I suppose, is that given by Paddy Dignam's apparition: metempsychosis. Or perhaps the theory of history so well set forth (after Hegel and Giambattista Vico) by the four eminent annalists who are even now treading the typepress in sorrow will explain part of my meaning" (*LI* 204). There is a jocular reference in one of his limericks: "A holy Hegelian Kettle / Has faith which we cannot unsettle / If no one abused it / He might have reduced it / But now he is quite on his mettle" (*PSW* 110). See also *FW* 12.21: "like so many heegills and collines"; 107.36–108.01: "who in hallhagal wrote the durn thing abyhow?"; *FW* 416.32–33: "The June snows was flocking in thuckflues on the hegelstomes."

118. Richard M. Kain, "The Position of *Ulysses* Today," 94.

119. Northrop Frye remarks that Hegel "is not the kind of source one looks for in Joyce." See "Cycle and Apocalypse in *Finnegans Wake*," 5. Joyce shares Hegel's totalizing spirit, but not at the cost of sacrificing the minutiae of everyday experience. In this respect, Joyce's outlook is diametrically opposite to that of Hegel and closer to Wittgenstein. While walking together in Dublin's Phoenix Park in 1948, Wittgenstein was asked by his Irish friend Dr. Drury: "What about Hegel?" Wittgenstein replied: "No, I don't think I would get on with Hegel. Hegel seems to me to be always wanting to say that things that look different are really the same. Whereas my interest is in showing that things which look the same are really different." M. O'Connor Drury, *The Danger of Words* and *Writings on Wittgenstein*, 157.

120. Aubert, 102, emphasis in original.

121. *CW* 142: "The moral question is the one he next takes up, at Pola. Using a sentence from Thomas Aquinas for text, he argues that, since the good is what is desirable, and since the true and the beautiful are most persistently desired, then they must be considered good. This is his only concession to the ethical aspect of art, but it is sufficient to make clear that he regards the good, the true, and the beautiful as intertwined." The second part of the latter sentence is entirely correct, but Joyce is concerned not with ethical goodness or truth but with the convertible concepts predicated of all realities— so-called transcendental properties, although he was certainly unacquainted with the history of these terms.

122. *Gen. An.* 2, 1, 731b28–30, my trans.

123. Aubert, 107. I see no reason to suppport Aubert's suggestion that "Joyce obviously exploits Bosanquet's presentation of Aquinas's view of symbolism" (103).

124. See Curran, *James Joyce Remembered*, 36–37, cited 39 above.

125. Curran, 37.

126. According to Russell (AE), Joyce had become "infected with Pater's Relative." On learning that AE sought the Absolute, "he again sighed, this time regretfully, and said that 'AE' could not be his Messiah, as he abhorred the Absolute above everything else." Richard M. Kain, "The Yankee Interviewer in *Ulysses*," 157.

127. See Jean-Michel Rabaté, *James Joyce*, 131; Michael Patrick Gillespie, *Inverted Volumes Improperly Arranged*, 4, 35. Other authors who have accepted Aubert's authority for Joyce's Hegelian inspiration include Barbara Laman (*James Joyce and German Theory*,

13–14, 17–18), Ginette Verstraete (*Fragments of the Feminine Sublime in Friedrich Schlegel and James Joyce*, 3), and Bruce Stewart ("A Short Literary Life of James Joyce," 23). Kevin Barry (*OCPW* 312n9) suggests that Joyce's definition of art as "the human disposition of intelligible or sensible matter for an esthetic end" (*SH* 77, *P* V.1182–3) is a condensation of chapter 3, "The Conception of Artistic Beauty," of Hegel's *Aesthetik*, translated in 1866 by Bernard Bosanquet and published as *Introduction to Hegel's Philosophy of Fine Art*. While it is possible to find similar terminology in Hegel, I suggest that it is more germane to Joyce's interests and education to seek an Aristotelian source. This definition had already been entered in his Paris notebook, and it is most unlikely that the twenty-one-year-old Joyce had already digested more than sixty pages of Hegel's dense text. Stephen's definition closely resembles that given by Aristotle in the *Nicomachean Ethics*: "All art deals with bringing something into existence; and to pursue an art means to study how to bring into existence a thing which may either exist or not, and the efficient cause of which lies in the maker and not in the thing made; for art does not deal with things that come to existence of necessity or according to nature, since these have their (efficient) cause in themselves" (*EN* 6, 4, 1140a10–16). According to Aristotle's fourfold scheme of substance, the efficient cause (in this case, the artist) introduces form into matter for the fulfilment of a goal or purpose. In his definition of art, Joyce coalesces Aristotle's four causes: *material* cause (that of which something is composed, or from which it is made), *formal* cause (manner in which it is fashioned or designed), *efficient* cause (agent responsible for its existence), and the *final* cause (purpose for its existence). In Joyce's definition, the material cause is *intelligible or sensible matter;* the formal cause is the activity of *disposition* by the *human* (efficient) cause for an *aesthetic end* (final cause). This allows Joyce to answer his own question whether houses, clothes, furniture, and so on are works of art. He replies that although they are human dispositions of sensible matter, they are works of art only when disposed for an aesthetic end (see Herbert S. Gorman, *James Joyce: A Definitive Biography*, 98–99; *CW* 146). The definition of art as the human disposition of intelligible or sensible matter for an aesthetic end is properly Aristotelian, although the same vocabulary was adopted by Aquinas. The notion of "intelligible matter" is adopted from Aquinas, who employs the term "matter" analogically to express any reality, including spiritual, that, when acted upon, is related as potency to actuality in the same manner as matter to form in the hylomorphic union of substance. Thus if ideas are manipulated in a certain manner, they may be described as "intelligible matter."

In her recent excellent monograph, *James Joyce and the Matter of Paris*, Catherine Flynn also elaborates upon Joyce's definition of art in Hegelian terms (52–54). I suggest that while Joyce's aesthetics indeed may be expounded from a Hegelian optic, it is clearly rooted in Aristotle, especially his application of the four causes. Theoharis Constantine Theoharis's remark is apposite: "Aristotle's works are the general source for Stephen's imperfectly empirical aesthetics" (*Joyce's Ulysses*, 23). I do not enter here into discussion concerning the source for Joyce's threefold division of art into the three genres of lyric, epic, and drama. The nominal division is already present in Plato and Aristotle, but Joyce's exposition shows clear evidence of modern influence. Robert Scholes and Marlena G. Corcoran state: "Stephen's whole theory of aesthetic forms [. . .] is German to the core. [. . .] It is explictly indebted to Hegel, Schelling, and Friedrich Schlegel"

("The Aesthetic Theory and the Critical Writings," 692). James Walter Caufield, however, argues convincingly that Schopenhauer was a more likely source. We know that Joyce had read Schopenhauer's writings and had one of his books in his Trieste library. See Caufield, "The Word as Will and Idea," 695–714.

128. Caufield, 711n5. Robert Spoo is less explicit in his evaluation: "Lionel Trilling wrote that *Finnegans Wake* is the realization of an 'anti-Hegelian' text, that 'its transcendent genial silliness is a spoof on those figments of the solemn nineteenth-century imagination—History, and World Historical Figures, and that wonderful Will of theirs which, Hegel tells us, keeps the world in its right course toward the developing epiphany of *Geist.' Ulysses*, too, combats these historical orthodoxies, and does so formally, by means of its textual praxis, as well as thematically, on the levels of plot and characterization." *James Joyce and the Language of History: Dedalus's Nightmare, 7.* The reference is to Lionel Trilling, "James Joyce in His Letters," 33.

129. Caufield, "The Word as Will and Idea," 696.

130. Mark Patrick Hederman, "The 'Mind' of Joyce: From Paternalism to Paternity," 247.

131. Eloise Knowlton, *Joyce, Joyceans, and the Rhetoric of Citation,* 37.

132. Andrew Gibson, *James Joyce,* 41.

133. Thomas E. Connolly, "Joyce's Aesthetic Theory," 271.

134. Ellmann, *Ulysses on the Liffey,* 12–13.

Chapter 7. Joyce's Quotations from Aristotle

1. The provenance of this large collection of previously unknown manuscripts is explained on the website of the National Library of Ireland: "The materials acquired by the Library were the property of Mr and Mrs Alexis Léon, and were acquired through the agency of Sotheby's, London. Mr Léon's parents, the late Paul and Lucie Léon, were close friends of Joyce from 1928 onwards. Mr and Mrs Alexis Léon decided that the National Library of Ireland should be given first refusal on the new collection because they hoped it would thus come to the Library to which Mr Léon's father had donated the extensive collection of James Joyce–Paul Léon letters in 1941." See Peter Kenny, "The Joyce Papers 2002, c. 1903–1928."

2. The notebook may be viewed on the website of the National Library of Ireland at http://catalogue.nli.ie/Record/vtls000356987/HierarchyTree#page/16/mode/1up (accessed May 1, 2021). See Crispi, "A Commentary on James Joyce's National Library of Ireland 'Early Commonplace Book': 1903–1912." A description of the notebook may be found on the National Library website, "'The Joyce Papers 2002': '*School exercise book for mathematics. Red-brown cover with black tape binding along outer spine. With printed cover title:* "L'ÉTUDIANT | [laurel wreath] | Papeterie-Imprimerie F. BÉNARD | 10, Galerie de l'Odéon, 10 | Maison principale: 16, Rue de Vaugirard." *31 numbered pages; 10 unnumbered pages with text; blank page; small fragment remaining from removed page; 2 unnumbered pages with text; 38 blank pages [i.e. 82 pages + fragment]. 21.5 x 17 cm. At head of front cover in MS:* 'Priez de rendre à | James A. Joyce | Rue Corneille, | Paris.'"

3. For a reproduction of page 8 of the notebook, neatly covered with sums and columns of receipts and expenses (in francs and £.s.d.), complete with a mock "seal" and

Joyce's signature, see the photograph opposite page 91 in Herbert S. Gorman, *James Joyce: Illustrated with Photographs*. The bottom line reads: "Remainder–0."

4. Herbert S. Gorman included only a selection of the Aristotle quotations in his biography of Joyce. They were reproduced in full by Richard F. Peterson from Gorman's manuscript. See "More Aristotelian Grist for the Joycean Mill." They are reproduced in Jacques Aubert, *The Aesthetics of James Joyce*, 131–37. In this chapter, I correct a number of errors in Aubert's version. These include some inaccurate quotations (referring occasionally to Barthélemy-Saint-Hilaire but giving what appears to be his own translation), as well as a number of incorrect page and text references. Confusion is initially caused for the reader by the absence of numbers indicating which of the three volumes of *Métaphysique d'Aristote* is cited. They are referred to in this chapter by Roman numerals.

5. Gorman, *James Joyce*, 94.

6. Victor Cousin, *De la Métaphysique d'Aristote*. There is a copy in the Special Collection of University College Dublin, with an *Ex Libris* stamp of the Catholic University, University College, Dublin; it is unlikely, however, that Joyce consulted this translation as a student in Dublin. Of the 230 pages of this book, 100 are occupied by a translation of books 1 and 12 of Aristotle's *Metaphysics*. The purpose of the publication was to present a report on the theses presented for a competition to the Academy in Paris in 1835.

7. I have changed Aubert's attribution of Quotation 27 from the *Physics* to the *Metaphysics*.

8. The volume contains the following: *On Sense and Sensible Objects, On Memory and Recollection, On Sleep and Waking, On Dreams, On Divination in Sleep, On Movement of Animals, On Length and Shortness of Life, On Youth and Old Age, On Life and Death, On Respiration.*

9. For a brief description of the contents of the notebook, see Peter Kenny, "The Joyce Papers 2002."

10. Since with few exceptions Joyce uses Barthélemy-Saint-Hilaire's translation, I give his name only with the first mention of a title. Victor Cousin is named each time his translation is quoted; for quotations 19 and 30, I cite both translations.

11. Unless otherwise stated, translations are mine.

12. Aubert locates the source for this quotation at 412a27; the French translation of 412b4–6 corresponds more accurately to Joyce's rendition.

13. Stanislaus Joyce, *My Brother's Keeper*, 152.

14. Interview, quoted *JJII* 204.

15. Robert McAlmon, *Being Geniuses Together*, 27.

16. Mary Lowe-Evans, *Crimes Against Fecundity*, 1.

17. Lowe-Evans, 9.

18. "The Boarding House," *D* 54.176–8, *D* 55.210–11.

19. Hélène Cixous, *The Exile of James Joyce*, 96–97.

20. *CW1*, 670.

21. See John Burnet, *Aristotle on Education*, 116. Joyce's review is reprinted in *CW* 109–10.

22. Loeb trans., modified. See *Hist. An.* 1, 1, 15, 494b16–18: "Of man's senses, touch is the most accurate; taste is second; in the others, man is surpassed by a great number of

animals." *CW1*, 787. Also *Part. An.* 2, 16, 660a11–13: "Flesh is softer in man than in any other animal, the reason for this being that of all animals man has the most delicate sense of touch." *CW1*, 1028.

23. Aubert, 132, incorrectly gives *De An.* 2, 11, 423b17, an earlier passage, as the source for this quotation.

24. Aquinas, *A Commentary on Aristotle's De Anima,* trans. Pasnau, 251.

25. Aquinas, 251.

26. Aubert correctly cites Joyce's source in Barthélemy-Saint-Hilaire's translation but gives an incorrect reference for Aristotle's text and the Loeb translation (*De An.*, 3, 3, 428b18, trans. 163). The passage cited by Aubert refers to the "perception of proper objects" but omits the word "always." The translation of the correct text may be found on page 157 of the Loeb edition.

27. My translation, incorporating lines from the Loeb edition.

28. Aquinas, *A Commentary on Aristotle's De Anima,* 382.

29. *CW1*, 686.

30. *CW1*, 698, modified.

31. Trans. Loeb, modified.

32. *Progression of Animals* 2, 704b11–18.

33. Trans. Loeb, modified.

34. *Met.* 1, 2, 982b11–28; *CW2*, 1554–55.

35. Aubert, 135, gives the correct page reference to Barthélemy-Saint-Hilaire (without volume number), but instead of citing the latter's translation, he appears to have provided his own translation of Joyce's phrase: "Le bois ne fait pas le lit, ni le bronze la statue." Joyce had also at his disposal the translation of Victor Cousin but does not seem to have used his version: "Ce n'est pas le sujet qui peut se changer lui-même; l'airain, par exemple, et le bois ne se changent pas eux-mêmes, et ne se font pas l'un statue, l'autre lit, mais il y a quelque autre cause à ce changement."

36. *CW2*, 1588.

37. Aubert, 135, gives the correct page reference to Barthélemy-Saint-Hilaire's translation (without volume) but appears to have translated Joyce's quotation back into French: "Il ne peut y avoir de moyen terme entre deux propositions contraires."

38. Loeb trans.

39. *Met.* 5, 5, 1015a20–b15.

40. *On Dreams* 3, 460b20–22, *CW1*, 732.

41. *Met.* 4, 6, 1011a32–33, *CW2*, 1596.

42. *Problems* 35, 10, 965a36–39, *CW2*, 1523.

43. For a modern account, see "That Freaky Feeling 1: Aristotle illusion," *New Scientist,* 34–35: "One of the oldest tactile illusions is the Aristotle illusion. It is easy to perform. Cross your fingers, then touch a small spherical object such as a dried pea, and it feels like you are touching two peas. This also works if you touch your nose. This is an example of what is called 'perceptual disjunction.' It arises because your brain has failed to take into account that you have crossed your fingers. Because the pea (or nose) touches the outside of both fingers at the same time—something that rarely happens—your brain interprets it as two separate objects." For discussions contemporary with Joyce, see W.

H. R. Rivers, "A Modification of Aristotle's Experiment," 583–84; M. Ponzo, "Intorno ad alcune illusioni nel campo delle sensazioni tattili, sull'illusione di Aristotele e fenomeni analoghi," 307–45.

44. Loeb trans., modified.

45. Aubert, 160.

46. Loeb trans., adapted.

47. See *EN* 6, 6, 1140b31–32: "Scientific knowledge is a mode of conception dealing with universals and things that are of necessity." Loeb trans.

48. Aubert cites *Phys.* 3, 1, 200.10–11, as Joyce's source for this quotation, intending presumably 201a10–11, which is entirely acceptable. However, since this phrase occurs between quotations from *Met.* 11 and *Met.* 12, it is reasonable to assume that Joyce took it from the same work. At *Métaphysique d'Aristote* III, 122, another, similar, version of the definition occurs: "La réalisation du possible en tant que possible, c'est le mouvement."

49. *CW2*, 1698, modified.

50. Aubert gives an incorrect location (*Met.* 12, 7, 1072b20) for this phrase.

51. Victor Cousin, *De la Métaphysique d'Aristote*, 69. See also 90 and 97 for further citations of this phrase.

52. *CW2*, 1695.

53. Patricia Hutchins, *James Joyce's World*, 86.

54. Loeb trans.

55. Aubert gives an incorrect page reference (335).

56. See 140 above.

Afterword

1. Theoharis Constantine Theoharis, *Joyce's* Ulysses, 25.

2. George Santayana, *Some Turns of Thought in Modern Philosophy*, 3.

Bibliography

Ackerley, Chris. "'Well, of course if we knew all the things': Coincidence and Design in *Ulysses* and *Under the Volcano.*" In *Joyce/Lowry: Critical Perspectives,* ed. Patrick A. McCarthy and Paul Tiessen, 4–62. Lexington: University Press of Kentucky, 1977.

Adams, Robert Martin. *Surface and Symbol.* New York: Oxford University Press, 1962.

Alston, William P. "Aquinas on Theological Predication: A Look Backward and a Look Forward." In *Reasoned Faith: Essays in Philosophical Theology in Honor of Norman Kretzman,* 145–78. Ithaca, N.Y.: Cornell University Press, 1993.

Aquinas, Thomas. *Quaestiones Disputatae de Veritate.* Ed. R. M. Spiazzi, Turin, 1949. Translated as *Truth.* Chicago: Regnery, 1952–1954.

———. *Of God and His Creatures: An Annotated Translation of the* Summa Contra Gentiles *of Saint Thomas Aquinas.* Trans. Joseph Rickaby, S.J. London: Burns and Oates, 1905.

———. *Summa Philosophica seu De Veritate Catholicae Fidei Contra Gentiles.* Paris: Lethielleux, 1906.

———. *Summa Contra Gentiles.* Trans. English Dominican Fathers. London: Burns, Oates & Washbourne, 1924.

———. *On Being and Essence: De Ente et Essentia.* Trans. Armand Maurer. Toronto: Pontifical Institute of Mediaeval Studies, 1949.

———. *A Commentary on Aristotle's De Anima.* Trans. Kenelm Foster, OP, and Sylvester Humphries, OP. London: Routledge & Kegan Paul, 1951.

———. *Truth.* Trans. Robert W. Mulligan, James V. McGlynn, Robert W. Schmidt. Chicago: Regnery, 1952–1954.

———. *On the Truth of the Catholic Faith: Summa Contra Gentiles,* Book One: *God.* Trans. Anton C. Pegis. New York: Image, 1955.

———. *On the Truth of the Catholic Faith: Summa Contra Gentiles,* Book Three: *Providence,* Part 2. Trans. Vernon J. Bourke. New York: Image, 1956.

———. *Commentary on the Nicomachean Ethics.* Trans. C. I. Litzinger, OP. Chicago: Regnery, 1964.

———. *Summa Theologiae.* Trans. Fathers of the English Dominican Province. Chicago: Encyclopaedia Britannica, 1988.

———. *A Commentary on Aristotle's De Anima.* Trans. Robert Pasnau. New Haven, Conn.: Yale University Press, 1999.

Ariew, Roger. *Descartes and the Last Scholastics.* Ithaca, N.Y.: Cornell University Press, 1999.

Aristotle. *The Complete Works of Aristotle*. 2 vols., ed. Jonathan Barnes. Princeton, N.J.: Princeton University Press, 1995.

——. *Métaphysique d'Aristote*. 3 vols. Trans. J. Barthélemy-Saint-Hilaire. Paris: Germer-Baillière, 1879.

——. *La Métaphysique*. Trans. J. Tricot, vol. 1. Paris: Vrin, 1940.

——. *Fragmenta*. Ed. Valentin Rose. Stuttgart: Teubner, 1967.

Attridge, Derek. *Joyce Effects*. Cambridge: Cambridge University Press, 2000.

Aubert, Jacques. *Introduction à l'esthétique de James Joyce*. Paris: Didier, 1973.

——. *The Aesthetics of James Joyce*. Baltimore, Md.: Johns Hopkins University Press, 1992.

Augustine, Saint. *Enarrationes in Psalmos*, XLI, 13, in *Corpus Christianorum* XXXVIII. Turnhout: Brepols, 1956.

Bacon, Francis. *Works*, vol. 6, ed. James Spedding, Robert Leslie Ellis, and Douglas Denon Heath. New York: Garrett, 1968.

Baines, Robert. "Hegel (and Wagner) in James Joyce's 'Drama and Life.'" *Journal of Modern Literature* 35, no. 4 (July 2012): 1–12.

Ball, Robert S. *The Story of the Heavens*. London: Cassell, 1900.

Barrett, Cyril. "The Aesthetics of St Thomas Re-Examined." *Philosophical Studies* 12 (1963): 107–24.

Beckman, Richard. *Joyce's Rare View: The Nature of Things in* Finnegans Wake. Gainesville: University of Florida Press, 2007.

Benstock, Bernard. *Joyce-Again's Wake: An Analysis of* Finnegans Wake. Seattle: University of Washington Press, 1965.

——. *James Joyce: The Undiscover'd Country*. Dublin: Gill & Macmillan, 1977.

——, ed. *Critical Essays on James Joyce*. Boston: G. K. Hall, 1985.

Bergson, Henri. *The Creative Mind*. London: Macmillan, 1922.

——. *Creative Evolution*. London: Macmillan, 1922.

Berkeley, George. *Philosophical Commentaries*. Ed. A. A. Luce. London: Nelson, 1944.

——. *The Works of George Berkeley Bishop of Cloyne*, vol. 1, ed. A. A. Luce. London: Thomas Nelson, 1948.

——. *Treatise Concerning the Principles of Human Knowledge*. London: Everyman, 1972.

Berrone, Louis, ed. *James Joyce in Padua*. New York: Random, 1977.

Boedder, Bernard, S.J. *Natural Theology*. London: Longmans, 1891.

Borach, Georges. "Conversations with James Joyce." *College English* 15, no. 6 (1954): 325–27.

——. "Gespräche mit James Joyce." In James Joyce, *Die Toten*, 329–34. Zürich: Diogenes, 1948.

Bosanquet, Bernard. *A History of Aesthetic*. London: Swan Sonnenschein, 1892.

Boswell, James. *Boswell's Life of Johnson*. Ed. George Birkbeck Hill, revised L. F. Powell, vol. 3. Oxford: Clarendon, 1934.

Boyle, Robert. *Selected Philosophical Papers*. Ed. M. A. Stewart. Indianapolis, Ind.: Hackett, 1991.

Boyle, Robert, S.J. "Worshipper of the Word: James Joyce and the Trinity." In *A Starcham-*

ber Quiry, A James Joyce Centennial Volume 1882–1982, ed. E.L. Epstein, 109–51. New York: Methuen, 1982.

Bredin, Hugh T. "Applied Aquinas: James Joyce's Aesthetics." *Éire-Ireland* 3 (1968): 61–78.

Brivic, Sheldon. *Joyce the Creator.* Madison: University of Wisconsin Press, 1985.

Broch, Hermann. *Geist and Zeitgeist: The Spirit in an Unspiritual Age.* Ed. John Hargraves. New York: Counterpoint, 2002.

———. *Schriften zur Literatur* I. *Kritik.* Ed. Paul Michael Lützeler. Frankfurt: Suhrkamp, 1975.

Budgen, Frank. *James Joyce and the Making of* Ulysses *and Other Writings.* Oxford: Oxford University Press, 1991.

Burgess, Anthony. *Here Comes Everybody.* London: Faber & Faber, 1965.

———, ed. *A Shorter* Finnegans Wake, by James Joyce. London: Faber & Faber, 1973.

———. *Joysprick: An Introduction to the Language of James Joyce.* London: Andre Deutsch, 1979.

———. *Re Joyce.* New York: Norton, 1965.

Burnet, John. *Aristotle on Education.* Cambridge: Cambridge University Press, 1928.

Busa, Roberto, ed. *Index Thomisticus* (https://www.corpusthomisticum.org/it/index.age) (accessed 1 May 2021).

Butcher, S. H. *Aristotle's Theory of Poetry and Fine Art.* London: Macmillan, 1923.

Byrne, J. F. *Silent Years: An Autobiography with Memoirs of James Joyce and Our Ireland.* New York: Farrar, Straus and Young, 1953.

Byron, Lord. *Selected Letters and Journals.* Ed. Leslie A. Marchand. Cambridge, Mass.: Belknap, 1982.

Campbell Fraser, Alexander. *The Life and Letters of George Berkeley.* Oxford: Clarendon, 1871.

Campbell, Joseph, and Henry Morton Robinson. *A Skeleton Key to* Finnegans Wake: *Unlocking James Joyce's Masterwork.* Novato, Calif.: New World, 2005.

Cappio, James. "Aristotle, Berkeley, and Proteus: Joyce's Use of Philosophy." *Philosophy and Literature* 5, no. 1 (1981): 21–32.

Catechism of the Catholic Church (parag. 242). Accessed May 1, 2021: http://www.vatican.va/archive/ccc_css/archive/catechism/p1s2c1p2.htm.

———. (parag. 467). Accessed May 1, 2021: http://www.vatican.va/archive/ccc_css/archive/catechism/p122a3p1.htm.

Caufield, James Walter. "The Word as Will and Idea: Dedalean Aesthetics and the Influence of Schopenhauer." *James Joyce Quarterly* 35, no. 36 (1998): 695–714.

Chapman, Immanuel. "The Perennial Theme of Beauty and Art." In *Essays in Thomism,* ed. Robert E. Brennan, OP, 335–46, 417–19. New York: Sheed and Ward, 1942.

Cheng, Vincent J. *Inauthentic: The Anxiety over Culture and Identity.* New Brunswick, N.J.: Rutgers University Press, 2004.

———. "History and Possibility: Shakespeare and the Stage in *Finnegans Wake.*" In *Joyce/Shakespeare,* ed. Laura Pelaschiar, 140–60. Syracuse, N.Y.: Syracuse University Press, 2015.

Chesterton, G. K. *The Innocence of Father Brown.* London: Cassell, 1911.

———. *The Victorian Age in Literature.* New York: Henry Holt, 1913.

Choisnard, D. *Synopsis Philosophiae Scholasticae ad Mentem Divi Thomae.* Paris: Roger & Chernoviz, 1892.

Cixous, Hélène. *The Exile of James Joyce.* London: Calder, 1976.

Clarke, Richard F., S.J. *Logic.* London: Longmans, 1987.

Clarke, W. Norris, S.J. *Explorations in Metaphysics: Being-God-Person.* Notre Dame, Ind.: University of Notre Dame Press, 1992.

———. *Person and Being.* Milwaukee, Wisc.: Marquette University Press, 1993.

Cody, Morrill. "James Joyce in the Twenties." In *James Joyce: Interviews and Recollections,* ed. E. H. Mikhail, 91–92. London: Palgrave Macmillan, 1990.

Coleridge, Samuel Taylor. *The Notebooks of Samuel Taylor Coleridge.* Ed. Kathleen Coburn and Anthony John Harding. Princeton, N.J.: Princeton University Press, 2002.

———. *Biographia Literaria.* London: Dent, 1956.

———. *Table Talk* I. Ed. Carl Woodring. London: Routledge & Kegan Paul, 1990.

———. *The Friend* I. Ed. Barbara E. Rooke. London: Routledge & Kegan Paul, 1969.

———. *Complete Works,* vol. 4, *Lectures upon Shakespeare and Other Dramatists.* New York: Harper, 1858.

Colum, Mary, and Padraic Colum. *Our Friend James Joyce.* New York: Doubleday, 1958.

Colum, Padraic. "With James Joyce in Ireland." *New York Times,* June 11, 1922, 52.

———. *The Road Round Ireland.* New York: Macmillan, 1926.

Conley, Tim. "*Finnegans Wake:* Some Assembly Required." In *James Joyce,* ed. Sean Latham, 132–52. Dublin: Irish Academic Press, 2010.

———. "Waking 'for an equality of relations.'" In *A Long the Krommerun: Selected Papers from the Utrecht James Joyce Symposium,* ed. Onno Koster, Tim Conley, and Peter de Voogd, 153–63. Leiden: Brill/Rodopi, 2016.

Connolly, Thomas E. "Joyce's Aesthetic Theory." In Thomas E. Connolly, ed., *Joyce's Portrait: Criticisms and Critiques,* 266–71. New York: Appleton-Century-Crofts, 1962.

Coppens, Charles, S.J. *A Brief Text-Book of Logic and Mental Philosophy.* New York: Schwartz, Kirwin & Fauss, 1891.

Cormack, Alistair. *Yeats and Joyce: Cyclical History and the Reprobate Tradition.* Aldershot, U.K.: Ashgate, 2008.

Costello, Peter. *James Joyce: The Years of Growth 1882–1915.* London: Kyle Cathie, 1992.

Council of Nicaea. Accessed May 1, 2021: http://www.papalencyclicals.net/councils/ecumo1.htm.

Cousin, Victor. *De la Métaphysique d'Aristote.* Paris: Ladrange, 1835.

Crispi, Luca. "A Commentary on James Joyce's National Library of Ireland 'Early Commonplace Book': 1903–1912" (MS 36,639/02/A), in *Genetic Joyce Studies* 9 (Spring 2009). Accessed May 1, 2021: http://www.geneticjoycestudies.org//articles/GJS9/GJS9_Crispi.

———. "A First Foray into the National Library of Ireland's Joyce Manuscripts: Bloomsday 2011." *Genetic Joyce Studies* 11 (Spring 2011). Accessed May 1, 2021: https://www.geneticjoycestudies.org/articles/GJS11/GJS11_Crispi#subject.

Curran, C. P. "Memories of University College, Dublin: The Jesuit Tenure 1883–1908." In *Struggle With Fortune: A Miscellany for the Centenary of the Catholic University of Ireland 1854–1954,* ed. Michael Tierney, 221–30. Dublin: Browne & Nolan, 1954.

———. *James Joyce Remembered.* London: Oxford University Press, 1968.

———. *Under the Receding Wave*. Dublin: Gill and Macmillan, 1970.

Damon, S. Foster. "The Odyssey in Dublin." In *James Joyce: Two Decades of Criticism*, ed. Seon Givens, 203–42. New York: Vanguard, 1963.

Dante, *The Divine Comedy*, vol. III: *Paradise*. Trans. Mark Musa. London: Penguin, 1986.

Davidson, Donald. "James Joyce and Humpty Dumpty." *Midwest Studies in Philosophy* 16, no. 1 (1991): 1–12.

Dawson, William. "The Society Restored (1897–1908)." In Meenan, James, ed., *Centenary History of the Literary and Historical Society of University College, Dublin 1855–1955*, 36–41. Dublin: A & A Farmar, 2005.

Deane, Seamus. Introduction. *Finnegans Wake*, by James Joyce, vii–l. London: Penguin, 1992.

Delaney, Frank. "Matters of Measurement." Review of *Voices on Joyce*, ed. Anne Fogarty and Fran O'Rourke, in *Breac. A Digital Journal of Irish Studies*, October 20, 2016.

Dennett, Daniel. *Consciousness Explained*. London: Penguin, 1991.

De Wulf, Maurice. "Les théories esthétiques propres à saint Thomas." *Revue néo-scolastique* 2 (1895): 188–205, 341–57.

———. *Introduction à la philosophie néo-scholastique*. Louvain: Institut Supérieur de Philosophie, 1904.

Diehl, Ernestus, ed. *Anthologia Lyrica Graeca* III. Leipzig: Teubner, 1952.

Diels, Hermann, and Walter Kranz. *Die Fragmente der Vorsokratiker* I. Zürich: Weidmann, 1971.

Donoghue, Denis. "Joyce's Landscapes." *Studies: An Irish Quarterly Review* 46, no. 181 (1957): 76–90.

———. "Joyce and the Finite Order." *Sewanee Review* 68 (1960): 256–73.

Doran, Michael. *Conversations with Cézanne*. Berkeley: University of California Press, 2001.

Drury, M. O'Connor. *The Danger of Words* and *Writings on Wittgenstein*. Ed. D. Berman, M. Fitzgerald, and J. Hayes. Bristol, U.K.: Thoemmes, 1996.

Duncan, Joseph E. "The Modality of the Audible in Joyce's *Ulysses*." *Publications of the Modern Language Association* 72 (1957): 286–95.

Eco, Umberto. *The Middle Ages of James Joyce: The Aesthetics of Chaosmos*. London: Hutchinson Radius, 1989.

Eliot, T. S. "*Ulysses*, Order, and Myth." In *Two Decades of Criticism*, ed. Seon Givens, 198–202. New York: Vanguard, 1948.

———. *Introducing James Joyce*. London: Faber & Faber, 1942.

———. *Collected and Uncollected Poems*. Ed. Christopher Ricks and Jim McCue. London: Faber & Faber, 2015.

Ellmann, Richard. Introduction. *My Brother's Keeper: James Joyce's Early Years*, by Stanislaus Joyce, x–xxii. New York: Viking, 1968.

———. *The Identity of Yeats*. London: Macmillan, 1954.

———. *James Joyce*. New York: Oxford University Press, 1982.

———. "*Ulysses*: A Short History." In James Joyce, *Ulysses*, 705–19. Harmondsworth, U.K.: Penguin, 1971.

———. *Ulysses on the Liffey*. London: Faber & Faber, 1974.

———. "The Big Word in *Ulysses*." *New York Review of Books*, October 25, 1984, 30–31.

———. *The Consciousness of Joyce.* London: Faber & Faber, 1977.

———. Preface. *Ulysses,* by James Joyce, ed. H. W. Gabler, ix–xiv. New York: Vintage, 1986.

Emerson, Ralph Waldo. *The Complete Essays and Other Writings of Ralph Waldo Emerson.* New York: Random, 1950.

Fallon, William G. "The Joyce I Knew." In *The Joyce We Knew,* ed. Ulick O'Connor, 37–59. Cork, Ireland: Mercier, 1967.

Fathers of the Society of Jesus. *A Page of Irish History: Story of University College, Dublin, 1883–1909.* Dublin: Talbot, 1930.

Feshbach, Sidney. "A Slow and Dark Birth: A Study of the Organization of *A Portrait of the Artist as a Young Man.*" *James Joyce Quarterly* 4 (1967): 289–300.

Fisher, Vardis. "Defenders of Truth Pay High Price." *Idaho Statewide,* July 22, 1948.

Flynn, Catherine. *James Joyce and the Matter of Paris.* Cambridge: Cambridge University Press, 2019.

Fordham, Finn. *I Do I Undo I Redo: The Textual Genesis of Modernist Selves in Hopkins, Yeats, Conrad, Forster, Joyce, and Woolf.* Oxford: Oxford University Press, 2010.

Foster, R. F. *W. B. Yeats: A Life II; The Arch-Poet 1915–1939.* Oxford: Oxford University Press, 1993.

France, Anatole. *Oeuvres complètes illustrées.* Paris: Calmann-Lévy, 1928.

Freud, Sigmund. *The Interpretation of Dreams.* New York: Avon, 1965.

Frye, Northrop. "Cycle and Apocalypse in *Finnegans Wake.*" In *Vico and Joyce,* ed. Donald Phillip Verene, 3–19. Albany, N.Y.: SUNY Press, 1987.

Gates, David. "Dylan Revisited," *Newsweek,* October 5, 1997.

Gibson, Andrew. *James Joyce.* London: Reaktion, 2006.

Gifford, Don. Ulysses *Annotated: Notes for James Joyce's* Ulysses. Berkeley: University of California Press, 2008.

Gilbert, Stuart. "The Latin Background of James Joyce's Art." *Horizon* (September 1944): 178–88.

———. *James Joyce's* Ulysses: *A Study.* Harmondsworth, U.K.: Penguin, 1969.

Gilby, Thomas. *Poetic Experience: An Introduction to Thomist Aesthetic.* London: Sheed and Ward, 1934.

Giles, J. A., ed. *History of the Ancient Britons* II. London: Bell, 1847.

Gillespie, Michael Patrick. *James Joyce's Trieste Library: A Catalogue of Materials at the Harry Ransom Humanities Research Center, the University of Texas at Austin.* Austin: Humanities Research Center, 1986.

———. *Inverted Volumes Improperly Arranged: James Joyce and his Trieste Library.* Ann Arbor, Mich.: UMI Research, 1983.

———. *Reading the Book of Himself: Narrative Strategies in the Works of James Joyce.* Columbus: Ohio State University Press, 1989.

Gilson, Etienne. *Painting and Reality.* New York: Pantheon, 1957.

———. *Thomist Realism and the Critique of Knowledge.* San Francisco: Ignatius, 1986.

Glasheen, Adeline. *Who Is Who When Everybody Is Somebody Else: Third Census of "Finnegans Wake."* Berkeley: University of California Press, 1977.

Goethe, Johann Wolfgang von. *Naturwissenschaftliche Schriften* II/3. Weimar: Hermann Böhlau, 1893.

Gogarty, Oliver St John. *As I Was Going Down Sackville Street.* London: Abacus, 1989.

———. "James Joyce: A Portrait of the Artist." In *Interviews and Recollections,* ed. E. H. Mikhail, 21–31. London: Palgrave Macmillan, 1990.

Gorman, Herbert S. *James Joyce: His First Forty Years.* New York: Geoffrey Bles, 1926.

———. *James Joyce: Illustrated with Photographs.* New York: Farrar & Rinehart, 1939.

———. *James Joyce: A Definitive Biography.* London: Bodley Head, 1941.

Groden, Michael. "The Complex Simplicity of *Ulysses.*" In *James Joyce,* ed. Sean Latham, 105–31. Dublin: Irish Academic Press, 2010.

Guthrie, W. K. C. *The Greek Philosophers from Thales to Aristotle.* London: Methuen, 1967.

Gwynn, Aubrey, S.J. "The Jesuit Fathers and University College." In *Struggle With Fortune: A Miscellany for the Centenary of the Catholic University of Ireland, 1854–1954,* ed. Michael Tierney, 19–50. Dublin: Browne & Nolan, 1954.

Hackett, Felix. "The Society Restored (1897–1908)." In *Centenary History of the Literary and Historical Society of University College, Dublin 1855–1955,* ed. James Meenan, 41–55. Dublin: A & A Farmar, 2005.

Hederman, Mark Patrick. "The 'Mind' of Joyce: From Paternalism to Paternity." In *The Irish Mind: Exploring Intellectual Traditions,* ed. Richard Kearney, 244–66, 345–47. Dublin: Wolfhound, 1985.

Hegel, Georg Wilhelm Friedrich. *Vorlesungen über die Geschichte der Philosophie 2.* Frankfurt am Main: Suhrkamp, 1986.

Heidegger, Martin. *Wegmarken.* Frankfurt am Main: Klostermann, 1976.

Herr, Cheryl Temple. *Joyce and the Art of Shaving.* Dublin: National Library of Ireland, 2004.

Hibbs, Thomas S. "Portraits of the Artist: Joyce, Nietzsche, and Aquinas." In *Beauty, Art, and the Polis,* ed. Alice Ramos, 117–37. Washington: Catholic University of America Press, 2000.

Higginson, Fred. *Anna Livia Plurabelle: The Making of a Chapter.* Minneapolis: University of Minnesota Press, 1960.

Hilary of Poitiers. *De Trinitate.* In *Patrologia Latina,* vol. 10. Paris: Migne, 1844.

———. *Nicene and Post-Nicene Fathers.* Second series, vol. 9, Hilary of Poitiers, John of Damascus. Ed. Philip Schaff and Henry Wallace. New York: Cosimo, 2007.

Hippocrates. *Nature of the Child.* Ed. Paul Potter. Cambridge, Mass.: Harvard University Press, 2012.

Hoffmeister, Adolf. "James Joyce." In *Portraits of the Artist in Exile,* ed. Willard Potts, 121–27. Dublin: Wolfhound, 1979.

———. "Portrait of Joyce." In *Portraits of the Artist in Exile,* ed. Willard Potts, 127–36. Dublin: Wolfhound, 1979.

Hope, A. D. "The Esthetic Theory of James Joyce." In *Joyce's Portrait: Criticisms and Critiques,* ed. Thomas Connolly, 183–203. New York: Appleton-Century-Crofts, 1962.

Hume, David. *A Treatise of Human Nature.* Ed. L. A. Selby-Bigge. Oxford: Clarendon, 1973.

Hutchins, Patricia. *James Joyce's World.* London: Methuen, 1957.

Ignatius of Loyola, Saint. *The Constitutions of the Society of Jesus.* Trans. George E. Ganss, S.J. St Louis: Institute of Jesuit Sources, 1970.

James, Henry. "The Art of Fiction." In *Partial Portraits*. Westport, Conn.: Greenwood, 1970.

James, William. *The Principles of Psychology*, vol. 1. London: Macmillan, 1901.

Jaspers, Karl. "Introduction to *The Great Philosophers*." *Existenz: International Journal in Philosophy, Religion, Politics, and the Arts* 12, no. 1 (2017): 13–49.

Jones, David Albert. *The Soul of the Embryo: An Enquiry into the Status of the Human Embryo in the Christian Tradition*. London: Continuum, 2007.

Joyce, James. "Early Commonplace Book" (I.ii. Notebook with accounts, quotations, book lists, etc., 1903–1904) (MS 36,639/02/A) National Library of Ireland. Accessed May 1, 2021: http://catalogue.nli.ie/Record/vtls000356987/HierarchyTree#page/16/mode/1up.

———. 'Subject Notebook' (Notebook II.i.1.) (MS 36,639/03) National Library of Ireland, available at http://catalogue.nli.ie/Record/vtls000357760#page/16/mode/ 1up (accessed 1 May 2021).

———. *James Joyce Archive 7*. New York: Garland, 1978.

———. *Stephen Hero*. Ed. Theodore Spencer, John J. Slocum, and Herbert Cahoon. New York: New Directions, 1963.

———. *Dubliners*. Ed. Margot Norris. New York: Norton, 2006.

———. *A Portrait of the Artist as a Young Man*. Ed. John Paul Riquelme. New York: Norton, 2007.

———. *Exiles*. Ed. Padraic Colum. London: Four Square, 1962.

———. *Ulysses*. Ed. Hans Walter Gabler. New York: Vintage, 1986.

———. *Finnegans Wake*. London: Penguin, 1992.

———. *Scribbledehobble, the Ur-Workbook for "Finnegans Wake."* Ed. Thomas E. Connolly. Evanston, Ill.: Northwestern University Press, 1961.

———. *Letters*, vol. 1. Ed. Stuart Gilbert. New York: Viking, 1966.

———. *Letters*, vols. 2 and 3. Ed. Richard Ellmann. New York: Viking, 1966.

———. *Selected Letters of James Joyce*. Ed. Richard Ellmann. New York: Viking, 1975.

———. *The Critical Writings*. Ed. Ellsworth Mason and Richard Ellmann. Ithaca, N.Y.: Cornell University Press, 1989.

———. *Poems and Shorter Writings*. Ed. Richard Ellmann, A. Walton Litz, and John Whittier-Ferguson. London: Faber & Faber, 1991.

———. *Occasional, Critical, and Political Writings*. Ed. Kevin Barry. Oxford: Oxford World Classics, 2000.

Joyce, Stanislaus. *My Brother's Keeper*. Ed. Richard Ellmann. New York: Viking, 1958.

———. *The Complete Dublin Diary of Stanislaus Joyce*. Ed. George H. Healey. Ithaca, N.Y.: Cornell University Press, 1971.

Kahn, Charles H. *Aristotle's Vision of Nature*. Ed. John Herman Randall, Jr., Charles H. Kahn, and Harold A. Larrabee. New York: Columbia University Press, 1965.

Kain, Richard M. "The Yankee Interviewer in *Ulysses*." In *A James Joyce Miscellany*, third series, ed. Marvin Magalaner, 155–57. Carbondale: Southern Illinois University Press, 1962.

———. "The Position of *Ulysses* Today." In *James Joyce Today: Essays on the Major Works*, ed. Thomas Staley, 83–95. Bloomington: Indiana University Press, 1966.

———. *Fabulous Voyager: A Study of James Joyce's Ulysses*. New York: Viking, 1967.

———. "Fifty Years of *Ulysses:* 1934–1984." In *Joyce's* Ulysses: *The Larger Perspective,* ed. Robert D. Newman and Weldon Thornton, 74–88. Newark: University of Delaware Press, 1987.

Kant, Immanuel. *Critique of Pure Reason.* Trans. Norman Kemp Smith. London: Macmillan, 1976.

———. *Kritik der reinen Vernunft.* Hamburg: Meiner, 1990.

Kearney, Richard, ed. *The Irish Mind: Exploring Intellectual Traditions.* Dublin: Wolfhound, 1985.

———. *Debating Otherness with Richard Kearney: Perspectives from South Africa.* Ed. Daniël P. Veldsman and Yolande Steenkamp. Cape Town: Aosis, 2018.

Kelly, John. *Joyce the Student: University College, Dublin 1898–1902.* Dublin: Gleoiteog, 2021.

Kenner, Hugh. "Joyce and the 19th Century Linguistics Explosion." In *Atti del Third International James Joyce Symposium,* Trieste, June 14–18, 1971, 45–60. Trieste: Università degli Studi, Facoltà di Magistero, 1974.

———. "The Cubist Portrait." In *Critical Essays on James Joyce,* ed. Bernard Benstock, 101–111. Boston: G. K. Hall, 1985.

———. *Dublin's Joyce.* London: Chatto & Windus, 1955.

———. *Joyce's Voices.* Berkeley: University of California Press, 1978.

Kenny, Peter, "The Joyce Papers 2002, c. 1903–1928." Accessed May 1, 2021: http://catalogue.nli.ie/Record/vtls000194606?ui=standard.

Kiberd, Declan. *Ulysses and Us.* New York: Norton, 2009.

Kimball, Jean. "St. Augustine and Love in Bloom." *James Joyce Quarterly* 25, no. 3 (1988): 375–78.

———. "Love and Death in 'Ulysses': 'Word Known to All Men.'" *James Joyce Quarterly* 24, no. 2 (1987): 143–60.

———. "Love in the Kidd Era: An Afterword." *James Joyce Quarterly* 29, no. 2 (1992): 369–77.

Killham, John. "'Ineluctable Modality' in Joyce's *Ulysses.*" *University of Toronto Quarterly* 34 (1965): 269–89.

Kitcher, Philip. *Joyce's Kaleidoscope: An Invitation to* Finnegans Wake. New York: Oxford University Press, 2007.

———. "Something Rich and Strange: Joyce's Perspectivism." in *Joyce's* Ulysses: *Philosophical Perspectives,* ed. Philip Kitcher, 207–51. New York: Oxford University Press, 2020.

Knowlton, Eloise. *Joyce, Joyceans, and the Rhetoric of Citation.* Gainesville: University Press of Florida, 1998.

Koestler, Arthur. *The Act of Creation.* New York: Macmillan, 1964.

Kohl, J. G. *Travels in Ireland.* London: Bruce and Wyld, 1844.

Kumar, Shiv K. *Bergson and the Stream of Consciousness Novel.* London: Blackie, 1962.

Kunkel, Frank L. "Beauty in Aquinas and Joyce." *Thomist* 12, no. 3 (July 1949): 261–71.

Lahr, Charles. *Cours de Philosophie.* Paris: Beauchesne, 1920.

Laman, Barbara. *James Joyce and German Theory: The Romantic School and All That.* Madison, Wisc.: Fairleigh Dickinson University Press, 1994.

Larbaud, Valery. "Larbaud on Joyce." In *James Joyce. The Critical Heritage,* vol. 1, ed. Robert H. Deming, 252–62. London: Routledge & Kegan Paul, 1970.

Leo XIII, *Aeterni Patris.*, Accessed May 1, 2021: https://www.vatican.va/content/leo-xiii/en/encyclicals/documents/hf_l-xiii_enc_04081879_aeterni-patris.html.

Lessing, Gotthold Ephraim. *Werke* 2. München: Winkler, 1969.

———. *Laocoön: An Essay on the Limits of Painting and Poetry.* Trans. E. C. Beasley. London: Longman, 1853.

Levin, Harry. *James Joyce.* Norfolk, Conn.: New Directions, 1960.

———. *James Joyce. A Critical Introduction.* London: Faber, 1960.

Levy, Antoine, OP. "Great Misinterpretations: Umberto Eco on Joyce and Aquinas." *Logos: A Journal of Catholic Thought and Culture* 13, no. 3 (2010): 124–63.

Lewes, George Henry. *Aristotle: A Chapter from the History of Science.* London: Smith, Elder, 1864.

Lewis, Wyndham. *Time and Western Man.* Boston: Beacon, 1957.

Livorni, Ernesto. "'Ineluctable Modality of the Visible': Diaphane in the 'Proteus' Episode." *James Joyce Quarterly* 36, no. 2 (1999): 127–69.

Locke, John. *An Essay Concerning Human Understanding.* Ed. Peter H. Nidditch. Oxford: Clarendon, 1975.

Lowe-Evans, Mary. *Crimes Against Fecundity: Joyce and Population Control.* Syracuse, N.Y.: Syracuse University Press, 1989.

———. *Catholic Nostalgia in Joyce and Company.* Gainesville: University Press of Florida, 2008.

Luther, Martin. *Letters* I. Ed. Gottfried G. Krodel. Philadelphia: Fortress, 1963.

———. *Works,* vol. 3. Saint Louis: Concordia, 1961.

Lynch, Brendan. *Parsons Bookshop: At the Heart of Bohemian Dublin, 1949–1989.* Dublin: Liffey, 2006.

Mach, Ernst. *Die Analyse der Empfindungen und das Verhältnis des Physischen zum Psychischen.* Jena: Fischer, 1903.

MacCarvill, Eileen. *The Collection of Joyce Exam Papers and University Calendars,* unpublished MS in private ownership (photocopy in James Joyce Foundation, Zurich).

MacIntyre, Alasdair. "Analogy in Metaphysics." *Downside Review* 69 (1950): 45–61.

Maddox, Brenda. "Love Makes the Joycean World Go Round." *Economist,* June 23, 1984, 85.

Magee, William Kirkpatrick. *Irish Literary Portraits.* London: Macmillan, 1935.

Maher, Michael. *Psychology: Empirical and Rational.* London: Longmans, Green, 1890.

Mann, Thomas. *Doctor Faustus.* Trans. John E. Woods. New York: Vintage, 1999.

Maritain, Jacques. *An Introduction to Philosophy.* London: Sheed and Ward, 1962.

Matthiessen, F. O. *The Achievement of T. S. Eliot: An Essay on the Nature of Poetry.* New York: Oxford University Press, 1959.

McAlmon, Robert. *Being Geniuses Together, 1920–1930.* London: Hogarth, 1984.

McCarthy, Patrick A. *Finnegans Wake.* Dublin: National Library of Ireland, 2004.

McDougall, William. *Body and Mind: A History and a Defense of Animism.* London: Methuen, 1911.

McGreevey, Thomas. "The Catholic Element in *Work in Progress.*" In *Our Exagmina-*

tion Round His Factification for Incamination of Work in Progress. London: Faber & Faber, 1929.

Mercanton, Jacques. "The Hours of James Joyce." In *Portraits of the Artist in Exile,* ed. Willard Potts, 206–52. Dublin: Wolfhound, 1979.

Mercier, Vivian. "Dublin under the Joyces." In *Two Decades of Criticism,* ed. Seon Givens, 285–301. New York: Vanguard, 1963.

———. "John Eglinton as Socrates: A Study of Scylla and Charybdis." In *James Joyce: An International Perspective,* ed. Suheil Badi Bushrui and Bernard Benstock, 65–81. Gerrards Cross, England: Colin Smythe, 1982.

Merton, Thomas. *The Seven Storey Mountain.* San Diego: Harcourt Brace Jovanovich, 1976.

Morrissey, Thomas J., S.J. *Towards a National University: William Delany SJ (1835–1924); An Era of Initiative in Irish Education.* Dublin: Wolfhound, 1983.

———. *Thomas A. Finlay SJ, 1848–1940: Educationalist, Editor, Social Reformer.* Dublin: Four Courts, 2004.

Morse, J. Mitchell. "Proteus." In *James Joyce's* Ulysses: *Critical Essays,* ed. Clive Hart and David Hayman, 29–49. Berkeley: University of California Press, 1977.

Nabokov, Vladimir. *Lectures on Literature.* New York: Harcourt Brace Jovanovich, 1980.

New Catholic Encyclopedia, vol. 4. Washington, D.C.: Catholic University of America, 1967.

New Scientist Staff. "That Freaky Feeling 1: Aristotle illusion." *New Scientist* 201, no. 2699 (March 11, 2009): 34–35.

Newman, John Henry. *The Idea of a University.* London: Longmans, 1889.

———. *Essays Critical and Historical,* vol. 1. London: Longmans, 1891.

———. *An Essay on the Development of Christian Doctrine.* London: Longmans, 1909.

———. *Apologia Pro Vita Sua.* London: Dent, 1934.

———. *Letters and Diaries of John Henry Newman,* vol. XI. Ed. Charles Dessain. London: Nelson, 1961.

Newman, Robert D., and Weldon Thornton. *Joyce's* Ulysses: *The Larger Perspective.* Newark: University of Delaware Press, 1987.

Newton, Isaac. *Opticks or A Treatise of the Reflections, Refractions, Inflections and Colours of Light.* London: William Innys, 1730.

———. *Mathematical Principles of Natural Philosophy.* Berkeley: University of California Press, 1960.

Nolan, Emer. *James Joyce and Nationalism.* London: Routledge, 1995.

Noon, William T., S.J. *Joyce and Aquinas.* New Haven, Conn.: Yale University Press, 1957.

———. Ph.D. thesis, 2 vols. Yale University, 1956.

———. "*A Portrait of the Artist as a Young Man:* After Fifty Years." In *James Joyce Today: Essays on the Major Works,* ed. Thomas F. Staley, 54–82. Bloomington: Indiana University Press, 1966.

Norris, Margot. *The Decentered Universe of* Finnegans Wake: *A Structuralist Analysis.* Baltimore, Md.: Johns Hopkins University Press, 1976.

Nussbaum, Martha C. "Between Detachment and Disgust: Bloom in Hades." In *Joyce's* Ulysses: *Philosophical Perspectives,* ed. Philip Kitcher, 29–62. New York: Oxford University Press, 2020.

O'Connor, Frank. "Joyce and Dissociated Metaphor." In *A Portrait of the Artist as a Young Man,* by James Joyce, ed. Chester G. Anderson, 371–77. New York: Viking, 1968.

O'Doherty, E. F. "Russell and the Great Mystery." *Studies: An Irish Quarterly Review* 46, no. 181 (1957): 27–33.

Oldenburg, Henry. *Correspondence of Henry Oldenburg,* vol. 3, ed. A. R. Hall and M. B. Hall. Madison: University of Wisconsin Press, 1966.

O'Rahilly, Thomas F. *A Miscellany of Irish Proverbs.* Dublin: Talbot, 1922.

O'Rourke, Fran. *Allwisest Stagyrite: Joyce's Quotations from Aristotle.* Dublin: National Library of Ireland, 2005.

———. "Joyce's Thomist Masters." In *Joyce in Context,* ed. John McCourt, 320–31. Cambridge: Cambridge University Press, 2009.

———. "Joyce's Early Aesthetic." *Journal of Modern Literature* 34, no. 2 (2011): 97–120.

———. "Aquinas and Platonism." In *Contemplating Aquinas,* ed. Fergus Kerr, 247–79 (London: SCM, 2003).

———. *Voices on Joyce.* Ed. Anne Fogarty and Fran O'Rourke. Dublin: University College Dublin Press, 2015.

———. "James Joyce and Aristotle." In *Voices on Joyce,* ed. Anne Fogarty and Fran O'Rourke, 139–57. Dublin: University College Dublin Press, 2015.

———. "Knowledge and Identity in Joyce." In *Cognitive Joyce,* ed. Sylvain Belluc and Valérie Bénéjam, 31–50. London: Palgrave Macmillan, 2018.

———. "Beauty from Plato to Aquinas." In *Ciphers of Transcendence: Essays in Philosophy of Religion in Honour of Patrick Masterson,* ed. Fran O'Rourke, 295–309. Newbridge: Irish Academic Press, 2019.

Owens, Joseph. *Aristotle: The Collected Papers of Joseph Owens.* Ed. John R. Catan. Albany, N.Y.: SUNY Press, 1981.

Pamuk, Orhan. *The Naive and the Sentimental Novelist.* Cambridge, Mass.: Harvard University Press, 2010.

Pater, Walter. *The Renaissance.* London: Macmillan, 1910.

Peake, C. H. *Joyce: The Citizen and the Artist.* Stanford, Calif.: Stanford University Press, 1977.

Peterson, Richard F. "More Aristotelian Grist for the Joycean Mill." *James Joyce Quarterly* 17 (1980): 213–20.

Philippe, M.-D. "*Analogon* and *Analogia* in the Philosophy of Aristotle." *Thomist* 33 (1969): 1–74.

Plato. *Theaetetus.* Trans. Francis Cornford, *Collected* Dialogues, 847–919. Princeton, N.J.: Princeton University Press, 1978.

———. *Republic.* Trans. Desmond Lee. Harmondsworth, U.K.: Penguin, 1974.

Ponzo, M. "Intorno ad alcune illusioni nel campo delle sensazioni tattili, sull'illusione di Aristotle e fenomeni analoghi." *Archiv für die Gesamte Psychologie* 16 (1910): 307–45.

Pound, Ezra. *Literary Essays.* Ed. T. S. Eliot. London: Faber & Faber, 1960.

———. "Pound on *Ulysses* and Flaubert." In *The Critical Heritage,* vol. 1, ed. Robert H. Deming, 263–67. London: Routledge & Kegan Paul, 1970.

———. *Pound/Joyce: The Letters of Ezra Pound to James Joyce.* Ed. Forrest Reid. New York: New Directions, 1970.

———. *Selected Prose, 1909–1965.* New York: New Directions, 1973.

Power, Arthur. *From the Old Waterford House.* Waterford: Carthage, 1940.

———. *Conversations with James Joyce.* Dublin: Lilliput, 1999.

Pribek, James. "Joyce and Newman." In *Voices on Joyce,* ed. Anne Fogarty and Fran O'Rourke, 187–99. Dublin: University College Dublin Press, 2015.

Rabaté, Jean-Michel. *James Joyce: Portrait de l'auteur en autre lecteur.* Petit-Roeulx: Cistre, 1984.

Rickaby, John. *General Metaphysics.* London: Longmans, 1890.

———. *The First Principles of Knowledge.* London: Longmans, 1896.

Rickaby, Joseph. *Aquinas Ethicus.* London: Burns and Oates, 1896.

———. *Moral Philosophy or Ethics and Natural Law.* London: Longmans, Green, 1903.

———. *Of God and His Creatures: An Annotated Translation of the Summa Contra Gentiles of Saint Thomas Aquinas.* London: Burns and Oates, 1905.

Rickard, John S. *Joyce's Book of Memory: The Mnemotechnic of* Ulysses. Durham, N.C.: Duke University Press, 1999.

Rivers, W. H. R. "A Modification of Aristotle's Experiment." *Mind* (ns.) 3, no. 12 (October 1894): 583–84.

Rodgers, W. R. *Irish Literary Portraits.* New York: Taplinger, 1973.

Rorty, Richard. *Philosophy and Social Hope.* London: Penguin, 1999.

Ryan, Judith. *The Vanishing Subject: Early Psychology and Literary Modernism.* Chicago: University of Chicago Press, 1991.

Sailer, Susan Shaw. *On the Void of to Be: Incoherence and Trope in* Finnegans Wake. Ann Arbor: University of Michigan Press, 1993.

Santayana, George. *Some Turns of Thought in Modern Philosophy.* Cambridge: Cambridge University Press, 1933.

Sarton, May. *I Knew a Phoenix.* New York: Holt, Rinehart & Winston, 1959.

Sartre, Jean-Paul. "Time in Faulkner: *The Sound and the Fury.*" In *William Faulkner: Three Decades of Criticism,* ed. Frederick J. Hoffman and Olga W. Vickery, 225–32. New York: Harcourt, Brace & World, 1963.

Schlegel, August Wilhelm von. *Vorlesungen über dramatische Kunst und Literatur.* Leipzig: Weidmann, 1846.

Scholes, Robert, and Richard M. Kain, eds. *The Workshop of Daedalus: James Joyce and the Raw Materials for* A Portrait of the Artist as a Young Man. Evanston, Ill.: Northwestern University Press, 1965.

Scholes, Robert, and Marlena G. Corcoran. "The Aesthetic Theory and the Critical Writings." In *A Companion to Joyce Studies,* ed. Zack Bowen and James F. Carens, 687–707. Westport, Conn.: Greenwood, 1984.

Schwarz, Daniel R. *Reading Joyce's* Ulysses. London: Macmillan, 1987.

Senn, Fritz. "Esthetic Theories." *James Joyce Quarterly* (1965): 134–35.

———. "Nausicaa." In *James Joyce's* Ulysses: *Critical Essays,* ed. Clive Hart and David Hayman, 277–311. Berkeley: University of California Press, 1974.

———. "Book of Many Turns." In *Critical Essays on James Joyce,* ed. Bernard Benstock, 120–36. Boston: G. K. Hall, 1985.

———. *Joycean Murmoirs.* Ed. Christine O'Neill. Dublin: Lilliput, 2007.

Sextus Empiricus. *Against the Logicians.* Cambridge, Mass.: Harvard University Press, 1983.

Sheehan, P. A. *Under the Cedars and the Stars*. Dublin: Browne and Nolan, 1903.

Sheehy, Eugene. *May It Please the Court*. Dublin: Fallon, 1951.

———. "The Joyce I Knew." In *The Joyce We Knew*, ed. Ulick O'Connor, 13–35. Cork, Ireland: Mercier, 1967.

Simplicius. *On Aristotle's Categories*. Trans. Michael Chase. London: Bloomsbury, 2003.

Simpson, John. "contransmagnificandjewbangtantiality: jaw-breakers and spelling bees." *James Joyce Online Notes*. Accessed May 1, 2021: http://www.jjon.org/joyce-s-words/c.

Smidt, Kristian. *James Joyce and the Cultic Use of Fiction*. Oslo: Akademsk Forlag, 1955.

Smith, Preserved, ed. *The Life and Letters of Martin Luther*. Boston: Houghton Mifflin, 1911.

Spencer, Herbert. *The Principles of Biology*. London: Appleton, 1864.

———. "The Genesis of Science." In *Essays: Scientific, Political, and Speculative* I. London: Williams and Norgate, 1883.

———. "Philosophy of Style," In *Essays: Scientific, Political, and Speculative* II. London: Williams and Norgate, 1891.

Spenser, Edmund. *Shorter Poems of Edmund Spenser*. Ed. William A. Oram et al. New Haven, Conn.: Yale University Press, 1989.

Spoo, Robert. *James Joyce and the Language of History: Dedalus's Nightmare*. New York: Oxford University Press, 1994.

Spurgeon, Caroline. *Shakespeare's Imagery and What It Tells Us*. Cambridge: Cambridge University Press, 1936.

Steinberg, Erwin R. "The Proteus Episode: Signature of Stephen Dedalus." *James Joyce Quarterly* 5, no. 3 (1968): 187–98.

Stewart, Bruce. "Joyce, James Augustine Aloysius." In *Oxford Dictionary of National Biography*, vol. 30, 778–800. Oxford: Oxford University Press, 2004.

———. *A Short Life of James Joyce*. Accessed May 1, 2021: http://www.ricorso.net/rx/az-data/authors/j/Joyce_JA/apx/biogrfy/biog12.htm.

———. "A Short Literary Life of James Joyce." In *James Joyce*, ed. Sean Latham, 19–44. Dublin: Irish Academic Press, 2010.

Stöckl, Albert. *Handbook of the History of Philosophy* I. *Pre-Scholastic Philosophy*. Trans. T. A. Finlay, S.J. Dublin: Gill, 1887.

Sullivan, Kevin. *Joyce among the Jesuits*. New York: Columbia University Press, 1958.

Swift, Jonathan. *The Works of Jonathan Swift*. Edinburgh: Nimmo, 1869.

Theoharis, Theoharis Constantine. *Joyce's Ulysses: An Anatomy of the Soul*. Chapel Hill: University of North Carolina Press, 1988.

Tindall, William York. *A Reader's Guide to* "Finnegans Wake." London: Thames and Hudson, 1969.

Trilling, Lionel. "Freud and Literature." In *Freud: A Collection of Critical Essays*, ed. Perry Meisel, 95–111. Englewood Cliffs, N.J.: Prentice-Hall, 1981.

———. "James Joyce in his Letters." In *The Last Decade: Essays and Reviews*, 1965–75, ed. Diana Trilling. New York: Harcourt Brace Jovanovich, 1979.

Van Mierlo, Wim. "The Subject Notebook: A Nexus in the Composition History of *Ulysses*—A Preliminary Analysis." *Genetic Joyce Studies* 7 (Spring 2007). Accessed May 1, 2021: https://www.geneticjoycestudies.org/articles/GJS7/GJS7_MierloSubject.

Vargas Llosa, Mario. *Bloom*. Dublin: Kingstown, 1966.

Vaughan, Roger Bede, OSB. *The Life and Labours of Saint Thomas of Aquin*. London: Longmans, 1871.

Verene, Donald Phillip, ed. *Vico and Joyce*. Albany, N.Y.: SUNY Press, 1987.

———. *James Joyce and the Philosophers at* Finnegans Wake. Evanston, Ill.: Northwestern University Press, 2016.

Verstraete, Ginette. *Fragments of the Feminine Sublime in Friedrich Schlegel and James Joyce*. Albany, N.Y.: SUNY Press, 1998.

Wagner, Geoffrey. *Wyndham Lewis: A Portrait of the Artist as the Enemy*. London: Routledge & Kegan Paul, 1957.

Ward, Anthony. *Walter Pater: The Idea in Nature*. London: MacGibbon & Kee, 1966.

Weininger, Otto. *Über die Letzten Dinge: Mit einem biographischen Vorwort von Moriz Rappaport*. Vienna: Braumüller, 1904.

———. *On Last Things*. Trans. Steven Burns. Lewiston, N.Y.: E. Mellen, 2001.

Weisheipl, James A. *St. Thomas Aquinas: Commentary on the Gospel of Saint John*. Albany, N.Y.: Magi, 1980.

Wells, H. G. Review of *A Portrait of the Artist as a Young Man*. *New Republic*, March 10, 1917.

Weninger, Robert K. *The German Joyce*. Gainesville: University Press of Florida, 2012.

Whitehead, Alfred North. *Science and the Modern World*. London: Free Association, 1985.

Woolf, Virginia. *The Essays of Virginia Woolf*, vol. 3. London: Hogarth, 1995.

Index Nominum

FRAN O'ROURKE is emeritus professor of philosophy, University College Dublin, where he taught for thirty-six years. He received his Ph.D. in philosophy (*summa cum laude*) from the University of Leuven and a Ph.D. in Anglo-Irish literature from University College Dublin. He has held Fulbright and Onassis fellowships. His publications include *Pseudo-Dionysius and the Metaphysics of Aquinas* and *Aristotelian Interpretations*. As well as philosophical influences in Joyce, he has specialized in the performance of traditional Irish songs that feature in his writings; he has given recitals in many places around the world, from Shanghai to San Diego (www.joycesong.info).

THE FLORIDA JAMES JOYCE SERIES
Edited by Sebastian D. G. Knowles

Joyce in Trieste: An Album of Risky Readings, edited by Sebastian D. G. Knowles, Geert Lernout, and John McCourt (2007)

Joyce's Rare View: The Nature of Things in "Finnegans Wake," by Richard Beckman (2007)

Joyce's Misbelief, by Roy Gottfried (2008)

James Joyce's Painful Case, by Cóilín Owens (2008; first paperback edition, 2017)

Cannibal Joyce, by Thomas Jackson Rice (2008)

Manuscript Genetics, Joyce's Know-How, Beckett's Nohow, by Dirk Van Hulle (2008)

Catholic Nostalgia in Joyce and Company, by Mary Lowe-Evans (2008)

A Guide through "Finnegans Wake," by Edmund Lloyd Epstein (2009)

Bloomsday 100: Essays on "Ulysses," edited by Morris Beja and Anne Fogarty (2009)

Joyce, Medicine, and Modernity, by Vike Martina Plock (2010; first paperback edition, 2012)

Who's Afraid of James Joyce?, by Karen R. Lawrence (2010; first paperback edition, 2012)

"Ulysses" in Focus: Genetic, Textual, and Personal Views, by Michael Groden (2010; first paperback edition, 2012)

Foundational Essays in James Joyce Studies, edited by Michael Patrick Gillespie (2011; first paperback edition, 2017)

Empire and Pilgrimage in Conrad and Joyce, by Agata Szczeszak-Brewer (2011; first paperback edition, 2017)

The Poetry of James Joyce Reconsidered, edited by Marc C. Conner (2012; first paperback edition, 2015)

The German Joyce, by Robert K. Weninger (2012; first paperback edition, 2016)

Joyce and Militarism, by Greg Winston (2012; first paperback edition, 2015)

Renascent Joyce, edited by Daniel Ferrer, Sam Slote, and André Topia (2013; first paperback edition, 2014)

Before Daybreak: "After the Race" and the Origins of Joyce's Art, by Cóilín Owens (2013; first paperback edition, 2015)

Modernists at Odds: Reconsidering Joyce and Lawrence, edited by Matthew J. Kochis and Heather L. Lusty (2015; first paperback edition, 2020)

James Joyce and the Exilic Imagination, by Michael Patrick Gillespie (2015)

The Ecology of "Finnegans Wake," by Alison Lacivita (2015; first paperback edition, 2021)

Joyce's Allmaziful Pluralabilities: Polyvocal Explorations of "Finnegans Wake," edited by Kimberly J. Devlin and Christine Smedley (2015; first paperback edition, 2018)

Exiles: A Critical Edition, by James Joyce, edited by A. Nicholas Fargnoli and Michael Patrick Gillespie (2016; first paperback edition, 2019)

Up to Maughty London: Joyce's Cultural Capital in the Imperial Metropolis, by Eleni Loukopoulou (2017)

Joyce and the Law, edited by Jonathan Goldman (2017; first paperback edition, 2020)

At Fault: Joyce and the Crisis of the Modern University, by Sebastian D. G. Knowles (2018; first paperback edition, 2021)

"Ulysses" Unbound: A Reader's Companion to James Joyce's "Ulysses," Third Edition, by Terence Killeen (2018)

Joyce and Geometry, by Ciaran McMorran (2020)

Panepiphanal World: James Joyce's Epiphanies, by Sangam MacDuff (2020)

Language as Prayer in "Finnegans Wake," by Colleen Jaurretche (2020)

Rewriting Joyce's Europe: The Politics of Language and Visual Design, by Tekla Mecsnóber (2021)

Joyce Writing Disability, edited by Jeremy Colangelo (2022)

Joyce, Aristotle, and Aquinas, by Fran O'Rourke (2022)

Lightning Source UK Ltd.
Milton Keynes UK
UKHW040047040123
414614UK00023B/301